Jewish Americans and Political Participation

Political Participation in America

Raymond A. Smith, Series Editor

Jewish Americans and Political Participation

A Reference Handbook

Rafael Medoff

Foreword by Edward I. Koch

A B C ⬥ C L I O

Santa Barbara, California • Denver, Colorado • Oxford, England

Library of Congress Cataloging-in-Publication Data

Medoff, Rafael, 1959–
  Jewish Americans and political participation : a reference handbook — Rafael Medoff.
      p. cm. – (Political participation in America)
  Includes bibliographical references and index.
  ISBN 1-57607-314-9 (hardcover : alk. paper); 1-57607-293-2 (e-book)
  1. Jews—United States—Politics and government. 2. Jews—United States—Politics and government—20th century. 3. United States—Ethnic relations. I. Title. II. Series.
  E184.36.P64 M45 2002
  973'.04924—dc21

                                                                2002006643

07   06   05   04   03   02   10   9   8   7   6   5   4   3   2   1

ABC-CLIO, Inc.
130 Cremona Drive, P.O. Box 1911
Santa Barbara, California 93116-1911

This book is printed on acid-free paper.
Manufactured in the United States of America

For my wife, Carin

She is more precious than pearls. Her husband's heart
relies on her and he lacks nothing.
She does him good, and never harm, all the days of her life.

—Proverbs 31:10–12

Contents

Foreword

Rafael Medoff, author of *Jewish Americans and Political Participation: A Reference Handbook,* who I have not met, wrote asking if I would write a foreword for his book. I'm an American Jew and one who has been a candidate in 23 elections beginning in 1962, so I immediately dove into the manuscript that accompanied his letter.

I was enthralled with the material, learning something new on almost every page. The history of Jews in office starts in the colonial and prerevolutionary period, and continues up to and including the candidacy of Joe Lieberman who ran for vice president on the Democratic ticket with Al Gore in the 2000 election against the Bush-Cheney Republican ticket.

Medoff points out, "No Jew has ever been nominated by a major party for president, and until Lieberman, none had been nominated for vice-president, although Senator Abraham Ribicoff reportedly declined George McGovern's offer to be his running mate in 1972. Only two Jews have ever declared their candidacy for the president, but in both cases withdrew from the race within a short time: Pennsylvania Governor Milton Shapp, a Democrat, in 1976, and Senator Arlen Specter, Republican of Pennsylvania, in 1996."

I am a friend of Joe Lieberman and raised money for his successful senatorial campaigns. He is an Orthodox Jew and Sabbath observer. He was seen during the investigations of President Clinton during the impeachment process as the conscience of the U.S. Senate. When he and Dick Cheney were put on the national tickets, they were quickly seen as class acts. The one debate between the two vice presidential candidates received far greater support and applause from the public and political savants than did any of the several debates between the two presidential candidates.

There were no polls that I can recall reporting that Lieberman would drag his ticket down because of anti-Semitism. Just the contrary. Most observers believed Lieberman was an asset and, in fact, Gore and Lieberman carried the national popular vote.

Unfortunately for the Democratic Party, the electoral college was carried by Bush and Cheney. A switch of one state—for example, Tennessee, Gore's home state, which voted for Bush—would have won the election for Gore and Lieberman, but it was not to be. But the closeness of the race and the goodwill directed at Lieberman shows how far Jewish candidates have come in acceptability in the United States, where Jews are barely 2 percent of the population.

In Congress, there are 27 Jewish members in the House of Representatives and 10 in the U.S. Senate. When I was in Congress, in the period 1969 to 1977, I was part of the Jewish caucus that at the end of my term had a membership of 22 Jews. Nearly every racial and ethnic group in the Congress established a caucus, meeting regularly to discuss issues that had particular relevance to their group.

The Greeks, of which there were three, had the smallest caucus. Two of three members, John Brademus and Paul Sarbanes, became U.S. Senators. During all the years that I served in the House, the Chairman of the Jewish caucus was Sid Yates, Democrat from Chicago, now deceased.

On occasion, there were disputes between the caucus members. One such dispute occurred between Bella Abzug and myself. We both represented liberal constituencies in Manhattan. She was running for the U.S. Senate in 1976 and I, far more moderate in my views than she, was opposed to her candidacy and pointed out in mailings to rabbis in New York City Bella's association with groups that were radical left and hostile to the State of Israel.

Bella herself was supportive of Israel, but active in those groups on other issues. She asked Sid Yates to call a meeting of the Jewish caucus to censure me for my criticism of her. I remember so vividly Sid Yates telling me, "I said, Bella, the last Sanhedrin met in 70 AD,'" and he was not going to use the caucus for the censuring of one member by other members.

Medoff has done a wonderful job in getting into other fracases that took place among Jewish members of Congress in the period pre and during World War II when the Jewish community and its political leadership were split on how strongly to speak out on the persecution of Jews by Hitler and Nazi Germany and on the U.S. response in helping the Jewish community (many would say the response was grossly inadequate). Some feared taking on President Franklin Delano Roosevelt, while others wanted a knockdown fight with him to save the Jews.

Finally, I recall a conversation I had with a newly elected member of Congress from Long Island, Jerry Ambro, a member of the Italian caucus. While we were seated in the House chamber listening to the debate, he asked, "How many of you are there?" clearly referring to the Jewish caucus. I replied, "Twenty-two, and how many of you are there?" He said, "Thirty-eight." I said, "What do you do when you get together?" He replied, "Mostly, we eat, and what do you do?" I replied, "Mostly, we cry."

Those were interesting days. How far we've come!

Edward I. Koch

Series Foreword

Participation in the political process is a cornerstone of both the theory and the practice of democracy; indeed, the word "democracy" itself means rule by the people. Since the formation of the New Deal coalition in 1932, the study of U.S. politics has largely been organized around the concept that there exist distinct "blocs" of citizens, such as African Americans, women, Catholics, and Latinos. This trend was reinforced during the 1960s when the expansion of the media and the decline of traditional sources of authority promoted direct citizen mobilization. And more recently, the emphasis on "identity politics" has reinforced the notion of distinct groups organized along lines of shared personal characteristics rather than common economic interests.

Although political participation is a mainstream, even canonical, subject in the study of U.S. politics, there are few midrange reference materials available on this subject. Indeed, the available reference materials do not include works that provide both a systematic empirical base *and* explanatory and contextualizing material. Likewise, because of the fragmentation of the reference materials on this subject, it is difficult for readers to draw comparisons across groups, even though this is one of the most meaningful ways of understanding the phenomenon of political participation.

The Political Participation in America series is designed to fill this gap in the reference literature on this subject by providing key points of background (e.g., demographics, political history, major contemporary issues) and then systematically addressing different types of political participation, providing both substance and context for readers. In addition, each chapter includes case studies that either illuminate larger issues or highlight some particular subpopulation within the larger group.

Each volume of the ABC-CLIO Political Participation in America series focuses on one of the major subgroups that make up the electorate in the United States. Each volume includes the following components:

- *Introduction to the group,* comprising a demographic, historical, and political portrait of the group, including political opinions and issues of key importance to members of the group
- *Participation in protest politics,* including marches, rallies, demonstrations, and direct actions
- *Participation in social movements and interest groups,* including involvement of members of the group in and through a wide variety of organizations and associations
- *Participation in electoral politics,* including a profile of involvement with political parties and voting patterns
- *Participation in political office-holding,* including elected, appointed, and "unofficial" offices from the local to national levels

The end of each book also includes an A-Z glossary featuring brief entries on important individuals and events; a chronology of political events salient to the group; a resource guide of organizations, newsletters, websites, and other important contact information, all briefly annotated; an annotated bibliography of key primary and secondary documents, including books and journal articles; excerpts from major primary documents, with introductions; and a comprehensive index to the volume.

Raymond A. Smith
Series Editor

1

Overview

A Demographic Portrait of American Jewry

At the beginning of the year 2001, the American Jewish community numbered approximately 6.1 million, 2 percent of the U.S. population. That represented an increase from a population of 5.5 million ten years earlier. Because of the relatively low Jewish birth rate, however, Jewish births and deaths reached comparable levels by the late 1990s, and the overall increase in the American Jewish population was due not to natural increase but to immigration, primarily from the former Soviet Union.

The largest U.S. Jewish communities are to be found in the major cities of the Northeast. About 40 percent of American Jews (2.4 million) reside in the Middle Atlantic states, especially in New York City, Philadelphia, Baltimore, and the greater Washington, D.C., area. The next largest concentrations, each comprising about 21 percent of American Jewry, are to be found in the South (primarily southern Florida) and the West (primarily the greater Los Angeles region). The other major areas of Jewish residence are the Midwest, at about 11 percent (primarily in Chicago and Detroit), and the New England region, with approximately 7 percent (concentrated in Connecticut and in the Boston area). The regions registering the most significant gains in recent decades are the Southeast and Southwest, as Jews from the Northeast, especially retirees, relocate to warmer climates. By way of comparison, it may be noted that in 1978, 52 percent of

1

American Jews resided in the Middle Atlantic states, 15 percent in the South, and 14 percent in the West. (The figures for the Midwest and New England in 1978 were about the same as they were in 2001.)

Studies of Jewish denominational preference have found the largest single segment of American Jewry to be those associated with Conservative Judaism, approximately 40 percent. About 35 percent prefer the more liberal Reform Judaism. Some 10 percent choose Orthodox, or traditional, Judaism; the remainder express no preference. About half of American Jews are members of a synagogue; an additional one-fifth have been members in the past. Those Jews affiliated with Conservatism are more likely to be older than the other denominations. Orthodox homes are more likely than others to have children who are seventeen years of age or younger. Reform and unaffiliated Jews have the highest levels of income, with the Orthodox at the lowest level. Politically, Reform Jews are the most liberal, followed by the unaffiliated, the Conservative, and then the Orthodox.

The American Jewish community is gradually experiencing an increase in both the numbers and influence of those Jews who are religiously more traditional and politically more conservative. There are several reasons for this trend. There is a correlation between levels of religious observance and birth rates, with religious Jews having the highest birth rate of any segment of the Jewish community. A second factor is that the rate of intermarriage with non-Jews (which currently stands at about 52 percent of all marriages involving American Jews) is highest among the unaffiliated and the Reform, and lowest among the Orthodox; and the majority of children of intermarriages do not remain within the Jewish fold. The phenomenon of assimilation—shedding most or all of one's Jewish identity—is likewise highest among the unaffiliated and the Reform; children who receive minimal amounts of Jewish experience and education are the ones most likely to discard their remaining Jewish affiliations as they grow to adulthood. Finally, there is a correlation between religiosity and involvement in Jewish communal institutions; the most religious are the most involved.

The Rise and Evolution of the American Jewish Community

Twenty-three Jews of Dutch origin established the first permanent Jewish settlement in North America, when they fled Brazil in 1654 on the heels of the Portuguese reconquest of the country from its Dutch rulers. The refugees from South America took up residence in the Dutch colony of New Amsterdam, which would be renamed New York after its capture by the English ten years later. Like millions of Jews who would settle in the United States in the centuries to follow, this tiny band of refugees fled adversity to find a new world of economic opportunity and relative religious and social tolerance, a climate in which the American Jewish community would grow and thrive.

The Jewish right to settle in England had been restored in 1655 after more than 300 years of exclusion, establishing the precedent for comparable treatment of Jews in the English colonies. Except for Puritan Massachusetts and Connecticut, where all non-Puritans—not just Jews—faced hostility, Jews were free to reside where they chose and begin creating the rudiments of communal existence. Small Jewish enclaves were soon to be found not only in New York but also in South Carolina, Pennsylvania, Rhode Island, and Georgia. Many of the earliest Jewish settlers were Sephardic, descendants of Jews driven out of Spain and Portugal in the fifteenth and sixteenth centuries who had settled in Amsterdam, and from there made their way to the Dutch colonies across the Atlantic. The leaders of London's Sephardim sought to alleviate poverty in their community by sending dozens of Jews to Savannah when Georgia was established in 1733.

During the late 1600s and throughout the 1700s, a trickle of East European Jews, fleeing oppression, war, and economic hardship, made their way to Colonial America. Given the difficulty of starting a new life in the uncharted wilderness of North America, the absence of a Jewish communal infrastructure, and the expense and hardship of travel from Europe to the New World, perhaps it is no surprise that American Jewry grew only slightly during the seventeenth and eighteenth centuries. Jews in Colonial America in the early 1700s, of whom there were approximately 1,300, still numbered fewer than 3,000 as late as 1790. The census of 1820 counted an estimated 2,700 Jews, 0.3 percent of the national population.

A smattering of Jews could be found in an array of professions, including a very small number involved in the slave trade, but most were merchants dealing in one aspect or another of transatlantic trade. In this they differed markedly from non-Jewish colonists, most of whom were farmers, along with a minority of artisans. An analysis of the wills of twenty-three Jewish men who died in New York between 1704 and 1774 has found that nineteen called themselves merchants. In this line of work, the Sephardim, sometimes described as one large, extended family, enjoyed the advantage of being able to utilize family connections to Sephardim in the Caribbean and Europe to facilitate business. It is no coincidence that most Jews in the Colonial era resided in port cities such as New Amsterdam, Charleston, Newport, and Philadelphia. Transatlantic marriages further cemented business ties, while simultaneously relieving the problem of finding a spouse among the tiny Jewish communities in Colonial America.

The fragmentary evidence from the period abounds with indications of acculturation. Congregational minutes detail fines imposed upon members found guilty of religious infractions, although the consequences for violating standards of behavior varied considerably. Some synagogues expelled the most egregious transgressors and denied them burial rights in the community cemetery; others assessed a variety of lesser punishments, such as forfeiture of the right to vote on synagogue affairs. Portraits show both men and women in the fashionable garb of the era, the men bare-headed and clean-shaven, the women with their hair uncovered, all deviations from traditional practice. Some synagogue architecture mimicked the latest European styles. Social interaction with Christians was not uncommon, and intermarriage was an increasing problem: during the 1700s and early 1800s, between one-fifth and one-third of marriages involving Jews were marriages to Christians. The intermarriage rate for frontier towns such as New Orleans may have been as high as 50 percent, according to some estimates. The national rate leveled off in the vicinity of one-third during the first decades of the nineteenth century, when many more potential spouses became available as a result of the influx of Jewish immigrants.

Although the Jews' right to vote and hold public office was restricted by the Colonial authorities (see Chapter 3), they considered themselves part and parcel of American political culture, and as the Revolutionary War neared, the Jewish community was split between those loyal to the Crown and those favoring independence. A large majority of Jews supported the rebels, although a noticeable minority remained faithful to England. An estimated 100 Jewish men fought in General Washington's ranks, and Jewish financiers helped bankroll the revolt, among them Haym Salomon, whose role has been a staple of American Jewish apologetic literature ever since. "Without penalty, recriminations, or untoward consequences, America's Jews could easily have chosen neutrality in the conflict between the colonies and the mother country, a choice that would have accorded well with their political non-existence," Eli Faber notes. "The fact that nearly all chose one side or the other, often quite visibly, indicates the degree to which colonial Jews felt that they belonged to early American society, in dramatic contrast to their centuries of exclusion in Europe." In Faber's view, the American Revolution "represents a watershed in the history of the Jewish people in America; it was a milestone in the emergence of the Jew as a citizen participating in the political life of his nation" (Faber 1992, 102).

The various states that composed the new nation gradually accorded the Jews equality in voting and office-holding (see Chapter 5), and the principles enshrined in the Northwest Ordinance (1781) and the Constitution (1789) reinforced freedom of religion as one of the nation's ideological anchors. The Jews of early America could derive additional solace from President George Washington's 1790 letter to the Jews of Newport, Rhode Island, promising that the United States would give "to bigotry no sanction, to persecution no assistance."

The German Jewish Immigration

The first major wave of European Jewish immigration to the United States, beginning in the 1850s, is popularly referred to as the German immigration, although a portion of the newcomers actually originated from Central European regions other than Germany. Some Jews left because of the pogroms that swept Prague on the heels of the 1848 revolution; others, especially those who had been active in the revolution, fled after the reactionary forces regained power the following year. But most German Jewish emigrants during the mid-1800s were motivated by economic causes. This is demonstrated by the fact that perhaps the most remarkable characteristic of the German exodus was the "pulling-after" phenomenon. Typically, one brother would emigrate, leaving behind siblings and parents. With their high birthrate—nine or ten children in a single family was not uncommon—most German Jews simply could not afford to move their entire family at once. After the most enterprising son established himself in the New World, he would gradually bring over the others. Such a pattern would not have played out had the German Jews believed themselves to be in imminent danger of severe persecution: they would simply have left en masse, even if they were penniless, which is what happened a few decades later in Russia. In Central Europe, by contrast, there was enough anti-Semitism to give emigration a push, but the main "pull" was the hope of a better life.

A surprisingly large number of the Jewish emigrants from Germany were single women. German government restrictions on the number of Jews who could get married in a particular city and the exorbitant fees charged for marriage licenses often caused Jewish women of marriageable age to emigrate, sometimes with a brother or two, in the hope of finding a match in America.

America's open-door immigration and unrestricted areas of settlement, together with its economic opportunities and freedom of religion, made it attractive as a destination. The public generally welcomed the approximately 200,000 new Jewish immigrants who came from Central Europe between 1830 and 1880; the popular attitude was that the United States was a large, underpopulated country that needed immigrant workers to build it up. By the mid-1800s, America was also far easier to reach than ever before; the first steamship to cross the Atlantic from Europe to North America arrived in 1819.

Case Study: Pulling Over

Joseph Seligman, age seventeen, left his hometown of Baiersdorf, Germany, in 1837 and sailed to New York. From there he made his way to the tiny Pennsylvania town of Mauch Chunk, where he had a cousin, and he soon found employment as a clerk in a grocery and supplies store. After a few months, Seligman had an idea. He noticed that farmers from outlying areas had to make frequent, long, and difficult trips into town to buy supplies. He figured that they would be willing to pay a little bit more for the convenience of having the goods delivered to them. And so, like many German Jewish immigrants before him, and many to follow, Seligman became a peddler. He used his small savings to purchase various goods and to send enough money back to Baiersdorf for two of his brothers to come over. The three of them then set out across the Pennsylvania countryside with their packs of goods for sale.

By 1840 the three Seligman brothers had made enough money to open a store, in Lancaster, Pennsylvania, and to "pull over" the other five brothers. The store soon multiplied into a chain of stores. By 1852 they had made so much money and become so deeply involved in the gold market, in making investments, and in buying and selling on credit that they were easily able to make the transition from merchants to bankers—a transition that many of their fellow German immigrants likewise made. Later, some of the more elitist of the descendants of these newly rich immigrants made a distinction between those who had "graduated" from the world of storekeeping and those who had stayed behind—such as the Strauses, proprietors of the Macy's stores.

Many of these unmarried immigrants began their new lives as peddlers. Frequently they moved westward, in part because there were business opportunities along the riverways; Cincinnati was second only to New York in the size of its Jewish community in the mid-1800s. The Midwest was also alluring because many non-Jewish German immigrants were settling there; the absence of a language barrier enhanced business opportunities. Unlike their East European coreligionists, who often lived physically and culturally apart from their non-Jewish neighbors, many German Jews had already become quite acculturated in Germany, and they felt comfortable among German-Americans. These German Jews spoke German at home, belonged to German-American cultural societies, read German newspapers, and made sure that their children received a German-language education.

Maintaining a traditional religious Jewish community in the New World was no simple task. In an open society in which church and state were separated, religious observance was purely voluntary. This contrasted sharply with the prevailing situation in Europe until the late 1700s. There, a Jew could choose only between membership in the traditional Jewish community or conversion to Christianity; there was no "neutral society," no middle ground where Jews could be less observant, or even nonobservant. America offered just such a middle ground.

Other factors also contributed to the erosion of tradition. Social and economic pressures, such as the six-day work week, strongly discouraged religious observance; economic mobility required assimilation. Many of the immigrants who made up the early American Jewish community were merchants, not pious scholars, and their very willingness to leave a Jewish environment to travel and settle in parts of the world that were Jewishly sparse indicates a certain tenuousness about their own commitment to tradition. A lack of notable rabbinical leadership (until the mid-nineteenth century) deprived the young American Jewish community of sources of guidance and inspiration that would have reinforced traditional modes of behavior; few rabbis of note were prepared to leave their students and congregants in Europe. The absence of Jewish religious institutions also posed a serious obstacle to sustaining traditional levels of observance; as of 1820 there were only six synagogues in the United States. Lacking private Jewish schools, parents sent their children to public schools (first established in the 1840s), where interaction with non-Jews, exposure to ideas considered heretical by traditional standards, and conflicts between school schedules and Jewish holidays further eroded religious observance.

Yet until the mid-1800s, traditional Jewish observance—what is to-day known as Orthodox Judaism—was the only official form of religious identity available in the organized American Jewish community. Reform Judaism, which began to emerge in Germany in the early 1800s, did not make its first organized appearance in the United States until the mid-1800s, and Conservative Judaism only in the early 1900s. American synagogues during the early years were thus all officially what would be called Orthodox, although a number of their members were personally lax in their observance. Reforms came gradually, introduced "from the bottom up"—that is, individual members of some congregations pressed for modest changes, first in the style, and later in the content, of the prayer services. Typically, changes were proposed not on the grounds that the traditional ways were somehow flawed, but rather that reforms were necessary to preserve Judaism, to keep within the fold Jews who might otherwise leave the Jewish community altogether.

Frequently the pressure for change would lead to a splitting of a synagogue into two separate congregations, one adhering to traditional ways, the other instituting reforms to "Americanize" their service. There was, however, a wide range of Americanized behavior. At one end stood those who would merely have their rabbi deliver his Sabbath sermon in English (as opposed to Yiddish or German) or would modernize their synagogue's decorum. At the other end of the spectrum were those who eliminated prayers that might seem un-American (such as praying for Jews to return to the Land of Israel), permitted men and women to sit together, abandoned traditional head coverings and prayer shawls, instituted the use of an organ during services, or even—in a minority of instances—changed their Sabbath day from Saturday to Sunday. Some of these changes were consciously intended to mimic Protestant churches.

Antebellum American Jewry

On the eve of the Civil War, there were some 150,000 Jews in the United States, about two-thirds of them recent immigrants from Central Europe. Most lived in the Northeast, especially New York. In addition to the aforementioned divisions between reformers and traditionalists over religious observance, the community was deeply torn over the issue of slavery. Southern Jews were overwhelmingly proslavery, while Northern Jews were divided. In a widely publicized sermon in 1861, the prominent Orthodox rabbi Morris Raphall cited the biblical justification of some forms of slavery as precedent for continuing the practice in the United States. The era's leading rabbis, traditionalist Isaac Leeser and reformer Isaac Wise, both privately sympathized with Raphall but eschewed controversies involving the non-Jewish public. By contrast, reformist rabbi David Einhorn argued vigorously for abolition, maintaining that the spirit of the Bible, not its letter, should prevail. When war broke out, Jewish communities around the country took their respective sides.

Early Eruptions of Anti-Semitism

By 1877, American Jewry numbered some 250,000. Jewish communities could be found in almost every state, with the largest (with a population of approximately 50,000) in New York City. Many of those who had arrived in the 1840s or 1850s were quite prosperous by the 1870s. There were a number of Jewish millionaires, and many others who were not millionaires but were quite well off. One survey of 18,000 American Jews in 1889, of whom four-fifths were German immigrants, found that 40 percent of the Jewish families had at least one servant, 20 percent had two, and 10 percent had three.

On the other hand, as Hasia Diner points out, the popular notion that most or all of the German Jewish immigrants quickly got rich is more myth than fact: some peddlers never rose much higher, many small storekeepers remained just that, and the proliferation of Jewish communal charitable societies testified to the impoverishment of a segment of American Jewry. Jewish women in nineteenth-century America, for that matter, were not all the pampered wives of the nouveau riche, supervising servants and attending tea parties; many, Diner shows, "participated actively in the labor force in peculiarly female and Jewish ways, primarily in family businesses." Overall, it could be said that American Jewry was a living example of how an ethnic minority could, by virtue of hard work and determination, succeed in America despite arriving with little money, little or no facility in the language of their new country, and the inevitable obstacle of religious prejudice.

Happily, manifestations of such prejudice did not yet constitute a serious problem for America's Jews. Part of the reason was the small size of the Jewish community, which made it easier for Christians to accept Jews as part of American society. Moreover, the United States was home to a variety of minority Christian sects, many of whom themselves had been persecuted in Europe and had fled to America, and were thus less likely to persecute others. The legal separation of church and state, from the beginning of American independence, kept Christian influence in the United States from becoming dominant, as it had been in Europe. Furthermore, the absence of any severe economic crises during the first century of American life also helped ensure social tranquility.

The success of the German Jewish immigrants did, however, breed a certain amount of jealousy. Some post–Civil War literature stereotyped Jews as glittering with vulgar jewelry, attracting attention by being too noisy or pushy, lacking social manners, and forcing their way into a culture that was not theirs. These sorts of anti-Semitic complaints about the upwardly mobile Jews unfortunately came at a time of struggle for social status in American life. Former members of the American middle class who had grown rich in recent decades were clamoring to gain admission to prestigious clubs and elitist social circles. It was a time of vastly increased interest in importing aristocratic European culture, emphasis on etiquette, the compiling of social registers, and a zealous interest in genealogy. Scapegoating the Jews for their attempts at social climbing offered an easy way to vent frustration over the broader changes underway in American society.

Historians disagree over the extent to which the German and Central European immigrants adhered to traditional Jewish practices in the New World. These immigrants' Jewish knowledge and levels of observance had already been weakened in Europe by the impact of the Haskalah (Enlightenment) and the early-nineteenth-century relaxations on social segregation, which enabled Jews to become more acculturated. Religious observance was no simple task in nineteenth-century America. Because of American Jewry's small numbers, kosher food could be difficult to obtain, and synagogues and mikvehs (ritual bath houses) were far from numerous. The most religious of the German Jews were the ones who opted to stay behind. Those for whom religious observance was extremely important would have been the most reluctant to venture out to a new country where, for all they knew, they would not be able to obtain what was necessary for their religious practice. Socioeconomic pressures, such as the six-day work week, made observance even more of a challenge. By the late 1800s, less than 10 percent of American Jews belonged to synagogues, and less than one-third of school-age Jewish children were receiving any kind of Jewish education. Although it was true that expensive new synagogues were being built, as Howard Sachar notes: "[As] in the case of Christian churches, the blue-chip real estate and lush decor bore only a casual relationship to piety" (Sachar 1992, 113).

Other historians, such as Hasia Diner (1992), take issue with this view, contending that most of the German immigrants "believed that to add on a new layer of [American] identity did not require a total stripping away of the old one." In her view they did not so much abandon their Judaism as transform it into a new brand of Jewish identity based on preservation of ethnic bonds and certain specific religious rituals. Many nineteenth-century Jewish immigrants did not observe the traditional dietary regulations (although some did) and transgressed the Sabbath restrictions. But most went out of their way to live near other Jews, carefully maintained traditional Jewish burial rites, married within the Jewish fold, and created fraternal lodges, of which B'nai B'rith and the Young Men's Hebrew Association (YMHA) are the best known. They also established a wide range of philanthropic endeavors to care for "the sick, widows, and orphans, distribution of free Passover matzo, interest-free loans, grants of clothing, shelter, fuel, and dowries for poor brides." Such activity was a form of Jewish self-defense as well: some Jewish orphanages, old-age homes, and benevolent societies were established in direct response to efforts by Evangelical Christians to proselytize indigent or ailing Jews in non-Jewish institutions. "In the nineteenth century," Diner concludes, "philanthropy became the glue that held American Jewry together" (100). For some, philanthropy became the core of a new form of Jewish identity; for others, it was the last vestige of a Jewishness that was in the process of being discarded.

Reforming Judaism

Although American life was conducive to assimilation, most German Jewish immigrants retained a sense of ethnic feeling, a desire to maintain the communal sentiment that they had enjoyed in Germany, not to mention a strong desire to have their children marry within the fold. In Europe the Jews had lived together, either in ghettos or segregated neighborhoods, so the sense of community was very much alive even among those who were less religious. But in America, where even the living arrangements were voluntary, it was necessary to consciously congregate in some manner, on some occasions, to remain part of the community. Thus the synagogue became the central focus of American Jewish communal life, the place where Jews would gather not only to pray but also to spend time together in social ways that might not be possible during the rest of the week. The synagogues that the German Jews developed reflected their looser religious style. Typically, such synagogues became affiliates of Reform Judaism, once the Reform Jewish movement created its own organization of synagogues, the Union of American Hebrew Congregations, in 1873. Until that time, they were not Reform congregations in any sense; they were simply synagogues that reflected the behavior and beliefs of their worshippers.

Typically, German Jewish immigrants would join their neighborhood synagogue, which was Orthodox because no other type yet existed. Then there would be pressure from congregants for changes in the services, usually relatively minor changes at first. The earliest and perhaps best known of these was the case of Congregation Beth Elohim, in Charleston, South Carolina. During the early 1800s, Charleston, with a community of about 600 Jews, was the largest Jewish community in the United States. In 1824, forty-seven members of Beth Elohim presented a petition to the board of directors, demanding a weekly sermon in English, a shortening of the prayer service, and the repeating of some of the Hebrew prayers in English. When the petition was rejected, the group broke away and formed its own congregation, the Reformed Society of Israelites. Once they decided to break away from Beth Elohim, they were free to reshape Judaism to suit their own needs and tastes. The practices they introduced in their prayer service clearly resembled those of a Protestant church in many respects: the introduction of a choir and an organ, men no longer wearing head coverings, and prayers mostly in English. They deleted all prayers that referred to the Jews returning to the Land of Israel, the coming of the Messiah, and the reinstitution of the ancient Temple sacrifices. The number of Reform-style congregations rose rapidly during the 1840s and 1850s as large numbers of German Jewish immigrants arrived, although many of the new congregations were not formally adherents of Reform Judaism and did not consider themselves to be advocating a separate form of Judaism. Many of them had initiated only modest changes and were still largely traditional.

Judaism as Philanthropy

The life of Felix Warburg illustrates the way in which philanthropy emerged as a surrogate form of Jewish identity for America's German Jewish elite. Warburg entered the German Jewish upper crust by marrying into it. In 1894 he wed Frieda Schiff, daughter of the American Jewish banking magnate Jacob Schiff, and was made a partner in

Schiff's investment firm, Kuhn, Loeb and Company. The Warburgs became an intimate part of an exclusive community of enormous wealth that was situated primarily on the mid- to upper-East Side of Manhattan. It included a number of private homes on Fifth Avenue that were nothing less than mansions—including Schiff's and, before long, Warburg's. Theirs was a world of chefs, servants, butlers, and private nurses for every child. With this entourage in tow, the "Jewish Grand Dukes," as they were sometimes called, regularly vacationed in select locales in the Adirondacks, the Jersey Shore, and Palm Beach, not to mention frequent journeys by steamship to Germany and Switzerland. Education for the young was entrusted only to tutors, private schools, and eventually Ivy League colleges. Socializing and marriage were kept strictly within the fold. Warburg's luxurious private residence was on Fifth Avenue. On weekends he could be found playing squash, horseback riding, or swimming at his Westchester County estate. They also maintained a vacation home at the Wood's Hole summer colony, in the southwest corner of Cape Cod, Massachusetts. Lighthearted, outgoing, and fond of practical jokes, Warburg entertained lavishly and took part in a whirlwind of sporting and cultural activities. A passionate opera fan, Warburg is said to have sometimes attended as many as three concerts in a single evening.

Warburg's approach to Judaism was typical of the German Jewish elite. Although his parents were Orthodox, Warburg had spent crucial periods of his teenage years with his grandparents in Frankfort, and there he had begun to taste the wares of the non-Jewish world. He studied European languages, learned to play the violin, and became a devotee of Renaissance culture. After settling in the United States, Warburg continued to pursue secular, rather than Jewish, cultural interests, and he quickly discarded the Orthodoxy of his youth. When his father-in-law, Jacob Schiff, who observed traditional religious practices, visited on the Sabbath, Warburg would make a perfunctory attempt to utter one of the required blessings. But it was no more than a gesture that departed from the otherwise complete absence of Jewish observance that characterized Warburg's religious life.

The world of American Jewish philanthropy gave Warburg the opportunity to assert his Jewish identity. Unenthusiastic about his role as an investment banker, Warburg was soon given the task of overseeing Schiff's distribution of vast amounts of charity. Warburg did so with relish. He later recalled charity as "the keynote of the household." His father, a wealthy Jewish banker, helped provide food and lodging for East European Jewish refugees passing through Germany on their way to the United States. Those scenes of Jewish emigrants "huddled together with their bundles in smelly masses," Warburg recalled, "made a deep impression on me." The Warburg children were imbued with the virtue of philanthropy at an early age. "[F]rom the first ten *pfennig* piece that we received as allowance, it was made our duty to put a tenth aside for charity, according to the old Jewish tradition, and these pennies were administered by us with a feeling of full responsibility, as though they consisted of large amounts," Warburg later recalled. "That rule has never left us." What Warburg would discover was that in the American Jewish community during the early 1900s, those who distributed the largest amounts of charity could use those funds to advance their social and political agendas.

For Warburg, as for so many of the Uptown stewards, philanthropic activity was the primary connection to the Jewish community. Warburg later recalled that when he arrived in America, he "yearned for an opportunity to become a party to planning and scheming" the future of his adopted country. Philanthropy, especially as it was practiced by the German Jewish upper crust in New York, would satisfy Warburg's yearning by giving him an opportunity to undertake social engineering through dollars. The waves of East European Jewish immigrants who arrived in the United States during the late 1800s and early 1900s would become the primary objects of Warburg's sympathy—and manipulation. Partly out of fear that the appearance and behavior of their coreligionists would irritate non-Jewish Americans, and partly out of genuine sympathy for their downtrodden brethren, the most successful of the German Jewish elite began devoting some of their resources to the creation of philanthropic institutions intended simultaneously to assist and Americanize the newcomers.

The German Jewish patricians were joined in such philanthropic endeavors by young activists from America's Progressive movement. These idealistic young adults, often from wealthy Protestant families, took up residence in what were called "settlement houses," institutions located in the heart of urban immigrant neighborhoods, where they devoted themselves to educating and "uplifting" the new arrivals from Europe. Warburg's interest in the settlement house movement brought him into contact with these "extraordinarily noble men and women," who became his lifelong friends and companions in the business of altruism. Warburg provided substantial financial assistance to a variety of institutions involved in helping, and Americanizing, immigrants: the Henry Street Settlement House, on the

Lower East Side; the Educational Alliance, also on the Lower East Side, a combination settlement house, night school, day care center, and gymnasium; the Young Men's Hebrew Association, which provided sports, cultural activity, and Americanization classes; the Jewish Theological Seminary, intended to train rabbis in the spirit of a more Americanized version of traditional Judaism; and the Kehilla, a community organization created to bring order, unity, and respectability to the chaotic world of the downtown ghetto.

Warburg was, at the same time, involved in a large number of nonsectarian projects. He told friends that he was "like Heinz pickles," which were advertised in fifty-seven varieties, because he "belonged to fifty-seven varieties of committees." A specially constructed cabinet in his office, featuring fifty-seven compartments, enabled Warburg to keep track of his charitable commitments to a wide array of museums, educational institutions, and civic improvement associations. To assist new immigrants of all nationalities, he gave financial support to the Immigrant Educational Institute and the North American Civic League for Immigration. Warburg accepted an appointment to the New York City Board of Education, chairing its committee for children with special needs. He also donated large sums to numerous cultural institutions, a reflection of his lifelong interest in music, art, and sports.

In Warburg one may detect a natural progression from helping all immigrants, to helping Jewish immigrants, to helping Jewish refugees in Europe. He utilized his mediating skills to bring together disparate Jewish relief agencies into a unified American Jewish Joint Distribution Committee, and to provide coordinated assistance to European Jewish communities devastated by World War I. Shortly afterward, Warburg brought similar unity of action to the local Jewish scene, bridging the differences between the major New York–area Jewish charities to produce the Federation to Support Jewish Philanthropies in New York. The ostensible purpose of the new Jewish federation was to streamline and centralize Jewish charity distribution. One of its unstated purposes was to give the German Jewish patricians firmer control over how communal funds were used. Warburg and his friends did not want wild Russian immigrants spending Jewish money on radical (that is, un-American) causes. As with the patricians' other favored charities, the federation served as an instrument of the social and political agenda of the German Jewish agenda, by financing institutions that helped promote Americanization.

The Russian Immigration

From 1800 through 1881, a total of about 250,000 Jews left Russia for various destinations. During the decade following the pogroms and anti-Jewish economic decrees of 1881, some 135,000 Russian Jews went to America and another 15,000 relocated to other countries. As persecution intensified, emigration reached tidal-wave proportions: from 1891 to 1914, 1.3 million Russian Jews immigrated to the United States. Looked at another way, it might be noted that the average annual emigration of East European Jews was 19,000 from 1881 to 1892, 37,000 from 1892 to 1903, and 76,000 from 1903 to 1914.

The peak years were between 1904 and 1908, when 642,000 Jews arrived. In 1880, on the eve of the Russian emigration, the American Jewish community numbered approximately 280,000, or 0.5 percent of the American population. By 1900 there were 1 million Jews in America. By 1915 there were 3.25 million, and American Jewry had become the largest Jewish community in the world. New York City, which had 80,000 Jews in 1880, had 1.4 million in 1914. By 1925 the newcomers would swell American Jewry to 4.5 million, more than 3 percent of the national populace.

Oppression was the primary cause of the massive emigration, although other factors played their part. Overpopulation in Russia, caused by recent medical advances, had made life more difficult; czarist totalitarianism in general showed no signs of abating, which caused Jewish political activists to lose hope; the often exaggerated success stories of earlier immigrants received widespread publicity in the Russian Jewish press; and improved shipping—the 1870s transition from sailing ships to steamships—made the long journey bearable. The majority of Russian Jews did not emigrate, however. The simple security of familiar surroundings militated against leaving; so did reports of the breakdown of religious observance in America and the circulation of hard-luck stories, especially from the approximately 15 percent of emigrants who returned to Europe. (The rate of return steadily decreased; it hit a high of about 15 to 20 percent in the early 1900s but dropped to 8 percent by 1908 and less than 1 percent by 1919.)

Case Study: "People Walk on Their Heads"

A particularly pessimistic report on the state of Judaism in late-nineteenth-century America, published in 1887, was that of Moses Weinberger, an Orthodox rabbi. Comparing the chaotic American Jewish community to the structured and pious shtetl he had left behind in Eastern Europe, Weinberger declared that in America "people walk on their heads." Weinberger bemoaned the entrepreneurial spirit he detected among many American Jews: "[M]oney is their god," he charged. He found many other problems as well. Thanks to church-state separation, the government did not enforce religious affiliation; any Jew was free to sever his ties to the Jewish community. Under the influence of American democracy, positions of power in synagogues were being doled out to unlearned individuals who in the old country would never have been considered qualified for the task. Kosher food supervision was in chaos; untrained preachers calling themselves "reverends" were replacing rabbis as congregational leaders; marriages were being conducted without regard for the requirements of Jewish religious law. Spirituality was being usurped by an emphasis on building luxurious new synagogues and the competitive hiring of "big name" European cantors to lead high-priced holiday services. Some historians see this "cantor craze" as a synthesis of Old World traditions and New World tastes; others characterize it as symbolic of the interwar synagogue's shift from participatory ritual to Judaism as performance.

Weinberger, a committed Zionist, wrote in Hebrew, which had not been in common use for many centuries; it was reserved for prayer and study of Scripture. As a result, his book was widely ignored at the time. Today it provides historians with a revealing glimpse of late-nineteenth-century American Jewry from the Orthodox perspective.

For 85 percent of Jewish immigrants, the port of arrival was Ellis Island. An 1890 Supreme Court decision gave the federal government jurisdiction over immigration. The government then established its main immigration checkpoint at Ellis Island, in the New York harbor. When new immigrants arrived there, they underwent a series of interviews and medical examinations that took days, sometimes even weeks. Newcomers could be refused admission if they advocated radical political ideas, had ever been arrested, had more than one wife, bore signs of medical ailments—about 1 percent were turned away for that reason—or even if they already had a job. When an immigration official asked if the newcomer had a job, it was almost a trick question—he might think he should answer "yes," so that he would not appear to be a burden on the American public; in fact, the better answer was "no," because it was illegal for American businessmen to contract for foreign labor.

Many of the new Jewish immigrants were taken care of during their first few weeks by HIAS, the Hebrew Immigrant Aid Society, a charitable agency established by Jewish philanthropists. Although initially troubled by the mass immigration, which they feared might provoke anti-Semitism as well as usurp their positions of power in the community, most American Jewish leaders felt genuine sympathy for the victims of Russian pogroms. In any event, they had little choice but to come to grips with the reality of a virtually unstoppable flood of immigrants. To aid the newcomers, and to Americanize them as quickly as possible, the German Jewish elite created HIAS, which offered shelter and an employment agency, and the Educational Alliance and Young Men's Hebrew Association, which provided instruction in the English language and training in American customs.

Most of the East European immigrants settled in New York City. This, too, troubled some Jewish leaders, who feared that the mass concentration of immigrants in a small urban area would create a sort of de facto ghetto that would perpetuate anti-Jewish stereotypes. In an attempt to divert the Russian Jews from New York, Jewish leaders created the Industrial Removal Office, which undertook the Galveston Project, settling a modest number of Jews in Galveston, Texas. Not many Jews, however, were interested in relocating to the rural Southwest. New York had a large, well-established Jewish community that could provide many types of Jewish communal services and fulfill religious needs; outlying areas could not. It also had a variety of industries in which they could find jobs. Moreover, many of the new immigrants already had friends and relatives living in New York.

Some 80 percent of the East European immigrants were between the ages of fifteen and forty-five, divided almost equally between the sexes, indicating that many of them were young families traveling together and intending to remain in the United States permanently. This contrasts with, for example, Italian immigrants, large numbers of whom arrived during the same years, but many of whom were married men traveling by themselves, with the intention of working for a while and then returning to their families in Italy.

These Jewish immigrants tended to reside in the same sections of each city, usually in areas that were relatively close to the downtown area in which they were employed. The Lower East Side of Manhattan, for example, was only a few minutes from the parts of Manhattan where many Jews were employed in the garment industries. In 1915, 350,000 Jews lived in the Lower East Side on less than 2 square miles of real estate. These crowded Jewish neighborhoods often suffered from problems with sanitation, not to mention disease and epidemics. It would, however, be an oversimplification to characterize the Lower East Side as a crowded and miserable ghetto. It was crowded, and for some people it was miserable. But there was also a rich and varied cultural life, there was the opportunity to be among one's own people, to meet a spouse, and to find employment among fellow Jews.

Many worked in New York's garment industry, often in sweatshops—small businesses located in cramped, dirty, and hazardous storefronts or basements. Their notoriously poor ventilation gave rise to the name "sweat" shops. Laboring as many as fourteen to sixteen hours daily, such workers typically were involved in the manufacture of specific pieces of garments that were later shipped elsewhere for final production. Smaller garment industries, also dominated by Jewish workers, could be found in Chicago, Cleveland, Philadelphia, Baltimore, and Boston.

The social and economic mobility of these newcomers has been amply demonstrated in Thomas Kessner's pioneering study of Jewish and Italian immigrants. The many similarities between the two groups make them prime candidates for comparison: they came to America during the same years, settled in the same cities in approximately the same proportions, established enclaves in lower Manhattan, and generally maintained their foreign language and religion in the face of pressures to abandon them. Both ethnic groups experienced a notable degree of mobility from blue collar to white collar, as well as some in the reverse, but Jews rose at a faster rate and far fewer Jews dropped from white to blue than did Italians. The Italians were mostly single men, unskilled, who came with a short-range goal of making some money and then returning; they lacked the sense of "no return" desperation needed to rise faster or higher. The Jews came with families, often with urban skills as well as experience in trades that they had been compelled to take up in Europe when some types of employment were closed to them. A number of Jews entered the labor market at the employer level, while Italians typically entered at the lowest rung. The vast majority of Jewish immigrants had no thought of returning to Europe; hence they were more stable and able to focus on long-range goals of personal advancement. Although many Jews relocated to suburbs as soon as they could, Italians tended to remain in their original areas of settlement longer. With their more limited aspirations and a greater sense of loyalty to family than to ethnic group, Italian children were often content to follow in their parents' occupations, while Jews more typically sought to rise above their parents' socioeconomic level.

Before 1900, Jewish-led labor unions made little headway in the mostly Jewish industries. Most of the workshops were very small, with only a few employees, which made it harder for the unions to organize. Often the boss and an employee were relatives, or friends, or at least came from the same town in Europe, making it harder to pit the workers against the boss. In addition, there was public hostility to labor unions, because the unions were sympathetic to socialism, and in the United States socialism during the late 1800s was associated with revolutionary violence, such as the Haymarket bombing.

But during the early 1900s, a number of factors boosted the involvement of Jews in the labor unions. The growth of large factories made it easier for organizers. The large factories ended the cozy relationship between boss and workers, putting distance between them. After the failure of the Russian Revolution of 1905, many veteran Jewish labor organizers fled to America and became involved in unions. There was more popular sympathy for unions, especially as a result of books like *The Jungle,* by Upton Sinclair (1912), which portrayed the miserable and dangerous working conditions in the Chicago stockyards. Many workers joined unions after the 1911 Triangle Shirtwaist Factory fire, in which 146 Italian and Jewish workers, mostly girls, were killed because the management had blocked off fire exits in order to discourage the workers from loafing on the fire escapes. By 1920 at least 250,000 Jews belonged to unions.

The East European Jewish immigrants found themselves bedeviled by economic pressures to assimilate similar to those their German predecessors had faced: the six-day work week, which pressured them to work on Saturday; Blue Laws that forbade them from opening their businesses on Sunday; the difficulty of obtaining leave from work on Jewish holidays. Furthermore, the turn of the century was a time when the "melting pot" philosophy—popularized by a play in which people of different nationalities literally jumped into a pot where they were melted together into a single American nation—had taken hold, increasing the pressure on immigrants to shed their Old World ways. And once again, the most religiously observant were the ones who stayed behind. And there was an additional factor encouraging the abandonment of religious traditions, one that did not obtain during the period of German immigration: because of the large concentration of East European Jews in New York City and a handful of other urban centers, there existed, for the first time, the option of a secular Jewish identity, one that revolved around speaking Yiddish, engaging in Jewish cultural activities, marrying other Jews, and living in heavily Jewish neighborhoods—thus enabling one to "feel" Jewish without personally observing religious strictures.

There were also a variety of factors that, even if they did not encourage religious observance, certainly slowed the process of acculturation. Unlike the Germans, the Russian immigrants often consisted of entire families—because they were fleeing persecution—and the cohesion of the family unit naturally reinforced traditional modes of behavior. When they arrived, they joined a large pre-existing ethnic community that was centered in the same small geographic location. They spoke their own language, partook of their own culture, and generally stuck to their own kind, in part because the rise of anti-Semitism, especially social discrimination, limited the opportunities for socializing with non-Jews.

As much as America had its impact on the East European immigrants, their impact on America and American Jewry could not be denied. To begin with, they now became a force at the ballot box. The suddenly much larger American Jewish community, with most of its members concentrated in key electoral states such as New York and Pennsylvania, now had to be taken more seriously by politicians.

The Russian Jewish immigrants also made themselves felt in the evolution of Reform Judaism. Radical trends in the movement had been evident since the adoption of its 1885 Pittsburgh Platform, which rejected the idea that a Jewish state would one day be revived; declared that Judaism was a religion only, not a nationality; rejected the idea that there would be a Messiah; and said that modern Jews were not bound by traditional Jewish law. Even more extreme, by the early 1900s, a minority of Reform temples were observing Sunday as their Sabbath; many others did not formally change their Sabbath day, but shifted their main focus to Sunday, by having the rabbi's major sermon of the week delivered at widely advertised Sunday-morning services.

The Russian immigration blunted these trends. Having just left an environment steeped in Jewish tradition, the Russians were not yet receptive to sweeping or radical changes. Those who joined Reform congregations exercised pressure from within to refrain from complete abandonment of tradition. The Russians' sympathy for Zionism also created pressure within the Reform movement that helped gradually reverse the movement's longstanding anti-Zionism. In addition, Reform leaders recognized that in order to attract East European immigrants to their congregations, they would need to step back from complete rejection of traditional practices and attitudes.

These changes were more pronounced among the East Coast Reform than at the movement's Cincinnati headquarters. In 1909 the handful of pro-Zionist rabbis teaching at Hebrew Union College had been purged from the staff. The traditional liturgy was radically revised, and the holidays of Purim and Chanukah, with their strongly nationalist overtones, were all but done away with. Then came the backlash. In 1920, Reform rabbi and American Zionist leader Stephen Wise established his own rabbinical training school, the Jewish Institute of Religion, in New York. It embraced Zionism and utilized a curriculum more relevant to the needs of students who were themselves of East European origin and were going out to serve Reform congregations in neighborhoods populated mostly by Russian Jews.

In addition to pressure from the Russians to refrain from straying too far from tradition, the rise of Nazism and the persecution of European Jewry profoundly affected the Reform movement by dealing a staggering blow to the optimistic worldview that had characterized early American Reform Judaism.

The Pittsburgh Platform, the 1885 declaration of principles by leading Reform rabbis, had reveled in "the spirit of broad humanity of our age" and averred: "We recognize in the modern era of universal culture of heart and intellect the approaching of the realization of Israel's great Messianic hope for the establishment of the kingdom of truth, justice and peace among all men." The platform argued that modern Jews should discard the "primitive" ideas of their ancestors and concentrate on facilitating the arrival of the Messianic era of universal brotherhood. This vision of a world marching steadily toward peace and harmony, harnessing medical and scientific achievements for the good of mankind, was shattered by the cruel reality of the 1940s, when scientific advances were used to implement mass murder. Soberly, the Reform movement reinstituted Purim and Chanukah in 1942, returned a number of excised nationalist-flavored passages to the prayerbook in 1946, and, in 1948, oversaw the merger of Hebrew Union College and the Jewish Institute of Religion. Reform Judaism had always prided itself on its willingness to change with the times; in the 1940s, it changed back with the times.

The Reform movement was not the only wing of Judaism that was influenced by pressure from the immigrants. Competition for the religious allegiance of the Russian immigrants changed Orthodox Judaism as well. In order to meet the needs and desires of the Russian immigrant masses, many Orthodox Jewish leaders began looking for ways that they could modernize Jewish religious practice, within the limits of what Jewish law allowed, so that it would appeal to the newcomers. Orthodoxy would have to be "Americanized" in order to survive. Synagogue decorum was improved; boisterous behavior during prayer services was actively discouraged; the rabbi's weekly sermon was delivered in English; and social activities were added. These changes helped ensure Orthodoxy's ability to endure in the face of the pressures on American Jews to assimilate. According to some estimates, in 1935 some 1 million American Jews considered themselves Orthodox, while the Conservative and Reform movements could claim just 300,000 and 200,000 members, respectively. Historian Jeffrey Gurock has shown how interwar American Orthodoxy, spearheaded by the outreach-minded Young Israel synagogue movement, "more than held its own" in its competition with Judaism's more liberal wings. Implementing a strategy of "modernization in the [style of the] service and conscious inclusion in congregational life of all Jews regardless of their personal religious deportment" (Gurock 1984, 48), Americanized Orthodoxy in the 1930s outpaced Conservatism (its chief rival) in the outer boroughs and suburban regions of metropolitan New York, the areas where the major battles for the religious allegiance of the second generation were fought.

Ideology and the Immigrants

The East European immigration included a number of radical-left political ideologues who adhered to various shades of Marxism and may be referred to, in general, as the socialists. They have attracted the lion's share of attention among historians, in part because their prolific literary output has enabled contemporary scholars to examine their views in some detail. It cannot be said, however, that they represented more than a particularly vocal and colorful minority. At the other end of the spectrum were the Jewish nationalists, partisans of the various factions of the Zionist movement. There was also a noticeable segment of the religiously Orthodox. Each of these factions seems to have had a relatively small number of hard-core adherents, along with a large number of fellow travelers or sympathizers.

Each of these movements also had its share of difficulty striking roots in the American Jewish community. Socialism, for example, was contrary to the American way of life, which had been working well for Jewish immigrants. The nativism and extreme anticommunism of the post–World War I years further discouraged Jews from viewing socialism favorably. Zionism, too, contradicted the goal of Americanization; immigrants were expected to shed their allegiances to foreign nationalist causes. Furthermore, those East European Jews who chose to come to America had also consciously chosen not to go to Palestine; the small number who felt most strongly about Zionism were not the ones arriving in New York. A similar point could be made about the level of religious observance among the East European immigrants: those who were the most devout were the least likely to leave the intensely Jewish environment of the East European shtetl. Orthodox Judaism faced the obvious problem of advocating a sectarian way of life in the face of the natural pressure on the immigrants to assimilate. That pressure was accelerated by the six-day work week and other socioeconomic factors in American society that conflicted with Jewish tradition.

So they Americanized. Many socialists toned down the revolutionary flavor of their rhetoric, although they could not substantially alter their ideology without losing their raison d'etre. Socialist opposition to America's entry into World War I severely undercut the movement's popularity, and by the time the war was over, many former socialists had moved over to the Democratic Party, where they could advocate many liberal causes without having their patriotism called into question. Zionism, too, underwent an Americanization process, to be explained in detail below.

Leadership in a Voluntary Community

Until modern times, Jewish communal leadership was in the hands of the rabbinical authorities. The Jews themselves venerated their rabbis and considered religious law to be the final arbiter in matters of communal policy. In any event, the rulers of the countries in which they lived had no qualms about recognizing the Jews' religious authorities as their communal leaders. Rabbinic functions in the premodern era thus ranged from the expected roles of judge, scholar, teacher, and pastoral adviser to the political roles of intermediary with the non-Jewish authorities and public defender of Judaism against Christian polemicists. But in modern America, the rabbi's role has shifted enormously. No legal role of consequence remains; rabbis may serve as judges in a private Jewish religious court, known as a *beit din,* but it has no real power because it is not empowered to enforce its rulings. Rabbis no longer serve as the community's political leaders. The role of pastor has been usurped, to a significant extent, by the rise of psychotherapy. Two vestiges from the earlier period do remain: the rabbi as teacher, although a large part of that is in the form of another innovation, the weekly sermon; and the public defender of Judaism, a role that rabbis assumed in the 1800s in particular, when public disputations over Judaism were more common. A new role for the rabbi has emerged: the rabbi as the performer of religious commandments. In the many Conservative and Reform synagogues where the vast majority of congregants are nonobservant, the rabbi's performance of religious obligations serves as a sort of conscience-reliever for the masses. Through the rabbi's religiosity, individual congregants can feel spiritually fulfilled—or perhaps spiritually absolved of being religious themselves.

The prominence of rabbis in the nineteenth-century American Jewish leadership made sense—at least for a time. Until the late 1800s, many of the major crises facing Jewry related to religious matters: overseas anti-Semitism often involved blood libels rooted in religious prejudice, while domestic struggles often revolved around Christian missionary activity or the imposition of Blue Laws (compulsory Sunday closings of businesses) and other attempts to make America more overtly Christian. In such an environment, it was no wonder that the Board of Delegates of American Israelites, established in 1859 to serve as the community's primary spokesman to the outside world, was dominated by rabbis. But as the nature of anti-Semitism shifted, in the late 1800s, from medieval-style religious bigotry to modern, secular variations such as racial pseudoscience and social discrimination, rabbis began to lose their special claim to community leadership.

There were additional reasons for the inability of the rabbinate to retain its prominence in the American Jewish leadership. Too many obstacles impeded attempts to transplant the old European model of community defense to the new and different environs of the United States. The entire notion of religious leaders serving as public and communal spokesmen ran contrary to America's ethos of strict church-state separation.

Further complicating matters was the ever-escalating phenomenon of religious conflicts within the rabbinate itself. By the late 1800s, the Reform movement had formally established its own, separate institutions—the Union of American Hebrew Congregations (1873); a rabbinical training school, Hebrew Union College (1875); and a rabbinical association, the Central Conference of American Rabbis (1889). Conservative Judaism did not yet exist as a separate ideological movement; its rabbinical academy, the Jewish Theological Seminary, was established (in 1887) as an Orthodox institution. But it gradually drifted away from Orthodox traditions, and by the early 1900s it was well established as religiously separate. The Orthodox, who were slower to create permanent institutions in America, tried unsuccessfully to install a prominent European rabbi, Jacob Joseph, as New York City's "chief rabbi" in the 1890s. But transplanting European ways to the new world proved impossible in a voluntary community in which religious leaders were not granted power by the secular authorities. Battles over a kosher food supervision tax and other internal disputes spoiled the "chief rabbinate" experiment; soon three different rabbis were laying claim to the title. In 1898 the Union of Orthodox Jewish Congregations of America was established. A rabbinical school, the Rabbi Isaac Elchanon Theological Seminary, was created in 1897 and expanded to become Yeshiva College (later Yeshiva University) in 1915. A religious leadership so deeply fractured could hardly be expected to provide unified leadership for the community at large.

By the late 1800s, the ethnic *shtadlan* emerged as a new and distinct type of Jewish leader. The *shtadlanim* were secular leaders, usually from Reform backgrounds and German-born, who joined the struggle for Jewish rights as a reaction to the spread of anti-Semitism. They established the first U.S. Jewish defense organization, the American Jewish Committee, in 1906, for the declared purpose of defending the rights of Jews around the world through diplomatic intercession and education. The ostensible reason for the committee's creation was the wave of pogroms in czarist Russia that year, and while the AJ Committee's founders were undoubtedly disturbed by the violence, the fact is that the intensified persecution of Jews in Russia had begun back in 1881. The real reason for the decision of this self-selected group to assert a position of communal leadership was their concern that the radical political activists who were prominent among the waves of recently arrived East European immigrants might attempt to seize the community's helm. They feared that irresponsible behavior by such agitators might provoke anti-Semitism from which all American Jews, respectable and militant alike, would suffer.

Wealthy, acculturated philanthropists such as Jacob Schiff, Nathan Strauss, and Felix Warburg subscribed to the notion prevalent in the nineteenth-century American Progressive movement that the "best" people should volunteer to solve society's problems. Many of their non-Jewish counterparts, friends, and associates were involved in Progressivism, and they looked to it as a model for how American Jews should behave. The AJ Committee's founders regarded themselves as the best the community had to offer, and they were volunteering to safeguard Jewish interests. They consciously did not choose an agenda based on fighting American anti-Semitism; that would have been too parochial, and also would have cast doubt on their optimistic view of America as a nation ready to embrace Jews and other minorities. Instead they focused on aiding distressed Jews overseas. Such humanitarian campaigns could be presented as consistent with Americanism, and with universalism as well.

An attempt to establish a unified community leadership did not fare well. It began with an anti-Jewish slur: the New York City police commissioner's remark, in 1908, that the city's criminal dockets were filled with East European Jewish immigrants. The Russians were outraged; the Germans were embarrassed that all Jews were besmirched by the newcomers' behavior. Suddenly "Downtown" and "Uptown" found common cause. The immigrants needed the Uptowners' financial largesse, political connections, and experience in public service to organize a serious defense agency; the German Jewish elite agreed to work together with the Russians in order to control them and find ways to correct their behavior. What emerged was the Kehilla (Hebrew for "community"), an organization intended to represent New York Jewry to the outside world while its Bureau of Social Morals worked with the police to stamp out Jewish crime and vice.

An array of problems gradually beset the Kehilla experiment. It could never meet the high expectations that accompanied its founding, especially in the face of competition from other Jewish defense groups that arose after World War I. Kehilla leader Judah Magnes was pressured to resign from his post in 1920, lest his staunch pacifism and opposition to American participation in the World War be perceived by the public as evidence of Jewry's lack of patriotism. Magnes's leadership had been crucial; the Kehilla could not survive long without him. At the same time, as the behavior modification aspects of the Kehilla's agenda failed to produce the quick and sweeping results for which the Uptowners had hoped, they shifted their financial support to the recently created Federation of Jewish Philanthropies of New York, a charitable body over which they had stricter control and which they perceived as a more effective tool of social pacification. By 1922 the Kehilla was no more.

Although the federation catered to New York Jewry's needs, the Jewish community also sponsored a slew of charities aimed at overseas needs. The devastation suffered by East European Jewry during World War I prompted the creation of three separate fundraising campaigns: an American Jewish Relief Committee, headed by the German Jewish elite; the Central Committee for Relief, organized by the Orthodox to meet the needs of the religiously observant, whom they feared other charities would neglect; and the People's Relief Committee, chaired by socialist congressmember Meyer London. All three factions came together in November 1914 to establish the unified American Jewish Joint Distribution Committee. Adversity would continue to compel unity in the years ahead. Local Jewish federations were created in individual Jewish communities around the country; with the onset of the Great Depression, they would unite in October 1932 as the Council of Jewish Federation and Welfare Funds. Likewise, the Kristallnacht pogroms of November 1938 would convince rival local and regional Jewish charitable fundraising campaigns to establish a single United Jewish Appeal, in 1939.

Meanwhile, an entirely new class of Jewish professionals were entering the community's leadership circles: lawyers. Donna Arzt (1986) contends that the disproportionate number of American Jews who took up public-interest law, beginning in the early 1900s, demonstrated "a kind of loyalty to the Jewish 'tradition' of public service." Arzt believes that public-interest law has provided American Jewish attorneys with the framework in which to express that "latent component of Jewishness" that cannot be lost through assimilation, "a timeless Jewish political style that will live on." The opposing point of view has been articulated by Jerold Auerbach: "For Jews who so preferred, and many did, the identification with American law and justice could even provide an escape from Judaism. Among Jews, it has been suggested, 'one way of hiding is to choose a universal mask'; as defenders of the American rule of law, and as champions of social justice, Jews located themselves securely within the prevailing liberal precepts of modern America." Auerbach points to the gradual transfer of Jewish legal authority from rabbis to acculturated Jewish attorneys that took place in the United States during the first decades of the twentieth century. The social and economic pressures under which immigrants labored, combined with the freedom to assimilate that the United States offered, helped accelerate the erosion of rabbinical authority. Many of the men who subsequently assumed positions of power in the American Jewish community were lawyers. The two most outstanding were Louis Marshall and Louis Brandeis. Marshall was a dominant force among the successful German Jewish immigrants associated with the AJ Committee, of which he was president from 1912 until his death in 1929. Marshall referred to the U.S. Constitution as the "holy of holies, an instrument of sacred import."

Brandeis's role as a Jewish leader is better known than Marshall's, and his part in furthering the rabbis-to-lawyers transition is perhaps more obvious. Who could have been more suited to such a role than a Jewish Supreme Court justice known as "old Isaiah"? Brandeis, devoted to the idea of running the American Zionist movement like a business corporation—or a law firm—filled its key positions with fellow lawyers who would help mold a new, Americanized Zionism distinct from the European variety. The speech-makers and nationalist ideologues of Old World Zionism were supplanted by attorneys and hard-headed businessmen for whom Palestine was either an attractive investment or a sort of experiment station for the noblesse oblige values of America's Progressive Era.

Thus, by 1915, with Marshall at the helm of the AJ Committee and Brandeis in charge of the American Zionist movement, "lawyers controlled the major organizational expressions of American Judaism," Auerbach writes. Rabbinical influence in the American Jewish community had been severely eroded, and "lawyers stepped in to provide a secular legal frame of reference for Jewish acculturation," as Auerbach puts it. "Their fervent attachments to the American legal system defined a new identification for American Jews."

As East European immigrants became acclimated in the United States, many felt uncomfortable at the idea of an elitist, self-appointed committee presuming to speak on their behalf. America's democratic ways offered an alternative model for choosing Jewish leadership. By the time of World War I, a grassroots movement for democracy in Jewish life was taking shape. American Zionists, unhappy with the AJ Committee's opposition to Zionism—the German-born elite feared that Jewish statehood would raise questions about their own loyalty to America—joined the new movement for a democratically chosen Jewish organization. In 1918, 400 delegates, most of them chosen by more than 300,000 voters in Jewish communities around the United States, gathered in Philadelphia for the first American Jewish Congress. By 1922 the AJ Congress transformed itself into a permanent body devoted to addressing a broad range of Jewish concerns, domestic and international. It also played a prominent role in Zionist educational and lobbying activity, and its presidents frequently served simultaneously in the leadership of the American Zionist movement.

American Zionism

Just as American Jews redefined their Judaism to suit American needs and conditions, so too did they Americanize their Zionism. Beginning in the early 1900s, American Jews took a gradually intensifying interest in Zionism, the international movement to re-establish the Jewish national homeland that had existed in Palestine in ancient times. The American version of Zionism was very much a product of the American environment. Helping downtrodden East European Jews begin a new life in the land of the Bible fit nicely with the ideals of philanthropy and humanitarianism popular in America. A Zionism that emphasized refugeeism was particularly in tune with the Progressive Reform movement of the late 1800s and early 1900s. "The American Jewish response to the Zionist idea always took its cue from the American scene," notes Naomi Cohen. "When Wilson talked of self-determination, when Truman took up the case of the displaced persons, when non-Jews expounded the theme of cultural pluralism, and when the American public grew accustomed to minority demands, overt Jewish support for Zionism rose." Even when the numerical strength of the American Zionist movement eroded, "it never evaporated entirely, for if confined to philanthropy or refugeeism it was unobjectionable" (N. Cohen 1975, 145). However, the idea that American Jews should themselves immigrate to Palestine was embraced by only a tiny segment of the American Zionist movement; Zionism in the United States was primarily a charitable enterprise to help those who needed a shelter to which they could escape from persecution. American Zionists certainly did not regard themselves as requiring a haven from oppression.

This was one of several ways in which American Zionism differed dramatically from the European variety. "Negation of the Exile" was a central tenet of classic European Zionist thought. Anti-Semitism, both in its violent manifestations and in the form of economic discrimination, was regarded as an inexorable force that would doom the Jewish communities of the Diaspora and compel mass Jewish immigration to the Holy Land. American Zionists could not possibly conceive of the American future in such bleak terms. They saw America, not Jerusalem, as their true homeland, and they were convinced that America, in turn, would be good to the Jews.

Another sharp contrast between Zionism in America and Europe concerned the focus of the Zionist movement. Early European Zionist leaders such as Theodor Herzl, Chaim Weizmann, and Vladimir Ze'ev Jabotinsky believed that international diplomacy was the key to securing a Jewish homeland, and they preferred to focus attention on political work. The American Zionist movement, especially under the leadership of Louis Brandeis as of 1914, regarded practical development projects in Palestine as the most urgent need. Brandeis returned from his first and only visit to the Holy Land, in 1919, convinced that Zionism's top priority must be the draining of swamps and the elimination of malaria. This emphasis on practicality and the view of Palestine as essentially a business project led American Zionists, in 1929, into an alliance with the self-described "non-Zionists," a group of wealthy businessmen and philanthropists led by AJ Committee president Louis Marshall who supported building up Palestine as a Jewish refuge, although they opposed the idea of a sovereign Jewish state, for fear it would raise questions about the loyalties of Diaspora Jews. Despite his disagreements with the Marshall-Warburg crowd, World Zionist Organization president Chaim Weizmann embraced the power-sharing alliance with the non-Zionists because of the Zionist movement's desperate financial straits. The investment of non-Zionist capital helped sustain the struggling Palestine Jewish community.

At the same time, membership in the primary U.S. Zionist group, the Zionist Organization of America (ZOA), declined precipitously during the 1920s. The drop was, in the first instance, a response to events abroad. In November 1917, the British issued the Balfour Declaration, pledging to facilitate the establishment of a Jewish national home in Palestine; shortly afterward they captured the Holy Land from its Turkish rulers. Most American Jews now concluded that with British help, a Jewish homeland had become inevitable, and therefore Zionism had achieved its goals; there was no longer any pressing reason to join a Zionist organization. There were domestic considerations as well. A rising nativist hysteria, which manifested itself in the U.S. government's 1920 Palmer raids against foreign-born radicals and the enactment of tight immigration quotas in 1921 and 1924, reminded American Jews that loyalties to foreign causes or countries were unwelcome. The sharp reduction in Jewish immigration to the United States because of the new quotas also had a detrimental effect on American Zionism, for it was the newcomers from Eastern Europe who still tended to feel the strongest sense of nationalism, while those who had been longer in America were usually more sensitive to the need to acculturate in order to gain acceptance in American society.

A conspicuous exception to American Zionism's declining fortunes was the ZOA's women's division, Hadassah. Established in 1913, Hadassah eschewed political and propaganda battles, instead focusing on operating health programs in Palestine. This struck a responsive chord among American Jewish women, offering them a practical and direct way to assist the development of the Jewish homeland. Differences with the ZOA leadership over administrative and financial practices, as well as the ZOA's reluctance to grant the women a greater say in the organization's decision-making process, led to the secession of Hadassah from the ZOA in the late 1920s.

American Zionism's downward spiral was halted by overseas crises. The Palestinian Arab pogroms of 1929 and the rise of the Nazis to power in Germany in 1933 required the urgent attention of the large and politically influential American Jewish community. Refugee Zionism offered American Jews a particularly convenient way to respond. They could raise funds to develop Palestine and facilitate German Jewish immigration, without having to worry about settling there themselves; they could focus on Palestine as oppressed Jewry's refuge rather than undertake the unpleasant task of seeking changes in the popular U.S. policy of immigration restriction; they could even use the Zionist cause as a substitute form of Jewish identification for those who had drifted away from traditional religious observance.

Nowhere in the American Jewish community was the impact of the European crisis more evident than in Reform Judaism's changing stance on the issue of Zionism. The Reform movement's anti-Zionism had deep roots. It had been an integral part of Reform Judaism since its birth in Germany in the early 1800s. German Jewish advocates of Reform Judaism were motivated to a significant extent by a desire to gain acceptance by German society. They believed that traditional Jewish practices and beliefs could be reformed to the point where they would sufficiently coincide with those of the German public as to eliminate anti-Jewish sentiment. This included formal repudiation of the traditional Jewish dream of returning to Zion and reviving the ancient Jewish state, which German Reform Jews feared would raise questions about their loyalty to Germany.

Anti-Zionism likewise constituted a central component in the ideology of American Reform Judaism. The movement's first major ideological statement was composed by nineteen leading Reform rabbis, meeting in Pittsburgh in November 1885. On the question of Jewish nationalism and territorial aspirations, the fifth of the Pittsburgh Platform's eight planks declared: "We consider ourselves no longer a nation, but a religious community, and, therefore, expect neither a return to Palestine, nor a sacrificial worship under the sons of Aaron, nor the restoration of any of the laws concerning the Jewish state."

Although the Pittsburgh Platform remained Reform's position on Zionism well into the 1900s, events abroad eventually provoked a reassessment. Since Reform's anti-Zionism was in large measure an attempt to make a positive impression on the non-Jewish world, the endorsement of Zionism by important segments of the non-Jewish world could hardy be ignored. England's 1917 endorsement of Zionism, the Balfour Declaration, which was seconded by the United States, led to the adoption, by the 1920 convention of the Central

Conference of American (Reform) Rabbis, of a resolution "rejoicing" at the decision by the League of Nations to grant the Palestine mandate to Great Britain. The resolution also asserted that it was "the duty of all Jews to contribute to the reconstruction of Palestine" while continuing to eschew Jewish nationalism. Two years later, the CCAR reached a formal agreement with the Palestine Development Council to promote joint projects for developing the Holy Land. In 1928 the CCAR passed a resolution praising the Jewish Agency for Palestine, the quasi-governing body for Palestine established by the British Mandate authorities; and Hebrew Union College awarded an honorary doctorate to world Zionist leader Chaim Weizmann. In 1930 the CCAR voted to include the Zionist anthem, "Hatikvah," in the Reform movement's hymnal.

These trends accelerated significantly after the rise of the Nazis to power in Germany in 1933, and especially after it became clear that Hitler would remain in power for the foreseeable future. The installation of a government officially devoted to the mistreatment of Jews— in, of all places, the land that Jews had always regarded as Europe's most cultured and enlightened—made the old dreams of universalism seem hopelessly outdated. Moreover, it underlined the urgency of establishing a haven for persecuted Jews. To cling to anti-Zionism despite such developments became increasingly untenable. In early 1935, 241 Reform rabbis—out of 401 CCAR members—signed a petition praising the accomplishments of Labor Zionism in Palestine. The 1935 CCAR convention took "no official stand on the subject of Zionism," thus officially acknowledging the movement's shift from anti-Zionism to non-Zionism. It also pledged to "cooperate in the upbuilding of Palestine." The Union of American Hebrew Congregations, the national association of Reform synagogues, in early 1937 adopted a resolution urging "all Jews, irrespective of ideological differences, to unite in the activities leading to the establishment of a Jewish homeland in Palestine." Later that year, the CCAR convention, meeting in Columbus, Ohio, declared that it was "the obligation of all Jewry to aid in [the] upbuilding [of Palestine] as a Jewish homeland by endeavoring to make it not only a haven of refuge for the oppressed but also a center of Jewish cultural and spiritual life." The Columbus Platform, as it came to be known, marked the culmination of the Reform movement's abandonment of anti-Zionism.

The backlash was not long in coming. Alarmed by the growing popularity of Zionism in the American Jewish community and the inroads it was making within the Reform rabbinate, several dozen Reform rabbis and lay leaders in 1942 established the American Council for Judaism, for the purpose of promoting anti-Zionism. The rise and fall of the American Council for Judaism illustrates a number of important trends and developments in the 1940s American Jewish community. The immediate catalyst for the council's establishment was the endorsement by the 1942 Reform rabbinical convention of a resolution calling for the creation of a Jewish army to fight alongside the Allies in World War II. The council activists feared that the establishment of such an armed force would raise questions about the loyalty of Diaspora Jews to the armies of their own countries. Although its membership remained small, the council enjoyed a notoriety out of proportion to its numbers, because of its close relationship with State Department officials and the prominent coverage it received in certain press outlets, particularly the *New York Times.*

Conceived by its rabbinical founders as a tool for promoting denationalized, classical Reform Judaism, of which anti-Zionism was only one aspect, the council became obsessed with Zionism only after it came under the control of lay Reform activists in 1943. Denouncing Zionism as a "retreat from emancipation," and "segregation in action," the council leaders regarded Zionism as an impediment to the assimilation of Jews into American society. By 1944, one of the council's founders was complaining that the organization had become "a refuge for atheistic and un-Jewish Jews who joined because they looked upon the ACJ as an instrument for assimilation."

Mainstream American Zionist leaders condemned the council for undermining the campaign for a Jewish homeland precisely at the moment when such a homeland was most desperately needed. Hitler's atrocities provided the most graphic and irrefutable arguments against anti-Zionism. It was no coincidence that many of the Reform rabbis who originally joined the council dropped out of it as the details of Hitler's genocide became public knowledge in the West in late 1942 and early 1943.

To combat the perception that it was indifferent to the suffering of Hitler's Jewish victims, the council found itself in the peculiar position of supporting increased Jewish immigration to the United States, by contrast with nearly all other Jewish organizations, which refused to call for immigration for fear that doing so would provoke domestic anti-Semitism. Significantly, however, the council did not lobby to permit the entry of more Jews until after World War II ended, and it played no role in any of the wartime campaigns seeking Allied rescue of Jewish refugees.

The refusal of most of the New York–based German Jewish elite to join the council, however, was not necessarily only a response to the persecution of European Jewry. Many of New York's wealthy German Jews had followed Louis Marshall and Felix Warburg in embracing non-Zionism and becoming partners in the Palestine enterprise in their agreement with the World Zionist Organization/Jewish Agency in 1929. Long before Hitler, they had come to believe that a Jewish national home was required to serve as a refuge for oppressed Jewry.

The council made two primary arguments. First, it insisted that Jews were members of a religion only and not a nationality, thus hearkening back to the formulation of classic Reform Judaism. Indeed, this argument was better suited to nineteenth-century American Jewry; by the 1940s many American Jews had jettisoned religious observance and instead embraced a secular ethnicity comparable to nationalism. The council's second major argument sought to play on Jewish fears, by contending that the creation of a Jewish state could endanger the citizenship or legal status of Jews living in the Diaspora. Non-Jews might suspect Jews around the world of maintaining a secret allegiance to the Jewish state, they warned. In the end, however, the council's dire warnings proved baseless. The creation of Israel did not compromise the legal or political status of American Jewry. Nor has it prevented Jews from becoming integrated in their countries of residence, or reversed any of the advances of the emancipation. Defeated and dispirited, the American Council for Judaism faded into obscurity shortly after Israel's establishment.

Interwar American Jewry

The economic success of the second generation was remarkable. The father worked in a sweatshop; the son was studying medicine, law, or another white-collar profession. A 1919 survey found that nearly 11 percent of students enrolled in professional or vocational courses were Jewish, even though Jews were only slightly more than 3 percent of the national population, and 85 percent of those Jewish students were studying medicine, dentistry, law, or engineering. There is scant evidence to support the popular assumption that Jewish achievements in business or scholastics were the product of the traditional emphasis in Judaism on education and study; that tradition venerated study of sacred texts, not secular professional skills. To whatever extent the phenomenon of widespread college enrollment by Jews was a reflection of any traditional Jewish emphasis on education, it was motivated at least as much, or more, by the simple lure of a desirable salary and all that went with it. Immigrants struggling for survival wanted their children to have it easier—and the children concurred. If by the 1930s the majority of the Jewish labor force was white collar, it was not because the Talmud mandates white-collar work, but simply because Jewish immigrants wanted to "make it" in America. Since so many of the second generation had jettisoned traditional religious observances, it hardly stands to reason that attitudes based on religion would determine their economic behavior. The only logical link between traditional Judaism and modern American Jewish economic activity would have been among that small portion of American Jews involved in businesses specifically aimed at Jewish observance, such as those concerning religious goods or kosher food. There is no persuasive evidence of a broader link between Old World Jewish values and the success of Jewish businesses in the New World.

"It was on the middle rungs of business that Jews found their niche," writes Henry Feingold (1992) in his definitive study of interwar American Jewry's economic advancement. By 1929 almost half of Jews were employed in trade, "more frequently as employees than as proprietors." Another one-fifth were in small manufacturing and sales. "By 1937, two-thirds of the 37,000 factories and 104,000 wholesale and retail establishments in New York City were owned by Jews, but only a third of their work force was Jewish." Commerce was far more attractive to Jews than the population as a whole. By the mid-1930s, "about 35 to 40 percent of the Jewish work force was in commercial occupations, compared with 13.8 percent of the general population. Commerce overshadowed manufacturing, which drew only 15 to 20 percent [of Jews], compared with 26.3 percent for the general population." The archetypal pattern of laborers eventually starting their own small business and then passing it down to their children was less frequent among Jewish immigrants and their children; the younger generation often aspired to more. "The heartbreak of parents whose sons rejected the family business was a familiar theme in Jewish literature and theater . . . . They became doctors, lawyers, accountants, and dentists."

East European immigrants and their children were not a noticeable presence in areas in which their German Jewish predecessors had been prominent, such as banking or department-store chains. But they did "gain important footholds in secondary industries, including the burgeoning automobile spare parts, used car, and private transportation business." Not many Jews rose in the steel industry, but "the scrap-metal business was 90 percent Jewish-owned." Jews also became prominent "in real estate development, construction, printing, shoe and textile manufacturing, hotel keeping and the entertainment business."

Ironically, anti-Semitic discrimination actually helped accelerate the process of Jewish economic advancement. Anti-Jewish restrictions "in the management of more established industries," such as heavy industry, railroads, automobiles, and petrochemicals, forced Jews to become "shoestring capitalists practicing free enterprise in the riskiest areas of the economy." Sometimes they succeeded beyond their wildest expectations—as in the case of the Hollywood film industry. Discrimination "could release enormous new energies to overcome the hurdles it imposed." When colleges imposed quotas to limit Jewish enrollment, "Jewish students simply worked harder to attain their goals. . . . [They] understood that they had to be better." The problem of anti-Semitic discrimination in the real estate world inspired Jewish merchants to purchase many of the downtown urban buildings in which their businesses were located; during the post–World War II real estate boom, that turned out to be an unusually profitable investment. The refusal of most banks to extend credit to Jews stimulated the establishment of Jewish-controlled credit unions and Hebrew Free Loan societies; by 1927 "there were in existence 509 [Jewish] loan societies, 83 percent of them affiliated with religious congregations," as well as "2,367 mutual benefit societies [which] extended small no-interest loans." This "ethnic economy" played a crucial supporting role in the success of Jewish entrepreneurship. Overall, Feingold concludes that "the best clue to a Jewish presence in a particular aspect of the economy relates to three factors: riskiness, since Jews were pushed or drawn to the more marginal areas; ready access to capital; or conversely, the need to raise little start-up capital" (Feingold 1992, 126–142).

One casualty of interwar Jewry's rise was the heavy Jewish presence in the labor movement, particularly the International Ladies Garment Workers Union and the Amalgamated Clothing Workers of America. The sweatshops of the needle trades were a first stop for Jewish immigrants on their way up the socioeconomic ladder. The garment industry unions organized strikes often and sometimes successfully, gaining improvements in wages, working hours, and employee benefits. But by the 1930s, most Jews had moved beyond the blue-collar workforce, leaving most of the previously "Jewish" unions with Jewish leaders and mostly non-Jewish members.

Interwar Anti-Semitism

Postwar America experienced a surge of nativism, fueled by fears of the communist takeover in Russia and a wave of tumultuous strikes in 1919 that made it seem to many as if violent revolution was just around the corner. The handful of Jews active in American communist or radical socialist groups received attention far out of proportion to their numbers, with some newspapers in the Midwest openly linking Jews and Bolshevism. In 1920 the *Dearborn* (Michigan) *Independent*, published by automobile magnate Henry Ford, began serializing *The Protocols of the Elders of Zion*, a forgery of czarist Russian origin that clamed to reveal a Jewish conspiracy to conquer the world. The paper's circulation of 72,000 when the *Protocols* series was launched reached 700,000 four years later, making it one of the largest newspapers in the United States.

Dozens of racist and anti-Semitic groups and publications sprang up during the interwar period. The Ku Klux Klan, expanding its list of targets to include Jews and Catholics, reached a peak of over 4 million members in the early 1920s. It wielded sufficient political influence to keep an anti-Klan plank out of the 1924 Democratic Party platform and to play a role that year in blocking the presidential nomination of New York governor Al Smith, a vocal opponent of the KKK.

Two highly publicized episodes especially jarred the Jewish community. In 1922 a Jewish soldier in the U.S. Army was charged, despite the absence of serious evidence, with murdering his commanding officer; after an unusually drawn-out process, he was eventually acquitted, over the protests of anti-Semites who called the verdict proof of Jewish manipulation of the courts. In 1928 a young Christian girl briefly disappeared from her upstate New York home shortly before Yom Kippur, and the town's rabbi was hauled in for questioning by the police and the mayor about the rumored Jewish practice of using Christian blood for religious purposes. Accusations normally associated with medieval Europe were being taken seriously in the modern, enlightened United States of America.

The public's escalating xenophobia provided congressional conservatives with the popular support necessary to enact strict immigration quotas. It was no coincidence that the quota figures were set up in such a way as to ensure that countries in Southern and Eastern Europe would receive the smallest allotments, while those in the north and west of the continent received the largest. The intellectual justification for restricting immigration was anchored in popular turn-of-the-century pseudoscientific theories that regarded Anglo-Saxons as racially superior to other ethnic groups. The quota system was a deliberate, and successful, effort to sharply reduce the entry of Jews and Italians in particular.

Nativist sentiment also found expression in the widespread discrimination against Jews, some of it surprisingly open. The president of Harvard University said publicly in 1922 that his institution would establish a quota to restrict the number of Jewish students admitted. Many other colleges, from Ivy League schools such as Columbia and Princeton to others all across the country, followed suit. Jewish faculty members were a rarity on American college campuses in the 1920s. Discrimination against Jews was practiced in many other fields of employment as well. Sometimes newspaper ads explicitly stated that Christian employees were sought; sometimes it was practiced more quietly, but just as effectively. Social clubs and resort hotels routinely excluded Jews, as did many of the "best" neighborhoods in cities across the country. It was not until 1948 that the Supreme Court outlawed the "restrictive covenants" that kept Jews out of certain residential areas.

With the onset of the Depression, economic hardship accelerated anti-Jewish scapegoating. More than 100 new anti-Semitic organizations were established between 1933 and 1941. The Michigan-based radio priest, Father Charles Coughlin, attracted millions of listeners to his anti-Jewish tirades over the airwaves. "Christian Front" hooligans sporadically desecrated synagogues, vandalized Jewish property, and assaulted Jewish passersby in sections of New York and Boston. The isolationist "America First" movement, whose leaders frequently accused Jews of trying to drag the United States into Europe's war, boasted a membership of some 850,000. Polls regularly found a majority of Americans regarded Jews as greedy or untrustworthy.

Case Study: Anti-Semitism in the U.S. Army

Since anti-Semitic prejudice could be found, to varying degrees, among a wide variety of social classes, economic levels, and ethnic groups, it is no surprise that it could be found among some government officials as well. This was a particular problem within the armed forces, although it was not well known at the time. As they struggled to come to grips with the changing nature of American society during the late nineteenth and early twentieth centuries, U.S. Army officers tended to see themselves as the guardians of the "true" America—white, Anglo-

Saxon, and Protestant—against the tide of immigrants crowding the nation's cities. They subscribed to the concept of Social Darwinism, viewing the history of mankind as one long struggle between biologically distinct races with predetermined levels of intelligence and other characteristics, with the white race constantly in danger of conquest, or at least "mongrelization." Students at the Army War College studied the pseudoscientific writings of popular racial theorists such as Madison Grant and Lothrop Stoddard about the superiority of the Nordic (or Aryan) race. The U.S. military action in the Philippines in the 1890s, which for many in the army marked their first substantive encounter with people whose appearance and culture were radically different from their own, further cemented racist preconceptions.

Anti-Semitism fit comfortably into such a worldview. The Jew, with his alien garb and language, not to mention religious beliefs and practices that had been the object of Christian disdain for so many centuries, was a ripe target for prejudice among the army officer corps. U.S. Army Major Charles E. Woodruff, whose Social Darwinist writings and lectures helped provide his military colleagues with a "scientific" basis for racism, wrote that Jewish "parasitism and ethnic disease" threatened to turn America into "another Poland." It was no wonder, Woodruff wrote, that other nations had always persecuted the Jews: "European nations have repeatedly undergone a disinfection in this regard. . . . It is not a persecution of the Jew as Jew, but an extermination of an invading disease."

During World War I and its aftermath, the army's Military Intelligence Division (MID) emerged as a center for gathering, endorsing, and circulating reports from czarist Russia and other sources about Jewish-Bolshevik conspiracies. What is most significant to note about the MID's bulging files of anti-Semitic memoranda, a recent study has found, is that "officers at home and abroad routinely did more than read, process, and pass on such information; they augmented it with observations and warnings of their own" (Bendersky 2000, 167–195). In the margins of these reports and in the cover letters attached to them by senior army officers, one could find evidence of widespread sympathy for the wildest imaginable accusations regarding international Jewish conspiracies.

The *Dearborn Independent*'s serialization of the *Protocols of the Elders of Zion* found a receptive audience among the officers corp. MID headquarters in Washington repeatedly ordered quantities of Ford's edition of the anti-Semitic czarist forgery for circulation among the army's top brass. *Protocols*-like conspiracy theories had already been endorsed in numerous reports to the MID from intelligence officers stationed at U.S. embassies in Europe, which in turn were treated seriously by senior officers and distributed to their colleagues. It was therefore probably no coincidence that Ford's New York office for "investigating" alleged Jewish conspiracies was staffed by former Justice Department and military intelligence officials.

The impact of these prejudices was soon felt in policy matters, some of them well beyond the areas that would normally involve the military, such as treatment of domestic radicals and national immigration policy. Recently retired senior army officers helped promote the anticommunist hysteria that brought about mass roundups and deportations of radical activists in 1920. The recently retired chief of military intelligence for the New York area, Captain John Trevor, provided riveting testimony about the alien menace at the 1921 congressional hearings that resulted in the enactment of America's first-ever immigration quotas, which were designed to drastically reduce the number of newcomers from Eastern and Southern Europe.

The rise of Nazism in Germany hardly fazed the army's upper echelons. Military attaches at the U.S. embassy in Berlin reported back to Washington that foreign press reports about the mistreatment of Jews were exaggerated. Major Ralph C. Smith, "the army's eyes and ears in Germany," reported to his superiors that Hitlerism was the German people's understandable response to "the sharp and rapid increase in Jewish influence." Germany was a land of "blondes like Jean Harlow" and youths who "march and sing and seem as happy as can be," Smith gushed. Such attitudes did not change, even though Nazi outrages multiplied. "Even after personally observing the human consequences of Nazi repression, attache attitudes toward Jews did not change appreciably from the views of earlier generations of officers." And their continuing anti-Semitism affected their recommendations regarding U.S. policy: "Throughout the Third Reich, attaches left the distinct impression that little could, or should, be done to change the conditions of Jews in Germany. . . . Nor should America address the problem by opening up its shores to provide a place of refuge for Jews, as this would only transplant the Jewish problem from Europe to America" (Bendersky 2000, 233).

Long after the Allies themselves had confirmed the authenticity of reports about Hitler's mass annihilation of the Jews, U.S. Army officials treated the news with skepticism and sought to downplay the victims' Jewish identity. For example, in 1944, the War Refugee Board—the token rescue agency established by FDR as a result of congressional and Jewish protests, but never given a meaningful budget—was reprimanded by the director of the Office of War Information (OWI) for giving the press details about the death camps. OWI claimed that the information was unconfirmed and might be the result of a conspiracy by the Germans to embarrass the Allies. The editors of *Yank: The Army Weekly* turned down a correspondent's report about the death camps on the grounds that it was "too Semitic": the reporter was instructed to "get a less Jewish story." The army's other major publication, *Stars and Stripes*, did not report on Hitler's atrocities until April 1945, and even then omitted the word *Jew* from its descriptions of the mass murder. The War Department's refusal to explore proposals to bomb Auschwitz also seems to have been influenced, at least in part, by the decades of ingrained anti-Semitism among senior army officials, which left a thick residue of indifference to the plight of the Jews under Hitler.

Many officers who had absorbed racist sentiments during their pre–World War II army education continued to exhibit such prejudices well into our own era; many retired generals cheered, for example, when the chairman of the Joint Chiefs of Staff, General George S. Brown, asserted in a 1974 speech that Jews control America's banks and media. But attitudes toward Jews and other ethnic minorities among the younger generation of officers seem to have changed with the times. As racism has become widely discredited and as American society has embraced the concepts of equality and pluralism, the army officer corps has followed suit in its teachings and in setting bounds for what is considered acceptable discourse.

Jews responded to the rising anti-Semitism in a variety of ways. Many adopted a more militant attitude, attending anti-Nazi rallies, supporting Jewish defense agencies, or joining the Zionist movement. Others chose to melt. Many Jews changed their names so that they could not be easily identified as Jewish; some employers actually insisted on it—for example, reporters for the *New York Times* who had Jewish-sounding first names were instructed to use their first two initials instead.

Jewish organizations moved cautiously in shaping their responses to anti-Semitism. Concerned that an overly energetic approach might ignite even greater hostility, Jewish groups such as the Anti-Defamation League (ADL) focused on distributing literature citing facts and figures to prove that Jews were loyal to the United States, opposed to communism, and appropriately represented in America's past wars. Whenever possible, Jewish groups would enlist sympathetic non-Jews to take the lead in publicly refuting anti-Semitic libels, on the assumption that the public would be more likely to take such arguments seriously if they heard them articulated by fellow gentiles.

Jewish organizations also actively initiated public interfaith programs with church groups, believing that there would be a trickle-down effect, with average Christians taking their cue from church leaders in their attitudes toward Jews. Such activities were regarded by Jewish groups as part of the antidote to anti-Semitism, since they would stress common interests and goals such as democracy, peace, and tolerance, and demonstrate to the public that Jews were just as committed as Christians to those aims.

The advent of radio offered the AJ Committee, one of the most active promoters of interfaith activity, a potentially powerful tool to advance its agenda. In 1937 it established a radio department to take full advantage of the opportunity to reach vast non-Jewish audiences. "Jewish leaders used the new medium to spread their message of interfaith understanding and pressed radio station managers, celebrities, and political leaders to sponsor their public interest segments," Marc Dollinger notes. "These appeals projected an 'all-American' image of Jews to millions of people who otherwise lacked personal relationships with Jewish people. For the first time in American Jewish politics, thousands and sometimes millions of people could be reached instantaneously. Radio offered Jewish leaders an unprecedented opportunity to highlight the symmetry between Judaism and American values" (Dollinger 2000, 67).

Case Study: Hebrew as the Antidote to Assimilation

In an attempt to combat rising assimilation among young Jews during the interwar period, Zionist activists launched a campaign, in 1929–1930, to have the Hebrew language taught in heavily Jewish public schools in New York City. In 1908, Jews had constituted one-third of New York City high school students, but ten years later that figure had risen to 53 percent as additional waves of immigration, and the offspring of earlier immigrants, swelled the number of Jewish teens in the city. Jewish organizations pressed for better salaries for teachers and the construction of more schools. Some 130 new public schools were built in New York City during the mid-1920s, among them Brownsville's huge Thomas Jefferson High, with a predominantly Jewish student body of more than 4,000. Jewish children attended both elementary and high schools in greater numbers than other ethnic groups. This was not the result of any religious motive, since the large majority of their parents were by no means religiously observant; it was, rather, a reflection of the fact that memories of recent persecution encouraged Jewish parents to place a premium on education as the ticket to social and material success.

Only about one-fifth of Jewish children attended private Jewish supplementary education, so it was not long before parents concerned about the dangers of assimilation began to see the public schools as a potential vehicle for strengthening their children's Jewish identity. When the New York City Board of Education turned down a proposal to teach Yiddish in public schools, on the grounds that it would hinder Jewish immigrants' assimilation into American society, Zionist student groups and educators began pressing for Hebrew instruction. Introduced on an experimental basis in two Brooklyn high schools in 1930, it was deemed successful and expanded in the years to follow. By 1938, Hebrew was being taught in forty New York schools and spread to Chicago, Boston, and other cities. In this, as in so many aspects of American Jewish life, the inexorable Americanization process soon took its toll. By the late 1940s, most Jewish students were more than a generation removed from the immigrant experience and had adjusted more or less fully to American life. The Hebrew language held no particular attraction for them, and enrollment in Hebrew classes in the public schools declined precipitously until the program was canceled altogether (Feingold 1992, 55–57).

The Impact of the Great Depression

The Stock Market Crash of 1929 and the Great Depression that followed hit American Jewry hard, but not quite as hard as it struck other ethnic minorities. A 1925 survey found 26.8 percent of Italian immigrants were unskilled laborers, while only 3.6 percent of Jews were in that category. By the 1930s an estimated 65 percent of Jews had moved into white-collar professions, which provided something of a cushion against the devastation of the Depression years. The Jewish proprietor of a small store was less likely to find himself penniless and on the street than an unskilled Italian-American laborer. One Depression-era survey reported that 21 percent of Italian-American families were receiving welfare, compared with 12 percent of Jewish families. Jewish institutions also helped ease the situation: employment bureaus sponsored by the Jewish Federation lent Jews a helping hand, which was particularly important in view of discrimination against Jews in various fields of employment.

The Depression inevitably left its impact on family life. Many Jewish housewives joined the labor force to help make ends meet. Young adults, unable to afford apartments of their own, were forced to postpone moving out of their parents' home. The cohesion of the family unit was preserved longer, but intragenerational tensions were sometimes exacerbated. Young Jews tended to enroll in college in greater numbers than other minorities, and with jobs scarce in the 1930s they were likely to stay in school, acquiring skills and education that would leave them far better equipped than their peers upon graduation. This was especially the case in New York, where the city-run colleges did not charge for tuition; on some campuses, Jews composed more than 80 percent of the student body. Some Jewish students, small in number but vocal and prominent, took part in radical-left campus political movements.

Jewish marriage and birth rates were noticeably affected by the economic crisis. Americans in general were less likely to marry during the Depression because of uncertainty over how they would make a living, but Jews were less likely than others. One survey found that only 8 percent of Jews under the age of 25 were married by 1935, compared with 12 percent of young non-Jewish adults. The contrast was even more stark regarding birth rates: there were sixty-nine Jewish births for every 100 among other whites in 1930. These trends reflected the same sense of insecurity about the future that other Americans felt, compounded by the uniquely intense anxiety that afflicted American Jews because of escalating domestic anti-Semitism. The massive proliferation of anti-Semitic propaganda groups during the Depression and the frightening popularity of the Jew-baiting radio preacher Father Charles Coughlin left American Jews feeling more intimidated than ever before.

The Depression altered the pace of Jewish suburbanization. By the 1930s most Jews in New York City had moved from their original neighborhoods to second areas of settlement—that is, from places like the Lower East Side of Manhattan to more spacious and comfortable areas in Brooklyn and the Bronx. The possibility of moving on to a third zone of settlement was rendered virtually impossible by the hardships of the Depression era. The result was that the neighborhoods in which Jews resided acquired ever larger Jewish majorities and an intensely Jewish political culture. This atmosphere encouraged neighborhood solidarity and activism, which made itself felt in rent strikes, organized physical resistance to evictions, and even a citywide kosher meat boycott in 1935. These efforts were sometimes instigated by local communist or socialist agitators but other times were simply the work of furious local residents displaying their ethnic and neighborhood loyalties.

The advent of New Deal social welfare programs changed the rules of the game. "New Deal programs relieved the acute financial distress that had attracted average Jews to radical campaigns," Beth Wenger notes. "Most Jews had never had a true ideological stake in the political agendas advanced by the Socialists and Communists; they joined radical campaigns that . . . addressed their immediate economic problems. The reformist accomplishments of the New Deal undermined the activist spark by meeting radical demands for federal jobs programs and unemployment assistance." The bonds of the budding alliance between Franklin Roosevelt and the Jews were significantly enhanced by the neighborhood activism that had rallied Jews around the very causes that Roosevelt's New Deal now championed. "The political campaigns conducted within New York's Jewish neighborhoods, whether by political clubs, radical activists, or organized parties, reflected the evolving dynamic of ethnic politics in the Depression era. . . . By the time the Depression ended, the Democratic and Jewish political agendas had become so thoroughly intertwined that for Jews, voting Democratic had become an expression of ethnic political ideals. For New York Jews, the emerging welfare state constituted a national affirmation of their ethnic political commitments and marked their coming of age as legitimate participants in mainstream American political culture" (Wenger 1996, 125, 135).

Responses to Nazism and the Holocaust

American Jewish responses to Nazism and the Holocaust are discussed in detail in Chapters 2 and 3, in which the community's generally hesitant reaction to the persecution of European Jewry is attributed in large measure to Jewish fears of provoking domestic anti-Semitism; the Jewish leadership's misplaced faith in the Roosevelt administration; and disunity among Jewish organizations. However, several additional factors, pertaining to the ways in which the American experience specifically impacted American Jews, should also be considered.

For example, Henry Feingold perceives a connection between the aforementioned rise of Jewish professionals and American Jewry's lethargic response to the Holocaust. "Professionalization and general skill enhancement entailed more than a change in job description and economic status. They meant a profound shift in mind-set in which self-actualization tended to be valued above group identity or religious belief. Loyalty and commitment to profession received the highest priority" (Feingold 1992, 145). Absorbed in their newfound, identity-forming professions, many Jews lost interest in Jewish communal concerns—precisely at the moment when a large, strong, and cohesive community was most needed to act on behalf of the persecuted in Europe.

One of the few areas in which American Jews maintained a coordinated and generally unified response to news of the Holocaust was in philanthropy. Umbrella organizations known as federations were established in Jewish communities around the country beginning in the late 1800s, to provide an array of local social services. The wealthy German Jews who provided the bulk of their budgets viewed the federations as a means of maintaining control and ensuring that needy Jews would not become a burden on the non-Jewish community. Eventually, in 1932, sixty-three federations and five Jewish welfare funds united to establish the Council of Jewish Federations (CJF) and Welfare Funds. In 1944 the CJF broadened its influence over communal policy-making by creating the National Jewish Community Relations Advisory Council, an umbrella for the other major Jewish organizations for dealing with issues affecting "community relations"—that is, broadly speaking, any issues affecting Jewish relations with non-Jews. Local federations were encouraged to establish their own local Jewish Community Relations Councils, as they were called, consisting of the local representatives of the major Jewish groups, to guide local community policy-making under the supervision of the national parent body.

Meanwhile, to address the needs of Jews overseas, three charities that had been created to aid Jewish communities devastated by World War I united in 1914 as the American Jewish Joint Distribution Committee. The allocation priorities of the "Joint," as it was known, became the focus of controversy when it decided, in 1924, to undertake the resettlement of 200,000 Russian Jews in agricultural communities in the southwest Soviet region of Crimea. The main movers and shakers behind the Joint were the German-American Jewish elite, and they saw nothing amiss in helping Russian Jews build a better life in their country of residence, something that the Joint did for other Jewish communities around the world. The Zionists, however, had always looked upon Russian Jewry as a huge reservoir of potential immigrants to the Holy Land; establishing them in Crimea could only undermine that goal. Furthermore, the size and scope of the project would necessitate such a large investment of funds that inevitably Palestine development would be short-changed. Zionist protests eventually persuaded the Joint leaders to somewhat scale down their level of financial support for the Crimea project and to allocate one-third of that budget, $1.5 million, for development of Palestine.

Unwilling to rely on the Joint's future largesse, the Zionists in 1925 established their own Palestine Economic Corporation, to sponsor development projects, and a fundraising arm, the United Palestine Appeal (UPA). The strife and inefficiency of having two rival fundraising campaigns for overseas aid was bad enough, but in the wake of the 1938 Nazi Kristallnacht pogroms, the prospect of dollars being wasted because of such unnecessary competition seemed especially irresponsible. Finally, in early 1939, the Joint and the UPA, prodded by the Council of Jewish Federations, created a single joint annual appeal, the United Jewish Appeal. The new spirit of cooperation established a pattern of increasing coordination of fundraising activities between the Council of Jewish Federations and the UJA in Jewish communities throughout the United States. As a result of these efforts, fundraising was streamlined and many more dollars were raised. Historians differ in their interpretations of the primary reasons for Jewry's remarkably active philanthropic tendencies. Some see it as a modern-day extension of the traditional religious precept of tzedakah, the biblically mandated giving of a portion of one's income to the needy. Others see it as primarily a reflection of the affluence of the American-born children of East European Jewish immigrants. For still others, it appears to have served almost as a surrogate form of Jewish identity; it was a way to express solidarity with the Jewish people and sympathy for the downtrodden—also entirely acceptable in the American ethos—without taking on the cumbersome rituals and traditions they had left behind in the ghetto of the Lower East Side.

Postwar American Jewry

From the point of view of the American Jewish community, the postwar period dawned as an era of potential and prosperity. By sharp contrast with the prewar years, when American Jews were confronted by a vigorous and rising wave of domestic anti-Semitism, in the postwar years anti-Semitism declined precipitously—at least on the surface—as hatred of Jews came to be identified with America's recently defeated enemy, as the revelations of the full extent of the Holocaust made anti-Semitism unfashionable, and as economic prosperity obviated scapegoating tendencies. The quotas that had restricted the admission of Jews to some prominent universities began to crumble, especially in view of the postwar shortage of doctors and the GI bill of rights, with its guarantee of admission for army veterans.

Two events that occurred almost simultaneously, just after Japan's surrender, helped make Jews feel more at home in America than ever before. In September, Bess Myerson, the daughter of Yiddish-speaking immigrants, was chosen Miss America. "It was remarkable for a Jew—especially the child of poor, radical, New York immigrants—to become the exemplar of American womanhood at a time of anti-Semitism and opposition to large-scale immigration of Jewish refugees," Gerald Sorin points out. "This, of course, was why American Jews were so enchanted by Myerson. Her individual triumph was also their collective victory over bigotry. Myerson symbolized the promise of American life, and she made them prouder as Jews and more confident about their future as Americans. Seemingly, there was nothing in America to which they could not now aspire." Meanwhile, Hank Greenberg, one of the few Jews in professional baseball, had returned from four years of well-publicized army duty to lead his Detroit Tigers into a hotly contested pennant race. He refused to play on Yom Kippur and then, ignoring the constant anti-Semitic heckling every time he came to bat, proceeded to hit home run after home run as he led his team to a World Series championship. To Jews, he was a hero, in large measure because his status as a genuine American sports hero demonstrated that Jews had "made it" in America. Bess Myerson and Hank Greenberg were "secular saints," wrote one journalist who recalled the impact of autumn 1945 on his consciousness. They were "symbols of a sudden legitimacy. . . . Hank and Bess were winners, like DiMaggio and Grable—only smarter. They were as American as apple pie and the Fourth of July—and as Jewish as knishes and Yom Kippur. They belonged to a race of victors, not victims. . . . For the first time, the Jews had successfully crossed over from ethnic favorites to national heroes without being isolated or absorbed: they had arrived without being assimilated or stereotyped" (Sorin 1992, 10–15).

The postwar cultural atmosphere was more conducive to tolerance than ever before. Will Herberg's classic study of religion in American society, *Protestant-Catholic-Jew* (1955), showed how religion had, by the 1950s, become an integral part of "the American way of life." For the vast majority of Americans, "the religious community [became] the primary context of self-identification and social location."

The pervasive national mood of conformism was compounded by a vigorous desire for the security of family life and a sense of belonging, especially amid the widespread anxiety over communism and the threat of nuclear war. Judaism, with its emphasis on family and biblically based morality, fit neatly into the American paradigm, especially when contrasted with America's main foe, the atheistic Soviet Union. A 1952 poll found that nearly all Americans born Christian believed in God (compared with 70 percent of American Jews). Those were the years when "In God We Trust" became America's official motto and the words "under God" were added to the Pledge of Allegiance. But in addition to their belief in God and the divinity of the Bible, Americans were developing a faith in religion itself, a conviction that religion is the basis for a life of virtue. From this mix emerged the popular notion of America as a "three-religion country," with each of the major faiths seen as legitimate expressions of the national faith—a remarkable statement about popular attitudes toward Judaism, considering its minuscule number of adherents compared with Protestantism and Catholicism. A potent symbol of how Judaism now stood shoulder-to-shoulder with America's major established faiths was the "Four Chaplains" story of World War II, which was well publicized at the time, frequently cited in the postwar years, and even immortalized on a postage stamp: a Catholic priest, a rabbi, and two Protestant ministers aboard the USS *Dorchester,* a troop carrier, sacrificed their lives by giving their life jackets to soldiers when the ship was torpedoed by a German submarine in 1942.

American Jewry underwent dramatic geographic changes in the postwar period. First was the relocation of many Jews from the Northeast to the South and West. Before World War II, New York City was home to 40 percent of American Jews. In 1950 more than two-thirds of American Jews lived either in New England or along the mid-Atlantic Coast in cities such as Baltimore and Philadelphia. But by 1990, only half still resided in the Northeast. South Florida and three cities in the Southwest—Los Angeles, San Diego, and Phoenix— were the major destinations of the Jewish migrants.

In 1946 more than 2,000 Jews were moving to Los Angeles each month, about 13 percent of the multitude of new residents. The Jewish population of the city, just 130,000 prior to the war, passed the 300,000 mark by 1951. Los Angeles had been home to 4.5 percent of American Jewry in 1948; that figure reached 7.9 percent by 1978. In 1970 there were 440,000 Jews in Los Angeles, and more than 500,000 ten years later. Surveys in the 1980s found 750,000 Jews living in the state of California as a whole, the largest regional concentration out-side Israel, the Soviet Union, and New York.

Miami's permanent Jewish population (that is, excluding the large number of cold-weather visitors from the North who stayed for months at a time), which had been 8,000 in 1940, reached 16,000 by 1945 and 55,000 by 1950. Five years later, the city had 100,000 Jews. That figure continued to climb in the years to follow: by 1960 there were 140,000 Jews living in Miami, making it the sixth largest Jewish community in America. In 1970 there were 230,000, and ten years later, nearly 290,000. By the 1980s, South Florida boasted the third largest Jewish community in the United States, after New York and California.

Many of these Jews were retirees in search of a warmer climate and more easygoing way of life. In addition, the advent of air travel facil-itated moving, and the large postwar influx of African-Americans and Hispanics into New York City neighborhoods that had previously been largely Jewish frightened many older Jews into moving out. Similar trends developed in cities such as Chicago, Philadelphia, and Cleveland. In Miami, the median age had risen from thirty-three to forty-six by 1959, while in Miami Beach—which was an estimated 80 percent Jewish by 1960—it rose from forty-three to fifty-four between 1950 and 1960. In 1965, 38 percent of the residents of Miami Beach were sixty-five or older, up from 28 percent five years before. Los An-geles differed. Initially, many of the new Jewish arrivals in Los Ange-les were older, but soon that changed, especially because of the lure of the Hollywood film industry, to which many Jews were drawn. The median age in Los Angeles actually decreased from thirty-seven to thirty-three by 1959.

Both regions gradually experienced an upsurge in kosher or "Jew-ish-style" restaurants, Jewish bookstores, synagogues, and Jewish day schools. But it was Los Angeles, with its much younger Jewish demo-graphic profile, where all three major branches of Judaism built new national institutions: the Conservative movement's University of Ju-daism (1947), Reform Judaism's Hebrew Union College-Jewish Insti-tute of Religion (1954), and Yeshiva University of Los Angeles (1978).

In the Miami area in particular, new Jewish residents frequently lived nearby one another. Some clusters of condominiums—typically heavily Jewish—have so many residents that they constitute their own voting districts. Gradually, however, both South Florida and Southern California attracted significant numbers of young Jewish professionals who helped build up diverse and thriving Jewish communities. The electoral implications of these trends are discussed in Chapter 3.

The other major postwar change in American Jewish geography was the exodus to suburbia, the "crabgrass frontier," as it was sometimes called. Between 1945 and 1965, an estimated one-third of American Jews moved from major cities to suburban neighborhoods. This was part of a broader trend in American society that saw some 12 million people move from urban areas to the suburbs from 1948 to 1958. In an era of prosperity and with the postwar baby boom underway, it was inevitable that large numbers of Americans would be ready for such a move. Automobiles were far more plentiful and affordable, which made it more possible to live farther from one's place of employment. The increased public demand for housing, after long years of doing without because of the Depression and then the war, could be satisfied only in suburban areas, and construction firms responded by focusing on development of previously uncharted outlying regions. Changes in the federal tax code made home purchases easier, and government benefits for veterans' housing also encouraged the trend.

"Protective covenants," in which property owners agreed to "protect" neighborhoods by refusing to sell to Jews or nonwhites, were gradually undermined by postwar legislation. New York City prohibited discrimination in private housing in 1957, followed shortly afterward by Pennsylvania, Colorado, Oregon, Connecticut, and Massachusetts. Towns in Westchester County, New York, such as Scarsdale and White Plains, which had almost no Jews prior to the war, soon had substantial Jewish communities, as did neighborhoods in Long Island and Queens. The latter had an estimated 50,000 Jews in 1923, 450,000 in 1957.

A massive upsurge in synagogue building accompanied the postwar suburbanization of American Jewry. An estimated $1 billion was spent on synagogue construction during the 1950s and 1960s. The new synagogues were built to fit Jews' new American lifestyle. In many cases distant from the residences of their members, these new suburban edifices were expected to be accessed primarily by automobile. Typically they included spacious rooms that would host a variety of modern functions. Conservative synagogues in particular were often called "Jewish Centers," suggesting a new role as both a social center and a house of prayer—a conscious decision by the Conservative movement's leadership to address the needs and preferences of a new generation. As a demonstration of identification with America, many of the new synagogues were designed as huge, visible symbols of Judaism, often in the shape of the Star of David or Mount Sinai. Some of the most prominent names in the world of architecture, including Frank Lloyd Wright, were enlisted to design these expensive structures.

For many, membership in a synagogue emerged as a uniquely suburban form of Jewish identity. In their inner-city apartments, Jews had typically lived in heavily Jewish neighborhoods that were filled with the sounds, sights, and scents of ethnicity. The neighborhood itself reinforced the Jewish identity of those who had grown lax in their observance of religious rituals, providing a secular, cultural substitute identity. Having left those ethnically distinct neighborhoods behind, the new Jewish suburbanites needed new ways to affiliate themselves with the Jewish community; synagogue membership provided the means. There was, however, a significant turnover in membership, because many families joined a local synagogue temporarily, for the purpose of their children's bar or bat mitzvah celebrations. In 1930 an estimated 20 percent of American Jewish families belonged to synagogues; by 1960 the figure was nearly 60 percent. The percentages were highest in smaller cities and suburbs, where Jews did not have an ethnic neighborhood to help reinforce their identity, and lowest in places like New York City, where the concentration of Jews in identifiable areas and the persistence of Jewish cultural trappings made synagogue membership more a luxury than a necessary identity-preserver.

The synagogues that enjoyed the most success were the Conservative. The Conservative movement's association of synagogues, the United Synagogue of America, grew from fewer than 200 member synagogues in 1945 to 443 just eight years later. It peaked at 775 in 1975 and has remained at or close to that number in the quarter-century since. Conservative Judaism was in many ways ideally suited for American suburbia. Although American society frowned upon ethnic separatism, it accepted, even encouraged, religion, and American Jews, anxious to fit in as good Americans, identified religiously, although not through personal observance of traditional rituals, which most Jews found burdensome and archaic. The modern suburban Conservative synagogue attracted a following by sponsoring a plethora of social activities, offering women a greater role in religious services, utilizing modern decor to make their buildings more attractive, shortening and altering the content of the liturgy to eliminate sections that seemed at odds with modernist notions, and instituting a late Friday evening prayer service that was convenient for members' work schedules, even if it began far later than the actual onset of the Sabbath.

Stationing itself as a middle-ground alternative to Reform and Orthodoxy, Conservatism never developed a clear or binding theology of its own—unlike Reform Judaism, which explicitly renounced traditionalist religious requirements, and Orthodoxy, which proclaimed its fealty to them. The Conservative movement's first official ideological platform did not appear until 1988, shortly after the centennial of the Jewish Theological Seminary, and even then it declined to take a clear-cut stand on crucial theological matters such as the existence of God and the revelation at Sinai, instead outlining the conflicting views held by various segments of Conservatism. The result has been a movement with a well-educated and traditionalist-leaning leadership and a far less observant laity, with each congregation's rabbi free to establish religious guidelines as he chooses.

This discrepancy, a hallmark of Conservative Judaism since its inception in the early 1900s and still in evidence a century later, has given rise to the phenomenon of the individual congregant as a spectator rather than a participant, enjoying a sort of vicarious Jewish experience on his infrequent visits to the synagogue, which usually takes place on the Jewish High Holidays or life-cycle events such as bar mitzvahs, weddings, and funerals. A 1953 survey of 1,800 lay leaders in Conservative synagogues, carried out by the Columbia University Bureau of Applied Social Research, found intense and widespread involvement with the United Jewish Appeal, local federation fundraising campaigns, and similar activities—significant evidence of the extent to which secular Jewish affiliations, such as involvement in communal and organizational work, had come to constitute a major component in the Jewish identity for these Conservative lay leaders. Regarding personal religious observance, the survey found that just one-third kept a kosher home (and even many of those ate nonkosher foods outside the home), one-fourth read Jewish books or periodicals, only about one-fifth frequently attended Sabbath services, and nearly three-quarters of those did not bring their children with them—an ominous sign of how Jewish identity would fare among the next generation.

The respondents to the 1953 poll were board members and officers of their synagogues—that is, the upper tier of the congregation in terms of ritual piety; the corresponding rates of observance among ordinary members have been consistently lower. Among Conservative Jews in Providence, Rhode Island, in the early 1970s, only 12 percent attended religious services at least once each week; 21 percent of first-generation Jews in Providence did so, compared with just 2 percent of the third generation. Some 37 percent of Providence Jews bought kosher meat, but just 27 percent kept separate dishes for meat and dairy, as religious law stipulates. The numbers declined with each successive generation. Sure enough, surveys of Conservative laity in 1990 and 1996 found that just 29 percent purchase kosher meat exclusively; 15 percent describe themselves as Sabbath-observant (even according to the relatively lenient standards of Conservatism); and 65 percent of children who recently celebrated their bar or bat mitzvahs in Conservative synagogues said that "it is okay for Jews to marry people of other religions." One prominent leader of the Conservative movement has described "most of our congregants" as "three-day-a-year-Jews"—that is, attending synagogue only on Yom Kippur and the two days of Rosh Hashana.

Orthodox Judaism experienced an unforeseen revival in America after World War II. An initial boost was received through immigration: among the estimated 150,000 to 200,000 Holocaust survivors who entered the United States during the late 1940s and early 1950s were tens of thousands who were Orthodox, many of them members of the Hasidic sects of Lubavitch and Satmar. Unlike the Orthodox Jews who had arrived during the late 1800s and early 1900s, the new wave typically did not assimilate into the American environment. The earlier waves of immigrants had come in defiance of their rabbis' urgings to remain in Eastern Europe, while those who came after World War II were reluctant immigrants, typically following their rabbinical leaders in leaving behind the destroyed but authentic Jewish world they had known. The America to which they came differed markedly from that which Orthodox immigrants had encountered in the early 1900s. Post–World War II Americans were considerably more accepting of antinomian behavior than earlier generations. At the same time, America's economy was now considerably more developed, creating more opportunities for religiously observant Jews to earn a living without having to compromise on their traditional ways.

The impact of the new Orthodox immigrants was felt almost immediately in the area of Jewish education. The newcomers were largely separatist in their orientation, living in specific neighborhoods and remaining aloof from the temptations of American culture as much as they could. Public schooling was unthinkable to them. As a result, all-day Orthodox schools mushroomed in the 1950s and 1960s: from fewer than 20 before the war to 257 in 1963 and more than 400 by the early 1970s. The largest expansion of Orthodoxy in America was yet to come, however, as large numbers of younger Jews in search of a spirituality more substantial than Conservatism embraced "modern Orthodoxy," or American Orthodoxy, observing the full complement of traditional rituals while maintaining an interest in many aspects of American culture. The rise of this Americanized version of Orthodoxy began in the late 1960s and has shown few signs of abating, more than three decades later.

These trends hardly accord with the expectations of leading Jewish sociologists in the 1950s and early 1960s. Marshall Sklare had foreseen a three-stage acculturation process: immigrants would at first reside in heavily Jewish neighborhoods, maintaining religious practices more for sociological reasons than out of genuine conviction; in the second stage, they would move on to homogeneous neighborhoods in which their synagogues would be formally Orthodox but religious observance among the members would be severely eroded; in the final stage, the next generation would be fully acculturated, while maintaining an ethnic identity through that comfortable balance of Judaism and Americanism known as Conservative Judaism. Sklare did not foresee that many young Jews would find in Orthodox Judaism a viable ideological alternative to what they perceived as the spiritual and intellectual shallowness of suburban Jewish life. Nor could he have anticipated the emergence of a powerful activist movement, the struggle for Soviet Jewry (see Chapter 2), which would awaken Jewish pride and identity among the younger generation and ultimately lead many of them to Orthodoxy.

Orthodoxy has been further strengthened by another surprising development: the spectacularly successful outreach efforts by the Lubavitcher Hasidim. Recent years have witnessed the remarkable phenomenon of these traditionally insular Hasidim actively venturing into the non-Hasidic world, seeking to bring Jewish knowledge and practice to Jews lacking in Jewish background and education. Often such efforts have taken the form of programs sponsored by Lubavitcher "Chabad Houses" on college campuses or in cities with small Jewish communities.

Sklare's famous 1957 study of a "typical" American Jewish community, which he called "Lakeville," when read together with his follow-up studies of the community in 1967 and 1979, helps to illustrate many of the sociological and demographic trends shaping American Jewry. In 1957, Jews made up close to one-third of Lakeville's population. Their primary forms of identification as Jews were residential—they lived close to many other Jews; personal associations—90 percent were close friends only with other Jews; and synagogue membership—two-thirds belonged to one of the five local synagogues, of which four were Reform (one of them associated with the nearly defunct anti-Zionist movement, the American Council for Judaism) and one Conservative. However, only 6 percent attended services regularly. Attitudes among the Jews of Lakeville reflected a vague, ethnically based identity: strong opposition to intermarriage and a conviction that the essence of being "a good Jew" is "leading an ethical life" and "not hiding one's Jewishness"—with "religious observance" the lowest-ranked criterion.

Sklare's return to "Lakeville" in 1967 documented signs of change, many of which were harbingers of even greater change in the offing. The synagogue associated with the American Council for Judaism had joined mainstream Reform Judaism; levels of community involvement were slightly increased; and intense pro-Israel sentiment was evident in the wake of the Six Day War. Sklare's follow-up study in 1979 found even more significant developments: Jews were now the majority of Lakeville's population; the Reform synagogues had embraced increased ritual practices; a Conservative day school, part of the movement's network of Solomon Schechter schools, had been established; and a small Orthodox congregation was in the process of formation. At the same time, the rate of intermarriage had increased significantly since the time of the previous study. "Lakeville" is situated in the Midwest, making it atypical of Jewish communities in some respects: the larger Jewish communities of the Northeast, where the majority of American Jews continue to reside, tend to be closer to tradition, and feature lower intermarriage rates, than those in more remote parts of the country. Still, the religious and social evolution of Lakeville Jewry mirrored a number of trends typical of contemporary American Jewry: those Jews who most strongly identify with the community are intensifying their levels of commitment and observance—hence the growth of both Conservative and Orthodox day schools, the spread of Orthodoxy in areas far from the inner city, and Reform's turn toward tradition; those Jews who are the most detached from the community are becoming ever more assimilated— hence the ever-increasing rate of intermarriage. The two opposite ends of the American Jewish community are heading even further in opposite directions. The great unknown is what will happen to those in the middle.

Reform Judaism, like its Conservative counterpart, expanded significantly in postwar suburbia, for mostly the same reasons. Demanding no personal religious observance and offering a way to affiliate with Jews that was acceptable in American terms, Reform grew rapidly in the 1950s and 1960s. Yet it never succeeded in surpassing Conservatism; surveys have consistently found that approximately 40 percent of American Jews currently identify themselves as Conservative, about 35 percent Reform, another 10 percent Orthodox, and the remainder identify with no specific faction. Reform's consistent place behind Conservative Judaism is in part because Conservatism's emphasis on ethnicity was somewhat closer to the secular ethnic sentiment of the younger generation than the more religion-oriented philosophy of Reform. American Jews in the 1960s were closer to being an ethnic group without religion than a religion without ethnicity. The perceived religious radicalism of the Reform rabbinate also worked to the movement's disadvantage. Suburban Jews who prefer a spectator Judaism, in which the rabbi's performance of rituals serves as a vicarious form of religious observance, are more likely to choose a Conservative rabbi, whose level of observance is usually much higher than that of Reform clergy. Surveys of Reform practice have found a small core of ritual practitioners and a large body of individuals, even among those in leadership positions in Reform synagogues, who observe almost no traditional practices. A 1987 poll of Reform leaders found that only 9 percent kept kosher. Even by stretching the term kosher to its broadest conceivable limits, that figure increases only modestly: in the 1950s, only one-fourth of Reform Jews observed any aspect of keeping kosher, such as refraining from bringing pork into their homes, while the 1987 study found that just over one-third said they refrain from eating pork products. Surveys of the Reform rabbinate have found decidedly nontraditionalist attitudes, including in regard to central doctrinal matters. In a 1972 study, for example, only one in ten Reform rabbis believed in God "in the more or less traditional sense," and among rabbis ordained between 1969 and 1971, just 3 percent.

The ordination of the first woman Reform rabbi, in 1972, was in keeping with the movement's support for egalitarian principles and women's equality. It also undoubtedly helped attract more women and younger people to the Reform movement, while at the same time alienating some who found women's ordination too radical a break from longstanding tradition. Eventually the Conservative movement likewise approved women's ordination, thereby eliminating one of the major remaining differences between the two factions. In another step belatedly echoing Reform Judaism, the Conservative movement in 1998 amended its standard prayer book to delete masculine names for God such as "Lord," "Father," and "King," substituting what it called "gender sensitive" terminology.

Other differences between Reform and Conservatism have persisted, however. In 1983, Reform Judaism declared that the child of a Jewish father and non-Jewish mother would be considered a Jew, despite the 3,000-year-old practice of regarding only the offspring of a Jewish mother as Jewish. Although framed as a theological decision, the endorsement of patrilineality was very much a concession to practical concerns: it had the potential to significantly increase the membership of Reform synagogues, which in many cases had been in steep decline. Here the Reform movement was, in a sense, trading quality for quantity, since studies have found that the children of Jewish-Gentile intermarriages typically display little interest in asserting a Jewish identity. Conservative Judaism, for its part, continues to reject the concept of patrilineal descent. The two movements remain far apart on the question of intermarriage as well, although their difference is less in theory than in practice. Officially, the Reform movement remains as opposed as Conservatism to marriages between Jews and non-Jews. In practice, however, a significant number of Reform rabbis consent to officiate between such marriages, often with the non-Jewish partner receiving only the most cursory training in Judaism before undergoing a speedy conversion.

Neither Reform nor Conservatism has suffered noticeable losses as a result of the small splinter theologies that have arisen in the Jewish community. Reconstructionist Judaism, set forth in a 1934 manifesto by radical theologian Mordechai Kaplan, contends that Judaism is not a body of laws but rather an "evolving religious civilization"; that Judaism should be redefined to encompass whatever Jews do and believe; and that God is not a supreme deity but rather whatever "power in the universe" inspires man to seek betterment of human existence. Although Reform Judaism traditionally advocated religion without humanity, Reconstructionism proposes humanity without religion. Too far removed from Jewish tradition ever to attract more than a relative handful of supporters, Reconstructionism has sustained itself on a small network of affiliated congregations and a rabbinical college in eastern Pennsylvania. Its graduates are frequently prominent in social and political activist causes. Even more minuscule is the movement known as Secular Humanistic Judaism. Established in 1969, it is essentially atheism with a Jewish veneer. It has some two dozen congregations in the United States and a small sister movement in Israel.

Postwar Anti-Semitism

Anti-Semitism fell into disfavor in the postwar United States as a result of its association with America's enemies in World War II. The gradual outlawing of discrimination in housing and employment during the 1950s and early 1960s further fostered a sense among American Jews that a new climate of tolerance had settled over much of the nation. An exception was the South, where polls found anti-Jewish prejudices to be more widespread than in any other part of the country. Three young civil rights activists, two of them Jews, were murdered by segregationists in Mississippi in 1964, while sporadic bombings of synagogues in at least nine Southern cities took place in 1957–1958 and 1967, the handiwork of white supremacists who accused Jews of promoting desegregation.

The Anti-Defamation League, which maintains an annual tally of significant anti-Semitic incidents, has reported a general decline in such episodes in recent decades, and its 1992 survey of the attitudes toward Jews of the American public concluded that only 17 percent of whites hold views so extreme that they could be described as "hard-core" anti-Semites. Still, it is a latent form of anti-Semitism, rarely expressed in acts of violence or publicly articulated in any fashion. Despite the assessment of sociologists and some Jewish organizational professionals that anti-Semitism is at its lowest point ever in U.S. history, polls continue to find that a majority of American Jews still perceive anti-Semitism to be widespread and a serious problem. Part of the reason is that polls about public attitudes toward Jews contain several inherent flaws. To begin with, as the historian Ben Halpern has pointed out, the polls are slanted by the fact that some respondents tell the pollsters what they think they are expected to believe—that is, what the pollsters want to hear, not what the respondents necessarily believe. What the polls reveal is not that anti-Semitism has declined but that anti-Semitism is not respectable (Halpern, 285).

Furthermore, tallies such as the ADL's cannot keep track of expressions of anti-Semitism that defy simple measurement, from street-corner anti-Semitic taunts that go unreported to attacks on Israel or Zionism that are only a fig leaf for anti-Semitism. Another reason that most Jews tend to perceive anti-Semitism as a serious menace is their concern over its potential. If one-fifth of Americans admit to sentiments that can be defined as "hard-core" anti-Semitism, and many others acknowledge harboring views that are at least moderately anti-Semitic, it is not unreasonable to expect that in times of unusual social or economic strain, such sentiments could come to the fore, with destructive results.

In the meantime, the Jewish community has focused its concern on the occasional anti-Semitic utterances by public figures, whose positions of power and prominence could give their prejudices an aura of legitimacy. Hence the Jewish outcry over Attorney General William Saxbe's 1974 comment about Jewish intellectuals being "enamored" of communism; the statement that same year by the chairman of the Joint Chiefs of Staff, General George Brown, that Jews control America's banks and newspapers; and the revelation, after Richard Nixon's resignation, of the anti-Semitic remarks he made in private during his White House years.

Case Study: General Brown's Mistake

General George Brown's allegation that Jews control the American news media shed light on an often misunderstood topic.

Jews actually came late to the world of American journalism. Especially during the interwar years, the media offered little in the way of professional stability or earning potential, and as a result Jewish parents steered their children down more reliable career paths such as law, medicine, and business. After World War II, the rise of the television networks gave the media increased prestige, and Jews gradually became increasingly prominent as reporters and editors, although not necessarily as owners. By the time of General Brown's remark, Jews owned only an estimated 3 percent of America's newspapers. The fact that the most important of the daily newspapers, the *New York Times,* is Jewish-owned, has undoubtedly fed erroneous assumptions about the role of Jews in the media. In any event, even the relatively few newspapers that are Jewish-owned can hardly be considered part of some sort of conspiracy to promote Jewish interests, since they scarcely promote them at all. The *New York Times,* to cite the most prominent of the Jewish-owned newspapers, was strongly anti-Zionist from the 1890s through the 1940s, and it has been sharply critical of many Israeli policies in recent decades.

Moreover, the Jewish owners of the *Times* were intensely, almost obsessively, fearful of being perceived as being "too Jewish." For many years, *Times* reporters with Jewish-sounding first names were ordered to use only their first initials in print—such as A. M. Rosenthal. Turner Catledge, for many years an editor at the *Times,* recalled in his memoirs how the newspaper's owner, Arthur Hays Sulzberger, periodically cautioned him to avoid hiring too many Jews. Well aware that such religious discrimination was illegal, Catledge was disturbed when, on one occasion during the late 1940s, one of the department chiefs under him admitted having actually told one job applicant that "I couldn't hire him because he was a Jew." When Catledge protested, the department chief replied: "Well, what am I supposed to do? I'm looking for a man to work the Jewish holidays" (Catledge 1971, 215–216).

Ari Goldman, a young reporter on religious affairs for the *Times,* felt a different kind of pressure when he began working for the "newspaper of record" in the early 1970s. Goldman, who describes himself as a "traditionalist," reached the conclusion that advancing his journalistic career required compromising religious observance—whether that meant covering a breaking news story on the Sabbath or sharing a nonkosher meal with a VIP—even if he were not actually instructed by his editors to do so. In his memoirs, Goldman noted that the Jewish editors at the *Times* sometimes "bend over backwards to be fair" on stories involving "Israel and Jewish issues." Goldman himself once refrained from reporting an anti-Israel tirade by the visiting wife of an Egyptian leader, evidently because he was concerned about how her statements might affect Egypt's image in the United States.

For many in the American Jewish community, the preposterousness of claims about Jewish control of the media is graphically demonstrated by the U.S. media's coverage of Middle East affairs, which in recent decades has often been unfriendly toward Israel and sympathetic to the Palestinian Arab cause. Several major Jewish organizations devote considerable resources to combating anti-Israel bias in the media, and one, the Committee for Accuracy in Middle East Reporting in America, or CAMERA, is devoted full-time to the task. These critics point out that, ironically, some Jewish journalists are among the least sympathetic to Israel's plight.

The prominence of far-right and extremist Christian anti-Semitic groups during the 1930s, along with postwar studies showing the highest levels of anti-Jewish prejudice among those white Christians who were the most religious, accustomed most American Jews to thinking of anti-Semitism as the province of Southern Baptist "rednecks" and elitist New England WASPs.

Hence the widespread shock in the Jewish community when, in the late 1960s, anti-Semitic expressions were increasingly heard from, of all places, the African-American community. Jews who had contributed so much to the black civil rights struggle, and had come to look upon

African-Americans as their natural allies in the common struggle against anti-Jewish and antiblack bigots, had never imagined the African-American community as a potential source of anti-Semitism.

Even more surprising was the discovery that the anti-Semitic outbursts by black militants in the 1960s were not the isolated utterances of aberrant radicals but expressions of a sentiment that was shared widely among African-Americans. A 1970 study of black residents of Los Angeles found that anti-Semitism was not only widespread among African-Americans but was actually highest among the young and educated. In Los Angeles, 73 percent of blacks in their twenties were found to be extremely anti-Semitic, compared with 59 percent of those in their thirties or forties, and 35 percent among blacks aged fifty or older. This contrasted sharply with Jewish leaders' assumption that anti-Semitism in general was more likely to come from those who were older and less educated, and who therefore subscribed to old-fashioned prejudices about Jews. Anti-Semitism unrelated to levels of education would be especially difficult to combat, since the Jewish organizations' standard "solution" for anti-Semitism had always been education.

Two studies commissioned by the AJ Committee in the late 1970s reached similar conclusions. Young blacks were found to be more anti-Semitic than young whites, and the gap was growing; anti-Semitism was found to be widespread among national African-American leaders, not just the rank and file; and anti-Semitism among blacks in general was increasing.

In an interesting sidelight, a 1986 study of black church-goers in Seattle, Buffalo, and St. Louis concluded that those African-Americans who were the most religiously devout were the least anti-Semitic. Although the 1986 survey was far from definitive, it did raise legitimate questions about popular assumptions regarding the basis for anti-Semitism. Previous assumptions had been rooted in, for example, the Glock-Stark study of the relationship between Christian religious beliefs and anti-Semitism, published in 1966 by the Anti-Defamation League; that study had concluded that classic theological teachings about Jews lay at the heart of contemporary anti-Semitic prejudice.

Case Study: Jesse Jackson and the Jews

For American Jews who instinctively associated anti-Semitism with whites on the far right, the anti-Jewish slurs made by the Reverend

Jesse Jackson, the militant left-wing black leader, came as quite a shock. It happened in the midst of the 1984 Democratic presidential primaries, in which Jackson was competing as a fringe candidate, hoping to increase his influence in the party although he had no chance of actually winning the nomination. In a conversation with a reporter, Jackson referred to Jews by the derogatory term "Hymies" and to New York City as "Hymietown." After initial denials, Jackson bowed to a storm of Jewish protests and publicly apologized for the statement.

If the controversy had been limited to the "Hymie" remark, many Jews might well have adopted a forgive-and-forget attitude, in the hope of smoothing over black-Jewish relations by sweeping the incident under the rug. The problem, however, was that upon closer examination, it turned out that Jackson had a long record of making unfriendly comments about Jews, Zionism, and Israel, many of which were publicized in newspaper advertisements by a protest group called "Jews Against Jackson." Jackson had railed about "Jewish slumlords," and when America's first black ambassador to the United Nations, Andrew Young, resigned after meeting a PLO official in contravention of U.S. policy, Jackson blamed Jewish pressure for Young's departure. He then ostentatiously flew for the first time to the Middle East, where he embraced Yasir Arafat, spoke at an Arab rally where extreme anti-Israel slogans were chanted, and was quoted as complaining that Jews were trying to "give America a guilt trip" about the Holocaust. The following year he publicly charged that Zionism is a "poisonous weed" choking Judaism, and he blamed Jewish pressure for the Democrats' support of Israeli action against PLO terrorists in Lebanon in 1982. In recent years, Jackson has repeatedly rankled the Jewish community by befriending Louis Farrakhan, the Black Muslim leader who has made numerous anti-Semitic remarks.

Jackson's continuing stature as the foremost spokesman for African-Americans, despite a series of scandals, has forced Jews to reassess some of their traditional expectations about the primary sources of anti-Semitism in America today, and about the willingness of so many blacks to support Jackson despite—or, in some cases, because of—his hostility to Jews.

What, then, of the camp with which Jews traditionally associated anti-Semitism, the political and religious far-right? Although American Jews are still far from comfortable, either politically or culturally, with conservative or fundamentalist Christians, they have discovered in recent years that such Christians do not entirely fit the stereotypes about them.

Consider the startling scene that accompanied the 1995 inauguration of Alabama governor Fob James, which offered a clue to some of the intriguing new questions that will face American Jewry. The gubernatorial inauguration ceremony, which would typically include an orchestra, a choir singing the national anthem, and an invocation by a clergyman, this time was something else altogether: the orchestra's horn section was accompanied by the blast of a shofar; the choir sang Israel's national anthem, "Hatikvah"; and a local bishop began his invocation by reciting the *Sh'ma* (a selection of biblical passages affirming faith in God, recited twice daily by traditional Jews). An outsider might have found the ceremony perplexing, but a glance at a map of Alabama would have yielded a significant clue: within a day's drive of the inauguration site one can find towns named Jericho, Mount Hebron, Joppa (derived from Jaffa), Pisgah, and Ruhama.

Governor James, like many of his fellow Alabamans, and like the original settlers of Alabama's many biblically named towns, was an evangelical Protestant with a keen interest in the Holy Land and the Jewish people. Such Christians, who are often described as fundamentalists because of their conviction that the Bible is the literal word of God, believe that the fate of the Jews is linked to the approaching messianic era. They perceive the rebirth of the Jewish state and the ingathering of the Jewish exiles as part of the chain of events preceding the End of Days, and as a result they strongly support Israel. At the same time, they expect the Jews to convert to Christianity as part of that same chain of events, and have therefore been at the forefront of efforts to proselytize Jews.

Tens of millions of such Christians are concentrated in the American South and Midwest (it is no coincidence that there are Hebrons in Indiana, Kentucky, Nebraska, Ohio, and other states, as well as Alabama), and in recent decades they have emerged as a powerful political force. Their new prominence has posed something of a dilemma for American Jewry. Many Jews, while impressed by Christian affection for Israel, are troubled by the fundamentalists' interest in proselytizing and by the positions Christian conservatives have taken on a number of domestic issues. Fob James himself raised one such issue during his gubernatorial campaign, when he praised a state judge for displaying the Ten Commandments in his courtroom. During his inaugural address, James called for the institution of a moment of silence (or voluntary prayer) in Alabama's public schools. The James inauguration, with its colorful Zionism and its church-state controversy, in some ways symbolized the dilemma with which

American Jews are grappling in their relations with the Christian right.

Evangelical Christians are reluctant participants in U.S. political life, provoked into the public arena by the social upheavals of the 1960s and 1970s. Alarmed by the relaxed morals and political radicalism of the younger generation, the liberalization of abortion, and the spread of racial tensions, Christian fundamentalists began making their presence felt in the public policy arena. They gained national prominence with the emergence of the Reverend Jerry Falwell's Moral Majority movement. Established in 1979, the Moral Majority helped mobilize Christian conservative voters on behalf of Ronald Reagan's presidential candidacy. With evangelical Protestants and like-minded conservative Catholics together numbering around 50 million, the Christian right was truly becoming a force to be reckoned with.

Many American Jews were alarmed by the evangelicals' vision of the United States as a "Christian republic." Jewish suspicions of Christian fundamentalist intolerance intensified when the Rev. Bailey Smith, leader of the Southern Baptist Convention, remarked in 1980 that "God Almighty does not hear the prayer of a Jew." Even if Smith was, as he claimed, merely reaffirming the traditional principle that embracing Christian doctrine is a prerequisite to attaining Divine acceptance, his choice of words nonetheless frightened and angered many American Jews. At the same time, many Jews were disturbed by what seemed like an assault on the very concept of church-state separation, as the fundamentalists lobbied for, among other things, government aid to parochial schools, a moment of prayer in public schools, and restrictions on controversial reading material in public school curricula. The fundamentalists were also vocal in their denunciations of homosexuality and abortion; the Rev. Falwell went so far as to refer to "the extermination of unborn babies" as if it were comparable to Nazi genocide.

As noted earlier in this volume, leading American Jewish organizations have fought for as strict a separation of church and state as possible, opposing school prayer and aid for private schools. On privacy issues, such as abortion and homosexuality, most Jewish groups have consistently endorsed noninterference by the government.

These differing perspectives on political issues are only part of the reason for the lack of common ground between American Jews and Christian conservatives. Social distance is also a factor. Many Jews are instinctively uncomfortable with Christian conservatives because of their personal unfamiliarity with them. The evangelicals are the

Christians with whom most Jews have had the least social contact. The pre–World War II generation of American Jews was raised primarily in urban areas in the Northeast, where the non-Jews they knew were typically Italian-Americans or Irish-Americans, frequently Catholics. The postwar Jewish generation, while often residing in the suburbs, frequently opted to live in neighborhoods that had significant numbers of fellow Jews, thereby limiting their social interaction with Christians. The largest concentrations of evangelicals, by contrast, have been in areas that happen to have few Jews: the rural South and Midwest. One will not find any synagogues in Zion, Iowa, although one will find many a church in which the worshippers pray fervently for the welfare of Israel's capital.

The evangelicals' interest in Israel was one of the few areas where American Jews and the Moral Majority found some common language. By coincidence, the evangelicals were gaining prominence in U.S. politics at about the same time that the Likud was first elected to power in Israel. The timing was significant, because during the international controversies over Likud's settlement policies, in the late 1970s and early 1980s, Christian fundamentalists emerged as some of the most vocal supporters of Israel in the United States. They developed an especially strong affinity for Prime Minister Menachem Begin, because of his articulation of Israel's biblical claims to the lands that he, and they, knew as Judea and Samaria.

Some Christian conservatives interpreted the escalating international criticism of Begin's policies in theological terms: well acquainted with the prophets' descriptions of Gog and Magog clashing at the End of Days, they expect to witness a global conflagration focusing on the Holy Land. The Christian right emerged as an unexpected source of support and comfort for many American Jews at a time when Israel was under fire—especially when some of that fire was coming from groups on the Christian left, such as the National Council of Churches and the American Friends Service Committee, which vocally endorsed pro-Arab positions.

Falwell and his colleagues from the Christian right of the early 1980s were subsequently supplanted (several were toppled in highly publicized sex-and-corruption scandals) by more sophisticated rivals. The Moral Majority organization was usurped by Pat Robertson's fast-growing Christian Coalition, with 850 chapters and 450,000 members nationwide. Its political influence extends even further, thanks to Robertson's cable television broadcasting network, which reaches 58 million American homes. The Christian Coalition played a role—experts dispute how significant that role was—in the numerous Republican victories in the 1994 congressional and gubernatorial elections.

Case Study: Jewish Fears of the Christian Right

Some Jewish organizations have responded with alarm to the renewed prominence of Christian conservatives in American politics. A booklet published by the Anti-Defamation League in 1999 charged that the Christian right "brings to cultural disagreements a rhetoric of fear, suspicion, even hatred." The ADL booklet warned that "the fragile structures of consensus are bulldozed by sectarian, absolutist declarations. In this way, we proceed down the road to the 'Christian nation' trumpeted by these prophets of rage." Here the ADL invoked what is perhaps American Jewry's most profound underlying fear concerning the Christian right: that it will turn the United States into a country that imposes Christian values upon its citizens. Most American Jews regard America's status as a formally secular country, with strict separation of church and state, as the key to enabling Jews to prosper. The conversion of the United States from a secular to a Christian nation would presumably be to the severe detriment of all non-Christian citizens.

The ADL report also found anti-Semitic individuals hovering on the fringes of some Christian conservative organizations, although it did not contend that anti-Semites are to be found within the leadership or mainstream rank and file of those groups. Jewish conservatives criticized the ADL's booklet. They accused the ADL of exaggerating the significance of the Christian right's extremist element and giving insufficient weight to the pro-Israel sentiment of the Christian conservatives.

Jewish Continuity

Ultimately, however, it seems that for the foreseeable future, the main concern for Jews vis-à-vis non-Jewish Americans will stem less from anti-Semitic rejection than from the problems accompanying American society's acceptance of Jews. Historically, the more comfortable Jews have felt in a given host country, the greater the number of Jews who have assimilated into the general culture, discarded their ethnic identity, and ultimately married non-Jews. Hence in recent years the slogan "Jewish continuity" has become a watchword in the Jewish organizational world, representing the sentiment shared by most American Jews that the persistence of Jewish identity should be a primary goal.

The increasing focus on "Jewish continuity" comes after many decades of assimilation and intermarriage that have eroded American Jewry. The progressively increasing intermarriage rate from generation to generation was already apparent in 1956, when a study of marriages involving American Jewish men found that while just over 1 percent of marriages involving men born abroad were to non-Jewish women, the rate increased to more than 10 percent among first-generation American Jewish men and to nearly 18 percent among the second generation. A comparable survey of Jews in Boston in 1965 found that only 7 percent of Jewish husbands between the ages of thirty-one and fifty were intermarried, while the figure for those under thirty was 20 percent. In the early 1960s, an estimated 10 to 15 percent of marriages involving Jews nationwide were mixed. Although the rates vary in different communities, with the highest figures in the West and Midwest and lowest in the Northeast, the national average intermarriage rate for subsequent decades was approximately 20 to 25 percent in the 1970s, 30 to 35 percent in the 1980s, and above 40 percent in the 1990s, reaching 52 percent in some locales.

Jewish-Gentile social contacts have become inevitable, Edward Shapiro notes, now that so many Jews are "living in suburbia, attending residential colleges rather than urban commuter institutions, and working in corporate and academic bureaucracies." Although Jewish critics of intermarriage have pointed to Jewish education as the solution, "those most prone to intermarriage were the least likely to be enrolled by their parents in Jewish schools or to be the products of intensely Jewish families." Many Jewish parents who oppose intermarriage are less than persuasive in their attempts to convince the next generation to feel likewise. "The ethnic and religious loyalties that they took for granted did not resonate to the same extent among their children." In addition, Shapiro points to an element of hypocrisy in such parental pleadings. "The liberalism that Jewish parents had passed down to their children encouraged intermarriage. Liberalism warned against intolerance, encouraged people to judge others as individuals and not as members of a group, and argued that religious and ethnic differences were anachronisms. How could liberal Jews attribute to anti-Semitism the reluctance of Gentiles to marry Jews and at the same time oppose Jews selecting Gentile spouses without appearing to be bigots themselves?" The parents' claims that differences in religion or ethnicity would be sources of tension in the marriage made little headway. "For the young, inter-marriage simply took the liberalism of their parents to its logical con-clusion, and they viewed parental opposition to intermarriage as hypocritical, particularly in those cases when their parents had not previously exhibited any strong religious or ethnic attachments" (Shapiro 1992, 231–232).

The problem has been aggravated by a seeming erosion of opposi-tion within the Jewish community to intermarriage. Many Reform rabbis will officiate at Jewish-Gentile intermarriages—without being penalized in any way by the Reform movement—and usually non-Jewish children from such couples are accepted as Jews by Reform synagogues. Most major Jewish organizations that in the recent past would have considered it unthinkable for an intermarried individual to hold a senior leadership position, have quietly abandoned that po-sition and accepted the intermarried into their highest ranks. Jewish groups vigorously protested the 1972 television program "Bridget Loves Bernie" because of its appealing portrayal of an intermarried couple; yet there were no protests against the late–1980s television series "thirtysomething," whose main characters included a Jewish man happily married to a Christian woman. Nor have Jewish groups protested the many other prime-time television shows in which in-termarriage has been depicted in a favorable light. The Jewish leader-ship's retreat on the intermarriage issue, even though it has been dic-tated by a sense of weary resignation rather than ideological conviction, has in effect sent a message to the next generation that intermarriage is no longer taboo.

Despite these trends, the overall size of the Jewish community continued to rise in the 1990s, albeit relatively slowly, from an esti-mated 5.5 million in 1990 to about 6 million in 2000. American Jewry's increasing divorce rate, decreasing marriage rate (and ever-higher median age of wedlock), and low rate of childbirth were tem-porarily offset by the influx of hundreds of thousands of Russian Jews from the collapsed Soviet Union and a steady stream of emigrants from Israel, some 500,000 of whom have taken up permanent resi-dence in the United States since 1948.

Paradoxically, then, the very freedoms and acceptance for which American Jews have labored so valiantly for so many years are facili-tating the assimilation that is eroding the Jewish community's num-bers. Still, the ethnic and religious resilience that Jews have often demonstrated in the past may well continue to manifest itself in the strengthening of Jewish identity and practice in certain segments of the community. Somewhat smaller numbers are likely to be offset by an intensification of personal commitment and political and social activism that will help ensure the Jewish community's continuing prominence and influence in American political culture.

References

Arzt, Donna. "The People's Lawyers: The Predominance of Jews in Public Interest Law." *Judaism* 35 (winter 1986): 47–62.

Auerbach, Jerold S. "Liberalism and the Hebrew Prophets." *Commentary* 89 (August 1987): 58–60.

———. "Prophets or Profits? Liberal Lawyers and Jewish Tradition." *Judaism* 127 (summer 1987): 360–365.

———. *Rabbis and Lawyers: The Journey from Torah to Constitution.* Bloomington: Indiana University Press, 1990.

———. Review of *Proskauer: His Life and Times.* In *American Jewish History* 68 (September 1979): 103–116.

Bendersky, Joseph W. *The "Jewish Threat": Anti-Semitic Policies of the U.S. Army.* New York: Basic Books, 2000.

Catledge, Turner. *My Life and the Times.* New York: Harper and Row, 1971.

Cohen, Naomi W. *American Jews and the Zionist Idea.* New York: Ktav, 1975.

Diner, Hasia. *A Time for Gathering: The Second Migration, 1820–1880.* Vol. II of *The Jewish People in America.* Baltimore, MD: Johns Hopkins University Press, 1992.

Dinnerstein, Leonard. *Anti-Semitism in America.* New York: Oxford University Press, 1994.

Dollinger, Marc. *Quest for Inclusion: Jews and Liberalism in Modern America.* Princeton, NJ: Princeton University Press, 2000.

Elazar, Daniel J. *Community and Polity: The Organizational Dynamic of American Jewry.* Philadelphia: Jewish Publication Society of America, 1995.

Faber, Eli. *A Time for Planting: The First Migration, 1654–1820.* Vol. I of *The Jewish People in America.* Baltimore, MD: Johns Hopkins University Press, 1992.

Feingold, Henry L. Review of *The Prophetic Minority* by Gerald Sorin. In *The Reconstructionist* 52 (September 1986): 31.

———. *A Time for Searching: Entering the Mainstream, 1920–1945.* Vol. IV of *The Jewish People in America.* Baltimore, MD: Johns Hopkins University Press, 1992.

Friedman, Murray. *What Went Wrong? The Creation and Collapse of the Black-Jewish Alliance.* New York: Free Press, 1995.

Glock, Charles Y., and Rodney Stark. *Christian Beliefs and Anti-Semitism.* New York: Harper and Row, 1966.

Gurock, Jeffrey S. "The Orthodox Synagogue." In *The American Synagogue: A Sanctuary Transformed,* edited by Jack Wertheimer, pp. 37–84. New York: Cambridge University Press, 1987.

72 ▓ Jewish Americans and Political Participation

———. "Pursuing Self-Interest." *Present Tense* 8 (1981): 29–30.
———. "The Winnowing of American Orthodoxy." *Approaches to Modern Judaism* 2 (1984): 41–54.
Halpern, Ben. "Anti-Semitism in the Perspective of Jewish History." In *Jews in the Mind of America,* edited by Charles Stember, et al. New York: Basic Books, 1966.
Kessner, Thomas. *The Golden Door: Italian and Jewish Immigrant Mobility in New York City, 1880–1915.* New York: Oxford University Press, 1977.
Locke, Hubert G. *The Black Anti-Semitism Controversy: Protestant Views and Perspectives.* Selinsgrove, PA: Susquehanna University Press, 1994.
Marcus, Jacob R. *The Colonial American Jew 1492–1776.* 3 vols. Detroit, MI: Wayne State University Press, 1970.
———. *United States Jewry 1776–1985.* Vol. I. Detroit, MI: Wayne State University Press, 1989.
Moore, Deborah Dash. *At Home in America: Second Generation New York Jews.* New York: Columbia University Press, 1981.
Sachar, Howard M. *A History of Jews in America.* New York: Knopf, 1992.
Shapiro, Edward S. *A Time for Healing: American Jewry since World War II.* Vol. V of *The Jewish People in America.* Baltimore, MD: Johns Hopkins University Press, 1992.
Sorin, Gerald. *A Time for Building: The Third Migration, 1880–1920.* Vol. III of *The Jewish People in America.* Baltimore, MD: Johns Hopkins University Press, 1992.
Sussman, Lance J. "Suburbanization of American Judaism: Synagogue Building 1945–1975." *American Jewish History* 74 (September 1985).
Waxman, Chaim I. *American Aliya: Portrait of an Innovative Migration Movement.* Detroit, MI: Wayne State University Press, 1989.
———. *America's Jews in Transition.* Philadelphia: Temple University Press, 1983.
Wenger, Beth. *New York Jews and the Great Depression: Uncertain Promise.* New Haven, CT: Yale University Press, 1996.

2

Protest Politics

merican Jewish involvement in protest politics has spanned a wide variety of issues, both domestic and international. The intersection of the Jewish community's own concerns about gaining acceptance in American society and the broader goal of shaping an inclusive, pluralistic America has resulted in a high level of Jewish involvement in protests related to immigration, church-state separation, and civil rights. At the same time, many American Jews and Jewish organizations have taken an active role in protest activity concerning the mistreatment of Jews overseas, especially the persecution of European Jewry by the Nazis, the oppression of Soviet Jewry, and the plight of Israel. Many American Jews have also been actively involved in protests focusing on issues not directly related to Jewish concerns. No other American ethnic group has assumed such an intense and long-standing involvement in so many political protest movements.

Domestic Issues

The roots of American Jewish involvement in protest movements reach all the way back to the very first Jews who settled in what was to become the United States. The handful of Jews who took up residence in the New Amsterdam colony in 1654 were, within weeks, ordered to depart by Governor Peter Stuyvesant, who cited both their poverty and their rejection of Christianity as grounds for expulsion.

The Jews of New Amsterdam, with the assistance of their coreligionists back in Holland, organized a petition of protest to the Dutch owners of the colony, resulting in the reversal of the deportation decree. The episode offered the fledgling American Jewish community several important lessons. First, unlike in Europe, where Jews feared violent backlash if they sought to assert their rights publicly, the prevailing atmosphere of tolerance in Colonial America made Jewish participation in public protest acceptable, and it offered at least the possibility that such protests might succeed. Second, protests backed up by political or economic power were the most viable—in this case, Jews were among the company's investors, and there was the expectation that Jewish settlers would contribute to the prosperity of the Dutch colony. Although tiny in number and newcomers to Colonial America, the Jews of New Amsterdam had successfully utilized political protest to promote their communal interests. It was an experience that would be duplicated by American Jews many times over in the centuries to follow.

Lingering anti-Jewish restrictions in the colony prompted additional protests by the Jews of New Amsterdam in the years following. A petition to permit Jews to serve in the colony's militia or be exempted from paying the tax for not serving was rejected, but necessity soon paved the way for equality: increasing conflicts with local Native Americans gradually resulted in the admission of Jews to the guard force. An appeal to the Dutch owners to overrule Stuyvesant's ban on Jewish real estate purchases succeeded, as did a protest over Stuyvesant's refusal to let the Jews establish their own cemetery. By the time that four Jews petitioned to gain burgher rights, in 1657, a weary Stuyvesant opted to grant the Jews' request rather than risk waging another losing battle.

Still, these skirmishes over the status of the Jews in New Amsterdam were by no means typical of Jewish public behavior in early Colonial America. The British regime that ruled the colonies as of the late 1600s permitted individual religious freedom but restricted public office-holding and voting rights to Protestants. Only in New York were Jews permitted to vote, and they continued to do so even after that right was formally revoked in 1737. The Jews elected to serve as New York City constables in the mid-1700s were the first to hold public office in the colonies. Excluded from political life, the tiny Jewish communities of Colonial America generally refrained from participation in the era's public controversies.

As tensions between the colonists and His Majesty's Government escalated during the 1760s, individual Jews became increasingly involved in the new struggle. Some Jewish businessmen in Philadelphia joined the protesters who declared a boycott of English goods in response to the first attempt, in 1765, to tax the colonists, and a handful of Jews in New York took part in protests against a British tax on tea in 1770. It was in response to the prominence of Jews among the anti-British activists in Savannah that the governor of Georgia issued a decree preventing Jews from settling in the colony and banning Jewish former residents from returning.

Many Jews also joined the rebels' military forces. As a demonstration of their opposition to British rule, some Jews voluntarily relocated to American-controlled territory from New York, Newport, Savannah, and Charleston when those cities were captured by the British, even though they risked no harm by remaining. A minority of Colonial America's 2,000 to 3,000 Jews supported the English. Historians have noted that perhaps the most remarkable aspect of Jewish involvement with either side in the struggle is the fact that so many Jews took sides despite the fact that they easily could have refrained from doing so. Although some of the colonists fought for independence, and others backed the British, many chose to remain neutral, and the Jews could have done likewise. The fact that they did not demonstrates how even at that earliest stage of American history, Jews felt at home in the nation's political struggles (Faber 1992, 102).

In early America federal law guaranteed equal rights for Jews, but state constitutions typically either restricted voting and office-holding to Christians (sometimes to Protestants) or required voters and candidates to take an oath of belief in Christian principles. Occasional Jewish protests resulted, as for example in 1784, when a Jewish congregation in Philadelphia wrote to the Pennsylvania Council of Censors to protest their state's constitutional requirement that legislators affirm the divinity of the New Testament.

The most serious test of Jews' status in the new nation was Maryland's Jew Bill, as it was known. Late-eighteenth-century Maryland law prevented non-Christians from serving as state officers, including lawyers and commissioned officers in the Maryland state militia, a restriction that was protested by one of the state's first Jewish residents, Solomon Etting of Baltimore, in a 1797 petition to the Maryland legislature. A bill to give Jews equal rights was defeated in 1802, 1804, 1818, and again in 1819. It passed only after its sponsors realized, in 1822, that they could gain support with a text that removed religious restrictions in general, without specifying Jews as the sole beneficiaries of the change. But before the bill could pass the requisite second vote, opposition emerged from deputies who feared that general equality would pave the way for "Turks and atheists" to settle in Maryland. A new version was drawn up, tailored to help Jews but disenfranchise atheists, by requiring affirmation of a belief in future Divine rewards and punishments. It became law in 1826.

The blurring of lines between religion and state aroused increased Jewish opposition in the decades to follow. When legislation was introduced in Congress in 1865 to make Christianity the official national religion, protests by the first national Jewish organization in the United States, the Board of Delegates of American Israelites, helped bury the bill in committee. The board also protested the persistence, in North Carolina and New Hampshire, of laws prohibiting non-Christians from holding public office. The protests had impact, and when a new North Carolinian constitution was drawn up in 1868, the Christians-only passages were deleted. New Hampshire, for its part, finally dropped the restriction in 1877. Tennessee law required that sessions of the legislature be opened by a Christian minister, but after Jewish protests the word *Christian* was deleted, and in fact a rabbi was soon invited to participate.

Laws requiring the shutting down of businesses on Sunday proved more intractable. These so-called Blue Laws were found in cities throughout the country, and although Jewish protests succeeded in bringing about their revocation in New Orleans and Richmond in the 1840s, they survived in many other locales. A proposed federal law to protect those who observed Saturday as their Sabbath was buried in committee in 1877, despite lobbying efforts by the two groups most affected, Jews and Seventh-day Adventists.

Attempts to secularize public schools were likewise slow to advance. Displays of Christianity in the schools ranged from observance of Christian religious holidays to readings from the Christian Bible. A test case in Cincinnati raged back and forth for several decades. The local board of education had, as of 1852, permitted Bible readings. After many years of Jewish protests, the board finally reversed the policy in 1869. Supporters of the readings challenged the reversal in court, and won; the board of education then appealed to the Ohio Supreme Court and emerged victorious.

In general, the first half of the nineteenth century was a period of relative political quiet for the American Jewish community. Small in number and nervous about their status in American society, Jews did not flock to protest movements even when they were privately sympathetic to their goals, such as abolitionism or the Mexican War. The Jews of the pre–Civil War period were primarily of German or Central

European origin, and they tended to be more conservative in their political outlook than their East European coreligionists, who would migrate to the United States in significant numbers only toward the end of the century.

There was evidence of change in the 1850s, when veterans of the failed German revolution of 1848 began arriving in America. Imbued with an activist spirit and political organizing experience, they were natural recruits for U.S. protest movements. Three of them, in fact, joined the ranks of John Brown's abolitionist militia in 1856, and another, Isador Bush, became an antislavery leader in Missouri. There were others, too: Moritz Pinner published the abolitionist *Kansas Post;* Philip Joachimsen, who served as assistant district attorney in New York, energetically targeted slave traders; and Ernestine Rose, a pioneer women's rights activist in the Jacksonian era, was an active abolitionist.

Still, these were individuals, not organizations representing large numbers of people. Most Jews chose to refrain from activism, pro or con, on the slavery question. There was a smattering of public protest activity by Jews in Cincinnati and Baltimore—a handful of Cincinnati Jews criticized Rabbi Isaac Wise's proslavery statements in letters to the *Cincinnati Daily Times,* while in Baltimore, Jews held a public protest meeting against abolitionist rabbi David Einhorn of Temple Har Sinai; some joined mobs that destroyed his printing presses and drove him from the city.

Direct attacks on Jews elicited a more active Jewish response. The speaker of the California House of Representatives, William Stowe, proposed in 1855 the institution of a head tax on Jews to deter them from settling in the state, setting off a string of Jewish protests in the local press as well as public protest meetings in San Francisco and Sacramento. During the Civil War, a YMCA staffer's complaint against a Jew serving as an ecumenical U.S. Army chaplain sparked Jewish protests against the little-known Northern regulation that such chaplains had to be Christian; President Lincoln responded by pushing through legislation to permit chaplains of all religions. In April 1862, residents of Thomsville, Georgia, accused Jewish shopkeepers of being unpatriotic and threatened to prevent additional Jews from settling in the town; the Jewish community responded with a public protest meeting and a letter to the local newspaper by thirty Jewish soldiers serving in the Georgia militia. Later that year, Union general Ulysses Grant responded to popular resentment over Jewish merchants allegedly taking advantage of the cotton shortage to sell cotton in war zones, by issuing General Order 11, which expelled all Jews from the region known as the Tennessee Department. The entire Jewish community of Paducah, Kentucky, was ordered to depart on twenty-four hours' notice. Local Jewish leaders, together with local dignitaries, among them Paducah Union League president Cesar Kaskel, protested directly to President Lincoln, who eventually revoked Grant's directive.

A major controversy erupted in 1867. Influenced by stereotypes about Jewish swindlers, a number of insurance companies began instructing their agents to refrain from insuring Jewish property. As word spread, Jewish protest rallies were held in Cincinnati, New York, St. Louis, Richmond, Cleveland, and other cities. Jews announced boycotts of the offending companies, and they set up a number of their own insurance firms. The economic pressure proved potent: when some insurance agents refused to deal with the companies in question, their stock dropped in value, and the anti-Jewish policies were subsequently withdrawn.

Jewish protests were similarly successful in the case of a resort hotel in upstate Saratoga, New York, which in 1877 denied admission to the prominent Jewish banker Joseph Seligman. Jewish protest meetings and threats to boycott the hotel's owner, the A. T. Stewart Company, persuaded the hotel to never again turn away Jewish patrons.

Labor Unions as Vehicles of Political Protest

The image of the Jewish radical on his Lower East Side soapbox is a staple of histories of the American Jewish immigrant experience. Scholars are divided, however, concerning such fundamental issues as the extent of radicalism in the Jewish community and the Jewishness of the radicals themselves. Irving Howe's best-selling *World of Our Fathers* propounds the theme of an immigrant community energized primarily by the dream of a socialist kingdom come. On the other hand, Thomas Kessner's study of Jewish and Italian immigrant mobility in New York concludes that the Jewish businessman, not the radical propagandist, was typical of the world of the turn-of-the-century immigrant. Daily economic survival, not some future utopia, was their chief concern. The radicals in the ghetto were squeaky wheels who attracted the most attention—both at the time and for many decades to follow—but they never attracted substantial numbers of ideologically committed members.

Case Study: What Drove Jews to Radicalism?

According to Gerald Sorin, even the most assimilated of the socialist immigrants retained—and were largely motivated by—a strong Jewish identification. Tracing the roots of Jewish radicalism's alleged Jewishness to the old country, Sorin depicts some young East European Jewish socialists leaving for America as having "marched off to departing trains with the Torah in one hand and a radical tract in the other." Although acknowledging that some Jewish socialists bitterly denounced Jewish tradition, Sorin believes that even those who were most hostile to Judaism must have had a sort of unconscious Jewishness, since they did not express hatred "toward Jews as a people."

Other historians take a more jaundiced view. Where Sorin regards the radicals' occasional references to passages from *Isaiah* as evidence of their continued reverence for Judaism, other scholars view the radicals' resort to biblical quotations as little more than a tactic to impress a constituency that was still largely religious, or at least traditional (Gurock 1987, 185). The radicals were generally ignorant when it came to Jewish tradition—"they could have recited all that they know about sacred doctrine while standing on one foot," Stephen Whitfield has noted, paraphrasing a famous Talmudic saying (Whitfield 144). Abraham Cahan, the dean of Lower East Side Yiddish journalism, described socialism as the immigrants' "new religion," and with good reason: in many ways, socialism was indeed precisely that, a new religion that many immigrant radicals substituted for the old one they so disliked. For some, it was the one religion that could lead them to a world without religion—radicalism "represented to them the path to modernism, to a world in which Jews would be fully accepted" (Feingold 1974, 166). In other words, radicalism was a means of escaping Judaism.

Most Jewish radicalism in the United States was imported. Disillusioned by the anti-Jewish violence and discrimination of the czarist regime, Russian Jewish radicals immigrated to the United States during the late 1800s and early 1900s, hoping to transplant the spirit of revolution to the New World. Some joined the *Am Olam* movement, which created a series of unsuccessful Jewish communal farming settlements, mostly in the Midwest and Far West. After the communes broke up, their members rejoined the urban centers of Jewish life and tried to rally the Jewish masses to socialism's side. It was not an easy task. Jewish immigrants, new to America and anxious to fit in, were understandably reluctant to associate with extremist ideologies that were regarded with hostility by most Americans. Moreover, the exhausting daily work schedule of the average immigrant left little time for extracurricular political activity.

Eventually the frustrated radicals realized that the best way to effect social and political change was by going through, not around, the ever-growing Jewish labor pool. Unions could be "instruments in the class struggle" (Feingold 1974, 167). If they could not overthrow the capitalist system in a workers' tidal wave of violent revolution, they could chip away at the old order by strengthening the unions and using them to force changes that would help the toiling masses. Jewish workers who might otherwise hesitate to link arms with radical agitators were ready to throw in their lot with the activists when the struggle was for their own rights, wages, and benefits. Since the masses had little interest in fighting for the overthrow of the capitalist system, the radicals focused on attainable short-range goals such as health and unemployment insurance; the forty-hour, five-day work week; pensions; and affordable housing cooperatives.

The average laborer's lack of interest in socialist ideology was only one of many obstacles that radical organizers encountered. Jewish immigrants and Jewish bosses had social, religious, and fraternal ties that made it harder for workers to see their employers as class enemies. Few laborers had ambitions beyond the immediate aims of their particular local strike, and they did not generally regard their walkout as a steppingstone in a broader struggle. Many Jewish immigrants belonged to *landsmanshaftn,* mutual-aid societies based on the immigrants' European town of origin. The benefits these groups offered their members often provided stiff competition for nascent labor unions. Ethnic animosity between Jews and other European-born laborers also hampered efforts to mobilize the workers.

An early success came in 1907 with a strike in New York's heavily Jewish garment industry by makers of children's cloaks. The seven-week walkout, backed by the increasingly powerful International Ladies Garment Workers Union, attained several important benefits for the workers, including a reduction in work hours. A 1909 strike by 20,000 female shirtwaist makers, and a walkout the following year by 65,000 male cloak makers, were marred by ugly clashes between strikers and scabs but again won important gains for the working masses. The cause of unionism was greatly energized by the 1911 Triangle Shirtwaist fire, in which 140 women garment workers were killed in a "holocaust of flame," as one activist put it, largely because of hazardous shop conditions and faulty fire escapes.

Yet the socialists failed in their attempts to channel the passions of the union struggles into an ongoing political protest movement. Attempts by Daniel DeLeon and his Socialist Labor Party to turn a group of Jewish unions into an arm of the party caused splits and chaos in the movement in the 1890s. Socialist candidates running in heavily Jewish areas attracted votes in proportion to their willingness to jettison standard socialist rhetoric and embrace parochial Jewish concerns.

The minority of German-born Jews who occupied American Jewry's highest economic and social strata felt a deep sense of embarrassment over the presence of radicals among the East European immigrants, not to mention acute discomfort at the thought of how non-Jews would regard the phenomenon of large numbers of impoverished and very Jewish-looking Jews crowding into America's urban centers. Nonetheless, these German-American Jews, who in 1906 established the American Jewish Committee as a vehicle for defending Jewish interests, fought vigorously in the early 1900s to maintain America's open door policy on immigration. As a matter of general principle, the AJ Committee leaders believed that America had a moral obligation to give refuge to the oppressed. Since they themselves were either immigrants or children of immigrants, they felt personal sympathy for Jews clamoring to escape Russia. A practical consideration weighed in, as well: the arguments against immigration were based heavily on popular racial theories that regarded all Jews, German as well as Russian, as inferior. Curtailing immigration on the basis of these anti-Jewish theories would strike a blow at the German Jews' efforts to gain full acceptance in American society. Louis Marshall, a prominent attorney and Jewish community activist who served as president of the AJ Committee from 1912 to 1929, actively lobbied Congress against bills intended to drastically reduce immigration. The AJ Committee's efforts resulted in the temporary defeat of major restrictions, but eventually the tide of public opinion proved overwhelming; Congress enacted immigration quotas in 1921, and further tightened them in 1924. (For details of the lobbying effort, see Chapter 3.)

The Role of the Rabbinate

Until the final years of the nineteenth century, protest activity in the Jewish community was typically the handiwork of lay activists and the grassroots, with relatively little involvement from the rabbinate. Conservative Judaism, as an organized and recognizable faction, did not yet exist, and most Orthodox rabbis were recent immigrants who had limited exposure to the broader American society and remained aloof from public political controversies. Reform rabbis in nineteenth-century America were occupied with burning theological disputes, such as whether to retain the Saturday Sabbath or switch to Sunday, and fending off competition from Unitarianism and the Ethical Culture Society. In general, the prevailing perspective in the Reform rabbinate until the late 1800s was that U.S. society was marching steadily into an era of prosperity and enlightenment, and had no need of protest meetings or movements to promote significant change.

By the early 1900s, the Reform rabbinate began to emerge as a significant new source of American Jewish social and political protest activity. Under the influence of the turn-of-the-century Progressive movement and the liberal Christian "Social Gospel" activists, Reform rabbis began embracing the notion of social activism as an expression of Jewish values. The fact that these Christian activists often looked to the pronouncements of the ancient Hebrew prophets as their guide made their cause even more palatable to Reform Jewry.

Historians have noted the discrepancy between the Reform rabbis' passionate support for social activism and their congregants' lukewarm interest. One interpretation is that the rabbis "were attempting to put forward the social relevance of the pulpit at a time when increasingly secular congregants were less affected by narrower religious subjects." Another view posits that it was "the rabbi's endeavor to forcefully reassert his own status against the wealthy businessmen who dominated his congregation and whose values reflected the capitalist ethos" (Meyer 1988, 288).

Whatever their motives, the Reform rabbis increasingly took stands on the high-profile political and social controversies of the day. In 1908 the Central Conference of American (Reform) Rabbis (CCAR) denounced child labor, and by 1918 the Reform rabbinate, following similar declarations by Protestant clergy in 1912 and Catholics in 1913, issued a full-fledged social-justice platform that called for, among other things, the institution of a minimum wage, an eight-hour work day, the elimination of child labor, and union rights. Choosing principle over popularity, the 1920 platform of the CCAR criticized the mass arrests of American communists during the postwar Red Scare; protested racist violence against blacks; and opposed restrictions on immigration. Later, the CCAR would become the first Jewish organization to approve conscientious objection to army service (1928) and the first national religious body in the United States to adopt a liberal position regarding birth control (1929).

One issue that Reform Judaism was not quick to embrace was women's suffrage. Although it would eventually distinguish itself as the first branch of Judaism to ordain female rabbis, the Reform movement endorsed women's right to vote only three years before the successful conclusion of the American suffrage struggle. The CCAR twice rejected prosuffrage resolutions before passing one in 1917. Many Reform rabbis shared the era's popular view of women as naturally subservient and homebound. Reform's hesitations about suffrage may also have been influenced by a practical consideration: the need to attract to its ranks East European immigrants, who now constituted the bulk of American Jewry and were generally closer to traditional Judaism's emphasis on women as mothers and homemakers. Interestingly, no Jewish women's organization publicly endorsed suffrage, evidently in deference to the ambivalence of most male Jewish leaders on the subject. Their silence may also have reflected a concern that high-profile Jewish organizational involvement in the suffrage battle might be resented by those elements within the women's rights movement who were unfriendly to Jews.

The prevalence of anti-Semitism, as well as the Christian evangelicalism of many suffragettes, kept all but a handful of Jewish women from joining the early feminist movement in America. Few in numbers and uneasy about their status in American society, Jews generally eschewed controversial causes in the early and mid-1800s. Judaism's traditional view of women's role helped to discourage interest in feminism. Early women's rights activists such as Rosa Sonneschein and Sadie American were the exception, not the rule. Increased Jewish participation in the broader women's rights movement was stimulated by two early–1900s activist campaigns: the National Council of Jewish Women's "holy war" against white slavery and Jewish prostitution, followed by the involvement of many Jewish women in the turn-of-the-century "settlement houses" initiated by the Progressive movement to provide social services, such as medical counseling and language classes, to immigrants in ghetto neighborhoods.

After honing their organizational skills in the settlement house movement and similar causes, women social activists, Christian and Jewish alike, naturally gravitated to the burgeoning suffrage movement. The recent successes scored by the Progressive camp in areas such as labor rights, electoral reform, and government supervision of foods and drugs, followed by the 1912 endorsement of suffrage by the Progressive Party and its presidential nominee Theodore Roosevelt, energized the women's vote activists for the climactic round of the suffrage struggle. Several Jewish women emerged as national leaders of the suffrage movement. Maud Nathan and Martha Klatschken, for two, were especially well known for their oratorical abilities and organizational know-how. Their imaginative protest tactics, such as delivering a nonstop twenty-four-hour-long streetcorner lecture, or giving what was called a "silent speech" while standing before a vacant store, helped draw attention to the cause. Rather than organize a distinctly Jewish branch of the suffrage movement, however, Nathan and her colleagues believed that it would be more effective to mobilize Jewish women to join the ranks of the women's vote movement as a whole. Their meetings in Lower East Side synagogues and assembly halls, sometimes featuring guest appearances by prominent Jewish figures such as Alice and Louis Brandeis or Louise and Stephen Wise, attracted many immigrant women to the suffragist cause.

There were outspoken Jewish opponents of suffrage, too—sometimes appearing alongside suffragettes at public meetings to present their point of view. They argued that the involvement of women in politics would lead to a breakdown of family life as well as put a dangerous amount of power in the hands of radical—and culturally inferior—immigrant women. Some even argued that suffrage would provoke anti-Semitism by encouraging East European Jewish women to engage in aggressive political activity that non-Jews would resent.

At the end of the day, however, it was the suffragettes and not their opponents who garnered the lion's share of support in the Jewish community, especially in the crucial suffrage battle in New York State. In New York's heavily Jewish areas, "from 76 to 93 percent of the total vote and half of all Jewish neighborhoods were pro-suffrage, while no identifiably Jewish districts were consistently anti-suffrage. . . . Jewish women [accounted for] at least 17 percent of the founding members of the [New York–based] Women's Suffrage Party district organizations and 64 percent of the membership in predominantly Jewish assembly districts. . . . The New York victory provided a major catalyst for the 1920 federal amendment. Without the immigrants' participation, it is doubtful if middle-class women alone could have gathered the grassroots political base that secured the victory" (Kuzmack 1990, 153–154).

While Jewish feminists fought for suffrage and Reform rabbis embraced social justice issues, Orthodox Jewish activists undertook a variety of protest campaigns closer to home. The demonstrably Christian environment encountered by immigrants who frequented the Henry Street Settlement house, in the heart of the Lower East Side, aroused Jewish protests beginning in 1903. The Union of Orthodox Jewish Congregations of America accused social reformer Jacob Riis, founder of the settlement, of proselytizing. Riis's vague reply only further stimulated Jewish suspicions, but Rabbi Stephen Wise, who was active in the settlement house movement and personally close to many prominent social gospel activists, insisted that the activity on Henry Street was an altruistic expression of Christian love that did not cross the line into missionizing. Wise's generally more favorable view of Christianity—a perspective common among many Reform rabbis— influenced his attitude toward Riis, while the Orthodox camp's instinctive distrust of Christian embraces shaped its opposition.

Yet even when Christian settlement house activists engaged in indisputably missionary work, the New York Jewish community was far from unified in its response. In 1906 a coalition of Downtown Jewish groups spearheaded by the Orthodox Union established the Jewish Centers Association, which sought to combat Christian proselytizing by publishing the names and addresses of missionaries in the Jewish press; infiltrating Christian settlement houses to document their activities; organizing protest rallies outside offending institutions; and establishing Jewish centers that would match the Christian activists' educational programs and humanitarian assistance with classes and assistance of their own—"school for school, picnic for picnic warfare," as it was described at the time (Gurock 1996, 158).

The one Jewish center they created, however, closed down after two years for lack of funds. The Uptown German Jewish elite refused to assist the Jewish Centers Association because they perceived it as being too opposed to Americanization efforts in general. The Uptowners also feared that the strident ways of the antimissionary activists would spoil relations with Christians and perhaps even provoke anti-Semitism. At the same time, the Centers Association was opposed by segments of the Lower East Side's Orthodox community: the Union of Orthodox Rabbis of the United States and Canada, known as the Agudath ha-Rabbanim, regarded the centers' activists as too Americanized, because they were willing to accommodate to the American environment in certain modest ways, such as offering classes in English rather than Yiddish. To those who hoped to transplant European Orthodox Judaism lock, stock, and barrel to the New World, even these seemingly small changes could not be countenanced.

Albert Lucas of the Orthodox Union, a leader of the antimissionary efforts, also helped spearhead a 1906 protest campaign against Christmas-related activities in public schools. Provoked by a Brooklyn school principal's exhortation to his mostly Jewish student body to be "more like Christ" and the local school board's refusal to reprimand him, Lucas pressed the Board of Education to order city schools to refrain from Christmas ceremonies. Lucas's appeals in the Jewish press aroused public attention, and angry parents packed the board's hearings to make their views known. Although the board delayed its decision, the schools announced plans to hold festive assemblies the day before Christmas, prompting a citywide one-day protest strike by parents. An estimated 20,000 to 25,000 Jewish children stayed home from school that day. The Board of Education responded with a directive forbidding or restricting most Christian religious activities in the schools.

Case Study: The Sabbath Alliance

Orthodox Jews who were prepared to actively combat those forces deemed threatening to Jewish well-being sometimes took the fight beyond the confines of the ghetto. In the early 1900s, Orthodox activists established the Sabbath Alliance, to protect the rights of Sabbath observers. The six-day work week that was standard at the time left only Sundays free, and most states had so-called Blue Laws forcing stores to close on Sunday. Thus if he observed the Sabbath, a Jewish shopkeeper would suffer the severe financial disadvantage of being open just five days a week. The alliance's initial lobbying efforts stumbled. Employers whom it approached were unwilling to make special allowances for their Orthodox Jewish workers, and America's moralist mood made it difficult to overturn Blue Laws. The Sabbath activists began to make progress only when they learned a crucial lesson in American political strategy: an alliance of disparate interest groups is far more powerful than one narrow lobby. By 1919 the Sabbath Alliance had changed the focus of its lobbying, and it began campaigning for a five-day work week. This new demand coincided perfectly with the agenda of the labor unions. The heavily Jewish unions in particular began pushing the five-day week, basing their case on economic arguments rather than appeals to bosses to have pity on their Sabbath-observing employees. Gradually the demand was embraced by the major unions, and eventually it triumphed.

The wealthy German-born Jews who created the AJ Committee were motivated to some extent by their fear that unless they formally took the leadership helm in the Jewish community, the vociferous and increasingly numerous East European immigrants would take control and, with their radical politics and uncouth demeanor, jeopardize relations between Jews and non-Jews generally. The ongoing tensions between German-born Uptowners and Russian-born Downtowners surfaced repeatedly in American Jewish affairs during this era. Regardless of their motives, however, the Uptown elite brought with them to the arena of Jewish defense activity the power of wealth and political connections. They used those weapons to great effect in their campaign for the New York State Civil Rights Act, legislation they initiated in 1907 to prohibit resort hotels from advertising restrictions on admission based on race or religion. When the legislature was slow to act, constitutional lawyer Louis Marshall and other AJ Committee stalwarts used their connections to place sympathetic editorials in major newspapers, mobilize endorsements from prominent citizens, and enlist the support of key state senators and assemblymen. The bill finally passed in 1913, and although its impact was not felt as broadly as its originators had hoped, the legislation was a significant early step in the battle against anti-Jewish discrimination, as well as an important public affirmation of the concept that prejudice was beyond the pale.

That same year, American Jews encountered anti-Semitism of a far more brutal nature in the case of Leo Frank, the Jewish manager of an Atlanta pencil factory who, on the basis of flimsy evidence and perjured testimony, was convicted of murdering one of his workers, a thirteen-year-old Christian girl named Mary Phagan. Incited by the rabble-rousing Georgia politician and publisher Tom Watson, who demanded capital punishment for "the perverted Jew," anti-Semitic mobs filled the courtroom and surrounded the courthouse during the trial, making a guilty verdict almost inevitable. Atlanta's Jewish community, intimidated by the hostile atmosphere surrounding the controversy, remained on the sidelines. The national AJ Committee declined to take a public stand on the case, but its president, Louis Marshall, did assist in Frank's unsuccessful appeals to the Supreme Court. The AJ Committee believed deeply in the efficacy of backstairs diplomacy as opposed to public protest, so Marshall and his colleagues focused their efforts on trying to quietly persuade prominent non-Jews and major newspapers to speak out. One result was a series of articles in the *New York Times* exposing the miscarriage of justice, although, at Marshall's urging, the *Times* refrained from suggesting that anti-Semitism had anything to do with the Frank affair. The AJ Committee leaders feared that Georgians would become even angrier if accused of bigotry. During the months following Frank's sentencing, national press coverage of the affair and mass rallies stimulated an extraordinary outpouring of protest: more than 100,000 letters and petitions bearing over a million signatures pleaded with the Georgia authorities to grant Frank clemency.

Just before Frank's scheduled execution, Governor John Slaton defied a torrent of death threats and commuted his sentence to life imprisonment, but shortly afterward a mob stormed the jailhouse, kidnapped Frank, and lynched him. Four weeks after the murder of Frank, the Jewish fraternal order B'nai B'rith established the Anti-Defamation League for the purpose of actively combating anti-Semitism. A sense that the quiet diplomacy preferred by most Jewish leaders during the Frank affair had proven insufficient helped stimulate the decision to create a new agency that would more forthrightly tackle manifestations of anti-Jewish prejudice.

Case Study: The Kosher Meat Boycott

On occasion, protest movements have erupted within the Jewish community itself. The Beef Trust's sudden increase of kosher meat prices from 12 cents to 18 cents per pound in May 1902 set off turmoil on the Lower East Side. Thousands of Jewish women rioted and ransacked butcher shops; eighty-five were arrested. The protesters proceeded to organize a full-scale boycott of kosher butchers, complete with picket lines, carefully organized neighborhood boycott committees, patrols to enforce compliance, and the interrupting of synagogue services to call attention to the controversy.

The boycott leaders were not seasoned political activists; they were mostly housewives with children responding to a crisis that directly and personally affected their lives. But in the style of veteran activists, they had hit upon an issue with broad appeal. Their campaign blurred the lines that normally divided Orthodox from socialist, and socialist from Zionist. They even enlisted the support of many butchers against the Beef Trust's price hike. By June 5 the trust had agreed to drop the price to 14 cents per pound. The women had achieved a significant victory and, in the view of historians, set the stage for the subsequent prominence of immigrant women in the labor movement.

The nonsectarian protest movement with which a significant number of American Jews have longest been associated is the black civil rights movement. Jewish involvement in African-American affairs began in earnest in the early 1900s, when prominent Jews played key roles in establishing, and leading, the National Association for the Advancement of Colored People (NAACP) and the Urban League. These Jewish activists were motivated in part by altruism, and in part by the conviction that elimination of racial discrimination would make for a society that would likewise reject anti-Semitism. "Working against Black exclusion and oppression provided a stalking horse on a more abstract level for American Jewish writers, thinkers, and doers who fretted over the power of anti-Semitism in America and Europe," according to Hasia Diner. They preferred to "downplay the extent of anti-Jewish action and sentiment in America" for fear that acknowledgment of its existence would further fuel its growth, and instead focused on discrimination against blacks by racist forces that could "crush [Jewish] aspirations for success in their latest diasporic home" (Diner 1992, 90). Eliminating mistreatment of blacks would ultimately pave the way for better treatment of Jews. In some instances, of course, the two groups' interests did directly converge, as for example when Jews fought against racially discriminatory laws that could be applied to Jews as well as African-Americans.

Joel Spingarn, a Jewish intellectual and social reform activist, became chairman of the NAACP board in 1914 and devoted the next two decades to constant public speaking, fundraising, and organizing for the black civil rights movement. The organization's Spingarn Medal for black achievement is named for him. The NAACP's legal division, which fought numerous landmark court battles over civil rights, was chaired by Jewish attorney Arthur Spingarn and included among its active members such prominent American Jews as future Supreme Court justice Felix Frankfurter, AJ Committee president Louis Marshall, and his son—also an AJ Committee leader—James Marshall. Other leading American Jews, including the philanthropic giant Jacob Schiff, American Jewish Congress president Stephen Wise, and American Zionist leader Julian Mack, frequently took part in the NAACP's public protests, legal battles, lobbying of politicians, and other activities.

After the conclusion of World War II, American Jewish involvement in the civil rights struggle intensified. In much of the public's mind, racism was associated with the defeated and discredited Nazis. Jewish organizations seized the moment to actively promote the virtues of an egalitarian society. The AJ Committee and Anti-Defamation League mounted a series of concerted press campaigns advocating tolerance, lobbied for fairness legislation, and sponsored impressive sociological studies to document the falsehoods and pernicious impact of racism. This Jewish crusade against prejudice utilized a wide variety of vehicles to spread its message, including advertisements in newspapers, subway trains, and buses with slogans such as "We Fought Together—Let's Work Together!"; public-service announcements on radio shows, as well as specially sponsored radio programs about tolerance; a series of one-minute cartoons against bigotry that were broadcast by television stations around the country; and short educational documentaries featuring celebrities. Uneasy about assuming too high a profile and convinced that their message would find a more receptive audience if it appeared to come from non-Jewish sources, the Jewish organizations often found nonsectarian allies to sponsor these activities. The ADL established two front groups, the Institute for Democratic Education and the Institute for American Democracy, for the purpose of promoting the antiracism campaign. The antiprejudice efforts began to peter out in the early 1950s, as some staff members began questioning the effectiveness of the mass media tactics, and as the high cost of radio and television advertising strained the Jewish groups' budgets. To make matters more complicated, anticommunist groups launched a public protest campaign against one of the antiracism documentaries after it was discovered that several of the Hollywood personalities involved in producing it had Communist Party connections.

The AJ Congress, for its part, believed that the war against bigotry could be prosecuted more successfully through legal challenges to actual discrimination, rather than efforts to change popular attitudes. The AJ Congress's Commission on Law and Social Action, established in 1944, engaged a battery of young, activist-minded attorneys headed by labor lawyer Will Maslow. The commission initiated civil rights lawsuits; drafted legislation to combat discrimination; and provided the research and expertise necessary to help local, state, and federal officials advance the antidiscrimination agenda. In some instances, the AJ Congress's actions related directly to Jewish concerns, such as its 1946 suit to cancel Columbia University's New York City tax exemption because of its quota system limiting Jewish enrollment in its medical school. Much of the antidiscrimination effort, however, targeted discrimination that could affect any religious, racial, or ethnic group, on the assumption that making American society fair to all was an intrinsically worthwhile goal as well as beneficial to the AJ Congress's Jewish constituents. The anticommunist atmosphere of the 1950s had something of a restraining effect on the AJ Congress's campaigns, however. Nervous about anti-Semitic propaganda linking Jews to communism—a fear intensified by the fact that a number of the communists or sympathizers targeted by Senator Joseph McCarthy happened to be Jews—the AJ Congress refrained from pushing for the kind of sweeping New Deal era–style changes in American life that it might have pursued in a different political climate.

The major Jewish organizations protested against some of the excesses of the McCarthy era but usually proceeded with caution, for fear that strident Jewish opposition to anticommunism might revive accusations of Jewish sympathy for communism. On the one hand, few American Jews felt any affinity for the ideology of communism, nor did they look with much sympathy upon the Soviet regime, with its harsh treatment of Russian Jewry and increasing arms sales to Arab regimes that threatened Israel. At the same time, Jewish groups noted the presence of anti-Semites among McCarthy's more extreme supporters and worried that the sweeping McCarthyite allegations about disloyalty and subversion represented the tip of an iceberg of intolerance that could ultimately victimize Jews and other minorities. Hence the Anti-Defamation League challenged the "vague criteria" employed when President Truman in 1947 established a program to scrutinize the loyalties of federal employees. Likewise, Jewish groups criticized the Mundt-Nixon bill to register and restrict "subversive" organizations, and an AJ Congress official testified before the Senate that the loose wording of the bill constituted "a great blow to freedom of speech." The National Community Relations Advisory Committee, representing eight major Jewish groups, protested the passage of the anticommunist McCarran bill in 1950 and urged Truman to veto it, which he did, although it was overridden.

Although groups such as the AJ Committee and the Anti-Defamation League tended to be more conservative in their choice of tactics, and sought to demonstrate their Americanism by cooperating with the House Un-American Activities Committee, the AJ Congress pursued a more activist and ideological civil liberties program. It called for the abolition of HUAC, filed briefs to assist the Hollywood Ten and others they regarded as the targets of unfair accusations, and fought against New York State's Feinberg Law, which prohibited communists from holding jobs in the public school system. The sharply different approaches of the AJ Committee and the AJ Congress were readily apparent in their responses to the rioting at two Paul Robeson benefit concerts in Peekskill, New York, in the summer of 1949, which raised funds for a pro-Communist group. The concertgoers were drawn largely from the left-wing Jewish summer colonies in the Peekskill area, and the rioters shouted antiblack and anti-Semitic slogans. Although left-wing groups portrayed the outbursts as a fascist assault on Jews and blacks, a grand jury investigation dismissed bigotry as a motive and blamed the procommunist nature of the concerts as the provocation for the violence. The AJ Committee, anxious to downplay any association in the public mind between Jews and communism, endorsed the grand jury's interpretation. But the AJ Congress denounced the violence as an attack on civil liberties and endorsed an inquiry by the American Civil Liberties Union, which concluded that anti-Semitism was the chief cause of the riots.

Jewish organizations were united, however, when faced with the trial of Julius and Ethel Rosenberg for passing U.S. nuclear secrets to the Soviets. Jewish groups remained conspicuously silent until communist groups began charging that the prosecution and sentencing of the Rosenbergs had been motivated in part by anti-Semitism. Anxious to prevent public perceptions of an alliance between Jews and communists, Jewish organizations protested the communists' assertions and issued pamphlets intending to prove that they had a fair trial and were sentenced without regard for their Jewish identity.

During the late 1940s and early 1950s, the major Jewish organizations also undertook to eliminate communist groups from the Jewish community. The AJ Committee's researchers prepared a report documenting links between the left-wing Jewish People's Fraternal Order (JPFO) and communists, and furnished the information to Jewish community councils around the country, which used it as a basis to expel the JPFO from their ranks. A similar exposé by the AJ Committee of the left-wing Social Services Employees Union caused numerous Jewish groups to sever their ties with that union. Communists and suspected communists were frequently fired from their jobs with Jewish organizations. The AJ Congress, while perhaps not as enthusiastic as other Jewish groups in its anticommunism, likewise cut its ties to procommunist groups and dismissed communist employees. Demonstrating Jewish patriotism and undercutting suspicions of Jewish radicalism were goals that all mainstream Jewish organizations shared.

As the black civil rights struggle shifted into high gear in the mid and late 1950s, American Jewish organizations played an increasing role. After the Supreme Court's 1954 antisegregation ruling in the famous *Brown v. Board of Education* case, the General Assembly of the Union of American Hebrew Congregations (UAHC) urged quick implementation of the ruling throughout the country, and the following year, the UAHC endorsed Martin Luther King's Montgomery bus boycott. Reform leaders were not entirely united in this respect: Reform rabbis in the South, responding to a wave of bombings of synagogues and fearing further anti-Semitic backlash if Jews continued to take a high-profile role in the civil rights battle, brought about the rescinding of the invitation to King to address the UAHC's 1959 convention. But in an indication that it intended to facilitate an increasing Jewish role in the civil rights movement and related struggles, the UAHC that year provided its liberal political action arm, the Social Action Commission, with its own building in Washington, D.C., and a significantly enlarged budget and staff.

Individual Jews assumed high-profile roles in the civil rights struggle. Atlanta attorney Morris Abram, often working in conjunction with the Anti-Defamation League, battled local ordinances that hindered black voter participation and spearheaded legal action that undermined the Ku Klux Klan by galvanizing the passage of local laws prohibiting the wearing of hoods in public. Abram became a confidant of Martin Luther King. Stanley Levison, a left-wing activist attorney from New York, was King's closest adviser.

The UAHC encouraged participation in the "Freedom Rides," the busloads of Northern liberal activists who traveled to the South to take part in antisegregation activities. The Freedom Riders attracted many Jewish volunteers, including a number of Reform rabbis; according to one study, between one-third and one-half of the Mississippi Freedom Summer Project in 1964 were Jews (Porter and Dreier 1973, xxii). Those who went did so at considerable risk; in the summer of 1963, three young Freedom Riders, Michael Schwerner and Andrew Goodman (who were Jewish) and James Chaney (who was black), were murdered by Klansmen. That summer's huge march on Washington gained the endorsement not only of the Reform and Conservative movements but also the AJ Committee, AJ Congress, and other mainstream organizations. At least seventy Reform rabbis and many other Jews participated.

One was Reform rabbi Israel Dresner of New Jersey, who had first been arrested at a Zionist demonstration outside British offices in New York in 1948, and courted controversy anew when he announced to his congregants in 1961 that he was joining the Freedom Riders. Dresner and a second rabbi from New Jersey, Martin Freedman, joined eight Christian clergymen in June 1961 in a sit-down protest at a segregated Tallahassee, Florida, restaurant, resulting in their arrest. It was to be the first in a series of arrests of Dresner for taking part in civil rights protests both in the South and in his native New Jersey, where he was clubbed by police at a protest against a segregated construction site. A handful of Conservative rabbis also took an active role in the movement. In the midst of the May 1963 protests over segregation in Birmingham, an appeal from Dr. King inspired twenty rabbis to leave the annual convention of the Conservative movement's Rabbinical Assembly and fly to Alabama to join the protesters. King's telegram to the 1964 Reform rabbinical convention in Atlantic City moved sixteen rabbis to join him in a series of demonstrations against segregation in St. Augustine, Florida. Arnold Jacob Wolf, one of those who chose not to heed King's call, later wrote about his ambivalence. He had become "incurably bourgeois," Wolf confessed. The security of American Jews was linked to keeping their "distance from the American Negro and the American poor." He found himself "terribly frightened by the new American Revolution. Like most revolutions in the past, this one is likely to do the Jew no 'good'" (Wolf 1964, 478–479). Yet the spiritual leader of Wolf's Conservative movement, Rabbi Abraham Joshua Heschel, soon became the best-known Jewish participant in the civil rights protests. In early 1965, Heschel led 800 demonstrators to FBI headquarters in New York to protest the harsh treatment of the participants in King's Selma-to-Montgomery protest march. At King's request, Heschel then flew to Alabama to join him at the head of the march. Shocked, like most Americans, at the televised images of Alabama police brutally beating the marchers, the AJ Committee and the National Jewish Community Relations Advisory Council, not usually the most active on matters of racial controversy, pressed President Johnson to intervene on the marchers' behalf.

Although united in their sympathy for the cause of African-American civil rights, American Jewish organizations were divided over how to respond to American involvement in the Vietnam War. The Reform movement once again took the lead: the UAHC openly criticized U.S. policy in Vietnam; the Central Conference of American (Reform) Rabbis endorsed the principle of conscientious objection to service in Vietnam; and the Reform movement's youth wing, the National Federation of Temple Youth, supported antiwar protests (as did its Conservative counterpart, the United Synagogue Youth of America). On the occasion of Chanukah in 1966, UAHC executive director Maurice Eisendrath went so far as to publicly compare President Johnson to Antiochus, the Greco-Syrian tyrant who is the villain of the Chanukah story. The leaders of New York's Temple Emanu-El, horrified by Eisendrath's statement, suspended their synagogue's

membership in the UAHC in protest. Other mainstream Jewish organizations, worried about appearing to be disloyal to their government—especially in wartime—took no stand on Vietnam. Some of
these groups were also reluctant to be seen as hypocritical for opposing U.S. military aid to South Vietnam while supporting aid to Israel.
Several of the more conservative Jewish organizations, including the
Zionist Organization of America (ZOA), Orthodox groups, and the
Jewish War Veterans, spoke out strongly in favor of U.S. military action against communist aggression in Southeast Asia and drew a connection between U.S. aid to Israel and U.S. aid to South Vietnam.
Members of the radical-left Jewish Liberation Project picketed the
ZOA's Manhattan headquarters to protest its stance on Vietnam.

Large numbers of individual Jews, especially college students, took
part in antiwar protests. Surveys in 1968 by the B'nai B'rith Hillel
Foundations found that Jewish students in the New Left were "highly
visible in its leadership and constituted perhaps one-third of its
ranks" (Spiegel 1968, 1). Sociologists Jack Nusan Porter and Peter
Dreier estimated that "Jews constituted at least 30 to 50 percent of
the Movement's ranks." These calculations were based in part on local studies, which found, for example, that 32 percent of the
protesters taking part in the Berkeley Free Speech Movement were
Jews (even though they were only 20 percent of the student body),
and that 45 percent of the students at the University of Chicago who
participated in 1966 protests against the draft were Jewish (Somers
1965, 547; Flacks 1967, 65). Many of the highest profile political radicals, such as Abbie Hoffman, Jerry Rubin, and Mark Rudd, were Jewish, although they seldom identified themselves as such.

A number of small Jewish organizations, among them Jews for Urban Justice (JUJ), the Jewish Liberation Project, and the National Jewish Organizing Project, sought specifically to attract Jews to left-wing
protest campaigns and to inject a Jewish flavor into their participation in such struggles. Typically this involved teach-ins seeking to
highlight alleged connections between Jewish traditions and contemporary protest activity, or demonstrations against the positions
taken (or not taken) by mainstream Jewish organizations on pressing
issues. The first public activity of Jews for Urban Justice was an October 1967 demonstration at a prominent Washington, D.C., synagogue, on Yom Kippur, to protest the "insensitivity of Jewish organizations to social problems." The group's militant rhetoric ensured
that it would be relegated to the fringes of the Jewish community—
by 1971 the JUJ was urging Jews to help "abolish the American em-
pire that now oppresses the Jewish people." Radical Jews picketed a

Jewish-owned supermarket near Los Angeles that was selling grapes harvested by nonunion workers during a labor action by unionized grape-pickers. Their signs quoted Isaiah's statement, "Thou shalt not eat the fruit of the oppressed." Among the most widely publicized protests by Jewish radicals was a May 1969 demonstration against the Oakland branch of B'nai B'rith for giving an award to a local college president who had used the National Guard to disperse a student protest; a November 1970 rally against a Philadelphia Zionist group giving an award to a conservative police chief; and a protest by some 500 Jewish activists in Los Angeles in September 1971, when Israel's foreign minister bestowed an award upon California's conservative governor, Ronald Reagan (Porter and Dreier 1973, xxxvii–xxxviii).

Case Study: Using Jewish Rhetoric on Behalf of Radical Activism

Since the late 1960s, left-wing activist Arthur Waskow has made a specialty of blending Jewish-sounding rhetoric and radical protest activity. Waskow designed a "Freedom Seder" for Jewish radicals in which traditional Passover themes were transformed into a story of "oppressed" American minority groups fighting the modern Pharaoh, the U.S. government. He was also the driving force behind a series of efforts to rally Jewish opposition to America's involvement in Vietnam. The premise of his "Jewish Campaign for the People's Peace Treaty" in 1971 was the notion that ordinary Americans could establish peace with North Vietnam, regardless of U.S. government policy. Waskow later transformed this group into "Trees for Vietnam," to raise awareness about the environmental damage caused by the war. Waskow was also a central figure in what he called Fabrangen. Although it is a Yiddish word that normally refers to a religious gathering by Hasidic Jews, Waskow adopted it as the name of his commune-style cultural and political action group in Washington, D.C. It initially received funding from the local United Jewish Appeal because of its efforts to attract unaffiliated young Jews, but the funding was withdrawn when Fabrangen members staged a demonstration on behalf of Palestinian Arab terrorist groups at war with the Jordanian government.

Why did New Left radicalism attract a disproportionately large number of Jews? According to the sociologist Seymour Martin Lipset, many of the young Jews taking part in protest movements such as the

Students for a Democratic Society (SDS) were rebelling against parents who employed the rhetoric of left-wing politics but refrained from acting on their convictions—"Families which, around the breakfast table, day after day, in Scarsdale, Newton, Great Neck, and Beverly Hills, have discussed what an awful, corrupt, immoral, undemocratic racist society the United States is," Lipset posits. "Many Jewish parents live in the lily-white suburbs, go to Miami Beach in the winter, belong to expensive country clubs, arrange bar mitzvahs costing thousands of dollars—all the while espousing a left-liberal ideology. . . . They sustain a high degree of tension between their ideology and their life style. This is their hypocrisy, and it is indeed the contradiction which their children are rebelling against" (Lipset 1971, 124).

Tom Milstein, an historian of the New Left, agrees with the notion that some Jews joined the New Left because of the influence of their parents' ideology of "progressive social change," but he proposes two additional categories: children of Jewish communists and fellow travelers who were following directly in their parents' footsteps; and those for whom New Left activism served as "a medium of assimilation for upper middle-class and lower upper-class youth of Jewish parentage into the dominant [Protestant] culture" (Milstein 1971, 299–300).

When prominent segments of the New Left turned against Israel in the late 1960s, however, many radical Jewish activists began to reconsider their involvement. Black militants who were openly hostile to Jews and Israel took over the leadership of the Student Non-Violent Coordinating Committee (SNCC), a leading civil rights movement, and SNCC publications were soon featuring allegations of Israeli atrocities against Arabs and crude cartoons of Africans being strangled by hands bearing dollar signs and the Star of David. A SNCC spokesman defended the propaganda as targeting only "Jewish oppressors" such as "those Jews in the little Jew shops in the ghettoes." At the September 1967 National New Politics Convention, which had sought to build a multiracial civil rights coalition, white radicals joined hands with black extremists in accusing Israel of waging an "imperialistic Zionist war" against the Arabs. African-American social activist Dick Gregory, a speaker at the conference, declared: "Every Jew in America over 30 years old knows another Jew that hates Negroes and if we hate Jews, that's just even, baby."

Many Jewish activists in the New Left were shocked and disillusioned that their colleagues sided with the Arabs rather than Israel. Actor and folksinger Theodore Bikel, one of SNCC's more prominent Jewish members, resigned in protest, accusing the militants of "spitting on the tombs" of the murdered Jewish civil rights volunteers

Michael Schwerner and Andrew Goodman. The UAHC's annual convention rejected a proposal to call for monetary reparations to compensate blacks for past discrimination. "Overnight many of my friends became enemies, partisans of the other side of the barricade," a shaken Menachem Arnoni recalled. "A whole world of associations collapsed around me. My former comrades, had they been pulling triggers instead of hitting typewriter keys, would have been shooting at me" (Arnoni 1971, 273–274).

Case Study: M. J. Rosenberg, Nat Hentoff: Disillusioned Jewish Radicals

M. J. Rosenberg, widely regarded as the father of the radical Jewish student press, exemplified the growing sense of Jewish disillusionment with the New Left in his February 1969 article in New York's *Village Voice*—itself a leading voice of the New Left—blasting those Jewish radicals "who put down everything Jewish" and "who are prepared to die for the Vietnamese, the Biafrans, the Greeks, and the Czechs yet who reject Israel." Rosenberg declared: "From this point on I shall join no movement that does not accept and support my people's struggle. If I must choose between the Jewish cause and a 'progressive' anti-Israel SDS, I shall choose the Jewish cause. If barricades are erected, I will fight as a Jew" (Rosenberg 1969, 14).

Similar outrage greeted a 1973 speech by antiwar activist Father Daniel Berrigan comparing Israel to Nazi Germany and branding the Jewish state "imperialist" and "a criminal Jewish community." The AJ Congress, which had been generally sympathetic to Berrigan's antiwar activity, called for cancellation of plans by a peace group to give Berrigan its Gandhi Award, and helped persuade liberal activist Dr. Donald Harrington to withdraw as presenter of the award. Nat Hentoff, the left-wing political activist and journalist, bitterly recalled how Jews had come to Berrigan's aid after his many arrests for antiwar activity, and wrote: "The next time the schmuck gets into jail, let the Catholics get him out" (Dellinger 1974, 6). An angry Berrigan announced that he would not accept the award.

Growing tensions between African-Americans and Jews in New York City further cemented the perception of a widening gulf between blacks and the New Left on one side, and Jews on the other. When a speaker at a February 1966 meeting of the Congress of Racial Equality, a leading black civil rights group, praised Hitler, Jewish organizations' protests persuaded CORE to quickly fire him. But despite Jewish protests over an anti-Semitic article the following year by John Hatchett, a black New York City schoolteacher, Hatchett was hired by New York University to direct its Martin Luther King Afro-American Student Center. Then a black school principal in the Ocean Hill-Brownsville section of Brooklyn, Rhody McCoy, fired ten Jewish teachers in 1968, on the grounds that predominantly black student bodies should be taught by African-Americans. Another seventy-three teachers, many of them Jews, who protested McCoy's action were barred from returning to their classrooms. A teachers' strike ensued, followed by angry confrontations between black and Jewish protesters outside the affected schools, the circulation of threats against the Jewish teachers, and the distribution of anti-Semitic leaflets demanding the "liberation" of predominantly black schools from Jewish "control." Coming on the heels of SNCC's embrace of the Arabs and a series of high-profile anti-Semitic statements by leaders of the militant Black Panthers, the New York City eruptions drove disillusioned Jewish activists from the civil rights movement. It also deepened the sense of frustration among middle-class and lower-middle-class inner-city Jews that liberal political leaders such as New York mayor John Lindsay were prepared to sacrifice Jewish concerns to appease militant sentiment among blacks. An October 1968 appearance by Lindsay at a Jewish center in Brooklyn ended in chaos as Jewish hecklers upset over the school strike shouted down both the mayor and U.S. senator Jacob Javits, who sought unsuccessfully to restore order.

A vocal but rapidly dwindling minority in the Jewish community still embraced the politics of militancy. Members of Columbia University's Jewish Radical Union disrupted services at Temple Emanu-El, the city's most prominent Reform synagogue, in 1969 to demand $100,000 in contributions for the Black Panthers' legal defense fund. The response was less than enthusiastic. A "Jewish Committee for a Fair Trial for Angela Davis" sought to raise bail money for the imprisoned black extremist with a full-page ad in the AJ Congress's monthly magazine, but the fifteen names listed as members of the committee pointedly included only fringe elements. A slightly more significant group of sixty-one Jewish liberals, including a smattering of high-profile sociologists and civil libertarians, announced in 1970 the formation of a "Council of Jews for Racial Justice" to accuse the New York teachers' union of fabricating anti-Semitic leaflets to rouse hostility against blacks. Not many New York Jews seemed persuaded by the accusation.

A different reaction to anti-Semitism on the left came from another segment of the Jewish student community, which sought to retain its role in left-wing causes while simultaneously defending Israel and Jewish ethnic interests.

A typical 1972 issue of the newspaper *Nitzotz* ("Sparks"), produced by the New York–based Radical Zionist Alliance (RZA), reported on RZA members marching against the Vietnam War, protesting the persecution of Soviet Jewry, picketing an Egyptian Airlines office to denounce Arab terrorism, and endorsing the boycott of nonunion lettuce. Jewish student activists threatened to invade the annual assembly of the Council of Jewish Federations and Welfare Funds in 1969; they were permitted to take part in the council's sessions, where they pressed for more funding of Jewish education, culture, and Soviet Jewry activity. Forty-five Jewish students were arrested for occupying the offices of the Federation of Jewish Philanthropies in New York City in 1970 to demand increased funding for Jewish education. M. J. Rosenberg, a student at the State University of New York at Albany, drew an audience of 300 at the founding meeting of his Hebrew Student Alliance, at which he announced: "We demand a Hebrew Studies program or we're taking over the administration building." Rosenberg later acknowledged: "The black students have radicalized us. They were so successful with their tactics and rhetoric, we used it too." And it worked: within a month, a Hebrew language course was begun at Albany, and the administration promised to launch a full Hebrew Studies program within the year. Protests by Jewish students on other campuses often yielded similar results (Rabinovich 1969, 8).

The final withdrawal of U.S. troops from Vietnam in 1975 put an end to the cause that had galvanized large numbers of young Jews to join the ranks of New Left protest movements. Individual Jews joined related political struggles, such as the campaigns for nuclear disarmament and black rule in South Africa, but the extent of Jewish participation in such movements did not even remotely approach the numbers that had marched against U.S. involvement in Southeast Asia. Jewish involvement in the left-wing protest campaigns of the late 1970s and 1980s was limited to small numbers of students and the expected coterie of veteran political activists. Most mainstream Jewish organizations shifted the bulk of their attention to Soviet Jewry, Israel, and other issues of more direct Jewish interest.

The exception, as in earlier years, has been the Reform movement, which has taken an ongoing interest in left-wing protest campaigns, occasionally with the support of additional Jewish groups. The Union of American Hebrew Congregations; the Central Conference of American (Reform) Rabbis; and the Rabbinical Assembly, the association of Conservative rabbis, endorsed the mid-1980s "Sanctuary Movement," which gave shelter to illegal aliens from Central American countries ruled by U.S.-supported anticommunist governments. Grassroots Jewish enthusiasm for the sanctuary campaign did not match that of the Reform and Conservative leadership, however, as only a handful of synagogues joined the several hundred churches pledging to open their doors to the immigrants.

The single sustained and organized effort in recent decades to revive Jewish interest in left-wing political campaigns was the creation, in 1979, of New Jewish Agenda (NJA), an organization intended to provide "a Jewish voice among progressives, a progressive voice among Jews." With that broad mandate, NJA activists around the country used the activist skills they had honed in the civil rights and antiwar struggles to advance the campaigns for nuclear disarmament, black rule in South African, gay rights, Central American guerrilla groups, feminism, and labor rights.

Energetic, devoted, and resourceful, NJA activists proved adept at infusing their 1960s-style agitprop with Jewish themes. On the occasion of the Feast of Tabernacles, when traditional Jews erect *sukkot*, symbolic dwelling places in which they dine, NJA activists set up sukkot outside the White House to dramatize the demand for disarmament. To publicize the dangers of nuclear weapons, they staged antinuclear educational programs on Tisha B'Av—the annual day of Jewish mourning for the destruction of the ancient Temple in Jerusalem—which they reconfigured as "Hiroshima Day." The Jewish "new year for trees," Tu B'Shvat, became the occasion for activists to undertake environmental awareness programs.

Individual NJA programs unrelated to Israel occasionally attracted the cosponsorship of local branches of major Jewish organizations, particularly the AJ Congress or affiliates of the Reform movement. But NJA's credibility within the Jewish community nationally was damaged by its calls for Israeli acceptance of Arab territorial demands, including ceding control of parts of Jerusalem, and its willingness to cooperate with Arab-American groups that were unfriendly to Israel. Its controversial demonstrations aroused considerable ire in the community, particularly its picketing of Israeli consulates to oppose Israel's military action against terrorists in Lebanon in 1982; a 1988 rally at the Philadelphia Holocaust Memorial to protest Israeli treatment of Palestinian Arab rioters and propose the creation of a "Palestinian Holocaust Memorial"; and the opposition of some NJA chapters to "Operation Exodus," the mainstream community's campaign to finance Soviet Jewish immigration to Israel, on grounds that it might impinge on Arab rights. The NJA's attempts to gain representation on local federation-sponsored Jewish community relations councils thus met with mixed results. The movement never attracted more than 4,000 to 5,000 members, nor was it able to muster substantial financial backing, and in 1993, New Jewish Agenda shut down its national headquarters. A small segment of the Jewish community, including former NJA members and other liberal activists, continue to take part in protest activities related to issues such as abortion rights, the environment, and defense spending, but these kinds of causes have not succeeded in generating significant Jewish participation.

Foreign Issues

Immigration from Central Europe in the 1840s and 1850s increased both the size and political influence of the American Jewish community. An increased willingness to publicly press their issues of concern followed. The earliest American Jewish protests focusing on Jewish concerns overseas came in response to the Damascus blood libel of 1840. When a Catholic priest and his servant were found murdered in the Syrian capital, Jews were arrested at random and tortured until they falsely confessed to killing the pair in order to use their blood in connection with Passover rites. U.S. Jews held protest meetings in numerous cities. When several of Switzerland's cantons forbade Jews from doing business in their territory, in the 1850s, angry U.S. Jews vigorously protested the action as a violation of the 1850 U.S.-Swiss commercial treaty. Articles in the newspapers, petition drives, and public protest meetings were supplemented by letter-writing campaigns to Congress and direct lobbying efforts seeking U.S. governmental pressure on the Swiss.

American Jews were especially aroused by the 1858 controversy over Edgar Mortara, an Italian Jewish infant secretly baptized by his family's Catholic servant and then taken away from the family by the papal police. More than 2,000 Jewish protesters rallied in New York, while a delegation of Jewish leaders from Philadelphia, accompanied by two members of Congress, traveled to Washington to seek presidential intervention. By reminding Jews of the inherent fragility of Diaspora life and the need for an effective mechanism to advance Jewish interests, the affair galvanized twenty-four synagogues to establish the first national American Jewish defense organization, the Board of Delegates of American Israelites.

Absorbed, like all Americans, in the travails of the Civil War, American Jews did not turn their attention abroad again until 1869, when Russia's plans to expel 2,000 Jews from their homes prompted American Jews to seek President Grant's intercession. Washington insider Simon Wolf, a leader of B'nai Brith's Washington, D.C., lodge, used his access to officialdom to undertake a lobbying effort. A protest by the Board of Delegates of American Israelites strengthened Wolf's campaign. Grant, hoping to make amends for his own attempt to expel Jews from parts of the South during the Civil War, agreed to intervene. Secretary of State Hamilton Fish, at first reluctant to roil Russo-American relations by raising the Jewish issue, relented in the face of Wolf's continual protests. Peppered with complaints from around the world and reluctant to risk a major row with the Americans in particular, the Russian authorities ultimately suspended the expulsions. The episode offered a number of important lessons. First, even if the United States did not have a direct interest in a particular foreign controversy, the sentiments of a group of American citizens might be sufficient to motivate U.S. action. Second, a politician once seen as inimical to Jewish concerns might well prove amenable to Jewish political pressure—indeed, precisely because of his past, he might even be more amenable than others. Finally, the emergence of the United States as a major world power meant that countries like Russia could be pressured to change internal policies in order to avoid harming relations with Washington. America's stature could create opportunities to exercise leverage abroad.

Still, not all such efforts met with success. The lengthy protest campaign against the persecution of Jews in Romania, for example, ultimately made little headway. The effort began in 1869 at the initiative of Rabbi Hayyim Zvi Sneersohn, an emissary from Palestine who had actually arrived in the United States to lobby for the removal of the U.S. consul in Jerusalem because of the latter's Christian missionary activity. Sneersohn's contacts with the wealthy and politically connected Seligman family facilitated a meeting with President Grant and Secretary of State Fish. Grant acceded to Sneersohn's request in the hopes of repairing his relations with the American Jewish community, which, remembering his Civil War expulsion order, had voted overwhelmingly for his opponent in 1868.

Encouraged by Grant's receptivity to Sneersohn, Jewish activists enlisted the Palestine emissary in their own effort on behalf of Romanian Jewry. Leaders of the Board of Delegates of American Israelites, together with Simon Wolf, recorder of deeds and unofficial Jewish lobbyist in the nation's capital, had been pressing for the appointment of a Jew as U.S. consul in Bucharest as a way of demonstrating American displeasure with Romania's mistreatment of its Jewish citizens. Their lobbying was now supplemented by Sneersohn's ability to utilize his connections with the Seligmans to open doors and gain audiences in the halls of power. This combined effort resulted in the selection of a B'nai B'rith official, Benjamin Peixotto, for the post.

Peixotto monitored the plight of Romanian Jewry, reported it to American Jewish leaders to stimulate protest rallies, and received from them the funds to sustain his energetic diplomatic intercessions on behalf of his persecuted coreligionists. Although Peixotto's efforts contributed to the 1874 enactment by the Romanian parliament of legislation theoretically helpful to the Jews, in practice it had little impact. On the other hand, his high-profile presence in Bucharest may have at least helped delay implementation of some of the government's anti-Jewish policies.

When in subsequent years U.S. Jews again sought their government's intervention on behalf of Romania's Jews, they could point to the Peixotto mission as a precedent for continued U.S. involvement in Romanian affairs. This happened at the turn of the century, as reports of the mistreatment of Romanian Jewry multiplied in the American press. American Jewish concerns for their Romanian brethren combined with the U.S. government's fears of a flood of penniless Romanian Jewish immigrants served to facilitate political action. Private pressure by U.S. Jewish leaders helped convince the administration to send Immigration Service official Robert Watchorn to investigate the plight of Romania's Jews first-hand. His reports further intensified American Jewish concerns but did nothing to ameliorate the situation in Romania. Behind the scenes, Jacob Schiff, Oscar Straus, and Simon Wolf pressed, shtadlan-style, for an official U.S. protest. As the months wore on and no sign of government action appeared, grassroots Jewish activists staged public protest rallies in New York, Philadelphia, and elsewhere to urge U.S. intervention— much to the chagrin of Schiff and his colleagues, who regarded backstairs diplomacy as the only effective means of advancing Jewish interests.

Meanwhile, U.S. Congressmember Lucius Littauer (R-NY) repeatedly questioned Theodore Roosevelt's administration regarding the likelihood of U.S. intervention, thus helping to keep the issue on the front burner and at the same time raising the unwelcome specter of Congressional intervention. The combination of public protests and private pressure by both Littauer and Jewish leaders eventually persuaded Secretary of State John Hay, in July 1902, to instruct the U.S. charge d'affaires in Athens to protest to the Romanian authorities about the treatment of their Jewish citizens, and urged the European allies of the United States to do likewise. The inability of Jewish leaders in Western Europe to persuade their respective governments to heed the U.S. appeal is regarded by some historians as an early indication of the shifting balance of power in the Jewish world, with the growing U.S. Jewish community beginning to usurp its European counterparts as the political powerhouse of international Jewry.

The Romanian affair also offered signs of the emergence of a new type of American Jewish leader. Previously, communal leadership was the more or less exclusive domain of those with religious authority—that is, rabbis. Here, for the first time, the individuals who played the key role in a Jewish political controversy were lay activists whose unique talent was the ability to parlay personal political contacts into behind-the-scenes leverage on government officials. Simon Wolf and his colleague Adolphus Solomons, a member of the District of Columbia's House of Delegates during the 1870s, were the key players, not the leaders of the Board of Delegates or the prominent rabbis of their time.

The plight of Jews in Eastern Europe continued to occupy the American Jewish agenda during the first two decades of the twentieth century. Government-incited pogroms in the Russian city of Kishinev in April 1903, leaving fifty Jews dead and almost 500 injured, triggered protest rallies by American Jews in cities from coast to coast. Yet neither the demonstrations, nor a B'nai B'rith petition signed by 12,000 "leading citizens," moved the Roosevelt administration even to submit a diplomatic protest to the czar, lest such action harm Russo-American relations. Unable to prod the White House, American Jewish leaders searched for other avenues of intercession. Jacob Schiff and a handful of other Jewish bankers began withholding investment capital from Russia, only to find themselves quickly replaced by French banking houses that were more than willing to fill the vacuum. In 1906 the recently established AJ Committee tried another angle: it successfully lobbied the major political parties to pledge to abrogate the Commercial Treaty of 1832, governing trade between the United States and Russia, on the grounds that Russia engaged in discrimination against U.S. citizens by its refusal to permit American Jews to travel freely in its territory. Years of additional protest activity, ranging from public rallies to lobbying Congress, culminated, in December 1913, with Congressional hearings and then the abrogation of the 1832 treaty—thereby significantly reducing

U.S. trade with Russia. With the eruption of World War I, however, the Wilson administration relaxed restrictions against loans to belligerent countries to enable American bankers to provide aid to the Allies, including Russia.

Not only did the opposition of the AJ Committee's leadership fail to change President Wilson's mind, but the administration initiated negotiations with Russia in 1915 to create a new Russo-American commercial treaty to replace the one abrogated by Congress four years earlier. Secretary of State Robert Lansing, mindful of that successful Jewish lobbying effort, instructed the U.S. ambassador to Russia, David Francis, to insist that the treaty satisfactorily address the problem of Russian discrimination against American Jews, "otherwise there would be no hope of securing Senatorial consent." Francis later attributed the breakdown in the treaty negotiations to the inclusion of the Jewish issue (Goldstein 1975, 43).

Intra-Jewish disagreements over public protests versus backstairs diplomacy formed part of the backdrop to the last great controversy that enveloped American Jewry during the World War I period. A coalition of East European immigrants dissatisfied with the elitism of the German-Jewish stewards, and Zionists unhappy with the anti-Zionism—or at best, non-Zionism—of the AJ Committee leaders, began clamoring in earnest for a new, democratically elected Jewish communal leadership. In 1917 they staged elections in Jewish communities all across the United States to choose delegates to the first American Jewish Congress. More than 330,000 ballots were cast, and the 400 delegates convened in Philadelphia in December 1918. The platform they adopted endorsed the Balfour Declaration and resolved to send representatives to take part in the Paris Peace Conference and to press for Jewish rights in postwar Eastern Europe. Four years later, the AJ Congress resolved to transform itself into a permanent Jewish defense organization—an ongoing source of competition with the AJ Committee for the sympathies of grassroots Jews and the ear of official Washington. That rivalry would make itself felt again and again in the years to follow.

A radical-left Jewish perspective on foreign affairs was articulated by a small but noisy faction in the community. Absorbed in the great labor struggles of the late 1800s and early 1900s, Jewish radicals at first devoted relatively little time to overseas issues, although they naturally took part in the many rallies protesting anti-Jewish persecution by the hated czarist regime. When World War I erupted, Jewish radical organizations and their political bedfellows, the Jewish-dominated trade unions, favored U.S. neutrality. America's entry into the war in 1917, however, confronted the Jewish far left with a choice between patriotism and radicalism. Faced with the reality of their own fragile status as new immigrants, not to mention the passionate nativist sentiment sweeping the country, most Jewish radicals thought caution the better part of valor and reluctantly endorsed the U.S. war effort. It became easier to hold such a position after the November 1917 Bolshevik revolution in Russia, since supporting the war no longer meant an alliance with the czar. A handful of principled pacifists, however, most notably the Reform rabbi Judah Magnes, continued to oppose the war and denounced the Allies' actions against the new Soviet regime.

The economic prosperity and Red Scares of the interwar years undermined Jewish radicalism, and the absence of any compelling overseas controversies served to refocus the radicals' attention on domestic affairs during the 1920s. But the Nazis' rise to power in Germany in 1933 presented an entirely new set of circumstances. American Jewish socialists and communists, with their fierce hatred of fascism, were among the earliest and most vocal opponents of the Hitler regime. They enthusiastically participated in the Jewish boycott of German goods, sent young toughs to bust up meetings of the pro-Hitler German-American Bund, and established a slew of front groups to spread anti-Nazi propaganda. All of this dovetailed perfectly with the anti-Hitler mood in the American Jewish community, making the radicals seem less out of step with the mainstream than ever before.

The activities of the Jewish radicals also helped soften the image of the Soviet Union in American Jewish eyes. U.S. Jewish socialist publications in the 1930s emphasized the role of the USSR as the chief foe of the Nazis, the much-ballyhooed outlawing of anti-Semitism in the Soviet Union, and the Kremlin's promotion of a Jewish "homeland" in the Biro-bidzhan region of eastern Siberia. When the Spanish Civil War erupted in 1937, there was considerable sympathy in the American Jewish community for the Soviet-backed Republican forces, and American Jews made up as many as one-third of the 3,000 members of the Abraham Lincoln Brigade, which saw action on the Republican side. The Soviets' crushing of Jewish culture, the purges and show trials with their many Jewish victims, the prohibition against Jewish emigration—all these received scant publicity in the West in the 1930s and barely intruded upon American Jewish consciousness.

Adolf Hitler's ascent to power aroused the ire and concern of the American Jewish community, but leaders of the major Jewish communal organizations were divided over how to respond. The positions they adopted often reflected their socioeconomic status. Those who were in the upper income strata and more fully integrated into American life tended to be the most cautious in their approach to political protests because of concerns that vocal protest activity might jeopardize relations with non-Jews. Those who were relatively new immigrants, less Americanized, or in the lower economic strata were less concerned about how they might be viewed by non-Jews and more inclined to advocate for Jewish causes publicly. There was an ethnic dimension to this division, as well. Those who were descendants of the German and other Central European immigrants who arrived in the United States in large numbers in the mid-1800s were generally more acculturated and less willing to "rock the boat." Those of East European origin or descent had for the most part reached the United States in the early 1900s, were less assimilated, and were more ready to raise Jewish concerns publicly.

Thus the AJ Committee and B'nai B'rith, which were largely controlled by the German-born or descended, opposed public protests against Hitler, which they thought would stimulate accusations that American Jews were trying to drag the United States into an overseas conflict. The AJ Congress, whose membership was largely of East European origin, inclined toward greater public activism. During the 1930s, the AJ Congress sponsored a number of "Stop Hitler Now" rallies at New York's Madison Square Garden and elsewhere to arouse public opinion against the German regime. The AJ Congress's charismatic and articulate leader, Rabbi Stephen S. Wise, frequently gave public addresses denouncing Hitler.

Wise was a devoted Zionist in the midst of the overwhelmingly anti-Zionist Reform rabbinate and a vigorous activist on a variety of social issues that were not always popular, including union rights, women's suffrage, and race relations. Wise began his rise to national Jewish leadership as a close ally of Louis Brandeis during the latter's years at the helm of American Zionism (1914–1920). During World War I, Wise led the movement to establish the AJ Congress as a pro-Zionist, democratically elected alternative to the existing major Jewish organizations. Wise's emergence was facilitated by his political relationships. His early and fervent support for Franklin Roosevelt and the New Deal gave him a level of access to the White House that no other Jewish leader enjoyed.

Shortly after Hitler's rise to power, two small organizations, the Jewish War Veterans and the newly formed American League for the Defense of Jewish Rights, began organizing a public boycott of German goods. The AJ Committee opposed such action on the grounds that "boycotting will strengthen the hands of anti-Semites, who make use of the myth that the Jews exert a so-called 'world economic influence,'" and its president assured the Deutsche Bank that the AJ Committee would do "all in our power to allay agitation." B'nai B'rith counseled American Jews to adopt a policy of "dignified silence" (Medoff 1987, 29–30). Stephen Wise, for his part, at first refrained from endorsing the boycott because it did not have "the sanction of our government." In his private correspondence, Wise wrote of the growing grassroots pressure for increased activism. "I cannot remember Jewry being so wrought up against anything happening to American Jews," he confided to colleagues. "You cannot imagine what I am doing to resist the masses. They want organized boycotts. They want tremendous street scenes" (Medoff 1987, 30). While Wise was away in Europe that summer, the AJ Congress leadership met and voted to join the boycott, ignoring his cabled plea to postpone their decision. With its superior resources, the AJ Congress soon assumed leadership of the boycott movement. Its Women's Division in particular actively rallied the community to boycott German goods and mobilized picketers to confront businesses selling the Reich's products.

One avenue of possible intervention that American Jewish leaders generally preferred not to discuss was immigration. The post–World War I atmosphere of nativism, isolationism, and anti-communism helped generate the enactment of tight U.S. immigration quotas in the early 1920s. Structured to favor immigrants from Northern and Western Europe, the new system had the effect of limiting the maximum number of immigrants theoretically permitted to enter each year from Germany to 27,370 and from Poland to 6,543. Those restrictions were tightened further by administrative fiat, when the Hoover administration in 1930 instructed U.S. consuls abroad to strictly enforce the requirement that those seeking admission first prove that they would not become "public charges" upon reaching the United States. This created a complex and often insurmountable obstacle for prospective immigrants, few of whom had relatives in the United States to provide the appropriate financial guarantees. During most of the 1930s the German quota remained largely unfilled: for example, 2,732 refugees were admitted from Germany in 1933; 4,134 in 1934; and 4,837 in 1935.

Both the Roosevelt administration and Congress, mindful of public opinion, opposed altering the quotas. The public's hostility to immigration intensified in response to the economic depression and widespread unemployment of the 1930s. American Jewish leaders, in turn, feared that Jewish proposals to liberalize immigration would provoke anti-Semitic accusations that Jews were trying to flood America with impoverished refugees. Sympathetic members of Congress who on occasion sought ways to admit even a slightly larger number of refugees were surprised to find that their efforts attracted no support—and sometimes even opposition—from Jewish leaders. When U.S. Representative Samuel Dickstein (D-NY) in March 1933 proposed the unrestricted immigration of those German Jews related to U.S. citizens, the AJ Committee lobbied him to "let your resolution die a natural quiet death," lest it "create a situation where it will be charged with force that American Jews want to sacrifice America's obvious and essential interests on behalf of their German Jewish co-religionists" (Medoff 1987, 25). Stephen Wise lobbied Congressmember Donald O'Toole (D-NY) to drop his April 1937 proposal to provide asylum for all German Jews fleeing persecution; Wise warned that "any effort to waive the immigration laws will result in a serious accentuation of what we know to be a rising wave of anti-Semitic feeling in this country" (Medoff 1987, 34).

Anti-Semitism was not the only problem American Jews faced in weighing how to aid their German brethren, especially during the early 1930s. They also had to overcome the widespread public skepticism over the severity of Hitler's mistreatment of the Jews. "The persecutions which are endured by Jews in Germany are probably slight as compared with the persecutions of minorities in a good many countries," an American Quaker leader wrote to a colleague in 1933. A *Newsweek* report on the Nuremberg laws claimed to see reason for "hope" that the situation was not so bad, that Jews might find "a soft spot in the [Nazis'] iron heel." If many Americans considered the reports of German Jewish suffering to be exaggerated, neither the public nor the Roosevelt administration would be inclined to look with sympathy upon proposals for U.S. government action to assist German Jewry.

Case Study: American Jewry and the Berlin Olympics

Officials of the American Olympic Committee repeatedly cited doubts as to the severity of Germany's anti-Jewish discrimination to fend off Jewish protests concerning the forthcoming 1936 Olympic games, which were scheduled to be held in Berlin. Although the AJ Committee and B'nai B'rith stood apart from the controversy, the AJ Congress, Jewish Labor Committee, Jewish War Veterans, and others campaigned for cancellation of the Berlin Olympics, or, failing that, a U.S. withdrawal from the games. The AJ Congress could comfortably take the lead on the issue, since it involved no conflict with the Roosevelt administration and relatively little risk of serious adverse reaction from the American public. The AJ Congress also constructed for itself a sort of political safety net by enlisting a variety of non-Jewish organizations and individuals to join the campaign against the Berlin Olympics, among them the (Protestant) Federal Council of Churches, the Catholic War Veterans, the National Association for the Advancement of Colored People, German-American opponents of Hitler, several governors and members of Congress, and a group of forty-one college presidents, as well as prominent periodicals such as the *New York Times* and the liberal Protestant journal *Christian Century.*

Unable to bring about either the relocation of the Olympics from Berlin or the withdrawal of the American team, the anti-Nazi activists sponsored a rival People's Olympics in Spain and a Jewish Olympiad, organized by the Jewish Labor Committee, in New York City. Individual American Jewish athletes who qualified to compete in the Berlin games were divided between those, such as track and field star Syd Koff, who boycotted Berlin to protest the persecution of German Jewry, and those, such as runners Marty Glickman and Sam Stoller, who decided to compete in the belief that their performance would undermine Hitler's theory of Aryan racial superiority. In the end, however, Glickman and Stoller were prevented from running by their own coaches, who bowed to Nazi pressure to keep Jewish athletes from winning any medals.

Part of the reason that Dr. Wise and his AJ Congress colleagues took the lead on the Olympics controversy was their recognition of the increasingly militant sentiment among the rank-and-file Jewish community. Wise knew that if he did not take the initiative, Jews might begin to look elsewhere for leadership. In New York City in particular, grassroots Jews seeking more vocal protests against Hitler already sometimes found their champion in Mayor Fiorello La-Guardia, whose verbal sparring with the Nazis delighted his Jewish constituents. When he blasted Hitler as a "perverted maniac" or declared that "the only authority in New York competent to deal with German press accusations [against him] is the deputy sanitation commissioner in charge of sewage disposal," LaGuardia was expressing what Jews felt. Jewish support for LaGuardia only intensified in response to the anti-Semitic attacks on the mayor (whose mother was Jewish), whether it was the Nazis calling him "a dirty Talmud Jew" or

Time asserting that his anti-Nazism was politically motivated, since "in New York City, as any political nose-counter knows, the hooked far outnumber the Aryan noses" (Stone 2000, 257, 263).

LaGuardia had an instinct for dramatic gestures that captured the spirit of the moment. Responding to a week of anti-Jewish riots in Berlin in July 1935, LaGuardia announced that he was denying a masseur's license to a German citizen, citing incidents of discrimination against American Jews in Germany. As the mayor undoubtedly had calculated, the Nazis reacted furiously to his small symbolic action, turning an otherwise minor episode into a full-fledged international confrontation, complete with a formal diplomatic protest by the German consul general in New York, a wave of overheated denunciations of LaGuardia in the German press, and an assertion by the State Department that it knew of no German violations of the rights of U.S. citizens. The same week that the masseur controversy raged, a crowd of several thousand angry New Yorkers demonstrated their feelings about Hitler by storming the anchored German ocean liner *Bremen* in the New York harbor, shredding its swastika flag and hurling it into the water.

Despite these occasional outbursts of popular militancy, mainstream Jewish leaders continued to guide communal policy along cautious lines, particularly when it came to the idea of asking the Roosevelt administration to come to the aid of German Jewry. Seeing no political gain in taking such action, and absent any apparent risk if he remained aloof, FDR stood aside. Until, that is, early 1938, when a fresh wave of anti-Jewish persecution in Austria followed the German occupation (known as the Anschluss) of that country, and some members of Congress and journalists began criticizing the administration's lack of interest in the plight of Austrian Jews seeking refuge abroad. Hoping to take the wind out of his critics' sails, Roosevelt in July 1938 hosted an international conference on the European refugee problem in the French resort town of Evian-les-Bains.

U.S. officials privately assured the attendees that none would be expected to alter their existing immigration restrictions, and that the financial backing for refugee resettlement would continue to be borne by private organizations, not governments. Numerous Jewish groups were permitted to send observers to the gathering, but the effectiveness of the Jewish delegations was hampered by a deep division between Zionist organizations that wanted to focus on Palestine as the solution to the refugee problem, and non- and anti-Zionists who preferred to explore other options. The British, however, refused to discuss Palestine, and the conference's only concrete action was to establish a committee that was supposed to negotiate with Germany for an orderly exodus of Jews from German territory. Underfunded and operating with only limited authority, the committee never came close to realizing that goal, although in the immediate aftermath of the conference, many American Jewish leaders regarded the committee's creation as a promising development. That turned out to be wishful thinking, for neither the committee nor the Roosevelt administration was prepared to act when, less than four months later, the Nazis unleashed savage nationwide pogroms against German Jewry, an orgy of violence and destruction known as Kristallnacht, the Night of Broken Glass.

The recently established General Jewish Council, a coalition of the four major U.S. Jewish defense groups, met three days after Kristallnacht to plan their response. They decided against staging any "parades, public demonstrations or protests by Jews," fearing a negative reaction from Americans who might resent agitation about a foreign cause. Concerned that any effort to liberalize the immigration laws might provoke anti-Semitism, the council concluded that "at least for the time being, nothing should be done with regard to this matter." Jewish leaders hesitated to raise the immigration issue even in private discussions. Samuel Rosenman, a senior figure in the AJ Committee who was also an adviser to the president, was asked by FDR if more Jewish refugees should be allowed to enter the United States in the wake of Kristallnacht; Rosenman replied that he opposed such a move because "it would create a Jewish problem in the United States." Indeed, when the SS *St. Louis,* carrying 904 German Jewish refugees, was refused entry into Cuba in May 1939 and hovered hopefully off the Florida coast, no Jewish leader urged Roosevelt to admit them to the United States. Likewise, the Wagner-Rogers legislation to grant entry to 20,000 German refugee children in the spring of 1939 received tepid support from American Jewish organizations and was buried in a subcommittee. By contrast, a 1940 campaign by *Pets Magazine* to place British pure-bred dogs in American homes for the duration of the war netted more than 1,000 offers of hospitality, a telling counterpoint to the defeat of Wagner-Rogers.

Some historians maintain that even a militant protest campaign by American Jews in 1939 was unlikely to have made any difference, since American public opinion was overwhelmingly antirefugee and could not be easily swayed. Congress, too, was passionately opposed to increasing immigration, and the few attempts made to introduce liberal immigration laws were quickly stifled. The State Department, which had day-to-day control over immigration matters, regarded immigrants as a menace to American society and repeatedly stymied attempts to admit larger numbers of Jewish refugees. President Roosevelt did have at his disposal a variety of methods to assist at least a modest number of refugees, short of unpopular steps such as tampering with the immigration laws. For example, FDR could have authorized a loosening of the way in which the quotas were administered, so that the maximum number of refugees were granted entry. Another possibility would have been to grant refugees entry to a U.S. territory, such as the Virgin Islands, on visitors' visas. Both the governor of the Virgin Islands and its legislative assembly endorsed proposals to that effect, but the State Department intervened to prevent such steps; FDR preferred to look the other way. Another option for Roosevelt would have been to pressure the British to open the doors of Palestine, but FDR was unwilling to risk tension in the Anglo-American alliance by raising the sensitive Palestine question.

The inability of mainstream American Jewish leaders to influence the Roosevelt administration regarding either immigration or Palestine policy created a vacuum in the Jewish community that grassroots activists sought to fill. A small group of New York–based Revisionist Zionists—affiliated with the world Zionist movement's militant wing, established by the firebrand Vladimir Ze'ev Jabotinsky—in 1938 established a group called the American Friends of a Jewish Palestine, to seek financial and political support for efforts to bring European Jewish refugees to Palestine in defiance of British immigration restrictions. Mainstream American Jewish leaders such as Zionist Organization of America vice president Israel Goldstein were deeply worried that the American Friends of a Jewish Palestine were attracting "a good many names of 'respectables' such as women of prominence in Hadassah, well-known lawyers . . . and other unwitting laymen. . . . [T]he penetration has been considerable."

Just as wartime conditions were beginning to make Jabotinsky's unauthorized immigration virtually impossible, the group found a new leader and a new cause. Hillel Kook, an emissary from Palestine who adopted "Peter Bergson" as his nomme de guerre, came to the United States in early 1940 and launched a campaign for the creation of a Jewish army to fight alongside the Allies against the Nazis. Bergson's Committee for a Jewish Army of Stateless and Palestinian Jews utilized dramatic techniques, such as full-page newspaper advertisements and protest rallies to focus public attention on the Jewish army issue. "JEWS FIGHT FOR THE RIGHT TO FIGHT" declared the headline of Bergson's full-page advertisement in the *New York Times* on January 5, 1942. The ad boasted 133 signatures, including three

U.S. senators, fourteen members of the House of Representatives, eleven rabbis, five Christian clergymen, and an assortment of well-known authors, journalists, and entertainers. Additional ads demanding a Jewish army would follow, in the *Times* and elsewhere, each generating enough contributions to sponsor the next. Jewish political advertising of this sort was an innovation. Jewish organizations usually resorted to newspaper ads only to announce specific events, and even then only in the Jewish press. The Bergson group was venturing into unknown territory, splashing a controversial political message across the pages of America's largest daily newspaper, where it would be read primarily by non-Jews—"just as you would advertise Chevrolet motor cars or Players cigarettes," as one of Bergson's deputies put it.

Although newcomers to the United States, Bergson and his colleagues quickly grasped the most basic principle of American political advocacy: a controversial cause is not likely to be embraced by the White House or Congress unless it has first gained substantial public acceptance. The Jewish army issue had to be taken out of the back pages of the Yiddish press and brought to the attention of large numbers of Americans. One month after the *Times* ad, Bergson supporter Congressmember Andrew L. Somers (Democrat of Brooklyn) introduced a resolution urging the creation of a Jewish army. Somers, Bergson's earliest and must enthusiastic supporter in Congress, was the son of a militant Irish nationalist and felt a natural kinship with Jewish opponents of England. When the Bergson group decided, in 1941, to assign a full-time lobbyist to Capitol Hill, Congressmember Somers volunteered the use of his office and secretarial staff. This was another innovation for Jewish activists: seeking Congressional action despite the opposition of the Roosevelt administration. The administration, anxious to avoid irritating the British, declined to support the Jewish army idea, although several officials, most prominently Secretary of War Henry Stimson, expressed their personal sympathy for the proposal. Although the Somers army resolution never came to a vote, it fired a warning shot across the administration's bow: militant Zionists were ready to press their agenda on Capitol Hill, with or without the approval of the White House.

Mainstream Jewish leaders were of two minds with regard to the Jewish army activists. On the one hand, they were instinctively distrustful of any intrusion onto the American Jewish scene by previously unknown foreigners who were associated with a controversial minority faction in the Zionist movement. Yet at the same time, many American Jewish leaders personally sympathized with at least some version of the Jewish army idea. Furthermore, the differences between the Bergson proposal and the more limited armed force advocated by the mainstream Jewish Agency were not substantial, nor could those differences be easily explained to the public. Another factor deterring mainstream Jewish leaders from publicly opposing the Committee for a Jewish Army was the leadership's perception that Bergson was winning widespread grassroots support in the Jewish community. As evidence of the Jewish army group's popularity mounted throughout 1941–1942, American Zionist attitudes toward the Bergsonites began to soften. The major Zionist organizations, while refusing to cooperate with Bergson, endorsed a version of the Jewish army idea, and leaders of the world Zionist movement privately lobbied the British for such a force, while the Bergson group kept up the pressure outside with its public protests. This two-pronged approach, although not coordinated, succeeded in eventually persuading London to establish the Jewish Brigade, an all-Jewish military unit that was part of the British Army and saw action against the Nazis during the final weeks of the war. Having done their job on the Jewish army issue but helping to stimulate the process that would eventually lead to the brigade's creation, the Bergson activists shifted their focus, in early 1943, to the Nazi annihilation of European Jewry (Medoff 2002, 74–79).

Reports of Nazi massacres of thousands of Jews at a time began reaching the American press in the summer of 1941, but they were generally confined to the back pages. Part of the reason for this lack of interest was that reports about the slaughter of hundreds of thousands of civilians were difficult to believe; many Americans remembered World War I atrocity stories that later turned out to be false. Deborah Lipstadt, in *Beyond Belief,* a study of U.S. press coverage of the Holocaust, characterizes such skepticism as the "'show me' syndrome"—unless actual physical evidence of the atrocities could be produced, the reports of what had happened were not believed. The prevalence of anti-Semitism in wartime America also helped blunt public interest in the fate of European Jewry. There were additional reasons for public apathy. Naturally the public was absorbed with news of the war effort, and it regarded the mass slaughter of Jews in Poland as one very small part of a much larger ordeal. "The right response to the Polish horror is a few straight words to say that it has been entered in the books, and then redoubled action on the Tunisian, Russian, Italian, and German fronts and on the production lines," the liberal Protestant *Christian Century* editorialized.

More detailed and verified reports of atrocities reached the West in ever greater quantities in late 1941 and early 1942. In the spring and summer of 1942, there were reports that the killing was not merely a series of individual massacres but part of a coordinated, systematic campaign by the Nazis to annihilate the entire Jewish population of Europe. Stephen Wise, who received credible reports to that effect in August 1942, consented to the State Department's request that he refrain from publicizing the information until U.S. officials could confirm it. Finally, in November, the State Department confirmed the accuracy of the reports. An official Allied statement on the subject condemned the Nazis and promised postwar retribution but offered no immediate steps to aid the Jews. Feeling no public pressure to take such action, Roosevelt left it to the State Department to explain to American Jews that (in the words of Assistant Secretary Adolph Berle) "[n]othing can be done to save these helpless unfortunates except through the invasion of Europe, the defeat of the German army, and the breaking of the German power. There is no other way." Crude anti-Semitic attitudes among some State Department officials further diminished the administration's interest in rescue. The president and his aides were so worried about being accused of fighting Hitler for the sake of the Jews that they deliberately downplayed the Jewish identity of the Holocaust victims; the statement that the White House issued to commemorate the first anniversary of the Jewish armed revolt against the Nazis in the Warsaw Ghetto did not even mention that the rebels were Jews. As Arthur Szyk, the Jewish artist and activist, complained: "They treat us as a pornographic subject. You cannot discuss it in polite society."

American Jewry's fervent support for Roosevelt soon began to show the first signs of cracking. Although the delegation of American Jewish leaders from major American Jewish organizations who met with FDR in December 1942 declared themselves satisfied with the president's expressions of sympathy and his promise to punish the killers after the war, the voices of the Yiddish press were considerably less satisfied.

The associate editor of the Yiddish daily *Der Tog* wrote: "And what about the Government of the United States? The Senate and the House of Representatives? Why hasn't a single voice been lifted in advocacy of the rescue of millions of Jews . . . and a mass migration to the United States?"

The decision by the leaders of the major Jewish organizations to refrain from challenging Roosevelt's position opened the way for action by the Bergson group, which began attracting widespread grassroots Jewish support during the spring of 1943 through a series of public rallies and newspaper advertisements demanding that the United States take direct action to rescue Jews from Hitler. These activities dovetailed with, and helped spark, questions in the press and Congress about whether there was anything the Allies could do to aid the refugees. Hoping to head off public pressure for action on the issue, the U.S. and British governments decided to cosponsor a conference to discuss the refugee problem.

Originally slated to be held in Ottawa, Canada, the conference site was changed to the island of Bermuda, where wartime regulations would restrict access by the press and potential critics. During the Bermuda conference, U.S. delegation member Senator Scott Lucas, a Roosevelt loyalist, warned Jewish leaders that diverting U.S. ships to carry refugees to safety would "prolong this war to the end that we might lose 100,000 boys." Ships were in fact available, but American Jewish leaders were not willing to risk facing such accusations in public. The conference produced little in the way of practical results. Neither the United States nor Britain was prepared to relax its immigration restrictions, and the British refused to consider Palestine as a potential refuge. The refusal of the sponsoring governments to make any of the proceedings public fueled speculation that nothing concrete would emerge from the conference, galvanizing Congressional and Jewish criticism of Allied policy toward European Jewry. The Bergsonites took out full-page newspaper ads calling Bermuda "A Cruel Mockery," and even some mainstream Jewish leaders used similarly strong language in expressing their disappointment. Bergson's new organization, the Emergency Committee to Save the Jewish People of Europe, attracted the support of a significant number of celebrities, prominent intellectuals, and members of Congress. News of Nazi atrocities generated sympathy for the committee's demand that the Allies take more vigorous action to aid Hitler's Jewish victims.

Three important factors helped this criticism of Roosevelt gather steam during 1943. First, the war effort: by mid-1943, the course of the war had turned clearly in favor of the Allies. With an Allied victory appearing inevitable, American Jews were less fearful that criticism of the president would be perceived as harming the U.S. war effort.

Second, prominent non-Jews were becoming increasingly critical of America's failure to rescue Jewish refugees. Having non-Jews challenge FDR made it psychologically much easier for Jews to do so, since it presumably diminished the danger that Jews would be accused of trying to influence America's war policy for the sake of their narrow interests. Aroused by news reports of the Nazi atrocities, a number of members of Congress and prominent American intellectuals affixed their signatures to the Bergson group's calls for U.S. intervention on behalf of European Jewry. The *New Republic* and *The Nation,* two of America's most influential political journals, published a steady stream of articles and editorials sharply criticizing Roosevelt's failure to help rescue Jews from Hitler. In August 1943, *New Republic* even ran a special twenty-two-page supplement denouncing U.S. policy and outlining various ways that Jewish refugees could be helped.

Third, growing tensions between the Roosevelt administration and the American Zionist movement over the future of Palestine began to overlap with, and aggravate, the Jewish community's relationship with the president. A British White Paper in 1939 had closed Palestine to all but a handful of Jewish immigrants for the next five years, and as the date for the expiration of that five-year-period approached, American Zionist groups intensified their calls for U.S. pressure on Britain to open Palestine. During the summer of 1943, press reports revealed that the United States and England were planning to issue a joint statement banning public discussion of the Palestine question for the duration of the war. The leaks helped prevent the planned statement from materializing, but the fact that it was under consideration further stimulated Jewish disillusionment with the Roosevelt administration.

Bergson raised the stakes on the eve of Yom Kippur, by organizing a dramatic march to the White House by more than 400 rabbis, to demand that the president establish a special governmental agency for the purpose of rescuing European Jews. The rabbis' request for a brief audience with President Roosevelt was denied. They did not know that FDR's decision was made on the recommendation of his two most prominent Jewish supporters, Judge Samuel Rosenman, a leader of the AJ Committee, and Dr. Stephen Wise, president of the AJ Congress. As Roosevelt loyalists, Wise and Rosenman wanted to protect the president from an embarrassing confrontation with the protesters. They also feared that the spectacle of hundreds of rabbis marching on Washington would arouse anti-Semitism. Rosenman had tried, unsuccessfully, to pressure the leaders of the march to "keep the horde from storming Washington," as he put it. When the rabbis persisted, Rosenman and Wise implored FDR to evade the marchers on the grounds that they were "a group of rabbis who just recently left the darkest period of the medieval world."

FDR's decision to snub the rabbis turned out to be a political blunder. It added a dramatic flair to press coverage of the event, transforming it from an exotic rabbinical gathering into a full-fledged clash between FDR and American Jewry. "Rabbis Report 'Cold Welcome' at White House" declared the headline of the story in the next day's *Washington Times Herald.* Criticism in the Yiddish-language press was especially biting. "Would a similar delegation of 500 Catholic priests have been thus treated?" asked a columnist in the *Yiddisher Kempfer.* Not a chance, declared the associate editor of *Der Tog:* "Somebody has failed us, and it was not the Rabbis." The leading columnist for the *Forverts,* the socialist Yiddish daily, which had been Roosevelt's strongest supporter in the Jewish community, feared that the episode was generating anti-FDR sentiment in the Jewish community. "In open comment it is voiced that Roosevelt has betrayed the Jews," he warned.

Capitalizing on the momentum generated by the march, Bergson's allies in Congress introduced a resolution calling for the creation of a government agency to save refugees from the Nazis. It won quick approval in the Senate but was stalled in the House thanks to the efforts of Representative Sol Bloom, a Jewish Congressmember who was a staunch Roosevelt loyalist. But Bloom miscalculated when he brought in Breckinridge Long, the State Department's most fervent opponent of rescuing the Jews, to testify against the Bergson resolution.

Long cited the number of entry visas that had been authorized since 1933, about 580,000, as if it were the number of refugees that had been admitted—when the actual number of those admitted was only a fraction of Long's figure. Long's maneuver initially had the desired effect, producing a front-page *New York Times* headline that read: "580,000 Refugees Admitted to United States in Decade." Ironically, David Wyman points out, it was "the first time that Holocaust-related news received such prominent notice in the *Times*" (Wyman 1984, 197). Mainstream Jewish leaders, whose attitude toward the Gillette-Rogers resolution had been lukewarm because it was sponsored by their archrivals, the Bergsonites, now vigorously denounced Long and the State Department.

As the battle over the resolution raged on Capitol Hill, other forces were also at work. The controversy galvanized Treasury Secretary Henry Morgenthau, who was already steaming over his recent discovery that anti-Semitism in the State Department was one of the major obstacles to U.S. action on behalf of Europe's Jews. Morgenthau was also worried that all the bad press FDR was getting would result in Jewish voters defecting to the Republicans in 1944. Morgenthau and his aides were motivated primarily by humanitarianism, but the president was more concerned about the election-year danger of the Congressional rescue resolution becoming, as Morgenthau put it, a "boiling pot on [Capitol] Hill" that could explode into a nasty scandal. Such a scandal would have publicly revealed the State Department's months of intentional obstruction of rescue. FDR preempted Congressional action by establishing the War Refugee Board, which, despite limited powers and meager funds, rescued many tens of thousands of Jews during the final months of the war.

In the spring of 1944, as Nazi deportations of Hungarian Jews to death camps got underway with the cooperation of the Hungarian authorities, there were scattered calls in the American Jewish press for Allied bombing of Hungarian railways, or a retaliatory bombing of Budapest. As it happened, Hungary was indeed bombed by the Allies, but as part of the general war effort, not as retribution for Hungarian collaboration in the slaughter of the Jews. Ironically, Budapest's expectation that the Allies would heed Jewish requests for retributive bombing of Hungarian cities helped persuade the Hungarian authorities to order a halt to the deportations on July 7. The Hungarian decision was also influenced by the embarrassing international publicity of Hungarian collaboration in the Nazi genocide; criticism by the Allies, the Vatican, and King Gustav V of Sweden; and Hungarian fears about being too closely tied to the losing side in the war.

Later that spring, and throughout the summer, there were proposals in the Jewish press that the Allies bomb the death camps themselves. The bombing idea was also repeatedly proposed privately to the War Refugee Board by Jewish organizations.

Assistant Secretary of War John McCloy rejected the proposals on the grounds that the War Department had undertaken "a study" that concluded that such bombing would require "the diversion of considerable air support essential to the success of our forces." In fact, no such study had been done. The War Department had already decided, in February 1944, that it would not allow the army to be used "for the purpose of rescuing victims of enemy oppression unless such rescues are the direct result of military operations conducted with the objective of defeating the armed forces of the enemy." In fact, on five different occasions beginning in August 1944, American bombers targeted German synthetic oil factories within the Auschwitz complex, less than five miles from the gas chambers. Despite the claim that nonmilitary objectives could not be part of military strategy, the State Department, which strongly opposed proposals to create a government agency to rescue Jews, in August 1943 established a government agency "for the protection and salvage of artistic and historic monuments in Europe."

American Jewish leaders nevertheless refrained from publicly challenging the administration's refusal to take military action against the death camps, fearing that any such criticism would provoke anti-Semites to accuse Jews of diverting wartime resources for their own narrow interests. The American Jewish Conference—a coalition of leading Jewish organizations—did sponsor a public rally in New York City on July 31, 1944, that drew a crowd of more than 50,000, but the rally's themes were carefully confined to general appeals to the Allies to help the refugees rather than any criticism of the Allies' failure yet to have taken such action. Intimidated by fears of anti-Semitism, handicapped by their devotion to Roosevelt, and weakened by intra-organizational rivalries, the American Jewish leadership accepted the late creation of the War Refugee Board as the maximum consideration they could expect their agenda to receive from the administration.

Of the many and varied protest movements in which American Jews have been involved, none has attracted more Jews, or more devotion, than Zionism, the movement to re-establish a Jewish state in Palestine.

Ironically, anti-Zionism was on the map in the American Jewish community long before organized Zionism ever appeared on the scene. Nineteen prominent American Reform rabbis, meeting in Pittsburgh in November 1885, issued a statement of religious principles that later came to be known as the Pittsburgh Platform. The platform argued that modern Jews should discard the "primitive" ideas of their ancestors and observe "only the moral laws" of the Bible. On the question of Jewish nationalism and territorial aspirations, the fifth of the Pittsburgh Platform's eight planks declared: "We consider ourselves no longer a nation, but a religious community, and, therefore, expect neither a return to Palestine, nor a sacrificial worship under the sons of Aaron, nor the restoration of any of the laws concerning the Jewish state." The Pittsburgh Platform's anti-Zionism would remain the official position of the Reform movement until the late 1930s, when the persecution of Jews in Germany by Hitler would compel the Reform leadership to re-examine the idea of Palestine as a haven for Jewish refugees.

Reform Judaism's opposition notwithstanding, fourteen local American Zionist groups, meeting in New York City in July 1898, established the Federation of American Zionists (FAZ), the first national

Zionist organization in the United States. Professor Richard Gottheil of Columbia University was elected president. The FAZ undertook a variety of educational endeavors, including the promotion of the Hebrew language, as well as activities aimed specifically at raising funds for Palestine development. The FAZ's women's division, Hadassah, was established in 1912. The FAZ's work was supplemented by a series of small Zionist organizations known as Achooza Societies that were established in the United States in the early 1900s for the purpose of purchasing cultivable land in Palestine; they established a number of communities that eventually blossomed into well-established towns in modern Israel.

The fledgling American Zionist movement had considerable difficulty attracting members during the early 1900s. The Jewish community was divided between Jews of Western and Central European origin who were well integrated in American society and uninterested in Jewish nationalism, and recent immigrants from Eastern Europe who in the struggle to eke out a living rarely had the time or financial resources to take an active role in American Zionism. Furthermore, the small and destitute nature of the Palestine Jewish community, and the bleak prospects for ending Turkish rule of the Holy Land, made the Zionist cause seem a hopeless dream. American Zionism's fortunes began to change after the outbreak of World War I. With the Berlin headquarters of the world Zionist movement cut off from Jewish communities in the Allied countries, the FAZ established, in New York, a Provisional Executive Committee for General Zionist Affairs, to serve temporarily as the central Zionist authority. The prominent attorney Louis D. Brandeis accepted the chairmanship of the Provisional Committee. The American wing of the movement was no longer Zionism's hapless stepchild. Brandeis's leadership of American Zionism, especially after he was named to the U.S. Supreme Court in 1916, helped make the movement acceptable to many American Jews who had previously feared that Zionism could compromise their status as U.S. citizens. Brandeis also attracted to the movement a coterie of talented businessmen and attorneys who used their organizational acumen to channel American Jewish sympathy for the plight of Jews in wartime Europe into practical support for the American Zionist movement. The FAZ's membership ranks quickly swelled. The movement grew even more popular when the British government, in November 1917, issued the Balfour Declaration, in which it pledged to facilitate the establishment of a "Jewish national home" in Palestine. The British conquest of Palestine from the Turks a short time later meant that Balfour's promise would be realized.

Brandeis was no stranger to political controversy, but prior to his emergence as a Zionist leader, none of his activism had been related to Jewish causes. In Boston he was known as "the People's Attorney" for his defense of consumers and small businesses, and his outspoken advocacy of social reform causes. Brandeis's first significant contact with Jewish matters came at age fifty-six, when he arbitrated the 1911 garment industry strike in New York City. Both sides in the dispute were East European Jewish immigrants, and Brandeis later reported that he was profoundly impressed by the ethical standards and idealism of strikers and bosses alike.

Contacts with Zionist emissaries, especially the Palestine agronomist Aaron Aaronsohn, aroused Brandeis's interest in the Zionist cause, but when American Zionists sought to recruit Brandeis as the leader of their movement, he initially hesitated, uncomfortable over possible conflicts between Zionist ideology and loyal Americanism. The social philosopher Horace Kallen helped Brandeis resolve the conflict with his argument that ethnic groups retaining their differences—what he called cultural pluralism—would in the end strengthen the overall fabric of American society. From his discussions with Kallen, Brandeis came to believe that "to be good Americans we must be better Jews, and to be better Jews we must become Zionists." At last he was convinced that there was no contradiction between Zionism and Americanism.

Brandeis's leadership reaped significant political and financial benefits for the American Zionist movement. His contacts with the Woodrow Wilson administration helped ensure U.S. support for the Balfour Declaration and the British Mandate over Palestine. His personal prestige, especially after he became the first Jew to be appointed to the U.S. Supreme Court, in 1916, significantly increased the popularity of Zionism in the American Jewish community. At the same time, his insistence that the organization operate at maximum efficiency and in accordance with strict business principles helped the American Zionist movement grow quickly. Boosted by the Balfour Declaration and the British capture of Palestine, the Zionist Organization of America (as the FAZ renamed itself) boasted more than 175,000 members by 1919, up from 12,000 only five years earlier.

Ironically, the Zionist movement's successes proved to be American Zionism's undoing. With England ruling Palestine and laying the groundwork for the creation of a Jewish homeland, and a generally peaceful climate between Arabs and Jews prevailing in Palestine during most of the 1920s, many American Jews no longer saw the need for an American Zionist movement. Although anti-Jewish violence by Arabs in Palestine erupted briefly in April 1920, and again in May 1921, they aroused relatively little reaction among American Jews because the rioting was of limited duration and scope. The U.S. press's incomplete and confusing coverage of the riots distorted the Jewish community's understanding of events in Palestine and hampered the possibility of an organized response. Most of what American Jews heard about Palestine during the 1920s was reassuring, and, partly as a result, the ZOA's membership ranks dwindled steadily. The organization did, however, score a significant political victory in 1922 when it persuaded both Congress and President Warren Harding to endorse the Balfour Declaration.

What thrust Zionism onto center stage in the American Jewish community was the outburst of massive, nationwide Arab violence in Palestine beginning at the end of August 1929. Some 133 Jews were slain in various parts of the country, including 69 in Hebron, where the centuries-old Jewish community had prided itself on its amicable relations with the local Arab populace.

Developments abroad had an unmistakable impact on American Jewry. In the Reform movement, for example, the spiraling Arab violence in Palestine and the rise of Nazism to power in Germany sharply accelerated the shift away from anti-Zionism that had been underway in the Reform movement for more than a decade. During the early 1900s, a small but vocal and growing minority of Zionist sympathizers within the Reform rabbinate, most prominently Stephen Wise and Abba Hillel Silver, began arguing against the staunch anti-Zionism of the 1885 Pittsburgh Platform. The international acceptance of Zionism symbolized by the Balfour Declaration and League of Nations Mandate eased the way for the Reform movement's change of heart. The 1920 convention of the Central Conference of American (Reform) Rabbis adopted a resolution "rejoicing" at the League of Nation's decision to grant the Palestine mandate to Great Britain and asserting that it was "the duty of all Jews to contribute to the reconstruction of Palestine," while continuing to eschew Jewish nationalism per se. In 1930 it voted to include the Zionist anthem, "Hatikvah," in the Reform movement's hymnal, and by 1935 the CCAR convention took "no official stand on the subject of Zionism," thus officially acknowledging the movement's shift from anti-Zionism to non-Zionism. It also pledged to "cooperate in the upbuilding of Palestine." In early 1937, the Union of American Hebrew Congregations, the national association of Reform synagogues, called on "all Jews, irrespective of ideological differences, to unite in the activities leading to the establishment of a Jewish homeland in Palestine." Later that year, the CCAR's annual assembly, meeting in Columbus, declared that it was "the obligation of all Jewry to aid in [the] upbuilding [of Palestine] as a Jewish homeland by endeavoring to make it not only a haven of refuge for the oppressed but also a center of Jewish cultural and spiritual life."

Just a week later, an unusual controversy in New York further illustrated the militant mood that was taking hold among grassroots Jews—and the potency of alliances between Jewish activists and politicians in need of Jewish electoral support.

The affair began when a New York City–owned radio station, WNYC, broadcast a program featuring three proponents of the Palestinian Arab cause inveighing against Zionism. The Jewish community erupted in protest. The feisty *Morgen Zhurnal,* making little effort to hide its point of view, reported that "Jewish listeners could hardly believe their ears," and that "the telephones at WNYC were ringing off the hook with calls from Jews wanting to know how it could air such an anti-Jewish abomination." Its rival, the daily *Der Tog,* published two editorials critical of WNYC. Orthodox and militant Zionist groups fired off telegrams of protest to the mayor's office. The protests inspired Brooklyn alderman Samson Inselbuch to introduce a resolution blasting the radio program and demanding that WNYC give equal time to the Zionist viewpoint.

The de facto alliance between the Jewish protesters and the Brooklyn alderman pointed to the emergence of new political forces in the American Jewish community. Passionate protesters and savvy politicians made for a potentially effective combination. The Orthodox, the militant wing of the Zionist movement (the Revisionists), and the journalist-activists associated with newspapers like the *Morgen Zhurnal* and *Der Tog* represented those Jews who were the most ethnically assertive. They were the most likely to be traditional in their religious observance, sympathetic to forceful Zionist activism, and in the lower economic strata. They were strongest in the Jewish neighborhoods of Brooklyn, the constituency to which Inselbuch was responding; not only did he represent an aldermanic district with a sizable Jewish population (Brooklyn's Williamsburg–Fort Greene area), but as a Brooklyn-wide candidate for city council, Inselbuch would soon need Jewish votes from all across the heavily Jewish borough.

What factors provoked the outburst of Jewish protests? No doubt the rise of anti-Semitism in Depression-era America helped generate the mood of Jewish anxiety that boiled over when the broadcasts were heard. Just a few weeks before the Arab radio speeches, synagogues in Manhattan and Brooklyn had been daubed with swastikas.

But the Jewish protests against WNYC should also be understood in the context of the worsening plight of Jews in Europe and the danger that Arab anti-Zionism posed to the effort to secure a refuge in Palestine for persecuted Jews; a large segment of the American Jewish community was convinced that Palestine was the answer to European Jewry's travails.

New York politics played a role in the controversy as well. Alderman Inselbuch was a man with political ambitions—and a keen awareness of the value of every vote. Elected to the New York State Assembly in 1933 by a margin of just ninety-three votes, Inselbuch lost his seat two years later by fifteen votes. He promptly ran for the New York City Board of Aldermen that same year and won—with just 51 percent of the ballots. Inselbuch understood all too well that every vote counted. By the time of the WNYC controversy, in June 1937, the Board of Aldermen was six months away from its scheduled dissolution, and Inselbuch was a Brooklyn-wide candidate for a seat on the board's successor, the New York City Council. A battle against Arab anti-Zionists could only enhance his candidacy in a borough with a large Jewish population. As a Republican seeking votes from Jews who usually cast their ballots for Democrats, Inselbuch could scarcely afford to squander the political opportunity that the WNYC controversy presented. His resolution received unanimous support from his Democratic colleagues, delighted at the opportunity to take a poke at the Republican LaGuardia administration.

The response of the mainstream Jewish organizations, however, introduced New York's political community to the divisions within Jewish opinion that made it difficult for a politician to know which position was most likely to gain Jewish votes or financial support. B'nai B'rith, the National Council of Jewish Women, the AJ Committee, and the AJ Congress asserted that the pro-Arab speakers had indulged in anti-Zionism (a legitimate, if distasteful, part of public discourse) rather than anti-Semitism (an unacceptable descent into racism), and therefore their comments fell within the bounds of free speech.

The evident chasm separating the attitudes of the militant grassroots in Brooklyn from the elite leadership circles based in Manhattan was in many respects a replay of the World War I–era disputes between the forces of Uptown and Downtown, only in a new locale and with a somewhat altered cast of characters. The wealthier, more acculturated Jewish establishment leaders were once again at odds with the vocal, ethnically aggressive, and politically militant grassroots; this time, however, the grassroots were not the immigrants on the Lower East Side, but rather the immigrants' children, living in an area of second settlement. Instead of discarding their ethnicity as they moved into the newer neighborhoods (as many sociologists had predicted), the second generation had responded to WNYC's Arab broadcasts with ethnic pride and assertiveness.

Increasingly during the 1930s, the international leadership of the Zionist movement, headquartered in London and Jerusalem, looked to the American Jewish community as a potential source of political power to advance the Zionist cause. Until the late 1930s, the Zionist movement had focused its lobbying and protests on the British government, trying to persuade the British to permit unrestricted Jewish immigration into Palestine and to fulfill England's promise, in the 1917 Balfour Declaration, to facilitate the creation of a Jewish national home. But despite the Zionist leadership's pleas, the British were responding to Arab violence by restricting Jewish immigration and land purchases. With Europe seemingly on the brink of war by late 1938, David Ben-Gurion, chairman of the Jewish Agency, Palestine Jewry's shadow government, concluded that the time had come for a major policy shift: "More and more, England must look to America as the only great power to which it could look for help in case of war," Ben-Gurion believed, "and more than ever America can demand certain things from England." He wanted to persuade American Jews to demand a Jewish Palestine.

Arriving in the United States in January 1939, Ben-Gurion immediately began urging American Jewish leaders to organize an international Jewish conference, in Washington, D.C., to declare an "aliyah war"—a campaign to send boatloads of Jewish immigrants to the shores of the Holy Land in defiance of British quota restrictions. Ben-Gurion expected that the English would hesitate to "combat *aliyah* with force" if "we ring ourselves round with the entire Jewish people, the entire *Yishuv*, [and] public opinion in America."

Much to Ben-Gurion's dismay, most American Jewish leaders were lukewarm to the proposal. Officials of the AJ Congress and the AJ Committee feared that such public gatherings would make Jews seem conspicuous, and would irritate the Roosevelt administration as well as America's ally, Great Britain. Ben-Gurion encountered similar opposition a year later, after the sinking of the Jewish refugee boat *Patria* and the death of its more than 200 passengers. He urged American Zionist leaders to issue a strong public statement and sponsor protest rallies around the country. Neither suggestion was adopted.

On the eve of World War II, American Zionist leaders had established an Emergency Committee for Zionist Affairs to serve as the world Zionist movement's temporary center. But the committee remained largely inactive during its first two years, because of American Zionist leaders' reluctance to criticize Britain during wartime and fear of accusations that they were trying to drag America into overseas conflicts.

Case Study: Responding to the Sinking of the Struma

The cautious approach on the part of many American Zionists during the early 1940s was illustrated by the response of the Washington, D.C., Jewish leadership in considering how to respond to the *Struma* catastrophe. The *Struma*, crowded with 750 Jewish refugees, sank off the Turkish coast in February 1942, after the British refused to grant the refugees entry visas to Palestine; all but six drowned. At an emergency session on March 9, the executive committee of the Washington Jewish Community Council debated how to respond to the tragedy. Activists such as Zalman Henkin of Poale Zion (the Labor Zionists) called for a public protest meeting. But local Zionist leader Rabbi Isadore Breslau favored a more cautious approach; fearing that a public protest might anger the British, Breslau—a close ally of Stephen Wise—suggested holding a nonpolitical "memorial meeting" instead. Others on the executive committee feared that any kind of public event could irritate non-Jews. Unable to reach a decision, the committee called for a meeting of the leaders of all the council's member organizations on March 19.

At the second meeting, Rabbi Norman Gerstenfeld, one of the city's most prominent anti-Zionists and spiritual leader of the Washington Hebrew Congregation, the capital's largest Reform synagogue, spoke out vigorously against any kind of public response to the *Struma* disaster. Gerstenfeld believed that Jews should not publicly raise specifically Jewish concerns. In the face of Gerstenfeld's opposition, Rabbi Breslau backed down from his previous endorsement of a council-sponsored memorial meeting. Instead, Breslau proposed that the council issue a mildly worded resolution expressing Washington Jewry's anguish over the *Struma*. He also proposed that the council recommend to local synagogues that they hold memorial services for the *Struma* victims, but insisted "that no resolutions nor protests would be appropriate at these memorial services." Breslau's proposal passed by a vote of 28 to 17.

But events in Europe soon changed attitudes in America. The Nazis' mass murder of Jews, the refusal of the Free World to provide a haven for Jewish refugees, and the continuing British blockade of Palestine combined to generate a mood of increasing militancy in the American Jewish community. Ben-Gurion's appeals for activism, and his calls for political pressure on Washington as a way of influencing London, began to find a receptive audience.

In May 1942, the member organizations of the Emergency Committee for Zionist Affairs convened an Extraordinary Conference of American Zionists at the Biltmore Hotel in New York City. The 600 delegates adopted resolutions denouncing the 1939 British White Paper as "cruel and indefensible"; urging "that Palestine be established as a Jewish Commonwealth"; and endorsing the creation of "a Jewish military force fighting under its own flag" alongside the Allies. Delegates from the women's Zionist organization Hadassah and the Marxist youth movement Hashomer Hatzair urged the Biltmore conferees to take a greater interest in the issue of Arab-Jewish relations, but the resolution that was adopted echoed the traditional position of the Zionist movement, expressing a general "readiness and desire" by Zionists for "full cooperation with their Arab neighbors."

At the time, many of the Biltmore attendees as well as commentators in the Jewish press saw little that was new or significant in the conference's resolutions. Many historians, however, regard Biltmore as a turning point in American Zionist affairs. It was the first national Zionist gathering in the United States after Pearl Harbor, and it represented a break from the cautious attitude that had enveloped American Zionists during the first months following America's entry into the war. The wording of the Biltmore resolutions also constituted a clear triumph of Ben-Gurion's more militant line over the more conservative approach advocated by Stephen Wise and others. In the months after the conference, the Biltmore resolutions became a sort of touchstone of Zionist commitment, with each of the major American Zionist organizations specifically pledging themselves to promote the Biltmore program.

For Jewish anti-Zionists, especially in the Reform rabbinate, where they were numerous, Biltmore was the last straw. Worried by the growing popularity of Zionism in the American Jewish community in general and within the Reform movement in particular, several dozen Reform rabbis and lay leaders established the American Council for Judaism in 1942. Through lectures, publications, and contacts with government officials, the council sought to persuade American Jewry and the U.S. government to oppose Zionism. Although its membership remained small, the council enjoyed a notoriety out of proportion to its numbers because of its close relationship with State

Department officials and the prominent coverage it received in certain press outlets, particularly the *New York Times*. The council's activities were strongly criticized by mainstream Jewish organizations. The council's primary argument, that the citizenship or legal status of American Jews would be endangered by the creation of a Jewish state, proved unfounded, and the organization faded into obscurity soon after Israel was established.

An important turning point for American Zionism came at the AJ Conference in 1943. Its original aim was to attain a measure of Jewish communal unity, not necessarily to promote Zionism, but more than 80 percent of the delegates elected or appointed to the conference represented Zionist organizations or their allies; passage of a strong Palestine resolution seemed certain. One faction of prominent Zionists, led by Stephen Wise, sought to soften the conference's stand on Jewish statehood, in the hope of assuaging concerns expressed by State Department officials and the AJ Committee. The Wise faction sought to broker a deal by which the Palestine resolution would make no reference to a Jewish state or commonwealth, in exchange for the support of the AJ Committee and other non-Zionists for language favoring unlimited Jewish immigration to Palestine. But a groundswell of pressure from the delegates, coupled with a fiery speech by Dr. Abba Hillel Silver, resulted in the passage of a strongly pro-Zionist resolution by a margin of 497 to 4 and crowned Silver the cochair of the American Zionist Emergency Council (AZEC), the coalition of major U.S. Zionist organizations.

It was not by chance that Silver's rise coincided with the escalating Nazi persecution of Jews, the apathetic response of the Roosevelt administration to news of Hitler's atrocities, and England's refusal to open Palestine to refugees from Hitler—all of which stimulated a mood of growing militancy in the American Jewish community during the late 1930s and early 1940s. Silver both symbolized American Jewish militancy and helped to encourage its spread. His speech at the 1943 AJ Conference, urging endorsement of Jewish statehood, was greeted with waves of thunderous applause that said as much about Silver's popularity as it did about the American Jewish mood.

Under Silver's leadership, American Zionism assumed a vocal new role in Washington. Mobilized by the AZEC, grassroots Zionists deluged Capitol Hill with calls and letters in early 1943 and late 1944, urging the passage of a Congressional resolution declaring U.S. support for the creation of a Jewish national home in Palestine.

The opposition of the War and State departments stalled the resolution in committee, but that did not deter Silver from campaigning, in the summer of 1944, for the inclusion of pro-Zionist planks in the election platforms of the Republican and Democratic parties that summer. Silver's ability to maneuver the two parties into competition for Jewish electoral support was a testimony to his political sophistication even if, much to Stephen Wise's chagrin, the Republican platform went beyond what AZEC requested by denouncing FDR for not challenging England's pro-Arab tilt in Palestine.

By contrast with Wise, who was a Roosevelt loyalist, Silver lobbied Republicans as well as Democrats and sought to use Congressional action as a means of pressuring FDR toward a more pro-Zionist stance. The hostility between Silver and Wise reached a boiling point at the end of 1944, with Silver resigning from the AZEC over Wise's acquiescence in the postponement of a pro-Zionist Congressional resolution. By the spring of 1945, however, a groundswell of grassroots Jewish pressure, galvanized by revelations of the full extent of the Holocaust, swept Silver back into power, this time as the AZEC's sole leader.

During the postwar period, Silver and the AZEC stepped up their pressure on the Truman Administration with a fresh barrage of protest rallies, newspaper advertisements, and educational campaigns. Silver's effort in early 1946 to link postwar U.S. loans to British policy in Palestine collapsed when Wise broke ranks to lobby against linkage. Nonetheless, Silver's energetic national campaign of rallies, lobbying, and political pressure in 1946–1948 helped win Congressional and public sympathy for the Zionist cause, blunted the State Department's attempts to turn President Truman against Zionism, and added to the international pressure on Britain to pull out of Palestine. Although the Truman administration wavered in its support for the 1947 UN plan to partition Palestine into Jewish and Arab states, a torrent of protest activity spearheaded by Silver and the AZEC helped convince the president to recognize the new state of Israel just minutes after its creation. Silver's protests against the U.S. arms embargo on the Middle East, however, were consistently rebuffed by the administration.

Truman's endorsement of Jewish statehood is the subject of debate among historians. Some cite factors such as Truman's Baptist background, with its sympathy for the idea of ingathering the Jewish exiles and re-establishing the Jewish state of biblical times; the pro-Zionist lobbying of several of his Jewish personal friends; his personal distaste for the State Department crowd; his perception that the press was generally pro-Zionist; and his strong support for the United Nations, which helped influence his positive response to the UN's partition recommendation. Other historians contend that the overriding factor was the cold political calculation that the Democrats would lose Jewish votes and contributions, both in the 1946 Congressional elections and the 1948 presidential contest, if the administration were perceived as anti-Zionist. This was the conventional wisdom that Silver's movement helped create.

Silver's reign marked a political coming of age for American Jewry. His lobbying victories infused the Jewish community with confidence and a sense that their agenda was a legitimate part of U.S. political culture—no mean feat for a community composed largely of immigrants and the children of immigrants. The Silver years left their mark on the American political scene as well. After the inclusion of Palestine in the 1944 party platforms, Zionist concerns assumed a permanent place in American electoral politics. Additionally, the swift U.S. recognition of Israel in 1948, a decision made, in large measure, with an eye toward American Jewish opinion, was a first major step in cementing the U.S.-Israeli friendship that has endured ever since.

Among the significant accomplishments of the American Zionist movement under Silver's leadership was its ability to attract the support of non-Jews. An issue that was of concern only to the numerically tiny Jewish community naturally had far less potential to influence government policy than an issue embraced by millions of Americans across denominational lines. American Zionist leaders recognized this political reality and worked hard to attract Christian support for their cause. Emphasizing both the Christian biblical attachment to the Holy Land and the humanitarian need for a refuge for Europe's downtrodden Jews, American Zionists elicited a sympathetic response from the American public. Zionist activist Emanuel Neumann revived the long-dormant American Palestine Committee in 1941 as a vehicle for attracting prominent non-Jews to support the Zionist cause. During the ensuing five years, the committee attracted to its ranks thousands of national and state officials, prominent intellectuals, and other public figures. The committee's work played a crucial role in the effort to win American public support for Zionism. In 1946 the American Palestine Committee merged with the Christian Council on Palestine, an organization of pro-Zionist Christian clergy, intensifying their public-information efforts as the American Christian Palestine Committee through radio broadcasts, sermons, and its publication, *Land Reborn.*

One of the American Zionist movement's most successful collaborations with non-Jews involved Walter Clay Lowdermilk. In late

1938, U.S. Secretary of Agriculture Henry Wallace had sent Lowdermilk, his assistant chief of soil conservation, to Africa, Europe, and the Middle East to examine whether climatic changes or human mistreatment of the soil were responsible for the transformation of ancient fertile regions into modern deserts. Lowdermilk was delighted to discover in Palestine that the Zionist pioneers were carefully practicing soil conservation as they sought to reclaim barren areas of the country. In a radio broadcast from Jerusalem, Lowdermilk dedicated to the pioneers what he called the Eleventh Commandment: "Thou shalt inherit the holy earth as a faithful steward, conserving its resources and productivity from generation to generation." Lowdermilk's Methodist upbringing had already instilled in him a measure of sympathy for the Jewish rebuilding of the Holy Land. His encounter with the modern Yishuv sealed his commitment to the Zionist cause.

Lowdermilk's final report of his journeys, completed in the spring of 1939, argued that Palestine could absorb as many as 4 million Jewish refugees if it used modern scientific methods to irrigate its desert regions, such as hydroelectric power and the diversion of water from the Jordan River. To that end, he recommended the establishment of a Jordan Valley Authority, modeled on the U.S. government's Tennessee Valley Authority.

Lowdermilk's conclusions were utilized by the Zionist movement to combat British claims that Palestine contained an insufficient amount of fertile land to absorb large numbers of immigrants. Justice Louis D. Brandeis characterized Lowdermilk's final report as "the best argument for Zionism I have ever read." The American Zionist Emergency Council provided him with research assistants and financial backing to facilitate the publication of a book based on his report. *Palestine: Land of Promise* reached the best-seller list in 1944. It eventually went through fourteen printings and was translated into seven languages. Lowdermilk and his wife, Inez, wrote and lectured widely on the Holy Land's future, and Inez even founded a Hadassah chapter in Berkeley, California, where they resided.

Lowdermilk's arguments ultimately played an important role in the November 1947 debate within the Truman administration over whether or not the Negev Desert should be included in the territory that the United Nations had recommended become a Jewish state. Zionist leaders convinced President Harry Truman to support Jewish retention of the Negev by showing him *Palestine: Land of Promise* and arguing that the desert region could be made fertile through methods recommended by Lowdermilk. Many years later, Israeli foreign minister Yigal Allon remarked that Lowdermilk's work had been "instrumental" in securing the Negev for the Jewish state.

Much of the Jewish political struggle in the United States during the late 1940s was a battle between American Zionists and State Department Arabists for the hearts and minds of the White House, Congress, and the American public. Through the press, the Zionists waged a crucial battle to create a conventional wisdom.

American Jews recognized that the coverage of Mideast events by America's leading daily newspapers—and, to a lesser extent, by America's radio commentators—helped to shape public opinion, which in turn helped to shape the foreign policy of the Truman administration. A major disadvantage for the Zionists was that Arthur Hays Sulzberger, publisher of the single most important newspaper, the *New York Times,* was firmly anti-Zionist, as was the newspaper's chief Washington correspondent, Arthur Krock. Zionist leaders regarded Krock's reporting as biased, and referred to him as the "mouthpiece of high officials in the State Department." Much to American Zionists' dismay, the *Times* published the unverified claims of "British sources" that communists were prominent in the Zionist underground and would transform the Jewish state into a Soviet satellite. Zionist leaders decried the attempt by the *Times* "to smear the Zionist movement with red paint," but once the paint was daubed, it was not easy to remove. The *Times* also published numerous editorials denouncing Zionism, and it lavished attention on a small anti-Zionist faction in the Jewish community, the American Council for Judaism, and upon Judah Magnes, the controversial advocate of Jewish-Arab binationalism. Although he represented only a minuscule portion of Jewish opinion in Palestine, Magnes was quoted in dispatches from Jerusalem so frequently that readers might have easily been led to believe that he enjoyed as large a constituency as David Ben-Gurion. The *Times* correspondent in Jerusalem, Clifton Daniel, went so far as to actively promote Chaim Weizmann as a conciliatory alternative to the more militant Zionist leadership of Ben-Gurion and Abba Hillel Silver.

Part of the battle for public opinion involved recasting the Jewish fight for independence in terms familiar to ordinary Americans. Peter Bergson's newest creation, the American League for Palestine, adopted "It's 1776 in Palestine" as its rallying cry, and Thomas Jefferson's memorable phrase "Resistance to tyranny is obedience to God" peppered their press releases. Dov Gruner, a Jewish militant scheduled to be hanged by the British, "might have been fighting in 1776 for American liberty and Nathan Hale might have been hanged in

1947, a martyr to Hebrew Freedom. . . . [T]hey fought a common oppressor." A brigade of Americans who volunteered to join the Irgun Zuai Leumi underground militia in Palestine was named the "George Washington Legion," while a group that organized boycotts of British goods was dubbed the "Sons of Liberty Committee," in imitation of the Colonial American boycotters of the same name.

Mainstream American Zionist leaders, too, came to the defense of the Jewish rebels as England's refusal to permit postwar Jewish immigration and the harsh measures it used to combat the Jewish underground fighters made Jewish violence seem less unreasonable. American Zionist leaders escalated their anti-British protests as the Palestine conflict intensified. Although not explicitly justifying Jewish violence, the Zionist leadership implicitly rationalized the militants' behavior by focusing hostile attention on the English as the real cause of the Palestine trouble. "Who Are the *Real* Terrorists?" asked the headline of a full-page ad by the ZOA in the *New Republic*. The ZOA's answer, of course, was the British, whose "illegal military measures and deportation of Jewish refugees to concentration camps" had "provoked acts of desperation by Jewish men and women."

By frequently utilizing phrases that compared British behavior to that of the Nazis, the American Zionist leadership implied that the violent resistance of the Jews to the British was as understandable as was Jewish resistance to the Nazis. A British law permitting searches without warrants was cited as evidence that "it is difficult to detect the difference between the laws of [Nazi] Germany and the lawlessness of Britain." Abuse of Palestinian Jewish civilians by British soldiers constituted "a Nazi pogrom." The Palestine Mandate administration was described as "a virtual Gestapo regime." The seizure of boatloads of unauthorized Jewish immigrants and their deportation to "concentration camps" in Cyprus was "patterned on the Nazi practice," declared Henry Monsky, leader of the AJ Conference.

It was not long before such rhetoric was being taken up by leading voices in the American intelligentsia. "Many Americans feel sympathetic to the fight that the Jews are carrying on in Palestine. They feel that in some respects it is like the fight the American colonies carried on in 1776," wrote former vice president Henry Wallace in the *New Republic* (of which he was then editor) in early 1947. I. F. Stone, the Washington editor of America's other major liberal weekly, *The Nation*, concurred. The Jews who had taken up arms against the British in Palestine "are no more gangsters than were the men of Concord or Lexington," wrote Stone.

Of course, American Zionists had always attempted to justify Zionism in American terms. In 1902, the Jewish refugees settling in Palestine reminded Richard Gottheil, president of the Federation of American Zionists, of "the Puritans [who] fled from persecution." The
Zionist pioneers "are building the new Judea even as the Puritans
built a new England 300 years ago," declared his colleague, Bernard
Rosenblatt, in 1907. "Hederah and her sister colonies are . . . the
Jamestown and the Plymouth of the new House of Israel." Louis
Brandeis spoke of "the Jewish Pilgrim Fathers" in Palestine, working
in a region that most closely resembled "a miniature California." If
there were occasional Arab attacks, Brandeis thought, that was inevitable, for the American pioneers "who found the Massachusetts
Bay Colony [likewise] had to protect themselves against the Indians."
Hadassah vice president Irma Lindheim, after visiting northern Palestine in 1922, said that the Jews there reminded her of "those of the
pioneer times of early New England, [who] went out each day, rifles
in hand, to cut their fields into furrows, and plant crops for their sub-
sistence."

How successful was the 1940s campaign to Americanize the Jewish
revolt? Extant polling data from the late 1940s is not sufficiently detailed to determine American public attitudes toward Jewish guerrilla
activity specifically. Attitudes toward several related issues, however,
are clear. Surveys indicate that the U.S. public's support for the creation of a Jewish state increased during 1945–1948. Twice as many—
and later, three times as many—Americans sympathized with the
Jews as with the Arabs. Only 7 percent thought that the British were
treating the Jews better than the Arabs, while more than five times
that number believed that the Arabs in Palestine were receiving better treatment. Of the 58 percent of Americans who said (in early
1946) that they had "followed the news about the disorders in Palestine," just 12 percent blamed the Jews, while 33 percent said that the
British were to blame (10 percent blamed the Arabs; the rest had no
opinion). The violent behavior of the Jewish forces in Palestine
would certainly have undermined American public sympathy for the
Zionist cause, if not for the information campaigns undertaken by
the Jewish underground's American friends. The one-two punch of
Zionist militants justifying Jewish violence in American terms, and
Zionist moderates focusing negative attention on Britain as the pro-
voker of Jewish violence, helped buttress U.S. public support for
Zionism against the erosion that would otherwise have been caused
by the steady stream of news reports about Jews killing British soldiers. The Jewish battle against the British, recast to resemble a rein-

carnation of America's own battle against England, helped redefine American public perceptions of the conflict in Zion.

As it became clear that the Arab regimes would violently oppose the creation of a Jewish state, Palestine's Jewish leaders turned to American Jews to help bankroll the expected military defense effort. And when six Arab armies invaded the newborn state of Israel in the spring of 1948, hundreds of American Jews volunteered to serve in the Israeli armed forces.

David Ben-Gurion and other emissaries from Palestine set up shop in the summer of 1945 in a Manhattan residential hotel. A few flights up from the ritzy Copacabana Club, the Zionists held weekly meetings with industrialist Rudolph Sonneborn and a group of several dozen New York businessmen and philanthropists whom he assembled to discreetly finance the purchase of ships to bring Holocaust survivors to Palestine in defiance of British immigration restrictions. The most famous of these refugee ships was the SS *Exodus,* later immortalized in a best-selling Leon Uris novel and a hit movie. A former excursion liner turned U.S. Navy battleship that was auctioned for scrap after World War II, the *Exodus* was purchased by agents for Palestine's Jewish fighting force, the Haganah, repaired and outfitted in Baltimore, and then dispatched to France to pick up 4,500 Holocaust survivors en route to the Holy Land. The all-volunteer crew included numerous idealistic young Americans, whose widely varied backgrounds were an indication of the broad emotional appeal of the Zionist cause; among them were a student who had interrupted his Orthodox rabbinical training at Yeshiva College and another who had left his Reform rabbinical training at Manhattan's Jewish Institute for Religion in order to join the effort. A clash with British soldiers attempting to seize the ship near the Palestine shore resulted in the death of one of the American crew members, Bill Bernstein. That tragedy inspired a huge protest rally at New York's Madison Square Garden that both memorialized Bernstein and served as a forum to denounce British policy in Palestine.

Case Study: American Jews Aboard the S.S. Exodus

The emotion-laden recollections of American crew member Eli Kalm help illustrate the powerful sentiments that motivated some American Jews to involve themselves in such a hazardous and controversial cause as the *Exodus* affair. "To me, it was a very rare privilege to see what it is like to be a DP [Displaced Person]," he said. The area in which the passengers were kept was like "living in a subway during the rush hours with all the fans turned off." Kalm was moved by the refugees' response when they were told that they were being taken back to France:

> Being a Bronxite, I know my Bronx Jews. I know my mother: she would yell like hell. But these were Jews I had not known, who had been through the rope. They stood there, dead quiet, tears came from a couple of women, and what did they answer? They all got up and sang *Hatikvah* [the Zionist song that later became Israel's national anthem]. I am used to hearing *Hatikvah* by now, but it runs chills down my spine. It is like hearing [American POWs singing] the *Star Spangled Banner* in a Japanese prison camp. (Medoff 1998, 12)

Although the refugees aboard the *Exodus* were sent back to Europe, the international attention that the episode garnered intensified the pressure on the British and contributed to London's decision, later that year, to leave Palestine for good.

Some American Zionists used theater as a means of protest. In late 1946, Irgun supporters in New York undertook the production of Ben Hecht's Zionist play "A Flag Is Born." Set in a European cemetery, the play began with two elderly and ailing Holocaust survivors on their way to Palestine, Tevya and Zelda, pausing to rest there on the eve of the Sabbath. In the midst of his prayers, Tevya has a series of visions in which he encounters sages, heroes, and kings from the Jewish biblical past. Their conversations serve as Hecht's platform to survey the lessons of Jewish history, the need for a Jewish state, and the cruelties of British rule in Palestine. The bridge between past and future is provided in the form of David, a distraught young Treblinka survivor who stumbles into the cemetery during the final part of the play. Tevya and Zelda die, but David is inspired to join the Palestine Jewish underground in its war against the British. In the play's dramatic final moments, David delivers a stirring Zionist speech and marches off to fight for Jewish freedom in the Holy Land, holding a makeshift Zionist flag fashioned from Tevya's *tallit*. The role of David was played by an up-and-coming twenty-two-year-old actor by the name of Marlon Brando.

At one point in *A Flag Is Born*, Brando's character, David, delivers an impassioned, heart-rending speech accusing American Jewry of failing to pressure the Roosevelt administration to rescue Jewish refugees from Hitler. "Where were you, Jews? Where were you when six million Jews were being burned to death in the ovens? Where

were you?" Brando demanded, beginning in a quiet voice and growing louder as he repeated the question. The accusation "sent chills
through the audience," Brando recalled. At some performances:

> Jewish girls got out of their seats and screamed and cried from the aisles
> in sadness, and at one, when I asked, "Where were you when six
> million Jews were being burned to death in the ovens of Auschwitz?" a
> woman was so overcome with anger and guilt that she rose and
> shouted back at me, "Where were *you?*" . . . At the time there was a
> great deal of soul-searching within the Jewish community over
> whether they had done enough to stop the slaughter of their people—
> some argued that they should have applied pressure on President
> Roosevelt to bomb Auschwitz, for example—so the speech touched a
> sensitive nerve.

Despite his limited knowledge of Jewish affairs, Brando had hit the
nail on the head. The postwar revelations of the full details of the
Nazi atrocities, combined with remorse over the American Jewish
community's failure to protest more vocally during the Holocaust,
had intensified Jewish passions over Palestine. In this atmosphere,
perhaps it was no surprise that Hecht elicited such an enthusiastic response when he stepped on stage to appeal for donations at the end
of the opening-night performance of *A Flag Is Born*. "Give us your
money," he said, "and we will turn it into history." They did give,
and Hecht kept his promise. Officials of the British consulate in New
York were annoyed to note the "crowds" that were "flocking" to see
Hecht's play (Medoff 2002, 155). Throughout the summer and autumn of 1946, British-American tensions over Palestine were approaching the boiling point, and *Flag* contributed its share to the
charged atmosphere. By presenting the Palestine conflict in simple,
dramatic images that ordinary Americans could easily understand
and remember, *Flag* broadened American public antagonism toward
England and sympathy for the Jewish revolt. The British, for their
part, did plenty to facilitate that antagonism. In June, Foreign Minister Ernest Bevin infuriated the American Jewish community when he
asserted that Truman administration officials were pressing for the
admission of DPs to Palestine only because "[t]hey did not want too
many Jews in New York." Nobody had yet forgotten Bevin's statement the previous November that "if the Jews, with all their sufferings, want to get too much at the head of the queue, you have the
danger of another anti-Semitic reaction through it all." His new slur
seemed to confirm Jewish suspicions that Bevin was not merely cold

to Zionist aspirations but was an anti-Jewish bigot as well, provoking a torrent of denunciations from the press, Congress, and the Jewish community, and injecting even more passion and outrage into American Zionist protests.

American Zionist anger, British intransigence on Palestine, and the American political calendar were on a collision course. Midterm Congressional elections were just a few months away, and many of President Truman's aides were increasingly worried that resentment over the administration's reluctance to confront the British on Palestine would spill over into support for Republican candidates. These political concerns spelled doom for the Morrison-Grady plan, a proposal drawn up in the summer of 1946 by British and American envoys that would have divided Palestine into semiautonomous Jewish and Arab provinces under continued British rule. Both London and the State Department pressed fervently for U.S. adoption of the plan, and at a July 30 cabinet meeting, an exasperated Truman complained of the Jews that "Jesus Christ couldn't please them when he was here on earth, so how could anyone expect that I would have any luck?" Yet while he was personally convinced that the Morrison-Grady plan was "really fair," Truman was increasingly sensitive to the volume of Zionist protests and their potential electoral impact. Henry Wallace, now secretary of commerce, had warned him in a private telephone conversation the previous day that Abba Hillel Silver had been "working with the Republicans" to whip up sentiment on Palestine, and Truman brought with him to the cabinet session "a sheaf of telegrams about four inches thick" that had been received from Zionist protesters. The meeting ended with Truman opting to reject Morrison-Grady, in deference to Wallace's warning that the plan was "political dynamite." Wallace later noted in his diary: "I emphasized the political angle because that is the one angle of Palestine which has a really deep interest for Truman."

London perceived the latest development as yet another instance of Zionist pressure preventing the Truman administration from acquiescing in Britain's Palestine policy. The new British ambassador in Washington, Lord Inverchapel, informed Bevin that Truman's rejection of the Morrison-Grady plan was "solely attributable to reasons of domestic politics," reminiscent of the administration's insistence on delaying the 1945 announcement of the Anglo-American Committee of Inquiry until after that year's New York mayoral election. Based on a talk with the State Department's Loy Henderson, Inverchapel told Bevin that since Stephen Wise was a Democrat and Abba Hillel Silver a Republican, "[n]either therefore could afford to compromise without the certainty that the other would at once derive political bene-fit from his decision. With both leaders thus solidly opposed to the joint recommendations the administration dared not take the risk of antagonising the powerful Zionist lobby in an election year."

Soon Inverchapel had more disappointing news: despite England's request that the United States seal the borders of its occupation zone in Germany to prevent the entry of more DPs from adjoining re-gions—which London feared would increase the pressure to admit them to Palestine—the Truman administration refused to take such action because of the likelihood of an American Jewish backlash. The worried ambassador also warned Bevin of unpleasant political fallout from Britain's announcement that it would deport to Cyprus all Jew-ish DPs who reached Palestine illegally. Because the Zionists "are so strong in this country and exercise so great an influence on domestic politics," Inverchapel urged London to consider making gestures needed to appease Jewish sentiment, such as inviting Jewish leaders to send a delegation to see the Cyprus detention camps for them-selves. London rejected the proposal for fear of creating a precedent of American Jewish involvement in Britain's Palestine policies, but it was clear that American Jews were, in fact, already deeply involved. Nowhere was their role more apparent—and more disconcerting to the British—than Truman's decision to issue a statement on the eve of Yom Kippur, barely a month before the midterm Congressional elections, for the first time implying U.S. support for the creation of a Jewish state. Secretary of State Dean Acheson privately admitted to Inverchapel that Truman had decided to take this step because he had learned that New York governor Thomas Dewey, the likely Re-publican presidential candidate in 1948, was about to make a prostatehood speech of his own. Truman's statement did not have the desired effect; the Republicans swept the elections, gaining con-trol of the House and Senate for the first time in nearly twenty years. From Britain's perspective, the conclusion of the election campaign did not signal relief from the problem of Jewish electoral pressure in-fluencing U.S. Mideast policy. In the two years leading up to the 1948 presidential election, both parties would be "promising the Zionists the moon" in order to secure Jewish support, Inverchapel warned Bevin. Into this volatile mix leaped the irrepressible Ben Hecht with his blend of drama and politics, not to mention his knack for making headlines and aggravating British officialdom.

After ten weeks of "colorful theatre and biting propaganda" (as *Time* described it) on Broadway, *Flag* was performed in other major cities around the country. A scheduled performance at the National

Theater in Washington, D.C., unexpectedly became the focus of an unusual intersection between the Zionist movement and the cause of black civil rights. Hecht, who was among a group of prominent playwrights pledged to withhold their works from theaters that discriminated against African-Americans, insisted that the Washington engagement be moved to the Maryland Theater in nearby Baltimore. When activists of the American League for a Free Palestine discovered that the Baltimore playhouse did restrict blacks to the balcony, they teamed up with the local NAACP to pressure the theater management to rescind the regulation. Exuberant NAACP leaders hailed the "tradition-shattering victory" won by the alliance of black and Zionist activists against theater discrimination a success that helped pave the way for the desegregation of other Baltimore theaters in the months and years to follow. "I am proud that it was my play which terminated one of the most disgraceful practices of our country's history," a beaming Ben Hecht declared after the opening performance in Baltimore.

Part of the money raised by the *Flag* project was used to purchase a ship for the purpose of ferrying Holocaust survivors to Palestine in defiance of British immigration restrictions. The SS *Ben Hecht* picked up 600 Holocaust survivors in France and sailed for the Holy Land, only to be intercepted by the British on March 8, 1947, just ten miles from the Palestine shore. The refugees were taken to a detention camp in Cyprus, while the crew members were jailed at the Acre Prison, south of Haifa—except for the American crew members, who were deported back to the United States. They were greeted with a rally in their honor hosted by acting New York City mayor Vincent R. Impellitteri, who declared: "As a war veteran myself, I can understand how you, war veterans, volunteered for this hazardous voyage with no reward for yourselves except the satisfaction of helping to attain American war aims including justice and freedom for all deserving peoples."

American Jews seeking to aid the upcoming Israeli war effort soon began focusing on the need to purchase and develop weapons. British restrictions on the acquisition of weapons by Jews in Palestine had left the community there dangerously unequipped for the expected Arab invasion. The Sonneborn group activated a network of sympathizers to acquire guns, ammunition, and explosives. One source was World War II veterans, many of whom donated weapons they had brought home with them as souvenirs. At the same time, local experts were engaged to develop prototypes of weapons that could be easily and cheaply mass-produced in Palestine itself, including a hand-held bazooka, a machine-gun, and the machinery to produce them. Derelict Bronx warehouses were used to store machinery that the federal government was auctioning as postwar scrap metal and as a storage depot for weapons and other military goods. With the constant influx of donated materials and the huge staff of volunteers sorting and packing them, the warehouses were often "busier than Sears Roebuck," one participant later recalled. To evade the State Department's arms embargo on Palestine, the Zionists cloaked the goods in crates marked "Used Machine Parts" or "Industrial Goods" prior to shipping them to the Holy Land. A particularly effective ruse was implemented with the assistance of Manhattan funeral parlor directors: Zionist activists, their faces as somber as real mourners, would gather at a prearranged "funeral," crowding around a hearse as the coffin was loaded—a coffin filled with weapons bound for the Irgun. Instead of going to a cemetery, such coffins would be taken to a local pier, where, still draped with a *dekke,* the black cloth traditionally put over a Jewish coffin, they were loaded onto ships and sent overseas. On several occasions, Jews involved in these activities were arrested, only to have the charges dismissed or to be let off with token fines by judges who were personally sympathetic to the Zionist cause. According to some accounts, New York mayor Bill O'Dwyer, who made no secret of his support for Zionism, once intervened to prevent the city's police from confiscating a warehouse full of guns and equipment awaiting shipment to Palestine.

Between 1,000 and 1,500 American Jews volunteered to serve in the Israeli armed forces. Many were trained at a disguised Haganah camp in upstate New York, then sailed for the Middle East posing as French farm workers. The publicity-savvy Irgun attracted many American recruits for its "George Washington Legion," a name intended to evoke memories of the Abraham Lincoln Brigade that fought against the pro-Nazi forces in the Spanish civil war during the 1930s. Former middleweight boxing champ Barney Ross, perhaps the most famous Jewish fighter in boxing history, was the featured speaker at Irgun rallies around the country, which attracted both publicity for the Zionist cause and idealistic young volunteers to fight. Ross's refrain, "All I've got left is my heart and two good hands to talk for me," resonated powerfully with the audiences—until the State Department eventually short-circuited the "George Washington Legion" by threatening to deny passports to any American who intended to fight in Palestine and to strip the citizenship of anyone caught taking part in the hostilities.

American Jewish volunteers also played a crucial role in Israel's fledgling air force. A group of American air force veterans used funds provided by the Sonneborn group to purchase and refurbish surplus World War II planes, then flew them to the Middle East via Central America. Eight Jews involved in this violation of the U.S. arms embargo were arrested, but they were given suspended sentences and fines rather than jail time by a sympathetic judge. Some of the smugglers stayed on to fly the planes in combat. In fact, there were so many English-speakers among Israel's first pilots that it was not until 1950, two years after the Jewish state was established, that Hebrew replaced English as the required language for army radio communications. Two American volunteers masterminded the July 1948 bombing of King Farouk's palace in Cairo; the bombs themselves caused only limited damage, but the raid struck a stunning psychological blow at the Egyptians, who until that point had been bombing Tel Aviv with virtual impunity. The Egyptians also relocated their powerful 88mm guns to defend Cairo against what they feared would be future Israeli bombing raids (there were none), thus keeping them out of action for the rest of the war. The best-known American Jew in Israel's army—the first general of a Jewish army in almost 2,000 years—was a tough Brooklyn street kid named David "Mickey" Marcus. He designed a command structure that turned the Jewish guerrillas into a modern army, personally wrote its training manuals, and helped plan the military strategy that saved Israel from destruction in 1948. Shortly before his death in a military accident in the summer of 1948, Marcus was awarded the rank of lieutenant general.

Back on the home front, large numbers of American Jews took part in a veritable whirlwind of activity to assist the Israeli war effort. Electronics experts helped develop a secret radio network to link isolated Jewish frontier settlements; former OSS operatives trained young agents of the Labor Zionist militia, Haganah, in the arts of espionage (such as how to use codes and ciphers, not to mention lock-picking, safe-cracking, and other dark arts), a task deemed too dangerous to conduct so long as the British still ruled Palestine. To lift the spirits of war-weary Israel, the world-famous symphony conductor Leonard Bernstein arrived for a two-month stint with the Israeli Philharmonic. Upon hearing the news of the dramatic Israeli capture of Beersheba in October 1948, Bernstein rushed his orchestra to the desert city to entertain the exhausted troops with stunning pieces by Mozart and Beethoven. The grateful soldiers made Bernstein an honorary member of the Palmach, the army's elite mobile strike force.

Many gave blood. Among the thousands who came to the Haganah blood bank in Manhattan was Jack Bass, a former slave laborer in a Nazi camp who was saved from death by two blood transfusions given him by the American soldiers who liberated Germany in 1945. A penniless refugee upon his arrival in New York, Bass gave blood, he said, "because I have no money to give." More than 300 New Yorkers took part in a Memorial Day picnic-dedication of thirty-two refurbished war-surplus ambulances to be shipped to Israel. In Brooklyn, the Pythian Sisters charity collected three tons of food and medical supplies for Holocaust survivors traveling to Palestine. Members of the local painters' union pledged to give the Haganah their double-time pay for a Saturday's work. In Manhattan, leading furriers announced that they would match every worker's contribution of a day's wages. Shaken by the Holocaust, moved by the plight of the survivors, inspired by the idea of a Jewish state reborn after 2,000 years, American Jews contributed in every way imaginable to the establishment of the state of Israel.

The relationship between the American Jewish community and the new Jewish state was complex from the start. The American Zionist movement, with the support of most American Jews, had devoted itself to assisting in the creation of Israel in the expectation that it would be a homeland for Holocaust survivors and refugees from the Muslim world—but not for American Jewry. In 1949 and again in 1950, delegations of leaders of the AJ Committee flew to Israel to personally protest statements by Israeli prime minister David Ben-Gurion urging American Jews to emigrate to the Jewish state. This was precisely what the AJ Committee had always feared, and what had prevented it from endorsing the goal of Jewish statehood until the eve of its creation—that American Jews might be seen as more loyal to a Jewish state than to America. Hoping to blunt the impact of Ben-Gurion's rhetoric, they persuaded the prime minister to issue a statement acknowledging that "the Jews of the United States as a community and as individuals, have only one political attachment, and that is to the United States of America." Not only did the AJ Committee leaders accomplish their immediate goal of compelling Israel's prime minister to retract what clearly were his heartfelt views, they also established the parameters of the Israel-Diaspora relationship. American Jews were prepared to raise funds to help the young state of Israel absorb new immigrants; they were not prepared to count themselves among those new immigrants.

At the same time, American Jewish organizations increasingly assumed the role of Israel's advocate in Washington. That was easy enough during Israel's first few years. America's recognition of Israel, just minutes after its declaration of independence, had provided an important boost of morale to the beleaguered Jewish state. Israel, although wary of angering the Kremlin, sided with the United States when the Korean War broke out in 1950, and Israel's first request for a modest $150 million in U.S. economic aid gained approval without serious opposition. But tensions soon began to emerge. American Jewish groups discovered that the Saudi government had extended its boycott of Israel and world Jewry to the point of barring Jews from the U.S. air base in Saudi Arabia; Jewish protests against this and other instances of boycott-related discrimination proved unsuccessful, however, because the State Department, anxious to preserve its relations with the Arab regimes, preferred to regard such behavior as an internal Arab affair with which it would not interfere.

The question of arms sales soon proved nettlesome. Not only did the Eisenhower administration decline to sell weapons to Israel, but when the Soviet Union began supplying arms to the Arab nations in earnest in the early 1950s, the United States sought to keep pace by increasing its own weapons sales to the Arabs. This development occasioned considerable criticism in the Jewish press, although, once again, such protests had no discernible impact on U.S. policy. After an Israeli counterterror action in Jordan left sixty-six dead in October 1953, the United States took the lead in promoting a UN resolution condemning the Israeli strike. The fact that Israel's raid came in response to three years of attacks by Jordan-based terrorists that had killed more than 400 Israelis did not dissuade the Eisenhower administration from temporarily suspending $26 million in U.S. economic aid to Israel, citing Israel's failure to suspend the construction of a disputed hydroelectric dam on the upper Jordan River. AJ Committee president Joseph Proskauer, embarrassed by Israel's actions, met with Assistant Secretary of State Henry Byroade and offered to press the Israelis to halt the construction in exchange for restoration of the aid. A subsequent delegation of Jewish leaders, accompanied by Senator Irving Ives (R-NY) and Representative Jacob Javits (R-NY), took a different approach in their meeting with Secretary of State John Foster Dulles. They confronted the administration for failing to challenge Arab violations of the Israeli-Arab armistice and ignoring Egypt's blocking of Israeli ships from the Suez Canal. Dulles heard similar criticism from the Republican candidate for mayor of New York, Harold Riegelman. The secretary of state instructed the U.S. ambassador to the United Nations, Henry Cabot Lodge Jr., to drop a planned U.S. resolution intended to force Israel to commit to permanently halting construction of the dam. Instead, U.S. and Israeli officials agreed that Israel would temporarily suspend construction while the issue was under UN consideration, in exchange for restoration of the $26 million in aid. Dulles told Lodge to make sure that the agreement was in place prior to the New York mayoral election on November 3—presumably fearing that the perception of ongoing tension between the Eisenhower administration and Israel would turn Jewish votes against the Republicans in New York.

New tensions erupted the following year, when Byroade—who by then had succeeded Dulles as secretary of state—publicly questioned the rationale for Jewish immigration to Israel and called on Israel to separate itself from world Jewry and become a "Middle Eastern state," fully integrated in the Arab world. Byroade had derived the latter argument, Jewish groups soon discovered to their horror, from information given to him by the anti-Zionist American Council for Judaism. The council's membership had diminished rapidly in the wake of Israel's creation, and its positions had seemingly been discredited, but its leaders had once again demonstrated a knack for finding sympathetic ears in high places. Byroade's statements came in the context of an apparent deepening chill in relations between the Eisenhower administration and Israel. The administration had rejected Israel's transfer of its capital from Tel Aviv to Jerusalem, and U.S. officials publicly suggested that Israel cede territory to the Arabs and permit Palestinian Arab refugees to settle inside the Jewish state. An October 1954 meeting between leaders of sixteen Jewish organizations and Byroade's successor, John Foster Dulles, ended on an ominous note, with Dulles warning that other, unnamed officials in the administration were far less sympathetic to Israel than he. A complaint by Dulles about the inconvenience of having to deal with multiple Jewish groups pleading Israel's case in Washington led to the establishment, in 1955, of the Conference of Presidents of Major American Jewish Organizations, to serve as American Jewry's primary spokesman on foreign affairs. At about the same time, mainstream Jewish leaders also established the first registered pro-Israel lobby in the nation's capital, the American Israel Public Affairs Committee (AIPAC).

The first serious confrontation between a U.S. administration and American Jewish leaders concerning Israel took place in November 1956, when Israel responded to repeated terrorist attacks along its border with Egypt by sending its forces to wipe out the terrorist bases and occupy the adjoining Sinai desert region. The operation was carried out in conjunction with Britain and France, which simultaneously dispatched their own forces to seize the Suez Canal to prevent Egyptian leader Gamal Nasser from nationalizing it. The Eisenhower administration quickly called on Israel to withdraw from the Sinai. American Jewish leaders, for the first time faced with the discomfort of a major public clash between the governments of Israel and the United States, sought to walk a middle line, defending Israel's action against Egypt but refraining from directly criticizing Eisenhower's pressure for a withdrawal. An important exception was the Zionist Organization of America, whose president, Emanuel Neumann, and past president, Abba Hillel Silver, publicly denounced the administration's pressure on Israel. At the same time, Nahum Goldmann of the World Jewish Congress privately pressured Israeli prime minister David Ben-Gurion to accede to Eisenhower's demand. Goldmann contended that it would be "impossible" to mobilize American Jewry to support an Israeli refusal to pull out of the Sinai. Goldmann may have underestimated the depth of pro-Israel sentiment in the Jewish community. The large volume of pro-Israel letters of protest sent to the White House and Congress, and the sudden and substantial increase in contributions to the main Israel-related fundraising agency, the United Jewish Appeal, indicated that grassroots Jews were rallying to Israel's defense. A February 1957 threat by Dulles to consider economic sanctions to force an Israeli retreat prompted AIPAC's lobbyists to mobilize members of Congress, including the Senate leaders from both parties, to publicly oppose the Eisenhower's pressure on the Jewish state. Still, Dulles persisted, warning that the administration might remove the United Jewish Appeal's tax-exempt status (crucial to the organization's ability to raise funds for Israel) and summoning a delegation of non-Zionist American Jewish leaders to request that they use their "helpful influence" to pressure Israel to withdraw. In March, Israel announced its willingness to retreat, which may have brought sighs of relief from some American Jewish leaders, but which also underlined the failure of the Jewish leadership to wage a sustained and effective campaign on Israel's behalf when confronted with an unfriendly U.S. administration. It was small consolation that Eisenhower agreed, in 1958, to sell Israel a token batch of 100 antitank guns, down from the 350 that Ben-Gurion had requested.

John F. Kennedy's administration proved more sympathetic—or at least less unfriendly—to Israel than its predecessor. On the one hand, Kennedy supported the UN condemnation of Israel's March 1962 retaliatory action against Syrian-backed terrorism. His administration also launched a major initiative to improve U.S.-Egyptian relations, including a $300 million aid package to the Nasser regime. On the other hand, that same year the Kennedy administration provided Israel with Hawk missiles, the first significant U.S. supply of military aid to the Jewish state. In addition, in response to protests by the AJ Committee, Kennedy cancelled the previous policy of accepting the ban on Jews serving at U.S. military bases in the Arab world. Israel's efforts to secure arms from the Lyndon Johnson administration were the subject of protracted negotiations that included active efforts by Johnson advisers to suppress protests by the American Jews. Johnson's liaison to the Jewish community, Myer Feldman, complained, "I have rarely been exposed to as much pressure as I have had recently on the question of tanks for Israel," referring to private phone calls and letters from Jewish leaders. Feldman reported to the president on his successful efforts to keep American Jewry and sympathetic members of Congress from speaking out on the issue: "It was only after considerable effort that members of Congress have been restrained against making speeches. . . . [T]he Anglo-Jewish press has killed several articles, and responsible leaders of the Jewish community have demonstrated their confidence in the Administration by keeping silent." Finally, in the autumn of 1964, the Johnson administration arranged for West Germany to transfer forty tanks to Italy, which were then forwarded to the Israelis.

The following year, the United States agreed in principle to direct sales of some military equipment to Israel, on condition that the Israelis refrain from publicly opposing U.S. military supplies to Jordan, and—as Undersecretary of State W. Averell Harriman put it—provided "that the Prime Minister [Levi Eshkol] put these matters into proper perspective for the key leaders of the [American Jewish] community"—in other words, that he persuade Jewish leaders not to oppose U.S. arms to Amman. Indeed, Jewish leaders did not fight the arms sale to Jordan, restricting their protests concerning the Hashemite kingdom to protests against an anti-Israel mural at the Jordanian pavilion at the 1964 World's Fair in New York City. Twelve national officers of the AJ Congress, including Democratic Congressional nominee James Scheuer and actor-folksinger Theodore Bikel, were arrested for defying the fair's ban on demonstrations. A sympathetic judge acquitted the twelve and declared the ban unconstitutional.

Amid Arab movement toward war against Israel in April and May 1967, a wave of "gloom and despair" swept American Jewry, the historian Melvin Urofsky notes. It was "the fear that twice in their lifetime the Jewish people would be slaughtered and they would be able to do nothing about it. . . . There was a widespread feeling that the lives of all Jews, that the fate of Judaism itself, hung in the balance. . . . American Jews felt themselves to be in a crisis of survival. . . . Israel stood, symbolically, as a redemption of the Holocaust; Israel made it possible to endure the memory of Auschwitz. Were Israel to be destroyed, then Hitler would be alive again, the final victory would be his" (Urofsky 1978, 350–351). On just four days' notice, the Conference of Presidents of Major American Jewish Organizations succeeded in attracting a crowd of 150,000 to a New York City rally to urge U.S. support of Israel. All across the United States, Jewish organizations held protest meetings, sponsored newspaper advertisements, and directed a torrent of letters to President Johnson and Congress. The Johnson administration did not, however, budge from its declaration that it would be "neutral in thought, word and deed" in the conflict nor from its refusal to provide Israel with weapons to meet the Arab threat.

There were many ways for American Jews to protest Arab belligerency and the international community's silence. Among the most dramatic was the phenomenon of 10,0000 American Jews spontaneously descending upon Israeli consulates around the country to volunteer to fly to Israel and help wherever they might be needed. A Jewish Agency official in New York described how a middle-aged man, accompanied by two younger men, showed up at his office on the day the war broke out and declared: "I have no money to give but here are my sons; please send them over immediately." The State Department's prohibition against Americans entering a war zone prevented most of the would-be volunteers from proceeding to the Middle East, but some 7,500 did go to Israel during the weeks after the war. The hundreds of American Jewish students already in Israel as the crisis unfolded chose to remain, almost to a man. These expressions of solidarity and self-sacrifice deeply moved the Israeli public, which had grown accustomed to the stereotypical image of American Jewry as a wealthy and marginally Jewish uncle, a distant relative who occasionally sent a modest contribution to ease his conscience. The outpouring of American Jewish charitable support for Israel dwarfed Israelis' fondest expectations. The first three weeks of the United Jewish Appeal's emergency campaign netted $100 million; that figure soared to $180 million, plus another $100 million in sales of Israeli bonds, by the end of that summer. Jewish leaders' efforts to rally public support for the Jewish state met with mixed results. Two of the largest church groups, the National Conference of Catholic Bishops and the National Council of [Protestant] Churches, declined to side with Israel on the eve of the war. A number of individual churchmen, including the Reverend Martin Luther King Jr., signed an open letter urging U.S. support for Israel. But King, mindful of the pro-Arab sentiment among black militants and concerned that the open letter conflicted with his pacifist principles, privately regretted signing the document and refrained from speaking out during the war itself, much to the chagrin of American Jewish leaders. A group of prominent liberal intellectuals, among them Lionel Trilling and Daniel Patrick Moynihan, signed a public letter of support for Israel, although Arthur M. Schlesinger Jr. refused to sign on the grounds that he could not continue to oppose U.S. intervention in Southeast Asia if he supported it in the Middle East.

Despite the absence of a sense of impending catastrophe as in 1967, American Jewish responses to the Yom Kippur War of October 1973 were characterized by a level of energy and commitment comparable to that of six years earlier. Meeting in emergency session the day after the armies of Egypt and Syria invaded Israel, the Conference of Presidents resolved to convene Jewish organizational leaders in Washington later that week to demonstrate their support for Israel and strategize for mobilizing the community at large. Meanwhile, that same day, an estimated 50,000 to 60,000 pro-Israel demonstrators organized by the American Zionist Youth Movement (AZYM) rallied in front of the United Nations. The AZYM's ability to attract so many people on such short notice was testimony to the shock and fear that gripped American Jewry during those first days of the war.

The 1,000-plus delegates attending the Conference of Presidents gathering in Washington resolved to mobilize their constituents to push for a quick U.S. resupply of Israel's arsenals, and to lobby representatives of those Western countries, Japan in particular, that were under strong Arab pressure to sever relations with Israel. (In the end, Japan did not break relations, but it did vocally support the Arab side.) With the Nixon administration's airlift of weapons—after an agonizing ten-day delay—the Jewish leadership's primary initial goal was accomplished.

Still, the war raged on, and American Jews sought to help. From coast to coast there were public rallies, newspaper advertisements, and emergency meetings with members of Congress. Thousands of Jewish protesters demonstrated outside the Syrian mission to the United Nations and at Red Cross headquarters in Washington to denounce Arab torture of Israeli prisoners of war. A midtown Manhattan rally on behalf of the Israeli POWs was held the day before New York City's municipal elections, guaranteeing that every local candidate, as well as other political leaders, would be on hand to lend more weight to the protesters' demands. Jewish college students played a conspicuous role in pro-Israel rallies around the country. Jewish activist groups had recently emerged on many campuses, partly as an expression of pride after the Six Day War, and partly in reaction to the eruption of anti-Semitism among black militants and the New Left. The lively and growing Jewish college press kept students informed and inspired throughout the crisis. Meanwhile, daily telethons around the country helped generate a massive outpouring of charitable donations—an astounding $107 million in the first week alone.

Case Study: Wartime Fundraising

The sociologist Daniel Elazar characterized the American Jewish fundraising successes during the 1973 Yom Kippur War as "a dramatic enactment of self-sacrifice, men borrowing money despite high rates of interest, women selling jewels, people mortgaging homes" (Elazar, 14). The mood of urgency was perhaps best illustrated by the decidedly unorthodox decision of the Young Israel movement, a network of Orthodox synagogues, to create bicycle brigades to collect pledges for Israel on Saturday, the day on which Jewish religious law normally prohibits any handling of money. The action was not, however, entirely unprecedented, for old timers in the community undoubtedly still recalled how Rabbi Abraham Kalmanowitz, one of the most prominent Orthodox rabbinical scholars in the United States, unabashedly transgressed Sabbath prohibitions in 1944 in the course of lobbying for U.S. intervention to save Jewish refugees from Hitler. Dangers to life, whether in Europe in the 1940s or Israel in the 1970s, have always been understood as taking precedence over the Sabbath regulations.

As in 1967, large numbers of volunteers crowded Israeli consulates to offer their services during the 1973 Yom Kippur War. But when it came to making use of foreign helpers, Israel's specific needs were such that during the first month of the war, fewer than 2,000 of the 30,000 to 40,000 who volunteered were actually accepted to serve.

Political developments during the two years following the war, especially the increasingly anti-Israel atmosphere at the United Nations, further galvanized American Jewry. The visit of PLO chairman Yasir Arafat to the United Nations in 1974 triggered a protest rally by some 100,000 Jews in New York City. The passage of a draft UN resolution equating Zionism with racism, in October 1975, sparked similar outrage.

A record 150,000 Jewish protesters rallied in Manhattan against the UN resolution the day after the vote, a startling figure considering the extremely short notice and the fact that the rally took place on a weekday, typically the day least likely to attract significant numbers of demonstrators. Jews also protested with their checkbooks: 60,000 Jewish tourists cancelled their planned visits to Mexico to protest that country's support for the draft of the resolution, prompting the Mexican government to reverse its position and vote against the final resolution.

It was in the aftermath of the Yom Kippur War that the first cracks in the American Jewish consensus became visible. Dissidents on the right staged a series of small but vociferous rallies against Secretary of State Henry Kissinger's pressure on Israel for territorial concessions to Syria and Egypt. To publicize their message, they borrowed heavily from the agitprop made famous by 1960s student activists, from dumping a truckload of soil in front of Israel's New York consulate to seating a protester with a Kissinger mask atop a live camel in front of Egypt's Mission to the United Nations.

At the same time, dissidents from the left sponsored protests blaming Israel's own policies as the obstacle to peace with the Arabs. These Jewish critics of Israel coalesced in a new organization called Breira, (Hebrew for "Alternative"). The name was intended as a rebuke to the popular Israeli saying, *ein breira,* meaning that in the face of Arab hostility, Israel had no alternative but to retain territory and military might. Breira's ranks consisted primarily of former 1960s Jewish radicals and liberal Reform and Conservative rabbis. They called for an Israeli withdrawal to the pre-1967 borders and the creation of a Palestinian Arab state in the vacated territories, with control of Jerusalem divided between Israel and the new state. They also criticized what they perceived as the centrality of Israel in American Jewish life. Because public Jewish criticism of Israeli policy had been so uncommon until then, Breira's activities caused a sensation in the American Jewish community. Meetings between Breira activists and officials of the Palestine Liberation Organization stirred particular controversy. Critics of Breira argued that its actions increased the pressure on Israel to make risky concessions, undermined Israel's position on Capitol Hill, and contravened the unwritten principle that those living outside Israel had no moral right to publicly attack Israeli government policies, since the Israelis alone would have to endure the life-and-death consequences of whatever policies were followed.

The Jewish left's criticism of Israel accelerated following the rise to power in Israel, for the first time, of the nationalist Likud bloc headed by Menachem Begin. The U.S. media's negative portrayal of Begin's policies, and the frequent clashes between Begin and President Jimmy Carter's administration over the establishment of Jewish communities in the territories that Israel had won in 1967, left a minority of American Jews uncomfortable about being identified with the Jewish state. For the first time, there appeared public letters of protest against Begin's policies, signed not only by Breira veterans but also by handfuls of individuals who had held positions in major Jewish organizations. The sympathetic response of some segments of the American press—including front-page stories in the *New York Times*—helped establish Begin's opponents as a force to be reckoned with in the Jewish community and beyond. By the time of Israel's military operation against PLO terrorist concentrations in Lebanon in the summer of 1982, actions once deemed unthinkable had become part of the Jewish political landscape. Members of New Jewish Agenda, one of Breira's successors, picketed Israeli consulates in several cities to demand Israeli withdrawal from Lebanon. Newspaper advertisements criticizing Israel's action in Lebanon—a frequent method of protest—featured as many as several hundred signatures each, giving the impression that they represented a sizable segment of the Jewish community. However, the noticeable overlap in the names appearing on the various ads made it difficult to assess the actual extent of the sentiments they expressed.

The conflict between Israel and the PLO in Lebanon also led to the emergence of an entirely new area of American Jewish protest activity: challenging the accuracy of media coverage of Israel. The American news media provided unusually extensive and graphic coverage of many aspects of the war, something that was made possible by the technological sophistication of television journalism in the 1980s, as distinguished from the techniques available during previous Israeli-Arab wars; the willingness of Israel to grant the media wide access to battle zones; and even the sheer length of the conflict, which gave editors extra time to focus on the story. The major television networks and newspapers alike consistently portrayed Israel's actions in Lebanon in a negative light. Critics of Israel, such as Thomas Friedman of the *New York Times,* claimed that Israel received negative coverage because it "deserved it," but there was a widespread sentiment in the American Jewish community that journalists who felt more sympathetic to the Arabs than to Israel were deliberately slanting the news.

"NBC in Lebanon," a video documentary produced in 1983 by a small nationalist group, Americans For a Safe Israel, analyzed NBC's coverage and found it to be marred by the injection of editorial comments into news coverage and NBC correspondents' excessive reliance on Arab sources. Not long afterward came several high-profile cases in which journalists unfriendly to Israel were found to have engaged in ethically questionable actions, including incidents of near-plagiarism by reporters for the *Chicago Tribune* and *Miami Herald*, and a *Village Voice* columnist was discovered to have received funding from an extreme Arab group. These developments seemed to confirm the validity of American Jewish concerns about media bias, and helped lead to the establishment of a new activist group dedicated exclusively to this issue, the Committee for Accuracy in Middle East Reporting in America, or CAMERA. Its detailed critiques of media coverage, newspaper ads challenging biased journalists, and mobilization of letter-writers have been effective in educating the public, and on some occasions have even brought forth public apologies from editors for inaccuracies in their reporting on Israel. The issue flared anew during the Palestinian Arab *intifada* of 1987–1988, when much of the American media's coverage seemed to be sympathetic toward those engaged in violence against Israel, and pro-Israel activists picketed the headquarters of the *Los Angeles Times, Miami Herald,* and *Newsday,* among others, to protest their Middle East coverage.

At about the same time, some American Jewish leaders became exercised over a possible change in the Israeli law granting citizenship to Jewish immigrants. The law, which grants citizenship to those born of Jewish parents or converted to Judaism, would recognize only those conversions done in accordance with traditional Jewish religious law, thus excluding conversions performed by Reform or Conservative rabbis. Although the change in the law would have affected a relatively small number of people—since few adherents of Reform or Conservative Judaism immigrate to Israel—the Reform and Conservative movements regarded the proposed legislative action as a symbolic rejection of their religious legitimacy. Jewish leaders affiliated with those movements organized a delegation of U.S. members of Congress to accompany them to Israel in 1988 to pressure the Israeli government to oppose altering the law. It was the first time that U.S. members of Congress were enlisted to lobby, in Jerusalem, against specific Israeli legislation, and it succeeded in persuading the Israeli government to shelve the proposed law.

One of the most vexing dilemmas in the history of relations between Israel and American Jewry has concerned Jonathan Pollard, a

U.S. Navy intelligence analyst arrested in 1985 for providing Israel with classified documents concerning military escalation by Arab and Muslim regimes, including their efforts to develop nuclear weapons. Shaken by fears that the case would arouse "dual loyalty" accusations, most major Jewish groups rushed to denounce Pollard and to demand that Israel surrender his accomplices, several of whom had fled the United States shortly before Pollard's capture. But the attitudes of Jewish leaders toward the Pollard case began to shift after Pollard received a surprisingly harsh sentence of life imprisonment, which exceeded the plea bargain agreement he had made with federal prosecutors. Jewish leaders were also troubled by the fact that Pollard received a harsher punishment for spying for an ally than others had received for espionage on behalf of regimes hostile to the United States. By the early 1990s nearly every American Jewish organization had publicly urged clemency for Pollard, and many Jewish leaders had personally visited him in prison to express their solidarity.

The Struggle for Soviet Jewry

Since the earliest days of Soviet rule, the Jews of Russia—the second largest Jewish community in the world, after the United States—have been subjected to systematic persecution. Jewish schools and most synagogues were shut down and confiscated by the government, the Hebrew language and Zionist activity were outlawed, prominent Jews suspected of dissenting from the government's positions were periodically subjected to show trials and executed, and emigration was prohibited. Until the 1960s, however, the American Jewish community had exhibited little serious or sustained interest in the plight of Soviet Jewry. Part of the reason, especially prior to World War II, was the dearth of information about the status of Jews in the USSR. During the 1930s and 1940s, the rise of Nazism and the subsequent Holocaust naturally became the preoccupation of American Jewry. The 1950s was a period of "blending in" for American Jews, and the quest for acculturation militated against the notion of launching noisy public protests on behalf of Jews overseas. In addition, some Israeli government officials discouraged American Jews from activism for Soviet Jewry during the 1950s, on the grounds that it would undermine Israel's efforts to improve its relations with the USSR.

American Jewish concern about the welfare of Soviet Jewry intensified in 1963, when the Soviet authorities launched a campaign against citizens accused of "economic crimes," which included putting hundreds of Jews on trial, sentencing ninety-one of them to death, and emphasizing their Jewish identity in the government press. These disturbing developments prodded Jewish leaders to establish the American Jewish Conference on Soviet Jewry, a coalition of representatives of Jewish organizations that was ostensibly charged with the task of arousing public opinion on behalf of Soviet Jewry. But the new group was not given a budget, a staff, or even an office. Lacking such basic resources, and faced with the fact that many of the major Jewish organizations opposed holding public demonstrations—which they feared would provoke an anti-Jewish backlash by the Soviets—the conference's handful of volunteers could not make much progress.

Yet there were stirrings at the grassroots level as well. That same year saw the creation of the Student Struggle for Soviet Jewry (SSSJ), inspired at least in part by the success of the African-American civil rights movement. The handful of young activists who founded the SSSJ had been involved in the civil rights struggle, where they witnessed first-hand the potential impact of grassroots activism. They brought to the cause of Soviet Jewry a similar spirit of idealism, optimism, and devotion. Recent Jewish history also weighed heavily on their minds; the official SSSJ handbook characterized the group's founders as "young men and women who learned from the Holocaust never to be silent again in the face of a threat to Jewish survival."

The year 1964 also saw the establishment of the Cleveland Council on Soviet Anti-Semitism, by grassroots activists who used borrowed space in their synagogue's choir loft for their meetings. It was symbolic of those early, unsophisticated days of the movement that the council's first major public event was held in a high school auditorium. On the other hand, the inclusion among the speakers of Christian religious leaders and a U.S. senator, not to mention a message from President Johnson, indicated that these Soviet Jewry activists were sufficiently savvy to recognize the need to form alliances with non-Jews and political figures to maximize the impact of the council's protests. Indeed, to facilitate the impression of Soviet Jewry as a broad-based nonsectarian cause, the council offered local Catholic and Protestant representatives seats on its executive board, and Cleveland mayor Ralph Locher served as the group's chairman. By 1965 the council's membership had passed 600, and it was helping to establish similar grassroots Soviet Jewry organizations in other cities. In 1970 six of these local activist groups united to establish the Union of Councils for Soviet Jews (UCSJ), which would serve as one of several activist alternatives to the mainstream Jewish leadership. By 1978 the UCSJ would represent twenty-two local Soviet Jewry groups.

Relations between the major Jewish organizations, on the one hand, and the activists of the SSSJ and UCSJ, on the other, were consistently strained. Their differing approaches stemmed in part from their relations with Soviet Jews themselves. Early on, the activists established close contacts with Soviet Jews who had been refused permission to emigrate. They concurred with the calls by "refuseniks" for high-profile activism and strong U.S. intervention against Soviet persecution. They saw themselves as the refuseniks' voice. By contrast, mainstream Jewish leaders tended to regard the refuseniks' perspective as unrealistic, and they were reluctant to press for U.S. government action that might upset U.S.-Soviet relations. Jerry Goodman, executive director of the establishment's National Conference on Soviet Jewry, contended that "one had to take the generally tough-minded positions articulated by the refusenik leaders with a grain of salt, since their understanding of the overall geopolitical situation was limited." Journalist Walter Ruby, who covered the Soviet Jewry movement in the United States during the 1970s and 1980s and also lived for a time in the USSR, faulted the major Jewish groups for declining to consult the refuseniks: "Not only did the American Jewish establishment groups fail to consult sufficiently, but all too often they evinced an arrogant and paternalistic attitude toward the refuseniks, treating them like impetuous children who needed to be guided and even dictated to." These conflicts burst into full public view at the May 1987 Solidarity Sunday rally in New York City, a huge annual demonstration organized by the major Jewish establishment groups. Former refuseniks were seldom invited to address the Solidarity Sunday crowd, for fear that they might advocate militant positions. But at the 1987 rally, a former Prisoner of Zion (the term used for someone imprisoned for seeking to emigrate), Yosef Mendelevich, grabbed the microphone and proceeded to lambaste American Jewish leaders for privately negotiating with Soviet leaders about the fate of Soviet Jewry without ever consulting Soviet Jews themselves.

On the other hand, as Micah Naftalin of the UCSJ recalled, there was a certain inherent strategic advantage to having both moderates and activists in the movement: "[It] was useful for the movement to have both establishment insiders who could deal in the corridors of power with the White House, Congress, and Kremlin, and the activists in the streets who provided the energy and passion to maintain the cause of Soviet Jewry in the public consciousness" (Ruby 1999, 202–203).

The nascent Soviet Jewry protest movement received a sudden and dramatic boost in 1969 from a small militant organization called the Jewish Defense League (JDL). Founded by a Brooklyn rabbi, Meir Kahane, for the purpose of physically defending Jews in deteriorating neighborhoods, the JDL expanded its agenda in late 1969 to include a confrontational new approach to the Soviet Jewish cause. Taking a page from the headline-grabbing antics of 1960s radicals, JDL activists disrupted appearances by visiting Soviet musicians, artists, scientists, and athletes; daubed "Free Soviet Jewry" slogans on Soviet airplanes at Kennedy airport; and symbolically re-enacted the biblical ten plagues by splashing red paint and releasing live mice and frogs in Soviet offices in New York City. Behind the facade of pranksterism, however, lay a calculated political strategy: Kahane aimed to force the issue of Soviet Jewry into the public spotlight, on the assumption that there was no hope for a satisfactory resolution to the problem until it was a prominent part of public consciousness. This ran counter to the philosophy of mainstream Jewish organizations, which traditionally favored "quiet diplomacy"—that is, working behind the scenes through diplomatic channels. In Kahane's view, the failure of quiet methods to secure Jewish emigration from the USSR demonstrated the flawed nature of such tactics.

The JDL regarded visiting Soviet cultural performers as an integral part of the then-burgeoning U.S.-USSR relationship known as détente. According to Kahane, the Kremlin's intention in sending musicians, artists, and the like was to create a gentler, kinder image of the Soviet Union in the eyes of the American public, in order to facilitate approval of trade credits and other benefits that the Soviets hoped to attain through détente. The JDL's bold aim was to create tension in the U.S.-Soviet relationship by disrupting performers, harassing Soviet diplomats, vandalizing Soviet property, and even bombing Soviet offices—thereby putting pressure on the Soviets to "pay for détente by letting Jews go." The JDL line was encouraged by some prominent Soviet Jews, such as Tina Brodetzkaya, whose appeal to American Jews to engage in "continuous harassing on all levels, be it the Soviet Embassy, a diplomat, a scientific delegation, or an artistic appearance" was published in the popular left-wing American Jewish student magazine *Response* in late 1970. An early success, from the JDL's point of view, came when Moscow announced the cancellation of the Bolshoi Ballet's planned 1971 tour of the United States.

Established Jewish organizations looked askance at the JDL's actions. The American Jewish Conference on Soviet Jewry publicly condemned the JDL's disruptions as "acts of vandalism and rowdyism" that were "harmful" to the cause of Soviet Jewry. Kahane shrugged off such criticism. Indeed, the expansion of the American Jewish Conference on Soviet Jewry in the summer of 1971 into a full-fledged organization with a budget and staff seemed to the militants proof that the JDL's actions were galvanizing mainstream Jewish leaders to assume a more active stance on behalf of Soviet Jewry. The AJ Conference, now renamed the National Conference on Soviet Jewry, researched and publicized information about the plight of Soviet Jewry, brought relatives of refuseniks to the United States from Israel for speaking tours, and engaged in a series of successful outreach projects aimed at galvanizing non-Jews, such as its Congressional Wives for Soviet Jewry.

Although at the national level mainstream Jewish leaders were sharply at odds with the militants, cooperation between the two sides sometimes occurred at the local level. For example, when the Moscow Circus visited New Haven, Connecticut, in early 1973, the Jewish Community Council and the JDL cosponsored the demonstration opposing the circus, and then–state senator Joseph Lieberman was among the protesters. Children attending the circus performance were handed black balloons inscribed with the words "Free Soviet Jewry."

Case Study: The Soviet Jewry Struggle as a Source of Jewish Unity

Some young Jews on the radical left found that they had something in common with the Soviet Jewry militants, despite the fact that a large portion of the JDL's membership were religiously Orthodox and politically conservative. *The Jewish Radical,* a leading Jewish student newspaper published at the University of California-Berkley, denounced as "treachery" the Anti-Defamation League's provision of information about JDL members to the Federal Bureau of Investigation. *The Jewish Radical* concurred with the JDL in opposing the Jewish establishment's preference for quiet diplomacy over public activism: "In similar fashion, American Jewish leaders during World War II muted their protests, thereby saving their beloved Roosevelt from embarrassment and wasting the opportunities of rescuing many thousands of European Jews who were subsequently slaughtered by the Nazis."

In this occasional meeting of minds between left and right one may note the potential of the Soviet Jewry cause to bring together grassroots activists across religious and cultural boundaries—and to draw them away from nonsectarian causes. Rabbi Kahane marveled at the diversity among the 1,300 people arrested at the JDL's mass civil disobedience on behalf of Soviet Jewry in Washington, D.C., in March 1971: "When row after row of proud young Jews—some with yarmulkes, some with long shaggy hair—march together for their people 5,000 miles away; when long lines of young Jews—some religious, some totally removed from religion—can stride together . . . When the strange and foreign causes are laid aside and it is [the persecution of Jews in] Leningrad and Riga that pull our young people—there is hope."

The ability to bring together in common cause so many disparate elements was undoubtedly one of the more remarkable aspects of the Soviet Jewry protest movement. A Jewish community riven by a multitude of seemingly insoluble political and religious conflicts nevertheless managed to unite in the fight to liberate Soviet Jews. Francesca Lunzer Kritz, who worked her way through the ranks of the SSSJ from "gopher" to "marshal and formation captain at rallies," was startled by the variety of protesters she encountered: "boys from Brooklyn and Queens wearing intricate kipot" side by side with "boys from the Reform Jewish movement who came to rallies wearing yarmulkes but ate hot dogs off the Sabrett cart." In her "post of coaxing marchers, I watched this patchwork of Jews. Rabbis and halter tops, Hadassah ladies and Zionist boys sang 'Am Yisrael Chai' together, said 'Amen' to Psalms together, hushed to listen to [Prisoner of Zion] Anatoly [Sharansky]'s wife, Avital, quietly speak of her husband. . . . By the end of a rally, everyone had heard one sob, one note, one word that brought the crowd together as one group, one people, one Judaism" (Kritz 1997, 14).

The JDL's militant tactics had an emotional appeal that some SSSJ members could not resist. In the "Young Jewish Activist" column that he wrote for a prominent Jewish weekly newspaper, Yossi Klein described taking part in a recent SSSJ picket line outside a performance by Soviet dancers at the Metropolitan Opera House in New York City in August 1972. Klein, who in the past had written sympathetically of the militants but had never personally joined them, decided that it was time to "stop writing about those Jewish youth who were driven by frustration to commit 'irresponsible' acts, and assume the role myself." He purchased a ticket, concealed several bags of animal blood in his pockets, entered the hall, and "threw the blood at the dancers."

The tactic of disrupting cultural performances gradually was adopted by many activists beyond the JDL. In Los Angeles, two activists in the Southern California Council for Soviet Jewry, Si Frumkin and Zev Yaroslavsky—the latter would become a Los Angeles city councilman—disguised themselves as maintenance men so as to gain access to a local auditorium prior to a performance by the Bolshoi ballet. They strung thin wires across the top from one end to the other, which they used the next evening to run "Save Soviet Jews" banners across the stage in the middle of the performance, while their cohorts unleashed loud buzzers, smoke devices, and dozens of balloons decorated with protest slogans. At their trial, the deputy district attorney showed the defendants an ironic telegram he had just received signed by two dozen leading Soviet Jewish refuseniks: "Free the Los Angeles Freedom Fighters—Justice for Frumkin and Yaroslavsky!" In another colorful stunt, Frumkin and Yaroslavsky once rented a motor boat to reach a Soviet freighter docked off the Los Angeles coast and painted "Let the Jews Go" on the Russian ship's side.

The three cities where official Soviet offices were situated inevitably became the focal points for Soviet Jewry protests: New York, Washington, and San Francisco. Washington was home to the Soviet embassy, and San Francisco to a Soviet consulate, but it was New York that became the center of the Soviet Jewry protest movement. Part of the reason was simply demographics: New York City has had the largest Jewish community in the United States since the late nineteenth century. With some two million Jews residing in the New York area, there was a much larger pool of potential demonstrators than in the District of Columbia or northern California. Hence midtown Manhattan was the site of the annual "Solidarity Sunday for Soviet Jewry," a march organized by the major Jewish organizations, starting in 1972, which consistently attracted crowds of more than 100,000. Because of New York's status as an international center of commerce and media, it was home not only to the Soviets' mission to the United Nations but also offices of the Soviet news agency Tass, the trade office Amtorg, the travel agency Intourist, and the airline Aeroflot. All of them were frequently the targets of picketers, and occasionally of vandals and even bombers, throughout the 1970s.

The Mission building was the site of one of the most important series of demonstrations of the Soviet Jewry movement's early years. In December 1970, nine Soviet Jews were tried for treason for conspiring to steal a plane to escape from the USSR. Some 6,000 Jewish protesters organized by the Conference of Presidents and the American Jewish Conference on Soviet Jewry rallied in midtown Manhattan and then marched twenty-five blocks north to the Soviet mission. Hundreds of impassioned JDL activists in the crowd attempted to crash the police barricades in front of the building, resulting in injuries, arrests, and increased media coverage. The news that all nine defendants had been convicted, with two sentenced to death and the others to lengthy prison terms, stirred emotions in the New York Jewish community to a fever pitch. The JDL, together with several student activist groups, launched a continuous 100-hour protest vigil outside the Soviet mission, no mean feat given the subfreezing temperatures in New York during the week of December. The number of protesters at the vigil at any one time fluctuated from several thousand to several dozen. One reporter's account offered revealing snapshots of the extraordinary diversity of the protesters:

> Stooped elderly men, shriveled graying grandmothers, hippies with unkempt hair and yeshiva boys with "peyot" tucked neatly behind their ears . . . . [O]ne boy wore a bright green jacket with big letters emblazoned on the back that said "Holy Cross School." . . . There was the hippie who sported a "Weathermen" button. . . . And there was the middle-aged smartly-dressed woman executive, employed by a "Jewish establishment" organization, who took her vacation especially at this time so that she could participate in the vigil all week long.

Asked about their motives for joining the vigil, some participants cited the failure of the previous generation of American Jews to speak out during the Holocaust; others focused on the failure of "quiet diplomacy" to secure Soviet Jewish freedom.

For the Soviet diplomatic personnel who worked and lived in the mission compound, it was startling and more than a little unsettling to have large crowds of noisy protesters in front of their building continuously from morning through night, day after day, with their complaints against the Kremlin broadcast to millions by the news media. The public outcry in New York, duplicated in city after city around the United States and in Europe as well, played a role in convincing the Soviet authorities that commuting the death sentences was a cheap price to pay to alleviate the public relations beating they were taking. Still, the commutations were a drop in the bucket compared with the Soviet Jewry movement's goal of freedom of emigration for all Jews in the USSR. Just days after the vigil concluded, the JDL upped the ante by launching a campaign of following and harassing Soviet diplomats and their families as they left the mission.

The angry Soviet authorities retaliated by harassing U.S. diplomats and journalists in Moscow. Jewish militants argued that the rising tensions between the two superpowers over the Soviet Jewry issue would eventually compel the Russians to ease up on emigration in order to ensure that détente proceeded smoothly. Jewish establishment leaders feared that the harassment would backfire and provoke even harsher Soviet policies.

Case Study: A Rabbi's Decision to Break the Law

During the mid-1980s, the Soviet Jewry protest movement underwent a significant change. The tactic of civil disobedience, once the exclusive domain of militant groups such as the Jewish Defense League and the Student Struggle for Soviet Jewry, was increasingly adopted by the mainstream community. In New York, dozens of rabbis who would ordinarily never dream of breaking the law volunteered to be arrested at sit-down protests at Soviet offices. The strategy succeeded in attracting media attention and thereby keeping the Soviet Jewry issue in the public limelight.

Rabbi Bruce Ginsburg later described the soul-searching that preceded his decision to join five fellow-rabbis in a sit-in at the offices of the Soviet news agency Tass in January 1985, resulting in their arrest for criminal trespass. "There are situations where violation of the law becomes a moral necessity," Ginsburg wrote. "After much soul-searching, five considerations convinced me of my moral obligation to 'run the lights' for Russian Jewry." First, "the situation is desperate. . . . [T]he gates of emigration have been virtually shut . . . one-fifth of world Jewry is on the threshold of cultural annihilation." Second, "too few have shown their outrage. . . . If the Jewish community isn't ready to *shrei gevalt* [vigorously protest], why should anyone else press the case when it is inconvenient to do so?" Third, "every conceivable legal avenue to draw attention to the cause has already been tried." "The news media have become bored" with the standard methods of protest, such as petitions and newspaper ads; it is necessary to adopt more dramatic methods. Fourth, "an effective civil disobedience movement will complement, rather than complicate, American negotiating efforts." The U.S. delegates to talks with the Soviets will be able "to explain to their Russian counterparts that they need some real concessions to appease the restless American public." Finally, "I was prepared to suffer the penalty, if necessary, for demonstrating the courage of my convictions. Readiness to accept the consequences of law breaking is a moral prerequisite of civil disobedience." Fortunately for Rabbi Ginsburg, the consequences were not severe: a sympathetic judge dismissed the charges "in the interest of justice" (Ginsburg 1985, 32).

In Washington, protest activity was initially hampered by a local ordinance prohibiting demonstrations within 500 feet of diplomatic property. Thus one of the earliest protests, a two-week vigil in July 1969 by the Washington Committee for Soviet Jewry (which became part of the UCSJ) on behalf of jailed Soviet Jewish refusenik Boris Kochubievsky, had to be held more than a block away from the Soviet embassy. In order to protest closer to the embassy without being arrested, local activists conceived the idea of standing across the street from the embassy silently and without placards, for fifteen minutes daily. The size of the crowd maintaining the vigil grew steadily, and a system was implemented in which each local synagogue and Jewish organization assumed responsibility for manning the vigil on a particular day. The restriction on demonstrating near the embassy was loosened slightly by a 1973 court decision permitting the distribution of leaflets in front of the embassy. Soviet Jewry activists stored large quantities of literature across the street from the embassy in the headquarters of a sympathetic labor group, the International Union of Electrical, Radio, and Machine Workers, whose secretary, David Fitzmaurice, was once arrested for hoisting an Israeli flag atop the building to protest the trial of the Leningrad Eleven.

The vigil site became the focal point for creative protests designed to arouse public interest in the plight of Soviet Jewry. Birthdays of prominent Prisoners of Zion were marked with special ceremonies. Relatives of refuseniks or former refuseniks who had emigrated would attend the vigil when visiting Washington. Emigre cellist Victor Yoran performed at the vigil to publicize his campaign to allow his wife, son, and mother to leave the USSR. When a Soviet basketball team came to town, the vigil participants showed up with basketballs, although the police prevented the protesters from noisily bouncing the balls. On the anniversary of the arrest of refusenik radiologist Maria Slepak, thirty uniformed nurses and doctors took part in the vigil.

In a dramatic challenge to the 500-foot restriction, two dozen rabbis, including the president of the Washington Board of Rabbis, marched to the Soviet embassy in May 1985 wrapped in prayer shawls and carrying Torah scrolls. They were arrested, tried, convicted, and sentenced to suspended sentences, probation, and a token fine—but, taking a page from the black civil rights movement, five of the twenty-four chose to serve their sentences in jail rather than accept the probation and fines, as a statement of principle against the restriction on demonstrators. Inspired by their example, some 132 demonstrators likewise chose to be arrested during the ensuing six months. Eventually, in 1988, the law was overturned.

Other Washington sites were frequently the scene of Soviet Jewry rallies, such as the Washington Monument and Lafayette Park, across from the White House. One of the largest demonstrations in U.S. history took place when an estimated 250,000 Soviet Jewry protesters gathered across from the White House on the eve of a summit conference between President Ronald Reagan and Soviet leader Mikhail Gorbachev. Washington, D.C., was also the scene of incidents of anti-Soviet violence, including the bombing of a building owned by the Soviet embassy, the breaking of windows at the homes of Soviet diplomats, and the disruption by paint-throwing protesters of diplomatic receptions for Soviet personnel.

The Soviet consulate in San Francisco was the scene of constant protests. Mainstream Jewish organizations sponsored protest rallies. Members of the Bay Area Council for Soviet Jews were arrested for chaining themselves to the consulate's front gates. JDLers harassed Soviet diplomats leaving the building, and on occasion hurled bottles of red paint at the front doors. College students built a mock jail cell and locked a "refusenik" inside. Jewish groups sponsored a daily vigil in front of the consulate from 1982 through 1990. A local Jewish summer camp brought hundreds of campers to the consulate for a protest rally each year. At Passover time, "freedom seders" were held in front of the consulate, rallies at Chanukah utilized menorah-lighting themes, and each year on the holiday of Simchat Torah, "rejoicing with the Torah," thousands of Jewish worshippers packed the streets around the consulate to take part in hours of singing and dancing with Torah scrolls.

An increasing number of American Jews personally visited the USSR, often under the auspices of the National Conference on Soviet Jewry, which briefed the participants beforehand, helped to arrange for them to meet with refuseniks, and helped to publicize the travelers' experiences when they returned. Such visits served multiple purposes. First, they were educational—a way to sensitize American Jewry to the plight of their brethren behind the Iron Curtain, since the visitors would invariably write and speak about their experiences. San Francisco student activist (and later professional Jewish activist) Douglas Kahn has described how the year after he returned was dominated by his efforts at "spreading the word—slide presentations to countless groups about my experiences, two-way weekly phone calls to refuseniks to tell them that they were not alone—sometimes packing my dorm room with friends and neighbors to give their greetings, planning a wide array of public events, collecting Judaica in special synagogue drives to send into the Soviet Union with travelers" (Kahn 1999, 184).

Second, the visitors were often able to smuggle in items that Soviet Jews could not obtain in any other way, such as religious articles or Western publications. Visits were also a way for American Jews to assist Soviet Jews directly, by boosting their morale. "They cannot visit us, but we can visit them," wrote Rabbi Saul Teplitz of Long Island, who went in 1969. "By our presence, we prove that they have not been forgotten, and that we stand by them in their plight." The visits often left a profound impression on the visitors themselves. Singer-composer Robyn Helzner, who visited the USSR in 1988 to give "underground" performances in the forbidden Hebrew language, later described the visit as a "life-changing" experience that convinced her to redirect her professional focus to Jewish music. The impact of such a visit was heightened by the element of danger. Douglas Kahn later recalled being trailed by KGB agents, and although his recollections may seem comical, a sense of peril could not be entirely avoided: "We were followed by five or six well-dressed men with newspapers neatly tucked under their arm, watching our every move. They fit every stereotype. And once, when walking back to our hotel with a refusenik, a car drove alongside us at the same speed as we walked" (Kahn 1999, 184).

Henry and Naomi Klein, who signed up to visit the USSR as tourists in 1972 but worried "about the morality of our spending dollars in such an anti-Semitic country," hoped to ease their consciences by agreeing to smuggle in a suitcase full of concealed items destined for the refuseniks Vladimir and Masha Slepak. "The clandestine route to the Slepaks' flat on Gorky Street was out of a spy novel," ending in a climb up a long, treacherous fire escape. Inspired by their meetings with the Slepaks and other refuseniks, "we became hooked on the struggle for Soviet Jewry." They were among the earliest activists in the Philadelphia Council for Soviet Jewry, and they initiated an "Adopt a Soviet Jewish Family" project that was soon picked up by Soviet Jewry activist groups around the country. This turned out to be a particularly effective tactic, because the American family would typically initiate a voluminous correspondence with their Russian Jewish counterparts, which would in turn provide a measure of security against the Soviet authorities: "Sure, the censors will open our letters, but this will be our protection," refuseniks told the Kleins. "They won't dare to touch us if they know that Americans care about us." A growing number of grassroots activists made their way to the ranks of the Philadelphia Council and, "together with their children, painted posters and marched and picketed, wrote letters to editors, Congressmen and the president, spoke at countless synagogues and organizational meetings, 'adopted' Soviet Jewish families, sent letters and parcels, and sometimes visited them in Russia" (Klein and Klein 1997, 8). Not surprisingly, the Philadelphia activists took full advantage of the presence in their city of the Liberty Bell, utilizing that symbol of freedom as the site for rallies, teach-ins, and other events.

Protests against U.S. companies doing business with the Soviet Union became a major part of the Soviet Jewry struggle. A campaign of rallies, letter-writing, and phone calls, waged primarily by the Bay Area Council for Soviet Jewry, played an instrumental role in persuading the Mack Truck Corporation to withdraw its plans to build a factory in the USSR. In Los Angeles, shareholder meetings of Occidental Petroleum became the scene of demonstrations after the firm concluded a fertilizer and chemical sales deal with the USSR in 1973. Protesters picketed the home of Occidental chairman Armand Hammer and splashed red paint across the lobby of the company's headquarters. A nationwide campaign against the Pepsi-Cola company's dealings with the USSR included a dramatic scene at the 1973 Super Bowl, when the more than 90,000 football fans at the Los Angeles Coliseum watched a rented plane circle the stadium with a huge banner reading "Don't Drink Pepsi—Pepsi Kills Jews!"

Among the striking features of the Soviet Jewry movement was the steady change in the positions of mainstream Jewish organizations. "Based on my personal experience, I believe the antiestablishment organizations played a critical role in pushing the establishment to embrace many tactics before they otherwise would have without such pressure," according to Rabbi Douglas Kahn, who spent many years with the Bay Area Council on Soviet Jewry before becoming an official of the mainstream Jewish Community Relations Council (Kahn 1999, 198). Indeed, when the SSSJ began organizing public rallies, some Jewish leaders admonished that publicity would anger the Soviets to engage in even more severe persecution. When the JDL began disrupting cultural events, many mainstream Jewish groups argued that it was inappropriate to take aim at nonpolitical targets. When activists were arrested for engaging in civil disobedience, major Jewish organizations contended that it was wrong to break the law. Yet by the mid-1970s, the established Jewish groups were sponsoring public rallies and disrupting Soviet cultural performances, although with more moderate tactics, such as unfurling banners inside the hall during intermission rather than during the performance itself. By the mid-1980s, the New York Board of Rabbis was organizing groups of prominent rabbis to be arrested en masse for chaining themselves to the gates of the Soviet mission, and leaders of the AJ Congress were deliberately flouting the 500-foot restriction in order to be arrested at the Soviet embassy in Washington. The Jewish establishment's embrace of the very activist tactics it had once denounced made activism legitimate, giving it the imprimatur of those segments of the Jewish community with the most political power and influence.

A combination of factors accounts for this stunning shift. Perhaps most important was the sudden rise in the number of emigration permits granted to Soviet Jews. Jewish leaders who had feared that activism would provoke an antiemigration backlash by the Soviet authorities found themselves confronted with statistics that indicated quite the opposite. Soviet Jewish emigration rose from 1,000 in 1970 to 15,000 in 1971, 25,000 in 1972, and 35,000 in 1973. There appeared to be a direct correlation between the intensity of American Jewish protests and the number of Jews permitted to leave the USSR. The activist Yossi Klein noted: "Jewish bureaucrats who persistently maintained that JDL would only 'make things worse' suddenly found themselves in a quandary." How could they oppose activism when activism seemed to be working?

Another important factor in the evolution of the established Jewish groups' position was the rapidity with which the Soviet Jewry protest movement became an inseparable part of mainstream American Jewish culture. The more it became an integral part of American Jewish life, the more it became impossible for the major Jewish groups to do anything but embrace it. Passover seders in private homes frequently featured an empty chair to represent Soviet Jews who were not free to celebrate the holiday. Jews in Detroit initiated the "Unlit Menorah" ceremony at Chanukah time. "Save Soviet Jewry" bumper stickers adorned cars, posters covered the walls of Jewish community centers, city billboards were rented to post Soviet Jewry slogans, news about Prisoners of Zion filled Jewish newspapers, and young people sported "Prisoner of Conscience" bracelets with the names of individual refuseniks. The struggle had its own songs, which quickly gained popularity throughout the community. "I made it my business to generate movement songs," SSSJ leader Jacob Birnbaum later recalled. He turned to an old friend, the famous "singing rabbi," Shlomo Carlebach, whose heartfelt rendition of "Am Yisrael Chai" ("The Jewish

Nation Lives") became the movement's unofficial anthem and further anchored the Soviet Jewry cause in the popular American Jewish consciousness.

Preholiday preparations in Jewish day schools routinely included having the children send greeting cards to refuseniks. American Jewish boys and girls celebrating their bar mitzvah or bat mitzvah symbolically "twinned" the ceremonies with the children of refuseniks, and spoke about the plight at the celebration. This kind of personal participation by young people often left a profound mark on the individual. A teenage participant in the daily vigil in Washington, D.C., remembered the day when it was her scheduled turn to take part: "My sister and I and a friend of ours took the day off from school and established ourselves at 16th and K. We fasted all day; we gave out leaflets to passersby; and we spoke to anyone who would listen. . . . I felt that I was a link in an important chain. Someone had stood in my place the day before; someone else would stand there tomorrow" (Helzner, 18).

Synagogues, as the most frequent gathering points for Jews engaged in specifically Jewish activity, became an integral part of the movement. Soon it was commonplace to see "Free Soviet Jewry" signs posted in front of synagogues and other Jewish institutions. The congregants at the Adas Israel Synagogue in Washington, D.C., left their services en masse one Sabbath morning in 1972 and chained the building's doors to symbolize the Kremlin's shutdown of synagogues. At Kehilat Jeshurun, a leading synagogue in Manhattan, a bulletin board at the building's entrance kept a running tally of the number of Sabbaths that Soviet Jewish refuseniks spent in prison. At one point, Kehilat Jeshurun's congregants held their daily morning prayer services for three months straight outside the Soviet mission to the United Nations, eleven blocks away. Many synagogues placed an empty chair on the podium, or set aside a front-row seat, permanently reserved for a Soviet Jewish refusenik. Such constant, visible reminders of the plight of Jews in the USSR helped to make the cause of Soviet Jewry a permanent fixture in American Jewish consciousness.

Natan (Anatoly) Sharansky once remarked that his KGB interrogators mocked him by asserting that the "noise" in his behalf in the West was the handiwork of "students and housewives." Yet it could be argued that students and housewives constituted one of the most crucial segments of the movement: students, with their energy and idealism; housewives, with the time to take part in political activism and the social networking skills needed to create a massive, grassroots campaign.

An additional important factor in shaping mainstream leaders' attitudes was the involvement of Congress in the Soviet Jewry struggle. The details of the Jewish community's lobbying for legislation to aid Soviet Jewry, known as the Jackson-Vanik Amendment, are discussed in Chapter 4. The relevant point here is that once members of Congress took a serious interest in the subject of Soviet Jewry, Jewish leaders' positions were dramatically affected. Mainstream groups had looked askance when activists called for linking progress in détente to the cause of Jewish emigration, arguing that such linkage would harm efforts toward world peace, create unpleasant tensions between the U.S. administration and American Jewry, and potentially trigger a backlash against the cause of Soviet Jewry. Once members of Congress in 1972 began crafting legislation linking U.S.-Soviet trade to emigration, no Jewish leader could oppose the effort without facing widespread criticism in the Jewish community. Members of Congress acting in response to what they perceived as the sentiments of Jewish voters and the moral principles inherent in the cause of Soviet Jewry unintentionally outflanked the Jewish establishment and compelled it to adopt a line it might never have otherwise embraced.

The alliance of Congress, the Jewish leadership, and the community at large ultimately proved too powerful a combination to be defeated. The constant torrent of negative publicity undermined the morale of the Soviet authorities; the political pressure generated by Congress, the media, and public opinion compelled successive U.S. administrations to constantly raise the issue with the Kremlin; and the economic pressure created by linking trade to emigration directly undermined the Soviet regime. In the short run, these factors helped crack open the Iron Curtain during the early 1970s, and in the long run they contributed to the downfall of the Soviet Union, which in the end was the full path to freedom for Soviet Jewry.

As individuals and through organizations, American Jews have maintained a consistently high level of participation in political protest activity. The influx of political radicals among the waves of East European Jewish immigrants in the early 1900s significantly increased the extent of Jewish involvement in political protests, although fears of provoking an anti-Semitic backlash sometimes tempered Jewish participation. Overseas concerns, primarily the persecution of Jews by Nazi Germany and the Soviet Union, and Israel's struggle for survival, have provided an especially powerful impetus for widespread grassroots Jewish participation in political protests.

References

Eighteenth Century

Faber, Eli. *A Time for Planting: The First Migration, 1654–1820.* Vol. I of *The Jewish People in America.* Baltimore, MD: Johns Hopkins University Press, 1992.

Marcus, Jacob R. *The Colonial American Jew 1492–1776.* 3 vols. Detroit, MI: Wayne State University Press, 1970.

————. *United States Jewry 1776–1985.* Vol. I. Detroit, MI: Wayne State University Press, 1989.

Nineteenth Century

Best, Gary Dean. "The Jewish 'Center of Gravity' and Secretary Hay's Roumanian Notes." *American Jewish Archives* 32 (April 1980): 23–34.

Chyet, Stanley. "The Political Rights of the Jews in the United States." *American Jewish Archives* 10 (April 1958): 14–75.

Cohen, Naomi W. *Encounter with Emancipation: The German Jews in the United States 1830–1914.* Philadelphia: Jewish Publication Society of America, 1984.

Diner, Hasia. *A Time for Gathering: The Second Migration, 1820–1880.* Vol. II of *The Jewish People in America.* Johns Hopkins University Press, 1992.

Gartner, Lloyd P. "Romania, America, and World Jewry: Consul Peixotto in Bucharest, 1870–1876." *American Jewish Historical Quarterly* 58 (September 1968): 25–116.

Greenberg, Evelyn Levow. "An 1869 Petition on Behalf of Russian Jews." *American Jewish Historical Quarterly* 55 (March 1965): 278–295.

Gurock, Jeffrey S. "Review of *The Prophetic Minority.*" *Jewish Social Studies* (Spring 1987): 184–185.

Howe, Irving. *World of Our Fathers.* New York: Harcourt Brace Jovanovich, 1976.

Isaacs, Joakim. "Candidate Grant and the Jews." *American Jewish Archives* 17 (April 1965): 3–16.

Seretan, Glen. "Daniel DeLeon: Wandering Jew." *American Jewish Historical Quarterly* 63 (March 1976): 245–256.

Sorin, Gerald. *A Time for Building: The Third Migration, 1880–1920.* Vol. III of *The Jewish People in America.* Baltimore, MD: Johns Hopkins University Press, 1993.

Tarshish, Alan. "Jew and Christian in a New Society: Some Aspects of Jewish-Christian Relationships in the United States, 1848–1881." In *A Bicentennial Festschrift for Jacob Rader Marcus,* edited by Bertram W. Korn. New York: Ktav, 1976, 565–583.

Twentieth Century (Pre–World War II)

Auerbach, Jerold S. "From Rags to Robes." *American Jewish Historical Quarterly* 63 (December 1976): 249–260.

————. *Rabbis and Lawyers: The Journey from Torah to Constitution*. Blooming-
ton: Indiana University Press, 1990.
Bloom, Leonard. "A Successful Jewish Boycott of the New York City Public
Schools, Christmas 1906." *American Jewish History* 67 (December 1980):
180–188.
Chernow, Ron. *The Warburgs*. New York: Random House, 1993.
Cohen, Naomi W. *Not Free to Desist: The American Jewish Committee,
1906–1966*. Philadelphia: Jewish Publication Society of America, 1972.
Dinnerstein, Leonard. *The Leo Frank Case*. New York: Columbia University
Press, 1968.
Feingold, Henry L. *Zion in America*. New York: Hippocrene, 1974.
Frankel, Jonathan. Review of *The Prophetic Minority* by Gerald Sorin. In *Amer-
ican Jewish History* 75 (December 1985): 235.
Frommer, Morris. "The American Jewish Congress: A History, 1914–1950."
Ph.D. dissertation, Ohio State University, 1978.
Goldstein, Judith. "Ethnic Politics: The American Jewish Committee as Lob-
byist, 1915–1917." *American Jewish History* 65 (September 1975): 36–58.
Gurock, Jeffrey S. *American Jewish Orthodoxy in Historical Perspective*. Hobo-
ken, NJ: Ktav, 1996.
————. "The Americanization Continuum and Jewish Responses to Christian
Influences on the Lower East Side, 1900–1910." In *Christian Missionaries
and Jewish Apostates*, edited by Todd Endelman, pp. 255–271. New York:
Holmes and Meier, 1987.
————. "Jacob A. Riis: Christian Friend or Missionary Foe?: Two Jewish
Views." *American Jewish History* 71 (September 1981): 29–47.
————. "The 1913 New York State Civil Rights Act." *AJS Review* 1 (1976):
95–113.
————. Review of *The Prophetic Minority* by Gerald Sorin. In *Jewish Social Stud-
ies* 49 (spring 1987): 184–185.
————. "Why Albert Lucas Did Not Serve in the New York Kehilla." *Proceed-
ings of the American Academy for Jewish Research* 51 (1984): 55–72.
Hunnicut, Benjamin Kline. "The Jewish Sabbath Movement in the Early
Twentieth Century." *American Jewish History* 69 (December 1979):
196–215.
Hyman, Paula E. "Immigrant Women and Consumer Protest: The New York
City Kosher Meat Boycott of 1902." *American Jewish History* 70 (September
1980): 91–105.
Kessner, Thomas. *The Golden Door: Italian and Jewish Immigrant Mobility in
New York City, 1880–1915*. New York: Oxford University Press, 1977.
Kuzmack, Linda Gordon. *Woman's Cause: The Jewish Woman's Movement in
England and the United States, 1881–1933*. Columbus: Ohio State Univer-
sity Press, 1990.
Leonard, Henry B. "Louis Marshall and Immigration Restriction,
1906–1924." *American Jewish Archives* 24 (April 1972): 6–26.
Mervis, Leonard J. "The Social Justice Movement and the American Reform
Rabbi." *American Jewish Archives* 7 (June 1955): 171–185.

Meyer, Michael A. *Response to Modernity: A History of the Reform Movement in Judaism.* New York: Oxford University Press, 1988.

Ruchames, Louis. "Jewish Radicalism in the United States." In *The Ghetto and Beyond: Essays in Jewish Life.* Edited by Peter I. Rose. New York, Random House, 1969, pp. 228–252.

Shapiro, Edward S. *A Time for Healing: American Jewry since World War II.* Vol. V of *The Jewish People in America.* Baltimore, MD: Johns Hopkins University Press, 1993.

Sorin, Gerald. *The Prophetic Minority: American Jewish Immigrant Radicals 1880–1920.* Bloomington: Indiana University Press, 1985.

Stone, Kurt. *The Congressional Minyan: The Jews of Capitol Hill.* Hoboken, NJ: Ktav, 2000.

Jewish Protests against Nazism and the Holocaust

Berman, Aaron. *Nazism, the Jews and American Zionism 1933–1948.* Detroit, MI: Wayne State University Press, 1990.

Berman, Gerald S. "Reaction to the Resettlement of World War II Refugees in Alaska." *Jewish Social Studies* 44 (summer–fall 1982): 271–282.

Breitman, Richard, and Alan M. Kraut. *American Refugee Policy and European Jewry, 1933–1945.* Bloomington: Indiana University Press, 1987.

Dawidowicz, Lucy S. "Could the United States Have Rescued the European Jews from Hitler?" *This World* 12 (fall 1985): 25.

Dinnerstein, Leonard. "Franklin D. Roosevelt and the Jews: Another Look." *Dimensions* 10:1 (1996): 3–8.

Feingold, Henry L. *Bearing Witness: How America and Its Jews Responded to the Holocaust.* Syracuse, NY: Syracuse University Press, 1995.

———. "'Courage First and Intelligence Second': The American Jewish Secular Elite, Roosevelt and the Failure to Rescue." *American Jewish History* 72 (June 1983): 424–460.

———. *The Politics of Rescue.* New Brunswick, NJ: Rutgers University Press, 1970.

———. *A Time for Searching: Entering the Mainstream, 1920–1945.* Vol. IV of *The Jewish People in America.* Baltimore, MD: Johns Hopkins University Press, 1993.

Finger, Seymour Maxwell, ed. *American Jewry during the Holocaust.* New York: Holmes and Meier, 1984.

Gilbert, Martin. *Auschwitz and the Allies.* New York: Holt, Rinehart and Winston, 1980.

Hecht, Ben. *Child of the Century.* New York: Simon and Schuster, 1954.

Lipstadt, Deborah E. *Beyond Belief: The American Press and the Coming of the Holocaust.* New York: Free Press, 1986.

Lookstein, Haskel. *Were We Our Brothers' Keepers?* New York: Hartmore House, 1985.

Lowenstein, Sharon R. *Token Refuge: The Story of the Jewish Refugee Shelter at Oswego, 1944–1946*. Bloomington: Indiana University Press, 1986.

Medoff, Rafael. *The Deafening Silence: American Jewish Leaders and the Holocaust*. New York: Steimatzky, 1987.

———. *Militant Zionism in America: The Rise and Impact of the Jabotinsky Movement in the United States, 1926–1948*. Tuscaloosa: University of Alabama Press, 2002.

———. "'A Foolish Encroachment upon the Allied High Command'?: American Jewish Perspectives on Requesting U.S. Military Intervention against the Holocaust." *Modern Judaism* 20, no. 3 (October 2000): 299–314.

———. "New Perspectives on How America, and American Jewry, Reacted to the Holocaust." *American Jewish History* 84, no. 3 (September 1996): 253–266.

———. "'Retribution Is Not Enough': The 1943 Campaign by Jewish Students to Raise American Public Awareness of the Holocaust." *Holocaust and Genocide Studies* 11, no. 2 (fall 1997): 171–189.

Peck, Sarah E. "The Campaign for an American Response to the Nazi Holocaust, 1943–1945." *Journal of Contemporary History* 15 (April 1980): 367–400.

Penkower, Monty N. "In Dramatic Dissent: The Bergson Boys." *American Jewish History* 70, no. 3 (March 1981): 281–309.

———. *The Jews Were Expendable*. Urbana: University of Illinois Press, 1983.

Ross, Robert W. *So It Was True: The American Protestant Press and the Nazi Persecution of the Jews*. Minneapolis: University of Minnesota Press, 1980.

Urofsky, Melvin I. *A Voice that Spoke for Justice: The Life and Times of Stephen S. Wise*. Albany: State University of New York Press, 1982.

———. *We Are One! American Jewry and Israel*. Garden City, NY: Anchor Press/Doubleday, 1978.

Wise, Stephen S. *Challenging Years: The Autobiography of Stephen S. Wise*. New York: Putnam's Sons, 1949.

Wyman, David S. *The Abandonment of the Jews*. New York: Pantheon, 1984.

Jews and the Civil Rights Movement

Berman, Paul. *Blacks and Jews: Alliances and Arguments*. New York: Delacorte, 1994.

Carson, Clayborne. *In Struggle: SNCC and the Black Awakening of the 1960s*. Cambridge, MA: Harvard University Press, 1981.

Diner, Hasia. *In the Almost Promised Land: American Jews and Blacks, 1915–1935*. Baltimore: Johns Hopkins University Press, 1995.

Friedman, Murray. *What Went Wrong? The Creation and Collapse of the Black-Jewish Alliance*. New York: Free Press, 1995.

Hentoff, Nat. *Black Anti-Semitism and Jewish Racism*. New York: Richard W. Baron, 1969.

Kaufman, Jonathan. *Broken Alliance: The Turbulent Times between Blacks and Jews in America*. New York: Scribners, 1988.

Lerner, Michael, and Cornel West. *Jews and Blacks: Let the Healing Begin.* New York: G. P. Putnam's Sons, 1995.
Locke, Hubert G. *The Black Anti-Semitism Controversy: Protestant Views and Perspectives.* Selinsgrove, PA: Susquehanna University Press, 1994.
Morris, Aldon D. *Origins of the Civil Rights Movement.* New York: Free Press, 1984.
Phillips, William M., Jr. *An Unillustrious Alliance: The African American and Jewish American Communities.* Westport, CT: Greenwood, 1992.
Ross, B. Joyce. *J. E. Spingarn and the Rise of the NAACP 1911–1939.* New York: Atheneum, 1972.
Svonkin, Stuart. *Jews against Prejudice: American Jews and the Fight for Civil Liberties.* New York: Columbia University Press, 1997.
Weisbord, Robert G., and Arthur Stein. *Bittersweet Encounter: The Afro American and the American Jew.* Westport, CT: Negro Universities Press, 1970.
Weisbrot, Robert. *Freedom Bound: A History of America's Civil Rights Movement.* New York: Norton, 1990.
Wolf, Arnold Jacob. "The Negro Revolution and Jewish Theology." *Judaism* 13, no. 4 (1964): 478–479.

Jews and the New Left

Arnoni, Menachem S. "Why the New Left Needs Israel." In *The New Left and the Jews.* Edited by Mordecai S. Chertoff. New York: Pitman, 1971, pp. 270–288.
Chertoff, Mordecai S., ed. *The New Left and the Jews.* New York: Pitman, 1971, 103–131.
Dellinger, Dave. "The Berrigan Debate: Bringing It All Back Home." *Liberation* 18:6 (February 1974): 6–7, 25–29.
Feingold, Henry L. "The Jewish Radical in His American Habitat." *Judaism* 22 (winter 1973): 92–105.
Flacks, Richard. "Liberated Generation: An Exploration of the Roots of Student Protest." *Journal of Social Issues* 23 (July 1967): 65.
Lipset, Seymour Martin. "'The Socialism of Fools': The Left, the Jew, and Israel." In *The New Left and the Jews.* Edited by Mordecai S. Chertoff. New York: Pitman, 1971, pp. 103–131.
Milstein, Tom. "The New Left: Areas of Jewish Concern." In *The New Left and the Jews.* Edited by Mordecai S. Chertoff. New York: Pitman, 1971, pp. 289–305.
Porter, Jack Nusan, and Peter Dreier, eds. *Jewish Radicalism.* New York: Grove Press, 1973.
Rabinovich, Abraham. "Borrowing Tactics from Campus Blacks." *Jerusalem Post,* (August 8, 1969): 8.
Rosenberg, M. J. "To Uncle Tom and Other Such Jews." *Village Voice,* February 13, 1969.
Somers, Robert. "The Mainsprings of the Rebellion: A Survey of Berkeley Students in November 1964." In *The Berkeley Student Revolt,* edited by Sey-

mour Martin Lipset and S. Wolin. New York: Anchor Books, 1965, 530–557.
Spiegel, Irving. "Hillel Leader Finds Confusion over Role of Jews in New Left." *New York Times,* December 19, 1968, 1.

The Soviet Jewry Protest Movement

Alexander, Edward. "Twenty-Four Hours with the KGB." *The Alternative: An American Spectator* 10 (May 1977): 22–23.
Dodek, Joan, and Ruth Newman. "Washington Jewry's Activities on Behalf of Soviet Jews, 1968–1991." *Record* 18 (1991): 7–16.
Friedman, Murray, and Albert D. Chernin, eds. *A Second Exodus: The American Movement to Free Soviet Jews.* Hanover, NH: Brandeis University Press and University Press of New England, 1999.
Ginsburg, Bruce. "Civil Disobedience on Behalf of Soviet Jewry: The Moral Dimension." *Jewish Press* 35 (March 1, 1985): 32.
Helzner, Robyn. "Still Vigilant after All These Years." *Record* 18 (1991): 17–21.
Kahn, Douglas. "Advocacy on the Community Level: A Personal Perspective." In *A Second Exodus: The American Movement to Free Soviet Jews.* Edited by Murray Friedman and Albert D. Chernin. Hanover, NH: Brandeis University Press and University Press of New England, 1999, pp. 181–199.
Klein, Naomi, and Henry Klein. "Present at the Creation." *Jewish Exponent of Philadelphia,* January 2, 1997, 8.
Kritz, Francesca Lunzer. "A Child of Sharansky Searches for Ways to Rally Her Own." *Forward,* January 3, 1997, 14.
Orbach, William W. *The American Movement to Aid Soviet Jews.* Amherst: University of Massachusetts Press, 1979.
Ruby, Walter. "The Role of Nonestablishment Groups." In *A Second Exodus: The American Movement to Free Soviet Jews.* Edited by Murray Friedman and Albert D. Chernin. Hanover, NJ: Brandeis University Press and University Press of New England, 1999, pp. 200–223.

American Jewry, Zionism, and Israel

Alteras, Isaac. *Eisenhower and Israel.* Gainesville: University of Florida Press, 1993.
Brown, Michael. *The Israeli-American Connection: Its Roots in the* Yishuv. Detroit, MI: Wayne State University Press, 1996.
Cohen, Michael J. *Truman and Israel.* Berkeley: University of California Press, 1990.
Cohen, Naomi W. *American Jews and the Zionist Idea.* New York: Ktav, 1975.
———. *Not Free to Desist: The American Jewish Committee, 1906–1966.* Philadelphia: Jewish Publication Society of America, 1972.

Elazar, Daniel J. "United States of America: Overview." In *The Yom Kippur War: Israel and the Jewish People*, edited by Moshe Davis, pp. 1–35. New York: Arno, 1974.

Feinstein, Marnin. *American Zionism, 1884–1904.* New York: Herzl, 1965.

Ganin, Zvi. *Truman, American Jewry, and Israel, 1945–1948.* New York: Holmes and Meier, 1979.

Halpern, Ben. *The American Jew: A Zionist Analysis.* New York: Herzl, 1961.

Halperin, Samuel. *The Political World of American Zionism.* Detroit, MI: Wayne State University Press, 1961.

Kaufman, Menahem. *An Ambiguous Partnership: Non Zionists and Zionists in America, 1939–1948.* Jerusalem and Detroit, MI: Magnes Press and Wayne State University Press, 1991.

Kenen, I. L. *Israel's Defense Line: Her Friends and Foes in Washington.* Buffalo, NY: Prometheus, 1981.

Kleiman, Aharon. *American Zionism: A Documentary History.* New York: Garland, 1987.

Knee, Stuart E. *The Concept of Zionist Dissent in the American Mind, 1917–1941.* New York: Robert Speller, 1979.

Kolsky, Thomas A. *Jews against Zionism: The American Council for Judaism, 1942–1948.* Philadelphia: Temple University Press, 1990.

Levin, Marlin. *It Takes a Dream: The Story of Hadassah.* Jerusalem: Gefen, 1997.

Medoff, Rafael. *Baksheesh Diplomacy: Secret Negotiations between American Jewish Leaders and Arab Officials on the Eve of World War II.* Lanham, MD: Roman and Littlefield, 2001.

———. *Militant Zionism in America: The Rise and Impact of the Jabotinsky Movement in the United States, 1925–1948.* Tuscaloosa: University of Alabama Press, 2002.

———. "New Yorkers and the Birth of Israel." *New York Times,* Israel at 50 Supplement, May 17, 1998, pp. 8–28.

———. *Zionism and the Arabs: An American Jewish Dilemma, 1898–1948.* Westport, CT: Praeger, 1997.

Penkower, Monty Noam. "The 1943 Joint Anglo-American Statement on Palestine." *Herzl Year Book* 8 (1978): 212–241.

Polish, David. *Renew Our Days: The Zionist Issue in Reform Judaism.* Jerusalem: World Zionist Organization, 1976.

Schechtman, Joseph B. *The United States and the Jewish State Movement: The Crucial Decade, 1939–1949.* New York: Herzl, 1966.

Shapiro, David H. *From Philanthropy to Activism: The Political Transformation of American Zionism in the Holocaust Years, 1933–1945.* New York: Pergamon, 1994.

Shapiro, Yonathan. *Leadership of the American Zionist Organization, 1897–1930.* Chicago: University of Illinois Press, 1971.

Slater, Leonard. *The Pledge.* New York: Simon and Schuster, 1970.

Urofsky, Melvin I. *American Zionism from Herzl to the Holocaust.* Garden City, NY: Anchor Press/Doubleday, 1975.

———. *Essays in American Zionism—Herzl Year Book.* Vol. VIII. New York: Herzl Press, 1978.

———. "Rifts in the Movement: Zionist Fissures, 1942–1945." In *Essays in American Zionism—Herzl Year Book VIII.* Edited by Melvin I. Urofsky. New York: Herzl Press, 1978, pp. 195–211.

———. *We Are One!* Garden City, NY: Anchor Press/Doubleday, 1978.

Whitfield, Stephen J. "The Radical Persuasion in American Jewish History." *Judaism* 126 (Spring 1983): 136–152.

Zaar, Isaac. *Rescue and Liberation: America's Part in the Birth of Israel.* New York: Bloch, 1954.

3

The Jewish Vote

he existence of a "Jewish vote" has long been a matter of dispute, but there can be no doubt that the perception of the existence of a Jewish vote has helped the Jewish community carve out a niche in the world of American politics. Some American Jews have vigorously denied that Jews cast their ballots on the basis of specifically Jewish interests, but these denials are sometimes motivated more by desire rather than conviction—that is, a desire to counteract suggestions of a Jewish vote for fear that non-Jews will regard Jews as insular or selfish. On the other hand, some segments of American Jewry have actively promoted the notion that the Jewish community has particular ethnic-based interests, and that many Jewish votes are indeed cast on the basis of a candidate's stance on those issues. Regardless of this intra-Jewish disagreement, most politicians have always assumed that at least a significant number of Jews do indeed predicate their vote, at least in part, on issues of specific Jewish concern. This assumption provides incentive to political candidates in some parts of the country to adopt positions they believe will elicit Jewish support. Although the Jewish community nationwide is less than 3 percent of the U.S. population, the concentration of many Jews in the two states with the largest number of electoral votes, New York and California, has elevated the importance of the Jewish vote in presidential elections. For reasons to be explored below, Jewish voting patterns throughout the past century have generally inclined toward liberal or

Democratic candidates, but signs of gradual and moderate change in that pattern are evident.

During the mid-1800s, the small American Jewish community was split about evenly between Republicans and Democrats, and "local conditions rather than national ideologies determined party affiliation" (Diner 1992, 145). Nor were Jews yet sufficiently numerous to constitute a factor of significance in presidential or congressional elections. Jewish communal leaders typically, and often with vehemence, denied the existence of an ethnically motivated Jewish voting bloc, fearing that the image of Jewish clannishness and political power would stimulate anti-Semitism. By insisting that Jews voted as individuals, not according to narrow group interests, Jewish leaders believed that they might impress upon non-Jews that American Jews were Americans first and foremost. Despite fervent denials from Jewish spokesmen, the assumption that there exists a "Jewish vote" has consistently—and increasingly—persisted, among both anti-Semites and aspiring politicians, for most of the past 150 years.

The first occasion on which a national discussion about a "Jewish vote" arose was in the presidential contest of 1868, when critics of the Republican candidate, General Ulysses S. Grant, sought to mobilize Jewish opposition to Grant by drawing attention to Grant's Civil War edict ordering the mass expulsion of Jews from the Kentucky-Tennessee region. Newspapers backing the Democratic presidential nominee, governor Horatio Seymour of New York, raised the issue, but they were not the only ones to do so. Isaac Mayer Wise, a prominent Reform rabbi and editor of *The Israelite*, also attacked General Grant, and Jews in several cities staged anti-Grant protest meetings. At the most notorious of these gatherings, held in Memphis, speakers urged "that the only position Grant deserved to be elevated to was the one occupied by Haman in the last moments of his career." Repeatedly prodded by his Jewish supporters to say something on the issue, Grant eventually felt compelled, in mid-September, to release a statement expressing regret over the expulsion edict, which he claimed he had signed "without reflection." The absence of detailed voter trend statistics from that era renders it impossible to determine whether the anti-Grant protests influenced Jews to oppose him, or if his statement of regret persuaded Jews to support him.

It was only after the mass immigration to the United States of East European Jews during the last decades of the nineteenth century and the early twentieth that Jews began to reside in specific voting districts in sufficiently heavy concentrations to permit the measurement of Jewish voting patterns. Socialist Labor Party leader Daniel

DeLeon, an assimilated Sephardic Jew, unsuccessfully ran for Congress from the Lower East Side in 1892 and 1894, garnering 10 and 18 percent of the vote, respectively. By contrast, socialist candidate Meyer London was elected to the House of Representatives—only the second socialist to win a congressional election—from a district on New York's heavily Jewish Lower East Side in 1914; he was re-elected in 1916.

To deduce from DeLeon's defeat and London's victories a significant rise in Jewish immigrant support for socialism would, however, be mistaken, as the 1917 New York mayoral contest demonstrated. The only Jew among the four candidates was a socialist, Morris Hilquit. But Hilquit was also a devout pacifist, at a time when the United States was at war. Jews who were deeply committed to pacifism, such as Rabbi Judah Magnes, backed Hilquit. But for most Jewish voters, Hilquit's pacifism was a drawback, not an asset. An outspoken Jewish pacifist politician might provoke accusations that the Jews were not loyal to America's war effort. There was also opposition from the Zionists, a small but growing force in the New York Jewish community, who disliked Hilquit because of his role in the withdrawal of the radical socialist faction from that year's American Jewish Congress. Hilquit received just 12.7 percent of the citywide vote. Only about 30 percent of his 145,000 votes came from the borough of Manhattan—where most of the city's Jews lived—and less than 20 percent of his Manhattan votes came from the heavily Jewish East Side. The Jews' rejection of Hilquit was by no means a rejection of socialism, however, for on that same election day, eleven socialists were elected to the New York State Assembly, seven were chosen as New York City aldermen, and another was elected municipal judge. Many Jewish voters had some sympathy for socialism, but they were interested in other issues as well, particularly issues directly pertaining to Jewish interests. Radical Jewish socialists such as Hilquit were often highly assimilated and out of touch with Jewish concerns. Hilquit had taken part in the controversial "Yom Kippur Balls" of the 1880s, in which young militants demonstrated their antipathy for Judaism with lavish banquets on a day traditionally reserved for fasting, prayer, and penitence. Although some Jewish socialists at least flirted with Zionism, Hilquit remained staunchly anti-Zionist. He even favored some restrictions on immigration—not a surprising position for a champion of labor, but unquestionably damaging to a candidate in a district heavily populated by immigrants. Daniel DeLeon's position on immigration had likewise harmed his chances in the congressional races of 1892 and 1894. Hilquit's congressional campaigns in 1906 and 1908 included no appeals to Jewish ethnic interests, and he had lost badly. Facing up to political reality, Hilquit began shifting his position on immigration, and by 1910 he spoke in language not far from that of advocates of keeping America's doors open. His campaigns for Congress in 1916 and mayor in 1917, while still unsuccessful, netted him substantial gains compared with his earlier races. Meyer London, by contrast, understood early on the need to address Jewish concerns; Hilquit realized it too late, and he paid the price.

In the presidential elections of the early 1900s, no pattern of Jewish voting was yet discernible. In the 1916 contest—the first election for which a reliable Jewish vote estimate is available—55 percent of Jews supported Democrat Woodrow Wilson, while 45 percent voted for his Republican opponent. Four years later, however, the Democrat, James Cox, captured just 19 percent of Jewish votes, far behind both Republican Warren Harding, who won 43 percent, and socialist candidate Eugene Debs, at 38 percent. In 1924 the Jewish vote fractured again: 51 percent of Jews voted for Democrat John Davis, 27 percent for Republican nominee Calvin Coolidge, and 22 percent for the Progressive Party candidate, Senator Robert La Follette.

A number of factors were responsible for the significant drop in Jewish support for third-party presidential candidates. The postwar Red Scares, with their anticommunist and antiforeigner hysteria, intimidated some Jews into casting aside their socialist sympathies lest they endanger their status as full Americans. For others, a tempering of the radical views of their youth was a natural part of the process of adjusting to life in their new country. In any event, the overall character of the Jewish community was changing. Immigration had dropped sharply during the war, and then it was drastically restricted by the enactment of tight quotas in 1921 and 1924. By the late 1920s, the great waves of East European immigrants had already been in America for a decade or more; there were simply fewer and fewer new immigrants—that is, fewer of those most likely to lean toward socialism because of their experiences in Russia. Those who voted for Debs or La Follette found a new home in the Democratic Party, which was aggressively courting ethnic minorities. In 1928 the Democrats took the unprecedented step of nominating a Catholic, New York governor Alfred E. Smith, as their candidate for president. Jews felt an affinity for Smith because he presumably understood the difficulties of being part of a religious minority group, and they gave him 72 percent of their votes.

Jewish support for the Democratic presidential candidate also reflected a broader phenomenon: the emergence of the post–World

War I Democratic Party as "a house for all peoples" (Allswang 1971). As part of a concerted strategy to woo the sizable ethnic voting blocs of urban America, Democratic Party strategists took sympathetic positions on issues of ethnic concern, included ethnic candidates on party tickets, and doled out patronage jobs accordingly. Immigrants who arrived in the years between the end of World War I and the imposition of immigration quotas became naturalized citizens during the mid to late 1920s and began to form their first serious long-term political attachments. The Democrats made their move at just the right moment, and the Jews were among the crucial constituencies they successfully recruited.

The new alliance between Jews and Democrats, which the nomination of Smith helped forge, continued with the choice of Franklin D. Roosevelt in 1932, and it soon evolved into the stuff of which political legends are made. Jewish support for FDR in subsequent presidential races was so strong as to give rise to a Yiddish joke that played on the word for world, *velt*, by describing a Republican politician as complaining that the Jews seem to have three "velt"s: this *velt*, the *velt* to come, and Roosevelt (Howe 1976, 393). More than 80 percent of American Jews voted for FDR in 1932, and more than 90 percent supported his re-election in 1936, 1940, and 1944. One reason for this high level of Jewish support was the fact that Roosevelt appointed a number of Jews to senior advisory positions; this attitude of inclusiveness had strong appeal to the Jewish community, particularly when contrasted with the Republicans' reputation as the party of white, Anglo-Saxon Protestants. The New Deal's emphasis on labor rights, unemployment insurance, social security, and similar worker benefits appealed strongly to a community that consisted in large measure of first- and second-generation immigrant laborers.

Roosevelt's approach to relations with Nazi Germany during the 1930s further cemented American Jewish affection for him: while the Republicans urged isolationism and were reluctant to enter into even verbal confrontations with Germany, Roosevelt issued a number of statements critical of the Nazis and was gradually moving the United States toward military preparedness. The president's refusal to permit the entry of substantial numbers of German Jewish immigrants during the 1930s was a source of some disappointment in the Jewish community, but FDR's position was generally interpreted by American Jews as unavoidable in view of the intense restrictionist mood in Congress.

The first signs of Jewish dissatisfaction with Roosevelt became apparent in 1943–1944, when FDR's reluctance to aid the refugees took on a particularly grim meaning in the wake of confirmation of the news of Hitler's genocide. Articles in the Yiddish-language press in the autumn of 1943 began raising questions about the Allies' apparent indifference to the plight of the Jews, and a columnist for one of the leading newspapers, *Der Tog*, bluntly warned the Roosevelt administration that it could no longer "take it for granted" that the Jewish vote would go for FDR in 1944.

One Jewish activist, surveying the political scene in December 1943 in the context of FDR's failure to aid European Jewry and reluctance to support Jewish statehood in Palestine, wrote: "It is typical today to hear public orators at Jewish public gatherings saying that Jesus was not the Messiah nor apparently is Mr. Roosevelt." Meanwhile, potential Republican presidential candidates Thomas Dewey and Wendell Willkie were suddenly championing Jewish causes; a distressed Vice President Henry Wallace noted in his diary "how vigorously Willkie is going to town for Palestine." FDR certainly heard his share of advice about the possibility of losing Jewish votes. At a White House luncheon for Winston Churchill earlier that year, FDR had spoken of the need to maintain good relations with the Arab countries in order to have a bloc of friendly states in the Mediterranean region; Churchill replied by pointing out that "there were more Jews than Arab votes in the Anglo-Saxon countries and we could not afford to ignore such practical considerations."

The issue shifted into high gear in December 1943, at congressional hearings over a resolution introduced by Jewish activists urging the creation of a government agency to rescue refugees from Hitler. Assistant Secretary of State Breckinridge Long, testifying at the hearings, gave intentionally misleading testimony about the number of refugees who had so far been admitted to the United States. Long's deception, quickly exposed by Jewish organizations, triggered a storm of protest in the press and galvanized Treasury Secretary Henry Morgenthau, who was already steaming over his recent discovery that anti-Semitism in the State Department was one of the major obstacles to U.S. action on behalf of Europe's Jews. Morgenthau was also worried that all the bad press FDR was getting would result in Jewish voters defecting to the Republicans in 1944. FDR's re-election was by no means a certainty, and New York state, with its large Jewish voting bloc, would be crucial. Morgenthau and his aides drew up a stinging report about the State Department's attitudes and met with Roosevelt adviser Ben Cohen to discuss how best to approach the president on the issue. Cohen told them: "[T]here is also a factor which you don't want to put in the memorandum [to FDR] which will influence the

President and influence [Secretary of State Cordell] Hull. We all know that during this political year minorities are being exploited. . . . [A]ll the politicians are trying to exploit the value of minority groups, and the situation has gotten to the point where something has to be done." Morgenthau, too, feared the election-year danger of the congressional rescue resolution becoming a "boiling pot on [Capitol] Hill" that could explode into a nasty scandal. Roosevelt's State Department would be revealed as having intentionally obstructed rescue.

At the urging of Morgenthau, Roosevelt undertook a gesture intended to pull the rug out from under his critics and deprive the Republicans of an opportunity to chip away at one of his most loyal constituencies. Rather than endure additional messy Congressional hearings over the rescue resolution, FDR announced the formation of the War Refugee Board (WRB), a governmental agency with the express task of rescuing Jews from Hitler. The creation of the WRB was greeted by the Jewish community as, in the words of the AJ Congress, "a healing balm applied to the wound which has long tormented American Jewry." Despite its limited powers and meager funds, the board rescued many tens of thousands of Jews during the final months of the war.

Case Study: How Others Viewed the Creation of the War Refugee Board

In politics, perception is sometimes as important as reality. Both in London and Washington, the creation of the War Refugee Board was widely perceived as an attempt to appease Jewish voters. In his year-end review of U.S. politics for 1943, the British ambassador in Washington, referring to increased protests on "the Palestine and European refugee issues," predicted "that some sort of reaction by the United States Administration to both these pressures is sooner or later bound to occur as four million voters in an election year are not to be ignored." Sir Herbert Emerson, who visited the United States subsequent to the establishment of the WRB, reported back to British foreign minister Anthony Eden that the Roosevelt administration had indeed succumbed to pressure for creation of the WRB because "the Jewish vote is large, and this is particularly the case in New York State, which is of first-rate importance in a Presidential election." The State Department's Breckinridge Long privately praised the establishment of the WRB as "a good move—for local political reasons—for

there are 4 million Jews in New York and its environs who feel themselves related to the refugees and because of the persecutions of the
Jews, who have been demanding special attention and treatment.
This will encourage them to think the persecuted may be saved and
may possibly satisfy them—politically." Long's interpretation dove-
tails with internal memoranda of Democratic Party officials in New
York state, showing that they were deeply concerned that the Republicans would win New York in November.

FDR's gesture provided American Jews with the reassurance that
they had longed for: that they did have a friend in the White House;
that the obstacles to rescue had been planted by nameless bureaucrats rather than by the president himself; and perhaps most important of all, that the establishment of the War Refugee Board was in effect a declaration by the highest authority in the land that American
Jewish concerns about the Nazi genocide were not un-American but
could fit comfortably within America's war policy, just as American
Jews could fit comfortably within the American body politic. Roosevelt scored some additional points with Jewish voters that summer,
when he announced that 982 European refugees, most of them Jews,
would be brought to a temporary safe haven in upstate New York. Although there were some rumblings of criticism by Jewish activists
who regarded the safe haven plan as too little, too late, there was
even more criticism in the Jewish community of Governor Dewey's
vice presidential running mate, John Bricker, when he denounced
the safe haven camp on the grounds that the refugees were not the
"palefaced women and frail children" that had been depicted in the
press but rather seemed to be "writers, lawyers, artists and intellectuals generally." Bricker's remarks about the refugees came shortly after
another unpleasant controversy in which Bricker at first accepted,
and only later disavowed, an endorsement from Gerald L. K. Smith,
one of America's most prominent anti-Semitic agitators.

The Bricker controversies were a reminder to the Jewish community that a significant part of the Republican Party was still in the
hands of those with whom Jews were the least comfortable, politically, socially, and culturally. Roosevelt might not be the Messiah,
and some of his positions on Jewish issues might have left something
to be desired, but when the alternative was the likes of John Bricker,
it is not surprising that the vast majority of Jewish voters cast their
ballots for FDR in November 1944, just as they had in the three previous presidential elections.

Case Study: The "Palestine Plank" in the 1944 Platforms

The ascent of the activist-minded Rabbi Abba Hillel Silver to the helm of the American Zionist movement in 1943 signaled the beginning of an important political realignment in the Jewish community. Silver, of Cincinnati, had endorsed Wendell Willkie for president in 1940 and enjoyed close ties to U.S. senator Robert Taft and other prominent Republicans—in sharp contrast to the Zionist leader Silver had usurped, Rabbi Stephen Wise, a loyal New Deal Democrat with ties to Roosevelt. For the first time, mainstream Zionists made a major effort to seek support for their agenda from the Republican Party. On the eve of the 1944 Republican convention, the Zionists lobbied energetically for a plank endorsing free Jewish immigration to Palestine and eventual Jewish statehood. The final text not only endorsed statehood but also directly criticized Roosevelt:

> In order to give refuge to millions of distressed Jewish men, women and children driven from their homes by tyranny, we call for the opening of Palestine to their unrestricted immigration and land ownership, so that in accordance with the full intent and purpose of the Balfour Declaration of 1917 and the Resolution of a Republican Congress in 1922, Palestine may be constituted as a free and democratic Commonwealth. We condemn the failure of the President to insist that the mandatory of Palestine carry out the provision of the Balfour Declaration and of the mandate while he pretends to support them.

By wooing the Republicans, the Zionists put the Democrats on the defensive—now they would have to include a comparable plank, or risk a backlash among Jewish voters. At their convention, the Democrats endorsed "unrestricted Jewish immigration and colonization" to be followed by the establishment of "a free and democratic Jewish commonwealth." For the first time, both major parties were openly recognizing the significance of the Jewish vote and actively courting it. The ramifications of the two parties' resolutions extended well beyond the American political scene. The ability of Zionist lobbyists to convince both major parties to go on record in favor of Jewish statehood also sent a powerful message to the British government, which ruled Palestine. England would need America's help after the war, and American Jewish political power was emerging as a factor in the shaping of America's postwar Middle East policy.

The future of Palestine emerged as the predominant issue of concern for Jewish voters in the immediate postwar period. Jewish rebels battled British troops for control of Palestine, while boatloads of Holocaust survivors seeking to enter the Holy Land in defiance of British immigration restrictions clashed with the British Navy in the Mediterranean, generating scenes of anguish that rallied world public opinion to Zionism's side. The turmoil overseas triggered a huge groundswell of support among American Jews for the cause of Jewish statehood, with serious ramifications at the ballot box. The Truman administration's support for its British ally stirred growing criticism in the Jewish community, and by the autumn of 1946, Democratic Party officials were warning the president that Jewish voters would support the Republican mayoral candidate in New York unless there was a clear shift by the president in favor of Zionism. Truman used the occasion of Yom Kippur, the Jewish holy day, which that year fortuitously fell just before the mayoral election, to issue a statement implicitly endorsing the idea of a Jewish state for the first time. Despite Truman's vague wording, the statement was hailed by the Jewish press as if it were a full-fledged embrace of Zionism. The following year, the Truman administration strongly supported the UN resolution recommending partition of Palestine into Jewish and Arab states.

As Jewish-British clashes intensified during the spring of 1948, however, the administration began to backpedal, proposing that the United Nations be granted a trusteeship over Palestine instead of partitioning it. Jewish voters in New York found the opportunity to respond when Member of Congress Benjamin Rabin, from the Bronx, resigned to take a seat on the New York State Supreme Court, forcing an off-year election to fill the vacancy. Former state assemblyman Leo Isaacson, nominated by the American Labor Party, devoted much of his campaign to denouncing the Truman administration's embargo on weapons to the Middle East, and he swept the four-candidate race with 56 percent of the vote. Political analysts saw the results as a boost for the third-party presidential candidacy of former vice president Henry Wallace, with whom Isaacson was allied. In the Jewish community, Isaacson's victory was trumpeted as a message to the Truman administration about the importance of the Jewish statehood issue to Jewish voters and the possible electoral ramifications if Truman adopted a pro-Arab policy.

Truman was able to recoup his standing in the Jewish community in May, by extending de facto recognition to Israel just minutes after its declaration of independence. The Truman administration's embargo on arms to the Middle East might well have hurt the Democrats at the polls had the danger to Israel persisted until election day. Instead, however, weapons provided to Israel by Soviet-bloc countries, particularly Czechoslovakia, helped make up for the refusal by the United States to provide arms, and by the autumn most of the fighting was over and Israel had clearly emerged victorious. At that point, Truman's embargo seemed to have had no practical impact, and Truman's speedy recognition of Israel served as a reassurance to Jewish voters of his basic sympathy for the new Jewish state.

Truman's share of the Jewish vote in November did not reach the level that Roosevelt had attained, but that was only because the third-party candidacy of former vice president Henry Wallace siphoned off some Jewish votes from the Democrats. Wallace did especially well in heavily Jewish neighborhoods in New York, Connecticut, and Los Angeles. The combined total of Jewish votes for Truman and Wallace was almost as large as that cast for FDR four years earlier.

The 1952 presidential contest between General Dwight Eisenhower, the Republican, and liberal Democratic senator Adlai Stevenson further confirmed American Jewry's overwhelming preference for the Democrats, although Stevenson won only about 64 percent of Jewish votes, a considerable drop from the levels attained by Roosevelt and Truman. Eisenhower's appeal as a hero of the U.S. victory over Nazi Germany may have helped draw some Jewish votes away from the Democrats. In 1956, however, America went to the polls just days after the eruption of the Sinai War, with the Eisenhower administration forcefully expressing its disapproval of Israel's pre-emptive strike against the Egyptian military buildup. But with Stevenson reluctant to defend Israel's action, the Middle East did not become an issue in the campaign. Indeed, Eisenhower actually did better among Jews than he had four years earlier, winning about 40 percent.

The Jewish majority for Stevenson in 1952 and again in 1956 marked the first instance of a significant deviation of Jewish voting patterns from those of the rest of the country in a presidential race. In 1952, among voters in general, there was a clear shift of Truman and Wallace votes to Eisenhower. But the number of Jewish voters who joined the shift was minuscule. The large Jewish vote for the Democrat, liberal U.S. senator Adlai Stevenson, could not be explained by income, education, age, or level of religious observance, since Stevenson received overwhelming support from Jews from all types within those categories. Lawrence Fuchs has argued that the widespread "Jewish support for internationalism and liberal government," which Stevenson embodied, is "deeply rooted in the history and character of the Jewish people." According to Fuchs, the Jews' "ethno-religious values of Learning, Charity and Nonasceticism" motivated their support for Woodrow Wilson, Senator Stevenson, and Roosevelt, with a special affection for the circle of intellectuals that formed FDR's brain-trust (Fuchs 1968, 73). The Fuchs theory linking Jewish traditional values to liberal voting patterns would begin to wear thin in the years to follow, as those Jews who were least attached to Jewish tradition continued to vote primarily for liberal Democrats, while those who observed tradition most strictly increasingly turned away from liberalism.

From 1952 through 1968, Jewish support for Democratic presidential candidates consistently ran 20 to 30 percent higher than that of the general population, reaching a peak difference of 42 percent in the Humphrey-Nixon contest of 1968 before narrowing in 1972, 1976, and especially 1980. Surveys of Jews' party affiliations have likewise found trends that are significantly out of step with the rest of the country. From 1952 through 1982, the percentage of Jews identifying themselves as Democrats was typically 55 to 60 percent, with 25 to 35 percent independents, and never more than 15 percent Republicans.

Although Jewish electoral support for Democratic presidential candidates in the 1960s reached levels comparable to those of the Roosevelt years, by the end of the decade it was possible to find some signs of change in Jewish voting patterns. Senator John F. Kennedy attracted 75 to 80 percent of Jewish votes in his 1960 race against Vice President Richard Nixon (compared with 50 percent of the general public), and Lyndon Johnson won 90 percent (and 61 percent overall) versus Senator Barry Goldwater in 1964. Nixon's association with the excesses of the McCarthy era, and Goldwater's ties to extreme conservatives, reduced the normally low level of Jewish support for the GOP even further. Senator Hubert H. Humphrey received 81 percent of the Jewish vote against Nixon four years later.

A somewhat more detailed explanation of Hubert Humphrey's Jewish support is possible thanks to the increasingly sophisticated voter data analysis undertaken by the late 1960s. According to an American Jewish Committee (AJ Committee) study, Humphrey received at least 70 to 75 percent of the Jewish vote, and perhaps as much as 80 percent or more (compared with 43 percent of the public at large). These figures were somewhat higher than the estimates of pre-election polls, some of which forecast a noticeable gain for the Republicans among Jewish voters. The AJ Committee attributed the final figures to two main factors: first, Jews who had supported U.S.

senator Eugene McCarthy in the Democratic primaries, and who may have been initially reluctant to express support for Humphrey when questioned by pollsters, returned to the Democrats when election day came; second, some Jewish voters underwent what the AJ Committee characterized as "polling booth trauma"—that is, Jewish voters who were not entirely enthusiastic about Humphrey and therefore indicated to pollsters that they would vote for Nixon then had a change of heart in the voting booth and could not bring themselves to vote for the GOP candidate. "The sentiment expressed in the polls but suppressed at the polling booths may be indicative of a new Jewish ambivalence with regard to liberalism in American politics," the study concluded (American Jewish Committee 1968, 9).

On the local level, however, election results as early as 1963 contained evidence of Jewish voters deviating from traditional liberalism. That year's election to the nonpartisan Boston School Committee focused on a charge by the local NAACP that de facto segregation was being practiced in the city's schools. Four of the five incumbent committee members emphatically rejected the charge; the fifth asked for a study of the matter. In the election for committee seats in November 1963, the candidates included all five incumbents plus a prominent black supporter of the NAACP. Galvanized by the controversy, more than twice as many Bostonians voted in the 1963 race as had cast ballots in the School Committee election two years earlier. The four incumbents who had criticized the NAACP's stand were elected; the fifth was not, nor was the African-American candidate. The majority of Jews, like the majority of other white ethnics, supported the incumbents. Heavily Jewish precincts voted 61 percent for the incumbents. Interestingly, however, areas with many Jewish voters were somewhat more liberal than other white neighborhoods, with 22 percent of Jewish votes in favor of the pro-NAACP candidates, compared with 13 percent in the mostly Italian and mostly Irish sections.

More early inklings of a possible shift away from Jewish electoral liberalism were apparent in Los Angeles in 1969, when conservative Sam Yorty defeated African-American councilman Tom Bradley for mayor. In the April 1969 nonparty primary, Bradley, running in a field of fourteen candidates, had received about half of Jewish votes, while Yorty, the runner-up, had won approximately one-fourth. As the date for the run-off election between the two approached, polls forecast that Bradley would receive from 72 to as much as 84 percent of Jewish votes. On the surface, the race bore all the characteristics that would anticipate overwhelming Jewish support for the Democratic candidate. The Republican was a conservative, and Jews had generally shied away from supporting conservatives; the Democrat was black, and Jews had generally supported African-American candidates in very large numbers. But by the autumn of 1969, Jewish concerns over rising inner-city crime, coming against a backdrop of well-publicized incidents of black anti-Semitism and Jewish disappointment with the New Left's toleration of extremism, combined to split the Jewish vote 54 to 46 percent for Bradley. There were comparable results in Philadelphia in 1971, when an estimated 50 percent of Jewish voters supported the mayoral candidacy of the conservative police commissioner, Frank Rizzo.

A 1973 survey by *New York* magazine of Jewish voters in New York City found indications of conservative leanings when it came to local concerns, especially on hot-button racial issues. Fully 65 percent of Jews said that they supported demonstrations by whites against a controversial low-income housing project in the mostly white (among them many Jews) Queens neighborhood of Forest Hills. In addition, 61 percent said that they supported antibusing boycotts in the Canarsie section of Brooklyn. The poll found that those Jews who were older or had lower incomes were more likely to be moderate or conservative in their voting preferences.

Analyses of the results in the New York and Los Angeles mayoral races of 1969 pointed to the emergence of a new factor in Jewish voting patterns: class. This contrasted with electoral patterns from the 1930s through the 1960s, when studies found that regardless of income levels, Jews voted overwhelmingly for liberal candidates. Among other white Americans, higher income levels have typically equaled more conservative political attitudes. In the 1969 Democratic mayoral primary in New York City, however, areas populated by significant numbers of lower-middle-class Jews, such as Boro Park and Far Rockaway, gave two to three times as many votes to conservative candidate Mario Procaccino as to his liberal rival, Herman Badillo. At the same time, the upper West Side of Manhattan, inhabited by many upper-middle-class Jews, voted three to one for Badillo. Similarly, in West Los Angeles and the city's suburban Valley communities, where Jews were typically younger, successful professionals affiliated with Reform temples, Bradley captured more than 80 percent of the vote; not surprisingly, these were neighborhoods located far from predominantly black areas. In the Fairfax section of the city, where Jews were typically older, not college graduates, earning lower incomes, and affiliated with traditionalist synagogues, Bradley won 50 to 60 percent of the vote. Fairfax is a section where "the possibility of school integration is real and in fact has occurred in many schools in the area" (Maller 1977, 162). Fear of the consequences of integration undoubtedly stirred many Jews to eschew traditional Jewish liberalism and instead vote according to perceived social and class interests, by supporting Yorty.

Was a new era in Jewish electoral trends underway by the 1970s? The political sociologist Murray Friedman, looking back from the vantage point of the mid-1980s, has described the period from 1945 to 1965 as a "Golden Age of American Jewry" in which there was "a notable decline in prejudice and discrimination. A civil rights revolution was underway that promised to realize the goal of equal opportunity for all. The United Nations had been put in place to wipe out the scourge of war. Buoyed by a wave of optimism and their growing integration in American society, Jewish political liberalism was at its zenith." By contrast, the years from 1965 to 1985, in Friedman's view, were an "Age of Anxiety," dominated by fears of crime, racial conflicts, and rising black anti-Semitism (Featherman 1984, iii).

Yet Jewish voting trends in national elections did not yet match those in Los Angeles and Philadelphia, suggesting that the results in those cities might be attributable to a dichotomy in local versus national concerns rather than a reflection of a general "Age of Anxiety." Perhaps they indicated that Jews casting ballots in elections for officials who would have a direct impact on their lives—such as the mayor of the city—were beginning to vote more like other Americans in their social and economic categories. When voting in national elections, which typically have far less direct or immediate impact on individual cities or neighborhoods, most Jewish voters tended to follow familiar patterns.

There were signs of change in Jewish voting in the 1972 national elections, but modest and tentative change at best. Some 80 percent of Jews voted for Democratic congressional candidates that year. Jewish voting in the presidential election, however, was not quite so lopsided: the AJ Committee's analysts estimated that 65 percent of Jews voted for liberal senator George McGovern, while 35 percent supported the re-election of President Nixon, the highest Jewish total for a Republican presidential candidate since the days of Abraham Lincoln. Nevertheless, Jewish voters remained almost a mirror image of the American public at large, only 38 percent of whom backed McGovern.

The AJ Committee detected several significant new voting trends within the Jewish community. First, "a defection from Democratic voting much more pronounced among middle-income and poor

Jews than among more prosperous ones." Second, although only a minority of Jews voted for Nixon, there were many others who chose not to vote rather than back McGovern, whose association with the New Left and unenthusiastic support for Israel made many Jewish voters wary. "[T]he rate of staying away [or voting in other races but not casting a ballot in the presidential contest] was substantially higher among middle-income and poor Jews," the AJ Committee found. "Especially for usually conscientious voters like these people, this in itself was clearly a form of voting. Adding the abstentions to the pulling of levers, we conclude that the middle-income and poor Jews voted for McGovern less than prosperous Jews."

As a means of comparison, the AJ Committee examined heavily Jewish voting districts in Brooklyn and Long Island where voters were generally similar in income, education, and age. It found a 61 percent rate of support for McGovern in the Brooklyn districts, down from the 84 percent that the previous Democratic presidential candidate, Hubert Humphrey, had received there in 1968. In the Long Island districts, McGovern attracted 69 percent, down from the 80 percent that voters there had given Humphrey four years earlier. "The Brooklyn people found it less difficult to pull the Republican lever," the AJ Committee study concluded. "We assume that the difference is to be accounted for primarily by the greater unhappiness, vulnerability, and disillusion of people who live in cities" (Himmelfarb and Yagerman 1972, 3).

In a later discussion of the 1972 results, one of the authors of the AJ Committee study, Milton Himmelfarb, pointed to an additional factor affecting the rate of Jewish abstentions from the presidential race: "Where the Democratic congressional candidate was a shoo-in most Jewish abstainers apparently stayed home. In districts where there was a contest, a good many Presidential abstainers apparently went to the polls to vote for Congressmen" (Himmelfarb 1989, 81). Overall, however, Himmelfarb found more continuity than discontinuity in that year's Jewish voting patterns: "Although American Jews had come economically to resemble the Episcopalians, the most prosperous of all white groups, their voting behavior continued to be most like the voting behavior of one of the least prosperous of all groups, the Puerto Ricans" (Himmelfarb 1989, 85).

The results of the 1974 midterm congressional elections seemed to confirm Himmelfarb's perspective; about 90 percent of Jewish voters supported Democrats. Stephen Isaacs attributed this lopsided figure to inflation during the Republican administration, post-Watergate disgust with the GOP in general, and what Isaacs called "penitence among those who forsook the Democratic Party in the 1972 Presidential election" (Isaacs 1974, 29).

When Jews went to the voting booths in 1976, however, the results were not quite what recent trends had seemed to foretell. There seemed to be good reason to expect overwhelming Jewish support for the Democratic candidate, former Georgia governor Jimmy Carter. Although most Jewish votes during the Democratic primaries had gone for Senator Henry Jackson, an outspoken champion of Soviet Jewry and Israel, the eventual victor, Governor Carter, positioned himself as a centrist and reiterated standard Democratic pledges of support for Israel; presumably Jewish voters would have found him more to their liking than Senator McGovern had been in 1972. Moreover, the Ford administration had recently suspended arms shipments to Israel for several months in order to increase pressure on the Israelis to surrender territory to Egypt; a Jewish backlash at the polls might have been expected.

How, then, to explain the fact that Ford managed to garner an estimated 30 percent of the Jewish vote, the second highest level of Jewish support for a Republican presidential candidate in the twentieth century? There may have been some Jews who felt uncomfortable with a candidate who was a Southern Baptist, a denomination traditionally associated with religious and cultural attitudes that discomfit many in the Jewish community. But those who might be troubled by Carter's religious views were more likely to be politically liberal and less likely to vote for a Republican. One factor explaining Ford's ability to capture a respectable share of Jewish support may be that the foreign policy clashes between his administration and Israel were generally attributed to Secretary of State Henry Kissinger, rather than to the president himself. In addition, the fact that Ford was not tainted by the Watergate scandal made it possible for Jewish conservatives to feel more comfortable in the ranks of the GOP. Furthermore, while a candidate such as Henry Jackson might have attracted Jewish Republicans because of his close and emotional link to Israel and Soviet Jewry, Carter, as the governor of a Southern state, had few occasions to take an interest in Israel or other Jewish matters and thus held no special attraction for wavering Jewish conservatives. Jews who normally voted Republican needed a compelling reason to defect; Carter did not give them one.

That was almost his undoing. For even though the Jewish vote for Carter was far out of proportion to that of the American public—70 percent as opposed to 51 percent—the vote was close enough in some states that even a partial Jewish swing to Ford could have changed the entire outcome of the election. If 10,000 Jewish voters had switched from Carter to Ford in Ohio, the president would have won the state and, with it, sufficient electoral votes to win the election. In New York state, 80 percent of Jews voted for Carter—but had the Jewish votes split 50–50, Ford would have captured the state and the election.

The results of 1976 demonstrated anew the strategic significance of the Jewish vote, despite its comparatively small size overall. The high level of Jewish participation in the political system significantly boosts the community's political power. Thus while surveys found that Jews were only 3 percent of the national population in 1980, they constituted more than 4 percent of all voters, because at least 80 percent of registered Jewish voters do cast ballots. Some studies have estimated that more than 90 percent of Jews actually vote, compared with 45 to 55 percent of Americans in general. These trends once prompted *The Economist* to remark: "A campaign rule of thumb is to multiply the Jewish voting-age population by three to get their true weight in a primary election and by two for a general election" (September 13, 1980).

The presidential election of 1980 marked the most significant shift of Jewish votes in U.S. political history. A series of controversies during the preceding two years augured change. In the spring of 1978, the Carter administration had proposed to sell advanced fighter aircraft to Egypt and Saudi Arabia. Fearing that the planes might one day be turned against Israel, Jewish activists mounted a major lobbying effort in Congress to block the sales. By coincidence, it was at the height of the plane sale battle that NBC Television aired "Holocaust," a miniseries dramatizing the Nazi persecution of European Jewry. The Jewish community's failure to block the jet sales, combined with the emotions generated by the broadcast of "Holocaust," deepened American Jewry's feeling of isolation and vulnerability—sentiments that helped generate widespread Jewish disillusionment with President Carter. Those feelings were compounded by Carter's escalating pressure on Israel, in 1979–1980, to make substantial concessions in its negotiations with Egypt; the revelation that the U.S. ambassador to the United Nations, Andrew Young, had, contrary to official U.S. policy, met with representatives of the Palestine Liberation Organization; and the administration's vote in favor of a U.N. Security Council resolution branding Jerusalem "occupied Arab territory."

In an effort to repair his relations with the Jewish community and regain their electoral support, Carter made a number of gestures calculated to soothe the Jewish community's outrage. Ambassador

Young was compelled to resign; Carter publicly apologized for the vote at the United Nations, insisting that it took place without his approval; and his administration helped bring about the establishment of the U.S. Holocaust Memorial Museum and the Justice Department's unit for tracking down Nazi war criminals, the Office of Special Investigations (OSI). Carter and his aides also assumed that his role in brokering the Camp David accords between Israel and Egypt, which most American Jews applauded, would make up for some of the anger provoked by his clashes with the Israeli government.

But actions such as the apology for the U.N. vote were perceived as cynical attempts to lure back Jewish voters, and credit for the creation of the OSI went largely to its chief sponsor on Capitol Hill, the popular Brooklyn member of Congress Elizabeth Holtzman. The cumulative impact of Carter's conflicts with Israel left most American Jews convinced that he was, in his heart, unsympathetic toward the Jewish state. Senator Edward Kennedy was the prime beneficiary of the anti-Carter mood in the Jewish community, winning the overwhelming majority of Jewish votes in Democratic primaries in New York, Florida, and elsewhere during the spring of 1980. When Carter nonetheless defeated Kennedy for the nomination, an unprecedented number of Jewish voters defected from the Democrats. Carter won only 40 to 45 percent of Jewish votes, the lowest total for a Democratic presidential candidate in modern times. Conservative Republican Ronald Reagan, who lacked foreign policy experience but spoke out strongly in support of Israel during the campaign, won 39 to 40 percent of the Jewish vote. Former member of Congress John Anderson, a liberal Republican running as an independent, won approximately 15 percent of the Jewish vote.

Reagan's conservative positions on domestic issues differed dramatically from those of most American Jews, accounting for his inability to win a majority of the Jewish vote. A series of Gallup polls during 1970–1973 found 51 percent of Jews describing themselves as liberal—by contrast with 27 percent of Catholics and 22 percent of Protestants. A *New York Times*/CBS survey in 1980 already hinted at the beginnings of a shift in attitudes among American Jews as well: only 38 percent now called themselves liberals, compared with 23 percent of Catholics and 17 percent of Protestants. Polls taken during the early 1980s found Jews much more inclined to advocate liberal positions on a variety of issues: 49 percent of Jews opposed increased defense spending as opposed to 33 percent of Americans in general; 58 percent of Jews, versus 35 percent of the public at large, opposed reductions in social spending; and 67 percent of Jews favored permitting avowed homosexuals to teach in public schools, while only 45 percent of all Americans felt that way. Yet the number of Jews who voted for Carter was far lower than the number who agreed with Carter's liberal positions on domestic issues. How to explain that discrepancy? Murray Friedman: "It is only when direct Jewish interests are involved, such as racial quotas and racial balance in the schools and direct threats to the security of Israel, that Jews tend to become more conservative" (Featherman 1984, v–vi). Carter's Middle East policy was perceived by many Jewish voters as a direct threat to Israeli security, thus prompting them to undertake the unprecedented step of voting for a conservative Republican.

The 1980 vote also signaled a trend toward political conservatism among younger Jews, and among the Orthodox. An estimated 36 percent of Reform, Conservative, and unaffiliated Jews voted for Reagan, while 60 percent of Orthodox Jews, and 94 percent of Hassidic Orthodox Jews, did so. Although 37 percent of Jews over the age of fifty voted for Reagan, 59 percent of Jews under thirty did so. Although only 17 percent of all Jews identified themselves as Republicans in 1980, 32 percent of those under thirty did so. In local elections in which no pressing Jewish issue was at stake, however, the traditional heavily Democratic voting trend in the Jewish community often persisted. In California's 1982 gubernatorial contest, for example, the liberal African-American mayor of Los Angeles, Tom Bradley, won 75 percent of Jewish votes in his unsuccessful race against conservative Republican George Deukmejian, and in New York, Mario Cuomo was elected governor with 64 percent of the Jewish vote over a conservative Jewish Republican, Lewis Lehrman. Overall, 72 percent of Jewish votes went for Democratic candidates that year.

Case Study: The Jewish Vote in Presidential Primaries

Several factors magnify the power of Jewish voters. The first is the concentration of Jewish voters in key electoral states: in 1980, approximately three of every eight voters in New York state were Jewish, although by 1984 that was reduced to two of eight—still quite a formidable force—because of an increasing number of African-American voters. Other important electoral states with sufficient Jewish votes to tip any given election include: Illinois, 5 percent; California, 6 percent; Pennsylvania, 7 percent; Florida, 10 percent; and New Jersey, 12 percent. Second is the high rate of Jewish voter turnout: although the figures vary from election to election, Jewish participation in voting is typically about 10 percent higher than the level for the general population.

Since more than 50 percent of Jews typically register as Democrats—compared with only about 10 percent registered as Republicans—Jewish voters have the potential to make a significant impact on the Democratic presidential primaries. Jewish voters typically feel freer to vote in accordance with ethnic concerns in the primaries than they do in a presidential contest. Some Jews are psychologically uncomfortable voting for a Republican presidential candidate, with whom they are likely to disagree on domestic issues even if the candidate is strongly pro-Israel; they would desert their party only if the Democratic nominee were blatantly inimical to Jewish interests. But no such worries obtain in a party's primary contest, where Jews can feel free to cast ballots for a candidate primarily on the basis of Jewish ethnic interests without abandoning traditional party loyalties. This creates a political dynamic in which Democratic presidential candidates vying for Jewish votes must evince particular sensitivity to matters of Jewish concern, since their positions on domestic issues are not likely to differ dramatically from those of their party rivals and therefore will not suffice, in and of themselves, to attract Jewish support.

In 1984, for example, one leading candidate, Senator Gary Hart, aroused Jewish criticism when he said that he regarded the Reverend Jesse Jackson as a potential running mate. Jackson had recently been the focus of national controversy for making derogatory statements about Jews, and Jews registered their dissatisfaction by supporting former vice president Walter Mondale over Hart by a more than two-to-one margin in the New York primary. The Jewish vote was squarely in Mondale's column in the primaries in California, New Jersey, and Pennsylvania, as well.

Jews did not vote for Reagan in 1980 so much as they voted against Carter. Hence it was not difficult for Walter Mondale to bring most Jewish voters back to the Democratic fold four years later. With his pro-Israel voting record in the Senate and his determination to distance himself from both Jesse Jackson and the memories of Jimmy Carter's Mideast policy, Mondale succeeded in persuading most American Jews that it was time to return to the Democratic fold. The New York Times/CBS poll found that 66 percent of Jews backed Mondale, while 32 percent supported President Reagan. With both candidates perceived as strongly pro-Israel, Jewish voters could afford the luxury of casting their ballots based on domestic considerations, such as their fear of Reagan's ties to evangelical Christian conservatives versus their fear that many Democrats were too receptive to the Reverend Jackson and his militant agenda. "Had the election occurred in the midst of the Democratic turbulence over Jackson's [anti-Semitic] remarks, and his failure to denounce the Rev. Louis Farrakhan, it is possible that Ronald Reagan would have received a greater portion of the Jewish vote," according to an AJ Committee report on the election.

But the Jackson dispute faded from public view long before the November election and seems to have had little effect on the Jewish vote, which in the end went for the Democrat by a more than two-to-one margin, true to American Jewish voting traditions. Indeed, Jews were the only group of white voters to give Reagan fewer votes in 1984 than they had given him in 1980. Interestingly, however, the results did offer some clues as to the likely direction of future Jewish voting patterns. An analysis by the Jewish Community Relations Council of New York calculated that while the overall Jewish vote for Reagan was 32 percent, it reached 43 percent in New York City. Reagan's Jewish supporters included 85 percent of the Orthodox.

In a related finding, Deborah Lipstadt, Charles Pruitt, and Jonathan Woocher (1984), analyzing how Jews describe themselves politically, concluded that while all Jewish liberals, some Jewish moderates, and even some Jewish conservatives identify themselves as Democrats, "only half or less of the Jews who call themselves conservatives identify as Republicans. It's as if conservatism has gained a measure of respectability within the Jewish community that Republicanism has not" (38). In their own survey of political views of the United Jewish Appeal Young Leadership, they found 22 percent to be conservatives but only 12 percent Republicans.

Irving Kristol, writing in 1984, cited three factors responsible for "uneasiness and discomfort" among Jewish voters. First, the emergence of Jesse Jackson, a militant, as the preeminent black leader, rather than a moderate in the model of the African-American activists with whom Jews had worked closely during the early 1960s. Second, the rise of the Moral Majority, a conservative Christian movement that was fervently pro-Israel but at odds with Jewish positions on most domestic issues. Third, the sharply anti-Israel turn of the United Nations in the 1970s, shattering the utopian view of that organization that had been common among many Jews since the 1947 UN resolution supporting the establishment of a Jewish state in Palestine.

Mayoral elections in the late 1980s and into the 1990s offered additional evidence of shifting Jewish attitudes. In Chicago, for example, where in 1983 the Jewish vote had provided the margin of victory for liberal African-American Harold Washington, by 1989 Jewish voters gave 83 percent of their votes in the Democratic primary to conservative Richard M. Daley (son of the former mayor), ousting the African-American acting mayor, Eugene Sawyer. In the heavily Jewish 50th Ward on Chicago's north side, Daley trounced Sawyer by an eight-to-one margin; likewise, he won 75 percent of the vote in the district known for its population of "lakefront liberals," many of them Jews. Local outbursts of black anti-Semitism played a key role in driving Jews into the Daley camp: the year before the election, Sawyer aide Steve Cokely accused Jewish doctors of injecting African-American infants with the HIV virus; Sawyer's six-day delay in firing Cokely disillusioned many Jewish voters. Several weeks later, an enraged black city alderman ripped down a student's satirical portrait of then-mayor Harold Washington in the Chicago Art Institute; one alderman's false assertion that the painter was a Jew made an ugly incident even uglier, and the political ramifications were felt the following year.

Comparable results in other mayoral elections in recent years have likewise confounded traditional assumptions about Jewish voters and liberalism. Republican mayoral candidate Bob Lanier won 70 percent of the Jewish vote in Houston in 1991. The GOP's Richard Riordan captured an estimated 50 percent of Jewish votes in the 1993 mayoral race in Los Angeles, where Jewish voters make up approximately 15 percent of the electorate. Four years later Riordan won 67 percent (according to another analysis, 71 percent) of Jewish votes in defeating Democratic state senator Tom Hayden. In New York City in 1997, with Jews casting an estimated 22 percent of the actual ballots, Republican incumbent Rudolph Giuliani took 76 percent of the Jewish vote in his victory over liberal (and Jewish) Manhattan borough president Ruth Messinger.

Philadelphia provides an enlightening case study of evolving patterns of Jewish voting at the municipal level. About 50 percent of the city's Jews voted for the conservative police commissioner, Frank Rizzo, when he ran for mayor in 1971, and Rizzo captured 53 percent when he ran for re-election in 1974. Rizzo's slice of Jewish support fluctuated in subsequent elections, depending on different local factors each time. In the 1983 Democratic mayoral primary, Rizzo lost despite winning more than 67 percent of the votes in heavily Jewish areas. Some pundits speculated that part of the reason for his Jewish support was Rizzo's vocal backing for Israel and the fact that his opponent, liberal African-American Wilson Goode, was endorsed by the Rev. Jesse Jackson, a prominent critic of Israel. Traditionally, however, local elections revolve around local issues, and it is likely that the major reason for Jewish support for Rizzo had more to do with Rizzo's reputation as a law-and-order candidate at a time of continuing anxiety among white, middle-class voters about crime. Still, the traditional tendency of Jews to vote for liberal candidates was at least somewhat substantiated by the fact that although Goode received only about 31 percent of Jewish votes, that was still the largest amount he received among white ethnic groups. He won only 11 percent in predominantly Irish neighborhoods, 9 percent in Polish areas, and less than 5 percent among Italian-Americans.

In the general election Goode fared no better among Jews, despite the fact that he was endorsed by Rizzo and that 74 percent of Philadelphia's registered Jewish voters were registered as Democrats. Facing moderate Republican rival John Egan, Goode received only 32 percent of the Jewish vote, although that was again higher than what he received from the Irish (15.5 percent), Poles (13.5 percent), or Italians (13.5 percent). Even the lowest level of Jewish support Goode attracted in any one Jewish area, 16 percent, was higher than the mean level of support he attracted among other white ethnics. When it came to governing their city, Jewish voters in Philadelphia overwhelmingly defied expectations about their traditional liberalism.

In national elections, however, Jews continued to vote in overwhelming numbers for the Democratic candidate almost instinctively, unless they found a compelling reason to do otherwise. Alfonse D'Amato, a conservative Republican, won only 7 percent of the Jewish vote when he ran for the Senate in New York against two Jewish opponents, liberal Democrat Elizabeth Holtzman and liberal Republican Jacob Javits, in 1980. As the new incumbent, D'Amato gradually gained a reputation as a strong supporter of Israel, increasing his ability to attract Jewish support. He captured 34 percent of Jewish votes when challenged by liberal Democrat Mark Green in 1986. By 1992, D'Amato was so firmly ensconced as a champion of Israel that he was able to take 41 percent of the Jewish vote against the state's Jewish attorney general, Robert Abrams, who entered the campaign with an array of Jewish community connections on his resume. But in 1998, when the challenger was a fellow member of Congress with as pro-Israel a voting record as his own, D'Amato had met his match; 76 percent of Jewish voters, finding themselves closer to U.S. representative Charles Schumer on domestic issues while the two candidates seemed indistinguishable on Israel, cast their ballots for the Democrat.

Presidential contests during the late 1980s and into the mid-1990s offered few surprises as regards Jewish voting patterns. Liberal Democrat Michael Dukakis, a governor with no record concerning Israel, netted the Democrats' standard share of the Jewish vote, about 64 percent. Republican victor George Bush won 35 percent of Jewish votes, benefiting from having served as vice president in an administration widely perceived as pro-Israel, and from not having any obvious ties to Christian conservative movements.

Bush's share of the Jewish vote dropped sharply four years later, however, to the lowest ever for a GOP presidential candidate. His secretary of state, James Baker, had implemented Mideast policies that Jews regarded as pro-Arab, and at one point he was even widely reported to have used a slur against Jews. Bush himself antagonized the Jewish community by making distinctly unfriendly remarks about the pro-Israel lobby. Jewish voters were further troubled by the fact that at the 1992 Republican convention, extreme conservative Pat Buchanan was permitted to deliver a major address, in which he issued a call for a religious war against liberal domination of American culture. In such an atmosphere, only diehard Jewish conservatives supported Bush. Surveys estimated that Bush received only 10 to 15 percent of the Jewish vote in 1992, with third-party candidate Ross Perot receiving about 5 percent. The Democratic nominee, Arkansas governor Bill Clinton, had no previous record on Israel, but against a Republican candidate perceived by Jews as unfriendly to Israel, Clinton had only to affirm his party's standard pro-Israel rhetoric to ensure overwhelming Jewish support. Clinton captured 80 to 85 percent of Jewish votes, carrying ten of the eleven regions in which more than four-fifths of all American Jews reside. It was the largest share of the Jewish vote since Lyndon Johnson won 90 percent of Jewish votes in 1964 against Barry Goldwater.

In 1996 the Republicans were able to improve their share of the Jewish vote only marginally. Bill Clinton's record on Israel was generally considered to be friendly, while the Republican candidate, Senator Robert Dole, was not known as being especially sympathetic to Israel. Indeed, he had at one point advocated a modest reduction in U.S. aid to Israel, and on another occasion had publicly blamed Israel when Islamic terrorists in Lebanon kidnapped and murdered an American. Although Dole sought to distance himself from those previous positions, he received just 17 percent of Jewish votes.

Looking back over the period from 1972 to 1992, political analyst Jay Lefkowitz found continuity as well as change: "The Democrats appear to have retained their historic lock on well over half the Jewish vote; but the rest can swing. What controls the swing is the fear factor—the extent and depth of Jewish apprehensions on specific issues. Some of these apprehensions, concerning Israel, say, or racial politics, tend to move Jewish voters to the Right. Others, concerning the role of religion in public life and—more recently—abortion, move them to or keep them on the Left" (Lefkowitz 1993, 40).

Although Lefkowitz points to the theoretical possibility of Jews shifting to the right or left depending on particular issues or circumstances, it seems that if there is a detectable trend of any sort in Jewish voting patterns, it is to the right, not to the left. Consider the surprising results of a 1995 study of Jewish opinion in the San Francisco area—perhaps the most liberal Jewish community in the United States politically—by the local Jewish Community Relations Council. Political self-identification among the area's Jews offered few surprises: only 10 percent described themselves as conservative, while 41 percent identified themselves as liberal and 43 percent moderate. When asked their positions on specific issues, however, the respondents' answers were more complex. Not surprisingly, only 24 percent of self-described Jewish liberals favored reducing the size of government, while 88 percent of Jewish conservatives supported reducing it—as did 72 percent of Jewish moderates. Less than half of the liberals endorsed the "three strikes" law (mandating long prison terms for third-time criminal offenders), as contrasted with 92 percent of conservatives—and 75 percent of moderates. Likewise regarding affirmative action, welfare reform, and environmental protection, most Jewish moderates sided with the conservative position rather than the liberal one. On some issues, however, such as illegal immigration, government vouchers for private school tuition, abortion, and the involvement of Christian fundamentalists in political life, moderates did lean toward the liberal position. But the fact that they leaned right so often seemed another indicator that traditional Jewish liberalism can no longer be said to dominate the community. As political analyst Earl Raab concluded: "There will continue to be much truth in the notion that if you scratch an American Jew, you will find a Democratic voter. The complicating news today is that if you scratch somewhat deeper, you will not always find a liberal" (Raab 1996, 45).

The races in 2000 offered some predictable results as well as some surprising ones—and instructive lessons concerning the future power of the Jewish vote. Polls found that Jewish identification with the two major parties remained at traditional levels: 62 percent of Jewish voters consider themselves Democrats (as compared with 39 percent of all Americans) and only 13 percent Republicans (as compared with 35 percent of all Americans). In congressional elections around the country, Democratic candidates captured 74 percent of Jewish votes, while the GOP won just 24 percent. The most watched contest involved first lady Hillary Clinton versus conservative Republican member of Congress Rick Lazio for the vacant Senate seat from New York. Lazio's voting record was pro-Israel, but he was not well known in the Jewish community as a particular champion of Jewish or Israeli causes. Mrs. Clinton's stature among Jewish voters was harmed by her expressed sympathies for the Palestinian Arab cause, but her repeated pledges of support for Israel and her association with an administration perceived by most Jews as generally friendly to Israel offset much of that damage. In the end she won an estimated 53 percent of the Jewish vote—less than any previous victorious Senate candidate from New York, but more than enough to ensure her triumph over Lazio. The Republican did beat Mrs. Clinton by a 60 to 40 margin in heavily Orthodox neighborhoods in Brooklyn such as Flatbush and Boro Park, but her showing in those areas was surprisingly strong in view of how politically liberal candidates typically fare among Orthodox voters.

Jewish votes in the presidential contest of 2000 fell along familiar lines. Vice President Al Gore, a stalwart Israel supporter during his Senate days and the number two man in what was widely perceived as a pro-Israel administration, and having chosen a Jewish running mate, Senator Joseph Lieberman, won 78 percent of the Jewish vote. George Bush, a Southern governor with no record on Israel, captured just 20 percent of Jewish votes. Green Party candidate Ralph Nader, attracting only a fringe element in the Jewish community, won 1 percent. Yet despite these lopsided numbers, the country was reminded of the potential power of the Jewish vote when Florida turned out to be the key electoral state, and the state's voting results became the subject of a series of heated court battles. The extraordinarily thin margin of victory for Bush demonstrated anew that even a relatively small ethnic voting bloc can have decisive influence in a close race. At one point in the postelection challenges, analysts argued on national television that overseas ballots cast in Israel by Jewish residents of Florida could tip the election. They did not—but the fact that they might have, and that the American public was repeatedly informed of their potential power, reinforced the image of the Jewish vote as a force to be reckoned with in American politics.

Although the division of the Jewish vote in the national race remained more or less true to tradition, the outcome of the New York City mayoral contest of 2001 provided further evidence of the rightward shift in Jewish voting patterns in nonpresidential races. In the New York race, ethnicity was no factor, since both candidates were Jewish. Nor were there any major campaign issues that aroused specific, or ethnic-based, concerns in the Jewish community. Hence the election results offered a portrait of the current general political orientation among Jewish voters when it comes to governing the city: 53 percent of Jews supported Republican Michael Bloomberg; 47 percent backed his liberal Democratic opponent, Mark Green.

The gradual shift in American Jewish voting from almost monolithic support for liberal Democratic candidates to a more divided and flexible electorate bears important implications for the future of the phenomenon known as the Jewish vote. Until recently, many Democratic candidates could safely assume that Jewish voters' support was more or less assured, and therefore they had no particular incentive to go to any unusual lengths to address issues of Jewish concern. At the same time, many Republican candidates had little incentive to pursue Jewish votes that they assumed were nearly impossible to win. But in recent years, the distribution of Jewish votes in mayoral and, to a lesser extent, congressional races has deviated from the patterns of previous decades. The gradual, ongoing changes in the American Jewish demographic profile, particularly the increases in the size and influence of that segment of Jewry that is both religiously and politically less liberal, are likely to result in the further fragmenting of the Jewish vote in local contests and, eventually, at the presidential level as well. A Jewish vote that is potentially within the grasp of either party's candidate will result in greater political power and leverage for the American Jewish community.

References

Allswang, John M. *A House for All Peoples: Ethnic Politics in Chicago 1990–1936.* Lexington: University Press of Kentucky, 1971.
American Jewish Committee (Information and Research Services). *Jewish Voting in the 1968 Presidential Election: A Preliminary Report.* New York: American Jewish Committee, 1968.
Diner, Hasia R. *A Time for Gathering: The Second Migration, 1820–1880.* Baltimore, MD: Johns Hopkins University Press, 1992.
Featherman, Sandra. *Philadelphia Elects a Black Mayor: How Jews, Blacks, and Ethnics Vote in the 1980s.* Philadelphia: American Jewish Committee, 1984.

Fuchs, Lawrence H. *The Political Behavior of American Jews*. Glencoe, IL: Free Press, 1956.

——. ed. *American Ethnic Politics*. New York: Harper & Row, 1968.

Himmelfarb, Milton. "American Jews: Diehard Conservatives." *Commentary* 100 (April 1989): 44–49.

Himmelfarb, Milton, and Howard W. Yagerman. *Preliminary Report on Presidential Voting by Jews in 1972*. New York: American Jewish Committee, 1972.

Howe, Irving. *World of our Fathers*. New York: Harcourt, Brace, Jovanovich, 1976.

Isaacs, Stephen D. *Jews and American Politics*. Garden City, NY: Doubleday, 1974.

"The Jewish Vote: Will There Be One?" *The Economist* (September 13, 1980).

Lipstadt, Deborah, Charles Pruitt, and Jonathan Woocher. "Election '84: Where Are the Jews?" *Moment* 9 (October 1984), 35–38.

Maller, Allen S. "Class Factors in the Jewish Vote." *Jewish Social Studies* 39 (winter–spring 1977): 159–162.

Raab, Earl. "Are American Jews Still Liberal?" *Commentary* 107 (February 1996): 43–45.

4

The Jewish Lobby

ince the late 1800s, lobbyists have sought to influence U.S. government policy on specific issues of Jewish concern, most often pertaining to the treatment of Jews in other countries. The ability of such lobbying to achieve its objectives has usually depended on the extent to which the issue in question was perceived by either Congress or the White House as coinciding with the U.S. national interest. The perception that there exists a cohesive and sizable bloc of Jewish voters with common views provides the political backdrop that gives politicians incentive to accede to requests by Jewish lobbying groups, just as the perception of the existence of other ethnic minority voting blocs has made it possible for those groups' lobbies to wield influence in Washington.

The earliest attempts by Jewish lobbyists to affect U.S. policy typically enjoyed limited success, precisely because American Jewish voters were not yet sufficiently numerous or organized to be regarded in Washington as a force with which to reckon. This was true of the 1850s protests over discrimination against Jews in Switzerland, the attempts to seek U.S. intervention in the 1858 abduction of Edgar Mortara by the Papal police, and the Jewish efforts in the 1860s and 1870s to secure U.S. action to counter the persecution of Jews in Romania. Washington insider and B'nai B'rith official Simon Wolf, the first Jewish lobbyist in the nation's capital (although unofficially so), pleaded for Jewish interests forcefully and eloquently during the late 1800s, but without the crucial ingredient of Jewish voting power behind him. Although the number of Jews in the United States began increasing significantly in the 1880s with the onset of substantial East European Jewish immigration, the newcomers did not receive voting privileges until seven years after their arrival. The political firepower that their sheer numbers could bring to the American Jewish community was delayed.

The German-descended American Jews who established the American Jewish Committee in 1906 were motivated to a great extent by their fear that the new East European immigrants would usurp their position of leadership in the community. Ironically, however, the arrival of those immigrants created the public perception of a large and growing bloc of Jewish voters, which gave political muscle to the lobbying efforts of groups like the AJ Committee. The wealth and personal connections utilized by the German-born elite could only go so far in Washington; the existence of a significant quantity of Jewish votes provided crucial reinforcement to Jewish lobbyists' efforts, in the language that all politicians understand. AJ Committee president Louis Marshall, who would spearhead the AJ Committee's lobbying efforts, frequently invoked the specter of the "Jewish vote" in his behind-the-scenes discussions in the halls of power. Marshall, like others in the upper crust of the Jewish leadership, publicly denounced any mention of a "Jewish vote" and even opposed the creation of Jewish political clubs, arguing that any such ethnic self-segregation would be perceived by the public as un-American. But such statements were little more than "lip-service," David Dalin notes. "Marshall's commitment to the ideal of Jewish political neutrality was much greater in theory than in practice," because in private, Marshall repeatedly demonstrated his ability to wield the Jewish vote as an effective weapon of political influence (Dalin 1992, 76–77).

Among the committee's first projects was a lobbying campaign to abrogate the Russo-American Commercial Treaty because of Russia's discrimination against American citizens by its refusal to permit American Jews to travel freely in its territory. Such discrimination affected only a handful of people, but it was targeted by the committee because of its symbolism: the U.S. government's toleration of such discrimination constituted official acquiescence in the notion that Jews were second-class citizens. What was at stake was the status of American Jewry, and that was an issue that galvanized the thoroughly acculturated Jews of the AJ Committee. As Dalin (1992) explains, Marshall, a prominent and well-connected Republican, had in 1904 warned the Republican presidential candidate, Theodore Roosevelt, that Jewish voters in New York City were sufficiently numerous to tip the balance in their state, and thus possibly decide the outcome of the race (63–65). Marshall made the same point to the 1908 nominee, William Howard Taft, with greater effect. When Taft's campaign promise to resolve the Russian controversy proved slow to materialize, Marshall sought other routes to increase the pressure, first by successfully lobbying the major political parties to urge abrogation, then by persuading Congress to focus attention on the issue by holding hearings, and finally by initiating a congressional resolution, which passed 300 to 1, instructing Taft to terminate the treaty. It was a striking demonstration of the emerging power of the Jewish lobby, particularly its ability to use Congress as a means of pressuring the White House.

Simultaneously, the AJ Committee mounted a lobbying effort against proposals to restrict immigration. Although embarrassed by the foreign dress and manners of the East European Jewish immigrants and fearful that the presence of radicals among them would harm American Jewry's public image, the AJ Committee leaders embraced the ideal of the United States as a refuge for the downtrodden and felt personal sympathy for Jews seeking to escape czarist Russia. There was also a significant element of self-interest: the opposition to immigration was rooted in racial theories that labeled all Jews, German as well as Russian, as inferior.

For more than a decade, Louis Marshall directed a lobbying effort in Washington against the many anti-immigration proposals considered by Congress. Marshall's arguments included appeals to humanitarianism but emphasized America's practical interests, arguing that immigrants provided cheap manual labor crucial to the nation's industry and that the European culture they brought with them would prove culturally and intellectually beneficial.

Marshall's lobbying strategy was anchored in his conviction that any public Jewish role in the fight against restrictionism would both undermine his lobbying and provoke anti-Semitism. The AJ Committee refrained from public activities on the issue, and Marshall's work was usually confined to behind-the-scenes contacts with individual members of Congress. The National Liberal Immigration League, headed by Jewish activist Nissim Behar, was a source of constant irritation for Marshall because it made no effort to hide its Jewish identity in its high-profile activities against restrictionism.

An early test of the AJ Committee's lobbying prowess came in 1906 with the introduction of a slew of anti-immigration proposals. As Henry Leonard (1972) explains, Marshall decided to focus his arguments on bills making literacy and sound physique requirements for admission (13–15). A literacy provision was unfair, he argued, because the inability of many Jewish immigrants to obtain education was the result of anti-Semitic discrimination. The good physique provision was unjust because immigrants unable to eat nonkosher food during the long journey to America might seem emaciated upon arrival, even if they were, in fact, generally of sound health. Marshall's lobbying of key legislators to "sit on" the bills kept them tied up in a congressional committee for much of 1906–1907. When a watered-down immigration bill finally passed, it no longer included the restrictions concerning literacy or physique.

As part of the compromise removing the most objectionable aspects of the bill, Marshall consented to a provision establishing a commission to study the immigration question. But that commission turned out to be a powerful new weapon in the restrictionists' arsenal when its forty-one-volume report, released at the end of 1910, blamed immigration from Eastern and Southern Europe for undermining America's well-being and urged the enactment of a literacy requirement. The AJ Committee sponsored publication of a study critical of the commission's findings without, of course, revealing the AJ Committee's connection to the critique. The committee's anti-restrictionist efforts were also boosted by the hiring, in 1910, of Fulton Brylawski—the first paid, full-time Washington lobbyist for a Jewish organization.

Brylawski faced steep odds. Public opinion strongly supported severe restrictionism, and anti-immigration sentiment in Congress was growing steadily. A literacy test requirement passed in early 1913; Marshall could derive only slight consolation that the final version did not include a proposal to oblige each would-be immigrant to present a "certificate of character" from the local police. Marshall turned to his constituents, looking to the Jewish community to provide the political muscle needed to counteract the anti-immigration crusade. He mobilized Jewish leaders to bombard President Taft with telegrams urging him to veto the legislation. Taft did so. Next came the battle to sustain the veto in the face of a major congressional effort to override it. Once again the AJ Committee enlisted Jews around the country to petition their representatives. The Senate had enough votes to override Taft's veto, but the House fell short by a handful of votes. Another literacy test bill passed the following year, only to be vetoed by President Woodrow Wilson. Marshall contacted Jewish activists in the home districts of anti-immigration members of Congress, and urged them to pressure their representatives not to override the veto. Once again, the veto was sustained in the House by the narrowest of margins. Although a literacy test requirement did finally become law in

1917—after Congress overrode another Wilson veto—Marshall succeeded in diluting its impact by securing an exemption for immigrants who were refugees from religious persecution.

The literacy battle was just a prelude to the most serious setbacks on immigration. Postwar nativism whipped up the public's anti-immigration sentiment to a fever pitch, and Congress responded by restricting immigration of each nationality to 2 percent of those residing in the United States as of 1910. The AJ Committee's lobbying failed to prevent President Warren Harding from signing the bill into law in 1921. Three years later the legislation was tightened by moving the cutoff date back to 1890. Would different tactics by the Jewish lobby, such as high-profile protests, have resulted in a different outcome? Not likely, Henry Leonard concludes: "Marshall's failure arose not so much from weaknesses in his techniques as from the circumstances and tensions in America which breathed life into nativism and over which he could exercise little control" (Leonard 1972, 26).

The immigration battles were not the only arena of Jewish lobbying activity during the early 1900s. At the behest of their British colleagues, American Zionist leaders lobbied President Woodrow Wilson and Secretary of State Edward House in the autumn of 1917 to endorse London's plan to issue a statement pledging to facilitate the building of a Jewish national home in Palestine. The divided British cabinet repeatedly sought Wilson's views on the subject as it weighed the pros and cons of a pro-Zionist declaration; American Zionist influence on the president and Colonel House thus played a crucial role. Lacking a staff of paid lobbyists, the leaders of the U.S. Zionist movement, Supreme Court justice Louis Brandeis and Rabbi Stephen Wise, assumed the task themselves. They utilized their personal contacts with the administration to repeatedly secure meetings with both the president and the secretary of state in order to make the case for Zionism. Wilson's view of Zionism as the fulfillment of biblical promises and his sympathy for the plight of East European Jewry intersected with his realpolitik interests, such as the establishment of a refuge that would divert immigrants from America's shores; the need to preempt a rumored German declaration of support for Zionism; and the belief that a pro-Zionist gesture by the Allies would encourage Russian Jews to pressure their government to remain in the war. Hence, with a relatively modest amount of lobbying, Brandeis and Wise were able to secure Wilson's approval, helping to pave the way for England's Balfour Declaration.

The American Zionist movement also undertook a major lobbying campaign in the spring of 1922 to win congressional endorsement of the Jewish statehood cause. Rabbi Simon Glazer of Kansas City used his connections on Capitol Hill to persuade Senator Henry Cabot Lodge and Representative Hamilton Fish to introduce a joint resolution supporting the Balfour Declaration, the British government's statement promising to facilitate the establishment of a Jewish national home in Palestine. Despite a counterlobbying effort by the State Department, the appearance of a prominent anti-Zionist rabbi among the witnesses at the congressional hearings on the resolutions, and the opposition of the New York Times (owned by a Jewish anti-Zionist family), the resolution passed unanimously that September. President Harding then endorsed it as well. Most members of Congress "saw little harm in the resolution, and much political advantage," Melvin Urofsky notes. "They had antagonized a number of ethnic groups in establishing immigration quotas in 1921, and by supporting Zionist demands, they could make at least partial amends to one of these groups, and seemingly at no cost or involvement by the country" (Urofsky 1975, 308). From the perspective of the Zionist movement, the resolution served multiple purposes. To begin with, it gave official American imprimatur to the Zionist cause, a fact that could be cited for decades to come as a precedent for continued U.S. support for Zionism or the State of Israel. At the same time, it helped legitimize Zionism within the divided American Jewish community. The non-Jewish world's stamp of approval helped wavering American Jews feel more comfortable with the Zionist cause. It also helped undermine Reform Judaism's traditional opposition to Zionism, and accelerated Reform's shift from anti-Zionism to non-Zionism, signs of which were already apparent.

Symbolic victories such as the Lodge-Fish resolution were far easier to secure than actual policy changes, as American Zionist leaders soon discovered. American Jewish attempts to induce a firm U.S. response to the August 1929 Arab pogroms in Palestine—which claimed 133 Jewish lives, including eight American citizens—ran into the brick walls of White House isolationism and State Department Arabism.

The Zionist Organization of America (ZOA) convinced Senator William Borah, chairman of the Senate Foreign Relations Committee, to join it in lobbying the administration to insist that a Jewish-selected American attorney testify before the British commission of inquiry into the causes of the violence; Secretary of State Stimson refused their entreaties. Some Jewish leaders, among them AJ Committee vice president Cyrus Adler, urged that a U.S. warship be dispatched to the waters off Palestine as a demonstration of U.S.

displeasure over the Arab violence; the White House showed no interest in the proposal.

In the aftermath of the Palestine riots, the ZOA appointed its first official lobbyist in Washington, Max Rhoade. His mission was to recruit members of Congress to oppose the increasingly pro-Arab shift in England's Palestine policy, but Rhoade did not get very far. It was bad enough that Rhoade's position was only part-time and that he lacked a real staff and a serious budget; but he was especially handicapped by the fact that the ZOA's dwindling fortunes—it had dropped from a national membership of 200,000 in 1918 to one-tenth that number a decade later—prevented it from providing him with the national network of Zionist activism necessary to give his efforts political muscle. "The organization neither dispatched small delegations (which its chapters could have provided) to wait upon local congressmen privately nor enlisted the ongoing aid of one or two prominent members of Congress to carry its case in the national legislature," Naomi Cohen recounts. "Men like [Representative Emanuel] Celler and [Representative Samuel] Dickstein, who had shown more than a cursory interest in the problem, were not cultivated or kept apprised of events. Dickstein's resolution in January, 1930, for an impartial international investigation of the Palestine issue was a misplaced gesture and a waste of potential ammunition" (N. Cohen 1988, 125). Since the British had already undertaken their own investigation, there was little chance of rallying significant congressional support behind an international inquiry, and even less chance that the British would go along with it; the ZOA's lobby expended its time, energy, and political capital on a resolution that was doomed from the start.

The rise of the Nazis to power in January 1933 "exposed the same shortcomings that had been manifest in 1929–30: divisiveness within the Jewish camp, political timidity, and an overreliance on 'enlightened public opinion'" (N. Cohen 1988, 176). In fact, the weaknesses of the American Jewish community were even more exposed in response to the Nazi persecution of German Jewry, as American Jews chose to refrain from exploring many of the opportunities for direct American action to aid the downtrodden. On the question of immigration, for example, American Jewish leaders hesitated to ask the United States to take in substantial numbers of Jewish refugees from Europe. When Representative Dickstein in March 1933 proposed the unrestricted immigration of those German Jews related to American citizens, the AJ Committee lobbied him to "let your resolution die a natural quiet death," lest it "create a situation where it will be charged with force that American Jews want to sacrifice America's obvious and essential interests on behalf of their German Jewish co-religionists" (Medoff 1987, 25). Stephen Wise lobbied Representative Donald O'Toole (D-NY) to drop his April 1937 proposal to provide asylum for all German Jews fleeing persecution; Wise warned that "any effort to waive the immigration laws will result in a serious accentuation of what we know to be a rising wave of anti-Semitic feeling in this country." Even behind-the-scenes attempts to increase immigration discomfited the Jewish establishment. Frances Perkins, the lone cabinet champion of refugee immigration, sought to employ a little-known bond procedure to permit the entry of more refugees, only to be discouraged from doing so by Jewish leaders who feared that word of the effort would leak out, resulting in anti-Semitic accusations that Jews were trying to flood the country with foreigners.

Ironically, however, when a number of members of Congress began promoting legislation to restrict propaganda by domestic Nazi sympathizers—the very propaganda that terrified and intimidated American Jewish leaders—the mainstream Jewish organizations lobbied against it. The General Jewish Council, a coalition of Jewish establishment groups, opposed the 1940 Flaherty bill, which would have broadened the government's ability to act against advocates of "discrimination against individuals of any religious creed." The council opposed the Flaherty legislation and similar efforts on the grounds that they unfairly limited freedom of speech. The Jewish leaders were not prepared to go further than the much more limited Gillie bill, which merely required publishers to list their name and address clearly on their mail, so that hate groups could not hide behind the shield of anonymity.

The most that Wise and his colleagues could accomplish was occasionally to delay the imposition of a policy change that was blatantly inimical to Jewish interests, as for example in the summer of 1936, when the British were poised to announce the suspension of all Jewish immigration to Palestine until the conclusion of an investigation by a recently appointed royal commission. Anguished by the news of the impending suspension and emotionally overwhelmed by his visit to Europe during the preceding weeks, Wise hurried to plead with President Roosevelt to intervene. Election-year politics and British self-interest combined to produce a surprising victory for Wise. With a presidential election just a few months away, FDR sensed an opportunity to reinforce his Jewish support at little cost; he directed Secretary of State Cordell Hull to urge the British to refrain from blocking Jewish immigration. Hull's intercession found a receptive audience because British prime minister Stanley Baldwin "decided that by a small gesture he could temporarily placate both the Zionists and their new-found friend, the president of the United States" (Urofsky 1975, 402–403). "Ultimately the gates of Palestine would close, but in the intervening years more than 50,000 Jews, mostly from Germany and Austria, were able to join the yishuv—men, women, and children who would undoubtedly have perished had the 1939 White Paper been issued three years earlier" (Urofsky 1982, 284). It was quite a triumph, considering that it had been accomplished with so little effort—no rallies, no Capitol Hill forays, no national protest campaign, just a single lobbying mission by Wise to Hyde Park. The Zionists were understandably ecstatic at the outcome, but they "rejoiced prematurely," failing to realize that it was simply a rare case of political self-interest in Washington and London briefly coinciding with Jewish interests. "In an election year, the President could chance coup de theatre with nothing to lose. If Britain had said 'No,' he had at least tried; the British, by merely granting a delay in their final determination, had sacrificed nothing, won Roosevelt's gratitude, and gave the President still another card to play in his bid for re-election" (Urofsy 1975, 403). The real test would come during the Holocaust, when Wise would belatedly discover that FDR "would have no compunction about ignoring the plight of European Jewry when it became politically useless or undesirable" (Urofsky 1982, 284).

The American Zionist movement finally hired its first full-time Washington lobbyist in early 1939. ZOA president Solomon Goldman, with the backing of Palestine Labor Zionist leader David Ben-Gurion, convinced his colleagues in the U.S. Zionist leadership to set up an office in Washington, known as the American Zionist Bureau. Under the leadership of an activist rabbi, Isadore Breslau, the bureau scored some initial successes, such as persuading 192 members of the House of Representatives to sign a letter urging England to keep Palestine's doors open to Jewish refugees. Breslau's work was hampered, however, by a lack of funds, simmering conflicts between the variety of Zionist groups that the bureau officially represented in Washington, and increasing doubts among American Zionist leaders over how aggressive the movement should be. Those doubts were fueled by the eruption of war in Europe. Many prominent American Zionists worried that vocal public activity on behalf of Palestine or European Jewry could provoke accusations that Jews were trying to drag the United States into overseas conflicts. Isolationist sentiment was at its peak in America, and the Zionist movement was to a significant extent paralyzed by fears of war-mongering charges. American Zionist leaders soon lost interest in Breslau's Washington lobbying operation; by mid-1940 it was sputtering, and by the end of that year it was officially shut down.

As Breslau's effort petered out, an alternative Jewish lobbying effort emerged. In the spring of 1940, the militant Revisionist Zionists, led by Vladimir Ze'ev Jabotinsky, dispatched one of their most promising young intellectuals, Benjamin Akzin, to Capitol Hill "to draw the attention of the makers of policy and of public opinion to the 'forgotten' Jewish angle of the war"—that is, the need for a Jewish army to fight in the war alongside the Allies, and the need for mass European Jewish immigration to Palestine. The Revisionists correctly perceived that the United States was replacing Great Britain as the major world power and that the position of the U.S. government on Zionist matters could force changes in Britain's Palestine policy. Akzin actually garnered the most sympathy among congressional isolationists and opponents of immigration, who saw the possibility of quick, massive Jewish immigration to Palestine as a way of ensuring that those immigrants would not come to the United States. Akzin was later succeeded as Revisionism's part-time Washington lobbyist by Benzion Netanyahu, the father of a future prime minister of Israel.

A second militant Zionist lobby appeared on Capitol Hill the following year, when a Revisionist splinter group led by Peter Bergson (Hillel Kook) established a Committee for a Jewish Army of Stateless and Palestinian Jews. Baruch Rabinowitz, a dynamic young rabbi who had left his pulpit in Maryland to become a Zionist activist, was hired by Bergson to seek congressional support for the Jewish army cause. The group's first "Jews Fight for the Right to Fight" advertisement in the *New York Times,* on January 5, 1942, included among its signatories three U.S. senators and fourteen members of the House of Representatives, recruited by Rabinowitz.

Jewish political advertising of this sort was an innovation. Jewish organizations usually resorted to newspaper ads only to announce specific events, and even then only in the Jewish press. The Bergson group was venturing into unknown territory, splashing a controversial political message across the pages of America's largest daily newspaper, where it would be read primarily by non-Jews—"just as you would advertise Chevrolet motor cars or Players cigarettes," as one of his aides marveled (Medoff 2002, 73). Furthermore, in recruiting members of Congress to endorse its campaign publicly, the Bergson group had hit upon a new and powerful way to promote a controversial Zionist goal. Congressional support legitimized the Jewish army concept among nervous American Jews, while simultaneously demonstrating to the Roosevelt administration that militant Zionists were becoming a political force to be reckoned with.

The *New York Times* ad was the first important step in that direction, followed one month later by the introduction of a congressional resolution, written by Representative Andrew L. Somers (D-Brooklyn), urging the creation of a Jewish army. That was another innovation for Jewish activists: seeking congressional action despite the opposition of the Roosevelt administration. The administration, anxious to avoid irritating the British, declined to support the Jewish army idea, although several officials, most prominently Secretary of War Henry Stimson, expressed their personal sympathy for the proposal. Although the Somers army resolution never came to a vote, it fired a warning shot across the administration's bow: militant Zionists were ready to press their agenda on Capitol Hill, with or without the approval of the White House.

Somers, Bergson's earliest and most enthusiastic supporter in Congress, was the son of a militant Irish nationalist, and he felt a natural kinship with Jewish opponents of England. When Baruch Rabinowitz began his lobbying effort, Somers volunteered the use of his office and secretarial staff. Given England's troubles administering Ireland, the British were understandably jittery about the possibility of Irish-Americans and Jewish-Americans uniting against their common enemy. Internal British government correspondence during the 1940s made repeated reference to indications of Irish-American support for maximalist Zionism. In a typical expression of such concerns, a report sent to the British embassy in Washington by a British consular official in New York who attended a Revisionist rally made much of the fact that one of the speakers, a U.S. Army major, had "suspicions of an Irish accent" (Medoff 2002, 74). The few contacts between Revisionist Zionists and their Irish-American sympathizers never actually materialized into substantive political collaboration, but the fear of such an alliance between these two influential ethnic groups contributed to the Zionists' pressure on London to change its Palestine policy.

The Bergson group's single-minded, and ultimately successful, campaign for a Jewish army pointed up a major difference in approaches between the dissidents and mainstream Jewish leaders. Bergson had a specific political goal and a focused agenda. He implemented a carefully planned strategy combining Capitol Hill lobbying, public rallies, and information campaigns, to take an issue that was completely unknown in 1941 and within two years turn it into a matter for serious consideration in the Jewish community, the press, and, most important, among Allied leaders. Mainstream Jewish leaders, anxious to avoid being usurped by the Bergsonites, eventually adopted the Jewish army issue as their own, and the combination of Bergson's public agitation and the establishment's behind-the-scenes lobbying convinced the British to establish the Jewish Brigade. Not only did the Jewish Brigade see action against the Nazis during the final weeks of the war but, in addition, many of its members actively assisted in postwar efforts to smuggle Jewish refugees into Palestine and later used their military training as soldiers in Israel's 1948 War of Independence.

In contrast with Bergson's aggressive and determined approach, the Jewish establishment, led by Stephen Wise, was essentially reactive. Wise and his colleagues had no specific strategy for seeking U.S. aid for European Jewry or securing U.S. pressure on England to open Palestine's gates. When a crisis arose, they struggled to come up with ways to respond, typically falling back on their personal contacts at the White House or on Capitol Hill rather than organizing public action. This sort of backstairs diplomacy tended to work better in times of calm than in times of urgency. When they had time on their side, Jewish leaders could quietly and patiently try to use their powers of persuasion on specific members of Congress or White House aides. But the torrent of reports about Nazi atrocities required the sort of swift response to which they were not entirely accustomed. The result was a vacuum of leadership in the American Jewish community, which the Bergson activists strove to fill.

In 1942–1943, as news of the Nazi mass murders began reaching the West, Bergson's Jewish Army group transformed itself into the Emergency Committee to Save the Jewish People of Europe, and Baruch Rabinowitz was directed to shift his attentions to the rescue of Jewish refugees from Hitler. Although many Democrats hesitated to defy the Roosevelt administration's line on Palestine or refugees, Republicans were often receptive to Rabinowitz's appeals. He also helped organize a dramatic march of 400 Orthodox rabbis to the White House just before Yom Kippur, 1943—the only time during the Holocaust that Jews staged a public protest at the gates to 1600 Pennsylvania Avenue.

The march helped to galvanize the Emergency Committee's most important project, a campaign for a congressional resolution urging FDR to take concrete action to rescue Jews from Hitler. Here Bergson's sense of realpolitik was on full display. Rather than wait for Roosevelt to offer some small gesture that would inevitably fall far short of European Jewry's needs, Bergson took the offensive, conceiving the idea of pressuring the administration to establish a special government agency devoted to rescuing the refugees. When Bergson drafted the congressional resolution urging the creation of such an agency, he deliberately omitted any reference to Palestine. He and his aides assumed, with justification, that the Palestine issue would cloud the rescue debate. Some members of Congress whose humanitarian sympathies would ordinarily motivate them to support rescue action might back away from a resolution critical of America's important wartime ally, Great Britain. Despite the political logic of Bergson's approach, Stephen Wise appeared at the rescue resolution hearings to testify against the measure. The split in the Jewish lobby had never before been so demonstrably aired on Capitol Hill. Wise focused on the injustice of omitting Palestine from the text, in view of the need to provide a haven for refugees, but as a *New York Post* editorial noted, he was also motivated by resentment that the dissidents were usurping his position as American Jewry's spokesman.

Not surprisingly, Wise's opposition helped stall congressional consideration of the resolution, as bewildered members of Congress tried to figure out what it was that American Jews really wanted. "I wish these damned Jews would make up their minds what they want," one senator privately complained. "I could not get inside the committee room without being buttonholed out here in the corridor by representatives who said that the Jewish people of America did not want passage of this resolution" (Wyman 1984, 200). But the bill had already gathered a political momentum of its own. State Department official Breckinridge Long, testifying at the hearings, presented wildly inflated statistics about the number of refugees who had been admitted to the United States. Long's gaffe compelled mainstream Jewish leaders to turn their attention from fighting Bergson to publicly refuting Long's misrepresentations. Nervous White House aides, warned by Treasury Secretary Henry Morgenthau that the embarrassing publicity over Long's testimony could harm Roosevelt's re-election campaign, convinced the president to preempt Congress by establishing a War Refugee Board to rescue European Jews from the Nazis. Although Roosevelt intended the board as little more than an election-year gesture, and although it was underfunded and understaffed, the War Refugee Board managed to save many tens of thousands of lives during the waning days of the war—as many as two hundred thousand, according to the estimates of some historians. Among the board's most notable accomplishments was its sponsorship of the life-saving activities of Raoul Wallenberg.

The Bergsonites were not the only successful Jewish lobbyists. The mainstream Jewish leaders scored the occasional victory as well, as for example in the case of the unexpected struggle over U.S. Mideast policy in the summer of 1943. Two emissaries of the Roosevelt administration, one from the Office of Strategic Services and the other from Army Intelligence, surveyed public opinion in the Middle East that year and separately urged the president to find ways to stifle American Zionist protest activity in order to avert a pro-Axis shift in Arab public opinion. State Department officials drafted a joint Anglo-American statement that would effectively postpone all public discussion of Palestine until war's end. Hearing the news, Zionist leaders mobilized Treasury Secretary Henry Morgenthau, Felix Frankfurter, and other Roosevelt confidants to lobby against the proposed declaration, while the Bergson group enlisted its influential ally, Senator Edwin Johnson, chairman of the Senate Military Affairs Committee, to combat the proposal. Word was leaked to Representative Emanuel Celler, who on the floor of the House of Representatives denounced the administration's planned "Silence, please" declaration as an attempt to "drown the clamor of the tortured Nazi victims pleading for a haven of refuge." Faced with vigorous wall-to-wall Jewish opposition, Roosevelt backed down, much to London's chagrin. The Jewish lobby, mainstream and militant factions alike, had successfully utilized their allies in Congress and, especially, within the administration to block a potentially calamitous shift in U.S. policy (Penkower 1978, 231).

As the war's end neared, the Emergency Committee to Save the Jewish People of Europe transformed itself into the American League for a Free Palestine, and Baruch Rabinowitz shifted the focus of his lobbying to the struggle for Jewish statehood. By that time, however, Rabinowitz was no longer alone. Mainstream Zionist groups, galvanized by news of the Holocaust and England's intransigence on Palestine, were taking a more activist approach. Abba Hillel Silver, chairman of the American Zionist Emergency Council (AZEC), personally spearheaded a lobbying campaign to intensify congressional pressure on the British.

In the autumn of 1943, Silver brought Rabbi Leon Feuer to Washington to direct a newly opened Zionist lobbying office there. Recognizing the link between grassroots activism and Capitol Hill leverage, Feuer first went to New York, where he spent six weeks organizing some 150 local activist committees around the country. Each was a mini-lobby of its own, and "it was impressed upon them that they must keep in constant contact with their Representatives and Senators [and] meet with them frequently on their home grounds where they are particularly sensitive to public opinion." During his first year alone, Feuer organized two national conferences of these activists to hone their lobbying skills, fine-tune political strategy, and galvanize them to intensify their efforts. Praising their success in helping to win congressional support for the Zionist cause, Feuer later hailed his grassroots activists as "unsung heroes of the struggle for the founding of Israel." As chief of the AZEC lobby in Washington, Feuer regularly turned to his national network of activists to provide the muscle to advance his agenda. "At a moment's notice and at their own expense they would send delegations to Washington to confer with their representatives and senators," he recalled. "They organized telegram and mail campaigns among both Jews and non-Jews. If we wanted to make a point with a certain congressman, a call from me to our committee in his home district would produce, within a few days, hundreds and sometimes thousands of communications from his constituents" (Feuer 1976, 110–111).

Until Silver's advent, Zionist lobbying efforts on Capitol Hill had tended to focus largely on liberal Democrats. Stephen Wise's close relationship with the Roosevelt administration and personal disdain for Republican positions on most issues tended to preclude contacts with the GOP. This put Jewish lobbying efforts at a considerable disadvantage, since the administration knew that there was scant likelihood of Jewish leaders rallying congressional opposition to Roosevelt's policies. But Silver's rise to power in the Jewish community altered those political dynamics. Although not formally a Republican, Silver had publicly endorsed Wendell Willkie for president in 1940 and enjoyed access to Republican leaders, particularly Senator Taft, who represented Silver's home state of Ohio. Beginning in early 1944, Silver and his aides met repeatedly with Taft, Governor Thomas E. Dewey of New York (the expected Republican presidential nominee), and members of the Republican convention's platform drafting committee. Netanyahu and the Revisionist Zionists likewise lobbied key Republicans concerning the convention platform. The resulting text actually went further than Silver had proposed, in that it not only endorsed statehood but also directly criticized Roosevelt's failure to insist that the British facilitate the creation of a Jewish homeland.

The Republican plank caused a major rift in the American Zionist movement, as Wise and other Democrats in the AZEC angrily accused Silver of trying to embarrass the president. He may indeed have embarrassed FDR, but in the process Silver proved a savvy political player, because the GOP's action forced the Democratic convention likewise to adopt a strong plank on Palestine. The ramifications of the two parties' resolutions extended beyond the American political scene. The ability of Zionist lobbyists to convince both major parties to go on record in favor of Jewish statehood also sent a powerful message to London. England would need America's help after the war, and American Jewish political power was emerging as a factor in the shaping of America's postwar Middle East policy.

Back on the Hill, however, the lobby's first major initiative ran into formidable obstacles. In January, AZEC arranged for sympathetic members of Congress to introduce a pro-statehood resolution that, while not directly affecting U.S. policy, would have important symbolic value by granting Zionism the imprimatur of the U.S. Congress. Such resolutions, Isaiah Berlin of the British embassy noted, "even if they were mere expressions of goodwill and no more," were useful "to inhibit [administration] officials from going too far, for fear of being attacked by name in Congress and in the press" (Berlin, 37). AZEC lobbyists rounded up broad support for the statehood resolution, only to see the administration kill it by having the War Department condemn it as inimical to the war effort. The resolution gained new life in October, when the War Department, assessing the latest changes for the better on the war front, withdrew its earlier objections. In view of the widespread congressional support for the resolution earlier in the year, Silver had assumed that it would pass easily; instead, the issue caused a major new rift in the Jewish lobby. Despite the War Department's new position, the State Department adamantly opposed the measure for fear of angering the Arab world, and it lobbied the Senate Foreign Relations Committee to postpone indefinitely consideration of the resolution. Unbeknownst to Silver, Stephen Wise acceded to the administration's request to quietly lobby key members of Congress to drop the bill. When the resolution was buried, an all-out battle erupted within the AZEC between the Silver and Wise camps, resulting in Silver's temporary ouster from the Zionist leadership. His departure triggered a tidal wave of grassroots demands for a more activist leadership. In the face of increasingly detailed revelations about the extent of Nazi atrocities, and Britain's refusal to change its Palestine immigration policy despite the official expiration of the White Paper in May 1944, American Zionists from coast to coast bombarded the ZOA leadership with letters demanding Silver's return. The Jewish press was filled with calls for reconciliation with the Silver group. Enthusiastic ovations greeted Silver at Zionist rallies. By the summer of 1945, he was back at the helm.

Capitol Hill was not the only place where Zionist lobbying took place during the crucial years leading up to Israel's 1948 declaration of independence. Across the country, AZEC activists persuaded thousands of state legislatures, mayors, civic organizations, churches, and unions to adopt pro-Zionist resolutions, write to the president and Congress, and speak out in their communities on behalf of the cause of Jewish statehood. They convinced thirty-nine governors to sign a letter to Truman urging him to press for free immigration to Palestine and a Jewish state. The Zionist movement attracted strong support from traditional Christians who regarded the ingathering of Jewish exiles and the rebuilding of the Holy Land as the fulfillment of Scriptural prophecies. American public sympathy for Zionist goals spread and intensified following the liberation of the Nazi death camps in the spring of 1945 and revelation of the full extent of Hitler's atrocities. Two AZEC front groups did yeoman work mobilizing public support for Zionism: the Christian Council on Palestine, which organized clergymen and at its peak had a membership of some 2,400; and the American Palestine Committee, with 75 regional chapters and 15,000 members nationwide, which rallied prominent non-Jews to the cause of Jewish statehood. Through rallies, petitions, newspaper ads, sermons, mass mailings, and the like, these groups proved to be a powerful component of the Zionist campaign. By influencing public opinion, these grassroots political action efforts made an impression in the halls of power in Washington. Jewish statehood was no longer the concern of merely one small ethnic group; now it was clear that Zionism enjoyed the active sympathy of many millions of Americans, too many for most politicians to easily ignore. When Senator Robert Wagner decided to sponsor a pro-Zionist letter to Truman, he was joined by 53 senators and 256 representatives; it was the kind of issue that had many potential advantages for politicians and few if any disadvantages.

The swirl of attention that the Palestine issue generated soon pushed the "Jewish vote" to the fore in American politics. As the cause of Jewish statehood gained widespread public and congressional support, the remaining pockets of anti-Zionism within the American Jewish community rapidly dwindled. Jewish opposition to Zionism traditionally had been largely based on concern that non-Jews would regard Zionism as un-American; the evidence of overwhelming American public sympathy for Jewish statehood made Zionism legitimate, or at least palatable, among those Jews who had been most worried about "dual loyalty" accusations. The AJ Committee and Reform Judaism, the two bulwarks of anti-Zionism during the early 1900s, began shifting to non-Zionism—support for a refuge, but not a sovereign state—in the 1920s. The persecution of European Jewry in the 1930s, the Holocaust, and the revelations of the liberated death camps sufficiently shocked most Jews—and generated sufficient sympathy from most non-Jews—to bring all but a relative handful of American Jews into the pro-Zionist camp. A Roper poll in November 1945 found 80 percent of American Jews in favor of Jewish statehood, and barely 10 percent opposed (the remainder being undecided). Furthermore, the highest rate of anti-Zionist sentiment, 18.5 percent, was found among those Jews who were the least important politically: residents of the South, where Jews did not yet have sufficient numbers to constitute a significant voting bloc. Local political contests in the Northeast could easily be tilted by the large number of pro-Zionist Jewish voters, and candidates thinking ahead to the 1948 presidential race would have to weigh the possibility that the Jewish vote could swing a state such as New York, which had the largest number of electoral votes in the nation.

As a result, a number of the Truman administration's policy decisions concerning Palestine were affected, to one degree or another, by concern about alienating Jewish voters. At a meeting of U.S. diplomats in October 1945, Truman reportedly replied to a complaint about the administration being too pro-Zionist: "I'm sorry gentlemen, but I have to answer to hundreds of thousands who are anxious for the success of Zionism; I do not have hundreds of thousands of Arabs among my constituents" (M. Cohen 1990, 89). The autumn 1945 decision to announce an Anglo-American Committee of Inquiry on Palestine, which Zionists were expected to greet with skepticism, was delayed by Truman—much to London's chagrin—lest it adversely affect the Democratic candidate in the November mayoral election in New York City. Under pressure from his political advisers, especially the chairman of the New York state Democratic Committee, Truman refused to endorse the 1946 Morrison-Grady Plan; formulated by U.S. and British representatives, it proposed Jewish and Arab enclaves under British rule, a plan sure to turn angry Jewish voters against the Democrats in the congressional and gubernatorial elections that November. Again with one eye on the Jewish vote, Truman used the occasion of Yom Kippur—just weeks before election day in 1946—to issue a statement that, while vaguely worded, was widely interpreted as an endorsement of the goal of Jewish statehood and hailed throughout the Jewish community. "The Yom Kippur statement marked a watershed in the political and diplomatic struggle for the Jewish state," Michael Cohen notes. "The British saw in the statement a demonstration of Jewish political power and gave up their quest for an Anglo-American consensus on Palestine. [British foreign minister Ernest] Bevin began issuing threats that the British would evacuate Palestine, and in February 1947 they did indeed refer the question with no recommendations to the United Nations" (M. Cohen 1990, 145).

The Republican landslide in the 1946 elections included over-whelming victories for the GOP's senatorial and gubernatorial candidates in New York, which infuriated the Democratic leadership but made Truman's advisers all the more desperate to recoup Jewish support before the 1948 presidential elections. New York Jewry's turn to the Republicans in 1946 thus increased the power of the Jewish vote and the leverage of the Jewish lobby. For all his private misgivings about the idea of a Jewish state, particularly his fear of a Mideast conflagration that would compel him to dispatch U.S. troops to the region, Truman acceded to his advisers' pressure to endorse the 1947 UN proposal for the partition of Palestine into Jewish and Arab states. The lobby's task was far from over, however. When State Department officials sought to amend the UN plan to give the Arabs the huge Negev desert (originally allotted to the Jewish state), the Zionists had to bring in their big gun, elder statesman Chaim Weizmann, to personally pressure Truman to intervene, which he did.

Weizmann had to be brought back to Washington the following March, when the State Department, with Truman's initial approval, proposed at the United Nations that Palestine be placed under an international trusteeship rather than be partitioned. Truman at first refused to see him; the Zionists had to enlist the president's boyhood friend Eddie Jacobson, to whom the doors of the White House were always open, to beseech Truman with an emotional plea to see Weizmann. The Zionist leader believed he had persuaded Truman to refrain from retreating from partition, but the very next day the U.S. ambassador at the United Nations proposed trusteeship before the Security Council. That sparked a wave of outrage in the Jewish community and an angry rift between the White House and the State Department; the problem was more one of coordination than policy differences, however, since Truman had in fact given the State Department the go-ahead on trusteeship. Truman, who was caught off guard by the backlash, appreciated the outcry's possible implications for the presidential vote just eight months away. He also took note of the February 1948 special congressional election in the Bronx in which Leo Isaacson, a supporter of third-party candidate Henry Wallace, scored an upset victory by hammering away at Truman's Palestine policy; the pundits interpreted the vote as evidence of Wallace's viability, as well as the escalating importance of the Palestine issue in American politics. Hence Truman hurried to publicly reaffirm his support for trusteeship, thus firmly ensconcing support for Jewish statehood as unchanged U.S. policy. When the Palestine Jewish leadership declared statehood on May 15, 1948, Truman was the first leader to extend recognition to the new state, just minutes after the announcement. The ecstatic response of American Jewry to the creation of Israel and to their president's warm rhetorical embrace of the new country overshadowed the administration's insistence on maintaining a complete arms embargo to the Middle East.

What did the American Zionist lobby accomplish with its 1940s campaigns? The congressional resolutions it sponsored did not directly alter America's Mideast policy. However, the many sympathetic declarations by the members of Congress whom the Zionists wooed, the protest letters they signed, their participation in rallies for Palestine, and other public activity that resulted from the Jewish lobby's Capitol Hill efforts certainly made a powerful impression on the White House. The president's perception of a pro-Zionist Congress became a factor in shaping policy.

Truman's speedy recognition of Israel was undoubtedly due in large measure to the work of the Zionist lobbyists, but how significant was that recognition? It could hardly make up for the military hardships Israel endured because of the U.S. arms embargo. At the same time, however, it is important to note the psychological impact of the Zionist movement's success with public opinion, Congress, and the White House. The Palestine Jewish leadership was deeply divided over whether to proceed with or postpone a declaration of statehood when the British left Palestine in May 1948. The leaders might well have refrained from declaring independence had they believed that the United States strongly opposed such a move; Israel might never have been established. The impact of the Jewish lobby in Washington and beyond gave Palestine Jewry the huge boost in morale needed to forge ahead with independence in the face of Arab threats.

The political legacy of the 1940s battles should not be underestimated. The struggles of those years established precedents and set new standards for Jewish political behavior in the United States. For the first time, both major political parties launched all-out efforts to woo Jewish voters. In addition, the Jewish lobby gained recognition as a force to be reckoned with in the nation's capital. Furthermore, the concept of a "Jewish vote" was firmly established as a legitimate and permanent part of the American political scene. The deep involvement of Americans in the fight to establish Israel in 1948 was also, in the end, the fight that made Israel part and parcel of the American political dynamic.

Case Study: An Unlikely Ally from North Dakota

Militant Zionist lobbyists found an unlikely ally to help them keep the Palestine issue high on the agenda of the U.S. Congress and gain publicity for the cause of Jewish statehood: William Langer, U.S. senator from North Dakota, a feisty, independent-minded Republican. Langer's interest in Jewish issues did not stem from any electoral concerns. North Dakota during the 1940s had a Jewish community numbering barely 3,000—less than 0.1 percent of American Jewry. Langer embraced Jewish issues out of genuine heartfelt sympathy for Hitler's victims and a simple conviction that it was unjust for England to prevent Jewish statehood.

Langer first became associated with the Bergson group in mid-1943. When Senator Scott Lucas took to the Senate floor to blast Bergson's newspaper ads taking issue with FDR's refugee policy, it was Langer who rose to the Bergson group's defense. The militant Zionists provided the North Dakotan with a steady stream of letters, memoranda, and newspaper clippings about the British and the Arabs, especially items reporting anti-American sentiment in the Arab world. Langer's office correspondence files testify to the persistent lobbying of the various Revisionist factions. The files bulge with letters and telegrams about Palestine from constituents in North Dakota, concerned citizens in other parts of the country, and various interest groups. During the crucial period from 1943 to 1948, appeals from the Revisionist factions and the Bergson committees outnumbered correspondence from mainstream Zionist organizations by a margin of nearly four to one. The militants recognized the need to combine their political talk with a personal touch. On one occasion after Langer delivered a stirring pro-Zionist speech on the floor of the Senate, Peter Bergson sent Langer a box of expensive cigars—the perfect gift for a man whom the *New York Times* would one day recall in these terms: "Visitors to the Senate could spot Mr. Langer by the cigar he always chewed. It was never lit and always still in the cellophane wrapper."

Langer soon emerged as one of the Senate's sharpest critics of England and most enthusiastic backers of the Jewish revolt. When the Bergsonites rented Madison Square Garden to stage a "public trial" of Britain's Palestine policy, Langer agreed to serve as a sponsor. When a handful of Jewish militants—including Stern group leader and future Israeli prime minister Yitzhak Shamir—escaped from their British detention camp in Eritrea only to be arrested in neighboring Ethiopia, Langer cabled Emperor Haile Selassie to set them free. When the assassins of British Mideast official Lord Moyne faced execution, Langer signed a telegram calling for commutation of their sentence on the grounds that the "background of agony, despair and death of millions of Hebrews in Europe and continued sufferings of survivors in that inferno constitute sufficient reason for leniency" (Medoff 2002, 168–169).

Despite protests by mainstream Zionist groups, Langer never shied away from closely collaborating with the Revisionists. He was, the British embassy complained, a "habitual 'signer'" of militant Zionist advertisements. He added his name to their letterhead. He delivered speeches based on their drafts. When British complaints resulted in an IRS investigation of the Bergson group's tax-exempt status, it was Langer to whom they turned for help.

The Postwar Fight to Liberalize Immigration

At the height of the Palestine struggle, in the autumn of 1946, President Truman had publicly broached the idea of permitting a significant number of Holocaust survivors to immigrate to the United States. Reluctant to engage in an all-out confrontation with the British over immigration to Palestine, yet anxious to demonstrate to Jewish voters that his administration wanted to provide concrete assistance to the survivors of Hitler's genocide, Truman considered immigration to the United States a politically feasible way to at least partially alleviate the suffering of the Displaced Persons (DPs). The estimated 65,000 Jewish DPs in the Allied zones of occupation in the summer of 1945 were joined by thousands of other survivors who had gone back to their hometowns, encountered local anti-Semitism, and opted to return to the camps. Postwar anti-Semitism in Poland provoked a steady stream of Polish Jews to seek shelter in the DP camps, especially after pogroms in the Polish city of Kielce in the summer of 1946. By early 1947, the DP camps were home to well over 200,000 Jewish refugees.

Encouraged by Truman's statements supporting immigration to the United States, the AJ Committee decided, in the autumn of 1946, to seek legislation permitting the entry of 100,000 DPs. As noted earlier, the AJ Committee had strongly opposed liberalizing the immigration quotas during the Hitler era, for fear of stimulating domestic anti-Semitism. Feelings of remorse over their earlier stance undoubtedly helped galvanize AJ Committee leaders to champion postwar immigration and motivated other Jewish organizations to join the effort. Some historians interpret postwar Jewish efforts for liberalized immigration as an attempt to preserve a certain image of America in their own minds: "For Jews, the symbolic power of America rested in its mythical affection for the downtrodden, the outsider, the foreigner, the immigrant. By waging a campaign to liberalize immigration laws, the Jewish community hoped to protect that myth both for themselves and for their desperate European brethren" (Dollinger 2000, 157).

The Jewish immigration lobbying effort included in its ranks the controversial American Council for Judaism, a small but well-funded organization established in 1942 to combat Zionism. Concerned that mass Jewish immigration to Palestine would increase the pressure to establish a Jewish state, the council decided to commit substantial financial assistance to the campaign for immigration to America led by the AJ Committee. It marked the first time that major Jewish organizations cooperated with the council, which had been generally treated as a pariah by most of the community because of its opposition to Zionism. For their part, many Zionist organizations privately fumed over the possibility that bringing refugees to the United States would undermine the campaign for Jewish statehood by diverting an important source of immigration away from Palestine. At the same time, they were uncomfortable about initiating a public dispute with other Jewish groups. The Zionist leadership also recognized that, for a variety of reasons, a number of DPs would not settle in Palestine even once its doors were opened. As a result, the Zionists opted to refrain from publicly airing their views.

The AJ Committee's newly formed Committee on Immigration, headed by attorney Irving Engel, set to work drafting legislation aimed at securing the admission of 100,000 Jews. Convinced that an emphasis on Jewish immigrants would stimulate criticism of the bill, and calculating that Jews constituted only about one-fourth of all European refugees, they opted to propose a bill that would permit the entry of 400,000 DPs. To further downplay the Jewish angle, the AJ Committee created the Citizens Committee on Displaced Persons (CCDP) to serve as the primary lobbying vehicle for the campaign. An array of church, labor, and business leaders were persuaded to take an active role in the CCDP. Broadening the committee's composition to represent a wide range of Americans would be crucial to the success of the legislation.

Case Study: The Problems of Coalition-Building

The Jewish leaders who initiated the campaign for the admission of DPs regarded the support of church groups as indispensable, and a number of Catholic and Protestant organizations joined the Citizens Committee on Displaced Persons at its inception. But most Christians had opposed liberalizing immigration throughout the Hitler years, and deeply ingrained attitudes did not change quickly. When the National Catholic Rural Life Conference finally passed a resolution on the DP issue in April 1947, it referred to the admission of "worthy" refugees, which it defined as those "who are not likely to undermine our democratic ideals and institutions"—that is, refugees who were fleeing communism. The prominent Protestant journal *Christian Century* supported admission of DPs on the grounds that most of them were "unable to return to their homes for fear of imprisonment and death at the hands of Communist governments." It was not until June 1947, fully seven months after the founding of the CCDP, that frustrated Jewish leaders were finally able to wrangle a statement out of the influential Catholic leader Cardinal Spellman urging that "these misery-ridden people" not be "forced against their will to return to countries, where, enslaved, their human rights will be denied them." The Jesuit periodical *America* went so far as to assert that even though many of the DPs "might be Nazis . . . to help them, specifically by taking some of them into our country, is a concrete challenge to Communism." Sympathy for Jewish victims of Nazism was in rather short supply; sympathy for Christian victims of communism, however, was another story. Recognizing that reality, American Jewish leaders accepted the church groups' anticommunist emphasis as a necessary tactic to facilitate DP immigration. They would soon discover, however, that there was a steep price to pay for inclusion of these Christian groups in the proimmigration lobby, as the proposed legislation was repeatedly altered to suit the preferences of both the Christian anticommunists and the restrictionist forces in Congress. The final version of the bill that passed scarcely reflected the Jewish leadership's original intentions (Genizi 1993, 74–75).

In an interesting reversal from years past, both the White House and the State Department supported the immigration initiative. Problems soon arose, however, because of anti-immigration sentiment in Congress. A measure consistent with the CCDP's recommendations was introduced in the spring of 1947, but it was heavily revised in the Senate Judiciary Committee to appease immigration critics. When it came out of the committee in March 1948, the total number of immigrants had been cut back to just 100,000, with half of the places reserved for agricultural laborers and the other half for individuals whose countries had been conquered by the Soviets. Both provisions, especially the former, were likely to drastically reduce the number of immigrants who would be Jews—which apparently was the intention of some of those involved in reworking the original bill. Now the Jewish-Christian coalition that the AJ Committee had assembled began to unravel; although Jewish organizations were deeply distressed by the composition of the bill, church groups, while expressing concern over the changes, called for passage of the legislation as it stood. During the final congressional committee discussions, the Jewish lobbyists helped secure several modest improvements, including an increase of the immigration total to 200,000, reduction of the percentage of farmers to 30 percent, and reduction of the percentage of refugees from Soviet areas to 40 percent. In a major setback, however, the list of those eligible for admission was expanded to include ethnic Germans who had settled in Nazi-occupied areas of other countries and had been expelled after the war—many of whom were unquestionably Nazi sympathizers.

When the legislation known as the Displaced Persons Act of 1948 was passed by Congress, the proimmigration lobby split again, this time over whether to urge President Truman to veto it. Church groups endorsed the bill. Two major Jewish groups, the Anti-Defamation League and the American Jewish Congress, called for a veto. But the AJ Committee opposed requesting a veto, for fear that such a demand would anger their Christian associates. The latter organization urged Truman to support the bill, while suggesting that it could later be amended. It became law on June 25, 1948. Almost immediately, the Jewish groups in the CCDP began making plans to amend the new act. Several Christian groups that had been part of the CCDP terminated their participation, however, and the others vehemently disagreed with some of the proposed changes. It took nearly a year for the CCDP member organizations finally to agree on which amendments to seek, and during the course of the negotiations, the Jewish groups dropped one of their key demands, the elimination of the ethnic German expellees from the eligibility list.

When the revised DP Act of 1950 reached the House-Senate conference committee, at which the legislation's language was to be finalized, a coalition of six Jewish organizations submitted a memorandum proposing a number of ways to improve the bill: stipulating the same strict investigation of suspected Nazi collaborators that the bill provided for investigating suspected communists; eliminating financial subsidies and tax exemptions for German expellees who immigrated to the United States; and altering the definition used for the German expellees so that it would not conform to the Nazis' pan-

German racial theories. As a result of strong pressure from congressional restrictionists, none of these proposed amendments were included. The final bill did, however, increase the total number to be admitted from 200,000 to 341,000, and it extended the eligibility deadline, as the Jewish groups had wanted; but it also doubled the number of German expellees who could enter.

What had begun as an initiative to bring succor to Hitler's victims in the end helped a relatively small number of Holocaust survivors, while providing assistance to a substantial number of Hitler's supporters and even collaborators. The coalition that had been assembled in order to ensure the bill's triumph had in the end facilitated its emasculation, and worse. Some historians have argued, however, that one of the beneficial aspects of the DP Act was its role in "changing the hostility of the American people as well as of Congress toward meaningful liberalization of the immigration laws. . . . By supporting the idea that the United States should offer a haven for political and religious refugees, this act paved the way for future persecuted people, particularly from the Communist countries such as Hungary, Cuba, Vietnam, and Soviet Russia" (Genizi 1993, 85).

The DP Act was conceived as temporary legislation to alleviate the immediate crisis of the DPs. It did not address the broader question of America's immigration system as a whole. In 1950 the Senate Judiciary Committee completed a comprehensive study of U.S. immigration laws, concluding that the quota system based on national origin, which had first been adopted in the 1920s, was still the best option. In early 1951, restrictionists introduced the McCarran-Walter Act, which restored the national origins system while adding new restrictions intended to further limit immigration from Asia and the Caribbean islands. Despite the horrors of the Holocaust and the absence of the economic stress that had fueled nativist sentiment during the interwar period, congressional and public opposition to increased immigration remained strong. Most Americans still subscribed to the concept at the heart of the 1920s immigration quotas—namely, "that there existed but one desirable national culture, the one that had been forged and nurtured by the original colonists and the 19th century immigrants from Northern and Western Europe." Between the 1920s and the 1950s, "there had occurred in America neither a marked increase in tolerance for immigrant cultures nor a bold and triumphant assertion of ethnic group individuality. . . . [T]he assumptions underlying the national origins system lay deeply entrenched" (Neuringer 1971, 343–344). If anything, restrictionism intensified during the 1950s as an expression of McCarthy-era fear of communist spies.

Jewish organizations lobbied against the McCarran-Walter Act on the grounds that it was based on racism. They were joined in their opposition to the bill by a number of liberal Christian groups, but some important organizations, such as the National Catholic Welfare Conference, strongly supported it. Faced with likely defeat, the antirestrictionist forces dropped their opposition to McCarran-Walter as a whole, and instead offered a series of amendments to modify its harsher aspects. All of the proposed amendments were defeated by large margins. Congress passed the McCarran Act, Truman vetoed it, and both houses of Congress overrode the veto by margins of more than two to one. Despite a number of attempts during the 1950s by Jewish groups, working with liberal members of Congress, to scrap the quota system, it was not until 1965, when the political and social climate in America had substantially changed, that the quotas were finally eliminated.

The Zionist Lobby's New Mission

Dropping "Emergency" from its name now that its initial primary task had been completed, the American Zionist Council (AZC) quickly shifted gears to focus on securing American assistance for the new state of Israel. An American Jew serving on the staff of the Israeli embassy in Washington, I. L. Kenen, was hired to direct AZC's lobbying operation. His first initiative was legislation providing Israel with $150 million in U.S. economic assistance. Kenen was careful to maintain a low profile. "We stand squarely behind legislation—never in front of it," was AZC president Louis Lipsky's motto. "I observed that precept, and for a decade my name never appeared in the press," Kenen recalled. "In those days 'lobbying' was a pejorative, but there are many peoples' lobbies today, and I like to think that we helped to popularize the people's right to petition their government, both on domestic and international affairs" (Kenen 1981, 70). Sympathy for Israel's plight in the face of Arab violence and massive immigration generated substantial congressional support for the Israel aid plan, compelling the administration to offer a counterproposal: $23.5 million for Israel, similar amounts for Iran and the Arab states, and $50 million for Palestinian Arab refugees. While mobilizing local Jewish communities to bombard their senators and representatives with telegrams urging passage of the $150 million, Kenen crafted a compromise: the $23.5 million that the administration offered, and $50 million for Israel to absorb Jewish refugees from Arab lands. Over the

State Department's continuing objections, Kenen's proposal won in a close vote, although budgetary cuts reduced it to about $65 million in the end. When Israel applied for additional aid the following year, the administration's attitude was entirely changed. With a presidential election just around the corner, the suddenly accommodating State Department, without prodding from the pro-Israel lobby, proposed a $79 million grant for the Jewish state, $73 million of which survived various budget cutbacks along the way.

To help fortify Israel's position on Capitol Hill, Kenen and his colleagues spent much of the summer of 1952 successfully lobbying the two major parties to adopt pro-Israel planks in their convention platforms. Once the election was over, however, the platforms' language could not suffice to win over the new administration. Amid a flurry of less-than-sympathetic remarks about Israel by Secretary of State John Foster Dulles and other officials, the new Eisenhower administration proposed reducing Israel's aid to $55 million for 1953–1954. While the AZC lobbyists were contacting congressional allies to have the aid amount raised, Dulles suddenly suspended all pending U.S. assistance to Israel in response to Arab charges that Israel was improperly diverting Jordan River waters for a hydroelectric power project. Unfortunately, the water controversy coincided with an Israeli counterterror raid that caused numerous Arab casualties, sparking a wave of criticism in the world press. Taken aback by the flurry of bad press and the State Department's harsh approach, the young and inexperienced pro-Israel lobby proved unable to muster significant congressional support for the Israel aid package. The Israelis saw no alternative but to halt the water-diversion project in order to restore U.S. assistance.

In the aftermath of the lobby's clash with Dulles over the water, friendly members of Congress relayed to AZC leaders rumors that they might face investigation for engaging in lobbying activities beyond the limit set for tax-exempt organizations. The danger was averted by establishing a new agency, the American Zionist Public Affairs Committee—soon to be changed to the American Israel Public Affairs Committee, or AIPAC, as it is known today—for the exclusive purpose of lobbying. Unable to enjoy tax-exempt status or receive funds from tax-exempt groups such as the AZC, the new lobby depended solely on private contributions to maintain its activities. That severely inhibited its ability to increase its staff or expand its lobbying efforts.

The Eisenhower years proved a rough period for the pro-Israel lobby. It could not muster sufficient congressional opposition to block the administration's 1954 sale of weapons to Iraq or to respond effectively to the revelation that the United States had been secretly sending military aid to Saudi Arabia for the past four years. Nor could it rally enough members of Congress to hold off Eisenhower's pressure on Israel to unilaterally withdraw from the Sinai after the 1956 war with Egypt. Nor did AIPAC have the staffing or influence to oppose the 1957 Eisenhower Doctrine, which offered vastly increased U.S. economic aid to Arab regimes supposedly endangered by the Soviets, while U.S. aid to Israel had gradually been reduced to just $25 million annually, some of it in loans. The trend continued in 1958, as U.S. economic aid to Egypt reached $63 million and continued to climb the following year, while grants to Israel were slashed to just $7.5 million in 1958 and were slated for elimination altogether in 1959. That outcome was narrowly averted when AIPAC mobilized members of the House Foreign Affairs Committee to intervene.

Especially in its early years, AIPAC often found that its legislative triumphs were more symbolic than substantive. In 1959 it contested Saudi Arabia's refusal to permit Jewish soldiers among the GIs at the U.S. military base in Dhahran, a policy that did not affect Israel but outraged American Jews. After a vigorous battle, the Senate passed an amendment blocking aid to any country that engages in racial or religious discrimination against Americans. But along the way, the sponsors agreed to a crucial compromise in the hope of attaining broader support: a sentence stating that the principles enunciated in the measure "shall be applied as the President may determine." The final version that passed thus constituted little more than a sense of congressional sentiment.

The 1960 Capitol Hill battle over Egypt's blockade of Israeli shipping likewise concluded without practical results: after strenuous lobbying to overcome objections by members of Congress who were either unsympathetic to Israel or reluctant to have the U.S. taking positions in an overseas dispute, both houses finally approved a general resolution—not even mentioning Egypt by name—condemning boycotts, blockades, and restrictions of international waterways; but it was a "sense of the Congress resolution," which had no impact on actual policy. A series of violent assaults on U.S. sites in Cairo and anti-American speeches by Egyptian leader Gamal Nasser, in 1964, prompted Congress to give initial approval to legislation cutting off U.S. aid to Egypt; but when President Johnson appealed to Congress to water down the bill, the Senate Appropriations Committee, with AIPAC's assent, inserted a loophole allowing the president to continue aid if he deemed it "in the national interest" to do so.

Legislative efforts to challenge the Arab boycott of Israel have been somewhat more successful. The boycott traditionally consisted not merely of the Arab nations' refusal to do business with Israel but also a secondary boycott, by which Arab regimes refused commerce with any company that also had dealings with Israel, and even a tertiary boycott of companies dealing with others that have business with Israel. Thus, in order to gain access to the large and lucrative business markets of the Arab world, U.S. firms would have to halt all business with Israel, and even with other firms that dealt with Israel. To combat cooperation with the boycott, AIPAC promoted a 1965 bill to require U.S. companies to refuse to reply to the questionnaire routinely sent by the Arab League boycott office to potential business partners to determine if they had any direct or indirect dealings with Israel. The questionnaire even asked whether any Jews were employed by the company. AIPAC's antiboycott bill passed its initial committee votes, but, under pressure from the Johnson administration, the term "require" was altered to "encourage and request." Thus the final version was reduced to a recommendation by Congress rather than an enforceable legal requirement. A loophole likewise encumbered a 1969 amendment to the Export Administration Act. The bill obliged exporters to report boycott requests from Arab regimes to the U.S. Department of Commerce—but it did not impose any penalties on those that failed to report.

AIPAC, together with other major Jewish organizations, periodically continued to press for legislative action against the boycott, although such efforts were sometimes complicated by a division within the Israeli government over the issue. Some Israeli officials supported a public antiboycott campaign, recalled longtime Anti-Defamation League leader Arnold Forster; but others, including Israeli ambassador to the United States Abba Eban, argued "that by openly opposing the boycott I was helping to publicize it, making it seem more potent, and thereby increasing its effectiveness." The ADL director went over Eban's head to then–foreign minister Golda Meir and "convinced her that if we did nothing, failed to fight, more and more companies would surely submit to the Arab boycott. . . . She promised to discuss the matter with Ambassador Eban. The effort to impede my activities stopped." Although Forster and his colleagues had no specific obligation to act according to the Israeli government's preferences, Jewish leaders usually defer to Israel's judgment in matters that primarily affect the Jewish state rather than American Jewry (Forster 1988, 258).

Capitalizing on public anger over the 1973–1974 Arab oil embargo, the pro-Israel lobby persuaded Congress to hold hearings on the Arab boycott in early 1975, and it convinced the chairman of the House Committee on International Trade and Commerce, New York Democrat Jonathan Bingham, to introduce legislation prohibiting American businesses from participating in the boycott. The Anti-Defamation League helped to stimulate support for the Bingham bill by releasing a study showing that more than 200 American companies, including twenty-five banks, were cooperating with the boycott. The most sensational finding was that the Commerce Department itself had included anti-Israel boycott stipulations in the tenders that it had been distributing for projects in Arab countries. The widespread media coverage of these revelations embarrassed the administration, whipped up public interest in the boycott issue, and helped generate support in Congress for Bingham's proposal. However, stiff opposition by the business community, backed by the Ford administration, initially stymied the Bingham bill. It gained new life during the 1976 presidential campaign, when Jewish advisors to candidate Jimmy Carter persuaded him to pledge his support for the antiboycott effort. At the urging of the Carter administration, Jewish leaders in early 1977 entered negotiations with the Business Roundtable, a group of prominent business leaders, to find a compromise formula on the boycott. The terms upon which they agreed were incorporated into the legislation, which was enacted in June 1977. The bill outlawed both direct and indirect compliance with any boycott of a country friendly to the United States, although it imposed only modest penalties on violators. Subsequent legislation further strengthened the antiboycott effort. Two 1993 bills prohibited the Defense Department and State Department from awarding contracts to companies that participated in the boycott, and a 1994 amendment banned U.S. arms sales to countries that take part in the boycott, but a "national interest" waiver in the latter bill rendered it toothless.

U.S. Military Aid for Israel

Securing U.S. military aid for the Jewish state proved a lengthy and arduous struggle for the pro-Israel lobby. The Johnson administration's provision of tanks to Jordan in 1966 prompted an Israeli request for American tanks, but the most it could obtain was permission to purchase them surreptitiously, via West Germany. Still hoping to win friends in the Arab world, the United States was not yet prepared to openly provide Israel with the means to defend itself. Despite AIPAC's efforts to stir Congress during the weeks of mounting

Mideast hostilities preceding the 1967 Arab-Israeli War, the administration could not be moved from its declared policy of remaining neutral "in word, thought, and deed" as the Arabs prepared to invade Israel. France, Israel's primary arms supplier, announced an arms embargo on the Jewish state on the eve of the war, compelling the Israelis to look to Washington for military assistance. The massive supply of Soviet weapons to Egypt and Syria further strengthened Israel's case for U.S. aid. In the spring of 1968, AIPAC launched a campaign to persuade the Johnson administration to sell Israel F-4 Phantom jet fighters. As congressional support for the proposal mounted, AIPAC successfully lobbied both major parties to endorse planes for Israel in their platforms. The leading candidates for the Democratic nomination, including Vice President Hubert Humphrey, quickly followed suit, substantially increasing the pressure on the administration to acquiesce. Although congressional action took the form of another symbolic "sense of the Congress" resolution, the combination of public and political pressure and election-year considerations persuaded Johnson to approve the sale. Beyond securing Israel's immediate military needs, AIPAC's fight for the Phantoms had broken down a significant psychological barrier obstructing U.S.-Israeli relations, established an important precedent for U.S. arms shipments to Israel, and helped cement the perception of U.S. weapons to Israel as an appropriate counterbalance to Soviet arms to the Arabs. Future Israeli requests for U.S. weapons would be much harder for the United States to deny, both because the Phantoms sale had legitimized the concept of such transactions and because it would be perceived as weakness in the face of aggressive Soviet behavior.

AIPAC had less success countering the Nixon administration's initial Mideast moves. The Rogers Plan, Secretary of State William Rogers's 1969 proposal for an Israeli surrender of virtually all territory won during the recent war, became U.S. policy despite Israel's characterization of such sweeping concessions as "national suicide" for the Jewish state. In a warning shot across the administration's bow, 1,400 AIPAC activists from around the country came to Washington and met with some 250 members of Congress to express their opposition to the Rogers Plan, and an AIPAC-organized letter opposing U.S. pressure on Israel attracted the signatures of 70 senators and 282 representatives. The following year a second congressional letter in a similar vein but going somewhat further, by specifically urging U.S. arms supplies to Israel, garnered the support of 70 senators and 280 representatives. These efforts sent a strong signal to the administration about the widespread support for Israel on the Hill, yet they did not suffice to change the basic thrust of U.S. policy in the region. Egypt's intensified shelling of Israeli targets across the Suez Canal in 1970–1971, known as the War of Attrition, led the administration to insist upon a cease-fire that was supposed to ensure no movement of Egypt's Soviet-made missile batteries into a 32-mile-wide zone along the canal. But when Egypt blatantly violated the truce, the United States chose to overlook the Egyptian infractions; the missiles it left in place would later be used with devastating effect against Israel in the 1973 Yom Kippur War. AIPAC's protests failed to persuade the administration to take action on the Suez missiles, but they did help convince Nixon to sell Israel additional jet fighters and tanks. That at least served the long-range purpose of reinforcing the legitimacy of Israeli arms requests to maintain a military edge in the face of Arab belligerency.

The major increase in U.S. military aid came as a result of the 1973 Yom Kippur War, when the Nixon administration undertook a massive airlift of weapons to help Israel fend off the Arab invasion. The grant from the United States to cover the cost of the aid totaled $2.2 billion. Subsequent annual aid packages to Israel reached comparable levels, gradually rising to a consistent $3 billion annually, $1.8 billion of it in military assistance and the remainder in economic aid. Part of the increase was to compensate Israel for the sacrifices it had made in surrendering Sinai territory and oil fields in the U.S.-brokered Israel-Egypt agreement of 1975; part compensated for Israel's retreat from the rest of the Sinai as part of the Israel-Egypt peace agreement of 1979. The continuing Arab arms buildup has forced Israel to spend large portions of its budget on weapons and to rely on the United States to maintain its level of $3 billion in annual assistance to Israel for more than two decades now.

Reducing the level of that aid is almost inconceivable in American politics today. U.S. military support for Israel has become a bedrock fixture of U.S. foreign policy, and no administration is likely to consider implementing a radical change in that policy without a seismic shift in public opinion and congressional sentiment. Polls consistently show most Americans, and an overwhelming majority in Congress, in favor of continued U.S. military assistance to the Jewish state. That sentiment has been so consistent over such a long period that it is difficult to imagine circumstances under which it could change so sharply as to enable or encourage a president to reverse long-standing U.S. policy toward Israel.

In simple political terms, Israel's enduring position as the largest single recipient of U.S. aid is testimony to the continuing significance of the Jewish vote, especially in presidential elections. If aid to Israel were widely perceived as directly inimical to U.S. national interests, the impact of Jewish votes would not suffice to secure such aid. But given the widespread perception of Israel as an ally of the United States, the weight of Jewish electoral support has become a decisive factor in U.S. Middle East policy. A major shift by the United States away from its traditional friendship with Israel would certainly result in a full-scale shift of Jewish voters away from that president. The desertion of Jimmy Carter by a majority of Jewish voters in 1980—most of them for a Republican candidate so conservative that few Jews would have ordinarily supported him—was a striking demonstration of the consequences of a president adopting policies unfriendly to Israel.

Case Study: The Anti-Israel Lobby

In the minds of its enemies, the influence of the pro-Israel lobby has risen to near mythic proportions in recent decades. The earliest complaints about the power of Israel's American friends date back to the late 1950s, when Senator J. William Fulbright, chairman of the Senate Foreign Relations Committee, began to distinguish himself as a vocal critic of the Jewish state and its allies in Washington. As aid to Israel increased significantly in the 1970s, Fulbright and other critics of Israel began focusing on AIPAC as a source of undue influence on U.S. foreign policy. Some of the criticism proved to be a double-edged sword, however. For while AIPAC did not enjoy being singled out for supposedly engaging in inappropriate behavior, the accusations also gave it a notoriety that helped create its reputation as a lobbying powerhouse. A lobby even a fraction as influential as Fulbright and company made it out to be was clearly a force to be reckoned with.

During the 1980s, two members of Congress who were among the most unfriendly toward Israel and AIPAC, Illinois senator Charles Percy and Illinois representative Paul Findley, were defeated by challengers whose campaigns were supported by friends of Israel from outside the state. For Findley, who has devoted his postcongressional life to anti-Israel activism, his defeat was proof of a Jewish conspiracy to silence those who differ with Israel's policies; his account of his conflicts with Israel's supporters was entitled *They Dare to Speak Out.* Findley's fears were misplaced; he is free to speak out against Israel both in and out of Congress, just as those who disagree with him had the right to oppose his re-election. Findley's defeat did contain a number of lessons, but none of them as nefarious as Findley and his supporters imagined.

First, Findley's fate demonstrated the growing sophistication of Israel's American supporters. Pro-Israel activists no longer confine their attention to races in their own congressional districts; now they carefully watch other congressional races around the country and contribute to candidates who most closely represent their views. Many special-interest groups do likewise.

Second, it demonstrated that the "Jewish lobby," which Findley denounced as if it were monolithic, in fact extends far beyond AIPAC's offices. AIPAC is a registered lobby, not a political action committee (despite its name, which by coincidence has the letters *PAC* in it), and as such it cannot contribute money to political candidates. It can, through its publications, focus unfriendly attention on those politicians who are hostile to Israel, but by law it cannot direct its members to support any particular candidate financially. An array of pro-Israel PACs has arisen in recent decades to perform that function. Groups such as WINPAC, the Women's Israel Political Action Committee, and NATPAC, the National Political Action Committee, monitor races around the country and raise money for their preferred candidates, although those amounts are strictly limited by campaign finance laws. The pro-Israel PACs are not controlled by AIPAC or the Israeli government; they are groups of private citizens interested in helping candidates whose views on the Middle East coincide with their own. If the pro-Israel PACs happen to oppose a member of Congress who was criticized in an AIPAC publication, that merely reflects the inevitable commonality of views between pro-Israel PACs and the pro-Israel lobby.

Third, the defeat of Percy and Findley demonstrated the increasing importance of Israel as an American election issue. Candidates and campaign managers everywhere took note of these developments and had to factor them into their calculations when weighing what positions to take regarding the Middle East. The defeat of Percy and Findley meant much more than the removal of two critics of Israel from Capitol Hill; it sent a message that was heard far and wide.

Sometimes the phrase "Israeli lobby" is used as a code word for "Jews," and harsh but legitimate criticism of Israeli policies slips into outright anti-Semitism. Pat Buchanan, who during the 1992 presidential campaign boasted that he was the only candidate "who had the guts to stand up to the AIPAC lobby," has frequently referred to Congress as "Israeli-occupied territory," a sort of contemporary variation of the stock anti-Semitic accusation about Jews controlling the government. On the eve of the 1991 Gulf War, Buchanan repeatedly accused the pro-Israel lobby of trying to drag the United States into the conflict, even going so far as to list Jewish-surnamed pundits as the nation's chief warmongers, and contrasting them with "kids with names like McAllister, Murphy, Gonzales and Leroy Brown" who would be the ones "doing the fighting." The remark was widely regarded as thinly veiled anti-Semitism.

Similar rhetoric appears regularly in the pages of the *Washington Report on Middle East Affairs,* a thick, glossy monthly magazine edited by several former U.S. ambassadors to Arab countries. Each issue contains a long list of private contributors whose financial assistance makes it possible for the magazine to be distributed free of charge to members of Congress, public libraries, and journalists from coast to coast. In addition to the standard denunciations of Israeli policies, the *Washington Report* has published articles belittling the magnitude of the Holocaust, listing the names of Jewish publishers of leading U.S. newspapers to demonstrate "Zionist" control of the media, and accusing Israel of "Nazi-style" genocide against the Arabs. Each issue is filled with wild conspiracy theories about Israel and pro-Israel lobby groups, accusing them of orchestrating everything from the Monica Lewinsky scandal to the assassination of John F. Kennedy. This kind of extreme rhetoric has made it even more difficult for the anti-Israel lobby to make inroads on Capitol Hill.

A Strategy of Avoiding Clashes

AIPAC's strategy over the years has been anchored in a determination to avoid conflicts with the incumbent president and his administration whenever possible. This attitude derives from a desire to preserve AIPAC's access to the White House; a conviction that the aims of the pro-Israel lobby are more likely to be attained through friendly compromise than bruising public conflicts; a fear that victories attained through public confrontation can leave a residue of bitterness that could endanger future Israel-related initiatives; and a belief that sustaining the public perception of warm U.S.-Israeli relations, even when those relations are not really so warm, can be a kind of self-fulfilling prophecy. When AIPAC has squared off publicly against an administration, it has been defeated more often than it has triumphed, and the lessons of those losses have not been lost on the AIPAC leadership.

AIPAC went all out against the Carter administration's proposed sale of advanced jet fighters to Egypt and Saudi Arabia in 1978. It helped mobilize a majority in the House International Relations Committee to urge withdrawal of the proposed sale, but after a major counterlobbying effort by the administration, the pro-Israel forces lost by a narrow vote in the Senate. Similarly, AIPAC campaigned against the Reagan administration's proposed sale of AWACS surveillance aircraft to Saudi Arabia in 1981, rallying a majority in the House against it but losing in the Senate.

By the late 1980s, the pro-Israel lobby found itself confronted by a new and unexpected nemesis: Jewish officials in the Defense Department and State Department who were sharply critical of Israel. Traditionally, few Jews had ever made it to the upper echelons of either department. One of the first was Deputy Undersecretary of Defense Dov Zakheim, who spearheaded a 1986–1987 campaign to pressure Israel to cancel production of a U.S.-financed fighter aircraft, the Lavi. Israel had initiated the Lavi in the hope of ending its reliance on U.S. aircraft; but the Defense Department resented congressional approval of funding for the project, contending that Israel should be compelled to continue purchasing U.S. fighter jets. Zakheim was the perfect choice to serve as the Defense Department's public point man for the attack on the Lavi; his beard, yarmulke, and prominence in the Washington-area Jewish community made it harder for supporters of Israel to argue that he was unsympathetic to Israel's concerns. Most of the pro-Israel lobby opted to remain on the sidelines as Defense Department officials used private pressure and orchestrated leaks to the media to provoke a split in the Israeli cabinet, which finally decided by a one-vote margin to scrap the Lavi.

The problem of Jewish government officials clashing with Israel intensified when James Baker was appointed secretary of state in 1989 and named as his chief Mideast advisers a number of Jews who were strongly critical of Israeli policies. Media reports about the new Jewish officials in the State Department emphasized their identification with Judaism and portrayed their rise as a breakthrough for Jews seeking positions in areas of government to which few Jews had gained access in the past. AIPAC chose to refrain from clashing with Baker's team rather than risk an open rift with the administration; the editor of the pro-Israel lobby's newsletter, *Near East Report*, was dismissed after writing a magazine article critical of what he called the State Department's "Jewish Arabists."

AIPAC's most difficult moment came in the autumn of 1991. Israel, staggering under the financial burden of caring for hundreds of thousands of new immigrants from the crumbling Soviet Union, asked the United States to guarantee $10 billion worth of loans. The

request garnered widespread support on Capitol Hill, thanks in part
to AIPAC's intensive lobbying, but also because of congressional ap-
preciation for Israel's decision to heed the U.S. request to stay out of
the Gulf War, even when that meant refraining from responding to
Iraqi missile strikes on Tel Aviv. But the Bush administration chose to
use the loan guarantee request as leverage against Israel's establishment of Jewish communities in the disputed Judea-Samaria (West
Bank) territories. The State Department's Mideast team chose
September 12, when AIPAC lay activists from around the country
were in Washington on their annual lobbying mission, for President
Bush to go full-force against Israel's American supporters. In a press
conference punctuated by carefully choreographed anger, Bush dramatically slammed his fist on the lectern as he complained that he
was "one lonely little guy" besieged by "powerful political forces"
who had brought "something like a thousand lobbyists" against him.
Bush's statements tapped into the fears and prejudices of those Americans who imagine Jews as power-hungry conspirators seeking to ma-
nipulate Congress and foreign policy. Not surprisingly, the White
House was deluged with letters and calls hailing the president for
"standing up to the Jews." But the most remarkable response was that
of those who had championed Israel's loan guarantee request. Leading congressional supporters of the loan guarantees, intimidated by
the president's outburst and fearful of accusations that they were taking orders from the Jewish lobby, quickly assented to the administration's request to delay consideration of the Israeli request for four
months.

For American Jewish leaders, the Bush denunciation was a public
relations nightmare. Whether deliberately or not, the president had
helped perpetuate an anti-Semitic stereotype and even suggested
that there was something improper about Jews exercising their right
to lobby. The heads of the Conference of Presidents of Major American Jewish Organizations immediately appealed to Bush to retract
his statement. The president waited nearly a week—until he could
be certain that his remarks had accomplished their goal of derailing
the loan guarantee request—before issuing a statement insisting that
he had not meant to disparage American Jewry's equal right to
lobby. The Jewish leadership could derive the psychological satisfaction of feeling that American Jews had been welcomed back into
American political culture as equals. But the Bush administration
was the clear winner. Congress, AIPAC, and the Jewish community
at large were too intimidated to resume fighting for the loan guarantees. For all of Bush's talk about the "powerful" Jewish lobby, it

took just one press conference by the president to effectively intimidate his opposition and demonstrate how uncertain the lobby's power really was.

The Oslo Accords and the Pro-Israel Lobby

Even as the loan guarantee battle subsided on Capitol Hill, the issue was drastically altering the dynamics of the U.S.-Israeli relationship and, with it, the role of AIPAC. The inability of the Israeli government to secure the loan guarantees caused a crisis of confidence among Israeli voters, especially among new immigrants from Russia whose social welfare was partly dependent on those funds. The result was the first national electoral triumph for the opposition Labor Party in nearly twenty years. AIPAC's traditional position had been that it would support the policies of whichever government Israel's voters chose. Labor ruled Israel from its establishment in 1948 until 1977, and AIPAC had grown accustomed to defending Labor's policies. AIPAC's leadership sometimes seemed less than enthusiastic in their defense of the policies of the nationalist Likud Party, which came to power in 1977 and won the next three elections. Returning, in 1992, to advocacy of Labor's positions was not especially difficult for AIPAC at first, since the new government's initial policies were not radically different from those of its Likud predecessors. But in 1993 the Labor government unexpectedly scrapped Israel's longstanding opposition to negotiations with terrorist leader Yasir Arafat, and signed an accord granting the Palestinian Arabs self-rule in exchange for peaceful relations with the Jewish state.

Almost overnight, AIPAC abandoned many of the arguments it had been making to lawmakers for years: the unreliability of Arafat's promises, the dangers of surrendering strategic territory, the right of Jews to establish communities in the disputed Judea-Samaria regions. Now AIPAC found itself making the opposite case and, in perhaps the most startling reversal of all, lobbying for U.S. government aid to the Palestinian Authority, to which Israel had agreed as part of the peace accord package. Some Israeli government officials began to suggest that perhaps the pro-Israel lobby had outlived its purpose. During times when Israel was at odds with the U.S. administration, AIPAC had been useful to counteract U.S. pressure; when Israel was in conflict with Arafat, AIPAC had been there to make Israel's case on Capitol Hill. But with the Israeli and U.S. governments in seeming harmony and Arafat's war against Israel apparently at an end, what would AIPAC be fighting for? There now remained relatively little difference between AIPAC's stance and that of two small left-wing lobbies that had recently been established in Washington: the Jewish Peace Lobby, which advocated Israeli acquiescence to all of the PLO's demands; and Americans for Peace Now, the U.S. wing of Israel's Peace Now movement, which urged Congress to reduce U.S. aid to Israel unless it made an array of concessions to the Arabs. These two groups, whose positions had been rejected by the vast majority of the Jewish community prior to the Israel-PLO agreement, suddenly found themselves nearly in accord with the Israeli government and its unofficial representative in Washington, AIPAC.

The immediate internal problem for AIPAC was that many of its constituents were uncomfortable with the sea change in its positions. Grassroots activists around the country who had joined with the pro-Israel lobby in order to lobby for Israel were now being told that the definition of "pro-Israel" had radically changed: now support for Israel meant support for the peace accord package, which, among other things, meant lobbying for aid to Arafat. Some AIPAC members followed along; others defected to a new pro-Israel lobby in Washington, the revived Zionist Organization of America (ZOA). Shortly after the accords were signed in the autumn of 1993, activists skeptical of Arafat's trustworthiness were elected to the leadership of the ZOA. They now strove to fill the vacuum created by AIPAC's shift to the left. What made the ZOA's new Washington lobbying all the more complicated for AIPAC was that it focused on issues that appealed to the AIPAC rank-and-file. AIPAC found itself caught between its desire to conform to the wishes of the Israeli government and the Clinton administration, and its fear of losing members and donors if it went too far or too fast in that direction.

An early test for AIPAC came with the January 1994 nomination of *Time* magazine columnist Strobe Talbott, a longtime and harsh critic of Israel, as deputy secretary of state. Talbott was well known to the AIPAC leadership; indeed, AIPAC's newsletter had criticized Talbott's attacks on Israel more than once. Moreover, this was no minor appointment; Talbott, an old personal friend of the president, would play a major role in the shaping of the administration's foreign policy and was already rumored to be next in line to become secretary of state. AIPAC, loath to take issue with the Clinton administration, endorsed Talbott; the ZOA launched a lobbying campaign against the nomination. The number of senators opposing Talbott, estimated at less than ten when his name was first put forward, rose to thirty-three by the time it was put to a vote, prompting media pundits to declare him too controversial ever to be promoted to secretary; indeed, he never was. It was a stunning accomplishment for the upstart ZOA and an embarrassment for AIPAC. For the first time, it was beginning to appear as if there were two pro-Israel lobbies on Capitol Hill.

The two lobbies crossed swords that summer, when the ZOA initiated legislation to make U.S. aid to the Palestinian Authority conditional on the PA's compliance with the peace accords. In a precarious balancing act, AIPAC publicly endorsed the Specter Amendment as a nod to its membership but then privately lobbied against it as a nod to the Israeli and U.S. governments. This unusual strategy might have succeeded had ZOA officials not shown up, unexpectedly, at the late-night House-Senate conference committee where the administration had hoped to bury Specter's amendment. Although the ZOA lobbied wavering members of Congress to support the bill, AIPAC's lobbyists were compelled to stand aside rather than risk its becoming known that they were undercutting the bill in contravention of their organization's public stance. The amendment passed, although the ZOA's enthusiasm over its triumph was somewhat dampened by the inclusion of a "national security" waiver, which the Clinton administration would use for years to come to authorize aid to the PA despite its violations of the accords.

The ZOA successfully carved out a sizable niche for itself on Capitol Hill during the mid and late 1990s by continuing to champion causes that AIPAC could not risk opposing without losing its constituents. The most compelling of these was the Clinton administration's failure to press Arafat to hand over Palestinian Arab terrorists involved in attacks in which U.S. citizens were harmed. Although on the surface it seemed to be a simple matter of injustice, the issue of American victims of terrorism also carried within it the seeds of broader controversy: it undermined Arafat's credibility by drawing attention to his sheltering of killers, and it raised questions about the administration's apparent willingness to refrain from pursuing killers of its citizens in order to shield Arafat from criticism. In the autumn of 1999, the ZOA initiated legislation requiring the State Department to report to Congress twice yearly on the status of efforts to catch terrorists in these cases. Although reluctant to lobby publicly for a bill that the administration strongly opposed, AIPAC could not afford to oppose it without seeming indifferent to the suffering of terror victims. Even Americans for Peace Now put up only a half-hearted protest that the legislation might interfere with the peace negotiations, but it beat a quick retreat when challenged by families of the victims, many of whom joined a potent political action group under the ZOA's auspices.

AIPAC today remains by far the largest and most influential of the Israel-related lobbying groups on Capitol Hill. The ZOA, however, has emerged as something of a contender for that throne, not because of the size or budget of its lobbying staff but because of its ability to hone in on issues that attract media attention, appeal to politicians on both sides of the aisle, and frighten off potential opponents. Those are crucial ingredients for a successful lobby.

The Case for Israel

Although much of AIPAC's resources are invested in struggles over specific pieces of legislation and aid packages, in between those battles its lobbyists invest their time in an educational process informally known as "making Israel's case." This involves one-on-one meetings between pro-Israel lobbyists and individual members of Congress or their senior aides, to update them on recent Mideast developments and present Israel's side of whichever controversy happens to be in the public eye at the moment.

Those making the case for Israel have always enjoyed a number of advantages. To begin with, Israel has much more in common with the United States than does the typical Arab regime, and those similarities make it easier for members of Congress to sympathize with the Jewish state. Israel's democratic system of government, freedom of the press, and Westernized culture are naturally more attractive to members of Congress than the totalitarianism and distinctly Middle Eastern culture of the Arab world.

Second, many members of Congress have been receptive to the argument that Israel is America's ally against common foes. From the 1950s until the collapse of the Soviet Union in 1991, pro-Israel lobbyists argued that Israel served the interests of the United States by deterring the expansion of Soviet influence in the Middle East. This perspective gained its widest audience in Washington during the Reagan administration. With the rise of Islamic fundamentalism and the increase in Muslim terrorist attacks against U.S. targets in recent years, the pro-Israel lobby has portrayed the Jewish state as Israel's comrade-in-arms in the battle against international terrorism. The Arabs' frequent use of terrorism horrifies the average American and strengthens the Jewish lobby's ability to rally congressional sympathy for Israel. Attacks striking closer to home, such as the Muslim terrorist attacks on the World Trade Center and Pentagon in 2001, naturally reinforced the perception that the United States and Israel are in the same trench.

Third, many Americans supported the creation of Israel, and have continued to endorse U.S. aid to Israel, as an appropriate response to the Holocaust. This view was motivated by sympathy for Hitler's Jewish victims as well as, in some cases, a sense of guilt over America's refusal to make any serious effort to rescue Jews from the Nazis. Over time, however, some of this sentiment has evaporated, because of the steadily dwindling number of Americans who were adults at the time of the Holocaust.

Fourth, for much of its existence Israel has been widely regarded as the underdog in its conflict with the Arabs, and most Americans instinctively side with an underdog. The huge advantage that the Arabs have always enjoyed over Israel in terms of manpower, weapons, and geography has garnered considerable sympathy for tiny Israel as it has struggled to survive against overwhelming odds. Its military victories in 1948, 1956, 1967, and 1973 were seen as all the more remarkable—to some, miraculous—in view of the Arabs' many advantages. However, Israel's traditional reputation as the underdog has steadily eroded in recent decades. Sophisticated and well-financed Arab information campaigns, aided by sympathizers in the media, have succeeded in focusing negative attention on various Israeli policies and portraying Israel as a powerful regime that oppresses defenseless Arabs.

Finally, there is the role of what is often called Christian Zionism. A significant number of Americans are Bible-believing Christians who regard the creation of the modern state of Israel as the fulfillment of Divine prophecy, and who consider it America's moral and religious obligation to help the Jewish state defend itself against its enemies. Although Israel's fate is by no means the single most pressing issue for most of them personally, they nevertheless constitute a reservoir of pro-Israel sentiment that can influence members of Congress. Moreover, pro-Israel lobbyists often find that members of Congress from the Midwest in particular often personally share such sentiments and are among Israel's most passionate supporters. Making Israel's case is considerably easier when a segment of Congress already subscribes to the pro-Israel view without even being lobbied to do so.

The Jackson Amendment

The single most significant victory in the history of Jewish lobbying in Washington concerned the plight of Jews in the USSR—although it owes its origins to a handful of Jewish congressional staffers, rather than Jewish lobbyists. In 1972 senior aides to senators Henry Jackson (D-WA) and Abraham Ribicoff (D-CT) and Representative Bertram Podell (D-NY) crafted legislation linking U.S.-Soviet trade to increased Jewish emigration. The Soviets were hoping that the Nixon administration, as part of its policy of détente, would approve "most favored nation" (MFN) status, which would enable the USSR to enjoy a range of trade benefits not available to most of America's business partners; the proposed legislation would deny MFN status to countries that prohibited freedom of emigration. Soviet Jewry activists were galvanized by the August 1972 decision by the USSR to impose an exorbitant "diploma tax" on any citizen with higher education who sought to emigrate. The new decree threatened to slash the rate of Jewish emigration, which, under international pressure (see Chapter 2), had increased from the traditional rate of less than 1,000 annually to about 15,000 in 1971 and an expected total of nearly twice that number in 1972.

Richard Perle and Morris Amitay, senior aides to Jackson and Ribicoff, respectively, arranged for Jackson to announce the proposed bill at a conference of Jewish leaders in Washington in September 1972. The speech "brought the members of the audience to their feet" (Korey, 10). Perle and Amitay helped override the few doubters at the gathering by reminding them of the American Jewish leadership's failure to speak out during the Holocaust. The lobbying effort swung into action. "Calls began going out to round up support," according to one journalist's account at the time. "In the next week senators reported receiving 20 or 30 letters a day on the issue; others told of visits or telephone calls from Jews in their states who had been active in their election campaigns" (Rosenbaum 1973, 14). Because the Soviet Jewry activist movement did not yet have a Washington-based lobbying operation, the work for the Jackson amendment was undertaken by AIPAC's Washington office, under I. L. Kenen and Ken Wollack, local Soviet Jewry activists in the Washington area, and Soviet Jewry groups around the country.

With national elections around the corner and widespread public criticism of the diploma tax, it was a politically fortuitous moment for Jackson's amendment; 72 of his Senate colleagues quickly joined as cosponsors. "Why did so many people sign the amendment? Because there's no political advantage in not signing," one senator explained. "If you do sign, you don't offend anyone. If you don't sign, you might offend some Jews in your state." In the House of Representatives, the bill was spearheaded by another Jewish congressional staffer, Mark

Talisman, aide to Representative Charles Vanik (D-OH). By January it had 144 cosponsors in the House. A *New York Times* report at the time described what happened next: AIPAC's chief lobbyist, I. L. Kenen, who played a major role in the Jackson amendment campaign, sent an urgent letter to about 1,000 Jewish leaders across the country. It included a list of 144 representatives who had agreed to sponsor a move identical to Senator Jackson's and said: "If your congressman has not yet joined in co-sponsorship, will you please urge him to do so without delay." Most of those who received Mr. Kenen's letter—his mailing list had been carefully cultivated over the years—were in position to pass the word to hundreds of others. By the third week in January there were few representatives who had not received dozens of letters and calls from important constituents (Rosenbaum 1973, 14). Within weeks, the bill had 270 cosponsors in the House.

Jackson's initiative directly challenged the Nixon administration's policy of détente, which had made no room for human rights issues. "Senator Jackson, spotting something the Soviet Union greatly desired, namely huge economic concessions by America, dropped a tiny little wrench in the smoothly reciprocating gears of American-Soviet friendship, grinding the whole thing to a shuddering halt," one pundit commented (Buckley 1974, 30).

The Nixon administration's vehement opposition to the Jackson-Vanik amendment ensured a lengthy and arduous struggle between the White House and Congress. In October 1972 the administration concluded a trade agreement with the USSR that, among other things, committed Nixon to pursue congressional endorsement of MFN status for the Soviet Union. Faced with growing support on Capitol Hill for the Jackson amendment and the administration's insistence that concessions on emigration were necessary to win MFN status, the Soviets quietly scrapped the diploma tax and increased the number of Jews permitted to leave. The number would eventually reach 35,000 for the year 1973.

Convinced that moving ahead with Jackson-Vanik would result in further Soviet concessions, Soviet Jewry activists continued their efforts to secure additional cosponsors and shore up those who might be wavering in the face of the Soviets' concessions and pressure from the administration. Howard Sachar (1992, 914) recounts the efforts undertaken to retain the support of Representative Wilbur Mills, chairman of the House Ways and Means Committee, a leading sponsor of the amendment, who started backtracking when the Soviets cancelled the diploma tax:

Morris Amitay learned that Wilbur Mills, who was vacillating in his support, had a close Jewish friend in Arkansas, David Herman, a retired shoe manufacturer. Arrangements were made for Herman to visit Mills in Washington. It was an emotional meeting, with Herman not hesitating to invoke the memory of the Holocaust. A day later the shaken Mills announced that he was back on board as a cosponsor.

According to Fine (2001, 16), Talisman located Jewish constituents of Vanik's who happened to own a factory in Mills's home district and persuaded them to hint to Mills that they would move the factory elsewhere if he abandoned Jackson-Vanik. Such anecdotes help illustrate the imaginative and energetic efforts undertaken by supporters of Soviet Jewry to keep the Jackson amendment on track despite the obstacles created by conflicting interests, competing pressures, and the complexities inherent in the legislative process.

Unable to pry loose Jackson's congressional allies with the Soviets' modest concessions, the administration opened phase two of its effort: splitting the bill's most enthusiastic and determined backers, the Jewish community. "Whether the balance now tips against the Jackson amendment depends . . . upon the attitude of the Jewish leaders in the United States," a *New York Times* political analyst noted in April 1973. "If the Jewish leaders begin to waver, many politicians will no longer feel under such a compulsion to challenge the President on what he has made into an important foreign policy issue" (Finney 1973, 1). Jewish leaders who were summoned to the White House in April were pressed by Nixon to abandon the legislation on the grounds that his private contacts with the Soviets would result in increased emigration. The group consented to issue a statement praising both the administration and Congress for their work on behalf of Soviet Jewry and saying nothing about Jackson's amendment— prompting a backlash of protests from the Jewish community that was so vociferous and widespread that the Conference of Presidents of Major American Jewish Organizations felt compelled to issue a statement explicitly endorsing Jackson-Vanik.

Nixon persisted in his efforts to create the perception of a divided Jewish community. In June, two of the Jewish leaders at the center of the earlier controversy, Republicans Max Fisher and Jacob Stein, sparked a new uproar by accepting the administration's invitation to dine with Soviet ruler Leonid Brezhnev during his visit to Washington. Other Jewish organizations roundly condemned Fisher and Stein, and Jewish student activists even picketed Stein's home.

This "year-long game of cat-and-mouse between the White House and the Jewish leadership" (Mehlman 1974, 30) reached its unpleasant climax in October. Shortly after airlifting military supplies to Israel to fend off the Arabs' Yom Kippur attack, the administration sensed a golden opportunity to drive a wedge between Jackson and the Jews. A handful of Jewish leaders were again summoned to the White House, this time to be told that U.S. support for Israel might be diminished if the Jackson amendment went forward. Several of the Jewish officials then appealed to Member of Congress Al Ullman, substituting for the ill Wilbur Mills as chair of the House Ways and Means Committee, to delay consideration of Jackson-Vanik. Following further pressure from the White House, a group of Jewish leaders agreed to propose to Jackson that he water down the amendment to meet the administration's concerns. As word of the Jewish leaders' intentions leaked, Soviet Jewry activists mounted a last-minute barrage of telegrams and phone calls to Jackson, urging him to stand fast, and they forced the convening of an emergency session of the establishment's National Conference on Soviet Jewry. Faced with overwhelming grassroots pressure, the conference leaders agreed to refrain from proposing any dilution of the Jackson amendment and instead proceeded to the meeting with Senator Jackson in full support of the bill. At the meeting, Jackson himself angrily chastised the Jewish leaders for considering pulling the rug out from under his efforts. With the Jewish community on board, the Jackson amendment moved full steam ahead. An attempt to weaken the House version of the bill was defeated handily, and Jackson-Vanik passed, intact, on December 11, 1973. The administration would have to offer Jackson and his allies something concrete to head off the amendment's passage by the Senate.

Case Study: Mobilizing Grassroots Pressure on the Jewish Leadership

When pressure by the Nixon administration caused some American Jewish leaders to waver in their support for the Jackson Amendment, a wave of angry protests by grassroots Soviet Jewry activists forced them to return to Jackson's camp. The episode illustrates the complex interplay of factors that shape the policies of the "Jewish lobby." Although Jewish lobbyists are not directly elected by their constituents and are not necessarily bound by anything other than their employers' particular preferences, there exists an understanding in the community—occasionally articulated in meetings of Jewish leaders and the Jewish media—that the actions of the Jewish lobby should generally reflect the sentiments of American Jewry at large. The case of the Jackson amendment was one of the few instances in which an aroused network of grassroots activists compelled the Jewish leadership and its lobbyists to take a particular stance.

The outrage that erupted over the Jewish leaders' position on Jackson was illustrated in an article by Yossi Klein in a national Jewish weekly, the *Jewish Post and Opinion*, on January 4, 1974. Klein's "Young Jewish Activist" column, a regular feature in the newspaper, offered readers a revealing glimpse of sentiment among young activists—some of them destined to become future leaders of the Jewish community. Although Klein's tone was sharp, sometimes even harsh, the points he made typified the anger felt by many in the Soviet Jewry movement.

The Jewish leadership's shift on the Jackson amendment was not "a result of the extenuating situation in the Middle East" or "some sort of confidential information that Jewish leaders were privy to," Klein asserted. "Our leadership always felt ill-at-ease with the idea of plunging the plight of Soviet Jewry into the very center of international relations, fearing to become too conspicuous" and nervous that anti-Semitism could result if it were widely perceived that the Soviet Jewry issue was interfering with peace between the superpowers. Hence, according to Klein, "Jewish leadership was prepared long before the current Arab-Israeli crisis to abandon Jackson in exchange for vague reassurances from President Nixon." He continued:

> Following the meeting last April between Nixon and Jewish officials, I had occasion to speak briefly with Richard Perle, Jackson's key aide on the Amendment issue. Perle spoke bitterly of the public defection of Jewish leadership from the Amendment and said that in their meeting with Nixon, "they melted like butter." However, because of recent developments, Jewish leaders were compelled to present a facade of continued support for Jackson.

Recalling American Jewry's response to the Nazi persecutions, Klein concluded:

> Those who pleaded ignorance and abandoned European Jewry to the Gas Chambers, now shamelessly abandon its survivors to Siberia. . . .

We must find the strength and courage to depose the arrogant men and women of the American Jewish Judenrat who are capable of selling us all out under the proper degree of pressure. One must thank God for the only Jewish leader left in America—Senator Jackson. But what does that say about American Jewry when it takes an Episcopalian from Washington to carry on the fight against its own leaders on behalf of the Jewish people?

To avoid passage of the legislation in the Senate, Secretary of State Henry Kissinger initiated negotiations with the Soviet authorities, on the one hand, and with Jackson and his supporters on the other, to reach a compromise on the Jewish emigration issue. Jackson insisted that the Soviets agree to let 100,000 Jews leave each year; the administration and the Kremlin offered 30,000. The talks moved slowly under the Nixon administration, but they made significant progress once Gerald Ford took office in August 1974. By October, Kissinger and Jackson had announced agreement, in the form of an exchange of letters in which Kissinger assured Jackson that the Soviets would liberalize their emigration restrictions, and Jackson stated that Congress understood this to mean that at least 60,000 Jews per year would be permitted to leave.

Meanwhile, however, unbeknownst to Soviet Jewry activists, another amendment restricting business with the Soviets was quietly winding its way through the legislative process. Sponsored by Senator Adlai Stevenson III, it imposed a $300 million ceiling on Export-Import Bank credits to the USSR even if emigration were liberalized sufficiently to comply with Jackson-Vanik. Stevenson's bill effectively wiped out the incentive for emigration that was the basis of Jackson's amendment. Upon the passage of the Stevenson amendment in December 1974, the Kremlin announced that it was canceling the October 1972 trade agreement, and the rate of Soviet Jewish emigration was slashed. Kissinger and other opponents of the Jackson amendment cited the Soviet move as evidence that the Soviet Jewry activists' strategy of pressure had backfired. Yet its achievements cannot be denied: the struggle for Jackson-Vanik firmly established the principle that the United States has a right to link aid to human rights abroad; it created a standard that the Soviets would have to meet if they ever hoped to improve relations substantially with the United States in the future; and it contributed to the economic pressures that eventually brought about the collapse of the Soviet Union.

The Jewish Lobby's Other Interests

The Jewish lobby has never restricted itself to lobbying on issues directly related to Jewish interests. Although American Jewish lobby groups are best known for their advocacy on matters pertaining to Israel or beleaguered Jewish communities abroad, they also have a rich history of involvement in issues not directly related to specific Jewish interests. Most notably, prominent American Jews played an active role in the civil rights movement from its inception, helping to found the NAACP and similar organizations and spearheading many of their interwar campaigns (see Chapter 2). Major Jewish organizations took advantage of the defeat and discrediting of Nazism to lead the post–World War II drive for fairness legislation, arguing that both racial and religious discrimination echoed Nazism, whereas American principles had always embraced tolerance and diversity. In 1946 the AJ Congress hired Will Maslow, a former official of the Roosevelt administration's wartime Fair Employment Practices Commission (FEPC), to head its lobbying arm, the Commission on Law and Social Action. During the late 1940s and early 1950s, the AJ Congress and other Jewish groups, especially the National Jewish Community Relations Advisory Council (NJCRAC), made a concerted effort to bring about enactment of a permanent federal FEPC. The NJCRAC even went out of its way to mollify segregationists by emphasizing that such legislation "has nothing to do with personal or social relationships" and would "not promote social equality," but would merely ensure equality of employment opportunities. Nevertheless, the opposition of Southern Democrats and many Republicans made it impossible to find sufficient congressional backing for a federal FEPC. By 1953, Jewish groups turned their attention to convincing individual states and cities to pass local FEPC-style regulations, with modest success.

They also lobbied for a federal anti–poll tax law and a federal anti-lynching law, although the latter was more symbolic than substantive, since by the 1950s lynching of blacks in the South had become rare. Indicative of the extensive Jewish involvement in promoting civil rights legislation is the fact that two of the most significant civil rights bills, the Civil Rights Act of 1964 and the Voting Rights Act of 1965, were conceived and crafted by Jewish and black activists with the Leadership Conference on Civil Rights, which for many years was located in the Washington, D.C., headquarters of Reform Judaism's lobbying arm, the Religious Action Center.

The AJ Congress also initiated a major lobbying effort, beginning in the 1950s and continuing to the present, against congressional attempts to provide government funding to parochial schools. The AJ Congress, joined by other leading Jewish groups, contended that strict church-state separation is the only way to ensure that the government does not favor any one religious group. Many of the Jewish church-state separationists were also motivated by their view of the public schools as a vehicle for the acculturation of Jews into American society that therefore merits unqualified and undivided government support. The issue of church-state separation provoked the first religious split in the Jewish lobby, as secular, Reform, and Conservative groups took part in the lobbying for strict separationism, while Orthodox organizations—those most closely aligned with Jewish parochial schools—began urging government aid to private schools.

Many of the Jewish lobbying groups in Washington have their own particular emphasis or special issues of interest. For example, the AJ Congress usually leads the charge on matters of church-state separation, while the Anti-Defamation League takes a particular interest in issues pertaining to religious and racial discrimination. Yet they and most of the other Jewish organizations with Capitol Hill lobbying offices share almost indistinguishable agendas and frequently join forces. The AJ Congress, AJ Committee, ADL, Reform's Religious Action Center, NJCRAC, B'nai B'rith, and the Jewish women's organization Hadassah all maintain high-level lobbying operations that usually advocate liberal positions on issues such as abortion, the environment, gay rights, defense, capital punishment, women's concerns, health care, government spending, and immigration.

The National Council of Jewish Women, while not a lobbying organization, has taken part in a number of lobbying efforts on women's issues throughout its history. As part of its early 1900s campaign against women immigrants being pressured into prostitution, the council successfully lobbied President Theodore Roosevelt to sign an executive order allowing "Boarding Matrons" to accompany the regular (male) inspectors who boarded newly arrived ships before they docked. The council took part in the 1911 campaign by social reformers for legislation to end child labor, provide housing for the poor, protect women laborers, and more. During the 1920s, the National Council of Jewish Women was the first women's organization to urge Congress to legalize birth control and participated in the interwar feminist lobbying coalition, the Women's Joint Congressional Committee. The council also took an active role in 1930s antiwar lobbying campaigns, pressing for reductions in the defense budget, arms embargoes on countries at war, and legislation for a national referendum prior to any U.S. declaration of war, as well as other pacifist goals such as U.S. endorsement of the World Court and the League of Nations.

In recent years, a handful of conservative Jewish organizations have joined the ever-splintering "Jewish lobby" in Washington. The Jewish Institute for National Security Affairs lobbies for increased military spending, while two Orthodox groups, Agudath Israel and the Orthodox Union, press for government assistance to parochial schools, support the death penalty and other strong anticrime measures, and take the Republicans' side on many other domestic controversies. On Israel-related issues, lobbies representing nearly all points of view on the broad spectrum of Israeli political opinion are constantly seeking to win over members of Congress.

Lawmakers today thus find themselves confronted by a sometimes bewildering array of Jewish lobbyists, each claiming to represent a significant segment of Jewish voters, even as they advance contradictory positions. Legislators are hard-pressed to decide if the bill, cause, or pet project being thrust before them at any particular moment truly reflects what their Jewish constituents desire. The situation is disadvantageous for the lobbyists as well. Unlike the 1940s, when Zionist lobbyists could honestly claim to represent the overwhelming majority of American Jews, or the 1970s, when Jewish advocates of affirmative action could claim to speak for virtually all of American Jewry, today's Jewish lobbyists are frequently spokesmen for nothing more than minority factions of their own community. This naturally reduces their political leverage and the power of their arguments. On issues, however, where there is widespread agreement in the community, the Jewish lobby continues to pack a powerful punch, backed by the threat of withholding large numbers of Jewish votes. But on issues that split the community, when a politician may alienate as many Jewish voters as he attracts by adopting a particular position, the lobby is likely to find it increasingly difficult to wield influence in American politics.

The "Jewish lobby," as such, has changed dramatically since its beginnings more than a century ago. From a lone, unofficial, part-time lobbyist in the days of Simon Wolf, to today's fully staffed multimillion dollar lobbying operation of AIPAC, as well as the full-time paid lobbyists from many other Jewish organizations, Capitol Hill has witnessed the evolution of the Jewish lobby into a sophisticated weapon of political influence. Yet growth has not necessarily ensured success, and a comparison of the earliest days of Jewish lobbying to contemporary Jewish lobbying efforts finds mixed results in both cases. Ultimately, the Jewish lobby's achievements are based less on the number of lobbyists or the size of their budget than on the merits of each specific issue and the degree to which that issue can be portrayed as coinciding with broader national interests.

References

Adler, Selig. "The Palestine Question in the Wilson Era." *Jewish Social Studies* 10 (October 1948): 303–334.
American Jewish Committee. "Jewish Voting in the 1968 Presidential Election: A Preliminary Report." New York: American Jewish Committee Research and Information Services, November 1968.
Arzt, Donna. "The People's Lawyers: The Predominance of Jews in Public Interest Law." *Judaism* 35 (winter 1986): (47–62).
Auerbach, Jerold S. "Liberalism and the Hebrew Prophets." *Commentary* 89 (August 1987): 58–60.
———. "Prophets or Profits? Liberal Lawyers and Jewish Tradition." *Judaism* 127 (summer 1987): 360–365.
Berlin, Isaiah. *Zionist Politics in Wartime Washington: A Fragment of Personal Reminiscence—The Yaacov Herzog Memorial Lecture.* Jerusalem: Hebrew University, 1972.
Brecher, Frank W. "Woodrow Wilson and the Origins of the Arab-Israeli Conflict." *American Jewish Archives* 34 (April 1987): 23–47.
Buckley, William F. "The Jackson Doctrine." *New York Post,* July 15, 1974, 30.
Cohen, Michael J. *Truman and Israel.* Berkeley: University of California Press, 1990.
Cohen, Naomi W. *The Year after the Riots: American Responses to the Palestine Crisis of 1929–30.* Detroit, MI: Wayne State University Press, 1988.
Dalin, David G. "Louis Marshall, the Jewish Vote, and the Republican Party." *Jewish Political Studies Review* 4, no. 1 (spring 1992): 55–84.
Dollinger, Marc. *Quest for Inclusion: Jews and Liberalism in Modern America.* Princeton, NJ: Princeton University Press, 2000.
Featherman, Sandra. "Philadelphia Elects a Black Mayor: How Jews, Blacks, and Ethnics Vote in the 1980s." Philadelphia: American Jewish Committee, 1984.
Feingold, Henry S. Review of *The Prophetic Minority.* In *Reconstructionist* 52 (September 1986): 31.
Feuer, Leon. "The Birth of the Jewish Lobby: A Reminiscence." *American Jewish Archives* 28 (November 1976): 107–118.
Fine, Arlene. "Honoring Cong. Charles Vanik." *Cleveland Jewish News,* March 24, 2001, 16.
Finney, John W. "Jackson's Strategy." *New York Times,* April 29, 1973, IV:2.
Forster, Arnold. *Square One.* New York: Donald J. Fine, 1988.
Frankel, Jonathan. Review of Gerald Sorin's *The Prophetic Minority.* In *American Jewish History* 75 (December 1985): 235.
Fuchs, Laurence. *The Political Behavior of American Jews.* Glencoe, IL: Free Press, 1956.

264 ▪ Jewish Americans and Political Participation

Genizi, Haim. *America's Fair Share: The Admission and Resettlement of Displaced Persons, 1945–1952.* Detroit, MI: Wayne State University Press, 1993.

Gurock, Jeffrey S. "Pursuing Self-Interest." *Present Tense* 8 (1981): 29–30.

———. Review of *The Prophetic Minority. Jewish Social Studies* 49 (spring 1987): 184–185.

Himmelfarb, Milton. "The Jewish Vote (Again)." *Commentary* 84 (June 1973): 81–85.

Himmelfarb, Milton, and Howard W. Yagerman. *Preliminary Report on Presidential Voting by Jews in 1972.* New York: American Jewish Committee Research and Information Services, November 1972.

Hochbaum, Martin. "The Jewish Vote in the 1984 Presidential Election." New York: American Jewish Congress, 1984.

Howe, Irving. *World of Our Fathers.* New York: Harcourt Brace Jovanovich, 1976.

Isaacs, Joakim. "Candidate Grant and the Jews." *American Jewish Archives* 17 (1965): 3–16.

Isaacs, Stephen D. "The Jewish Vote in '74." *Hadassah Magazine* 56 (December 1974): 11, 29.

Kenen, I. L. *Israel's Defense Line: Her Friends and Foes in Washington.* Buffalo, NY: Prometheus, 1981.

Korey, William. "Let Our People Go." *National Jewish Monthly* 115 (January/February 2001): 10–11, 39.

Kristol, Irving. "The Political Dilemma of American Jews." *Commentary* 95 (July 1984): 23–29.

Lebow, Richard Ned. "Woodrow Wilson and the Balfour Declaration." *Journal of Modern History* 40 (December 1968): 501–523.

Lefkowitz, Jay P. "Jewish Voters and the Democrats." *Commentary* 104 (April 1993): 38–41.

Leonard, Henry B. "Louis Marshall and Immigration Restriction, 1906–1924." *American Jewish Archives* 24 (April 1972): 6–26.

Lipstadt, Deborah, Charles Pruitt, and Jonathan Woocher. "Election 84: Where Are the Jews?" *Moment* 9 (October 1984): 35–38.

Medoff, Rafael. *The Deafening Silence: American Jewish Leaders and the Holocaust.* New York: Steimatzky, 1987.

———. *Militant Zionism in America: The Rise and Impact of the Jabotinsky Movement in the United States, 1925–1948.* Tuscaloosa: University of Alabama Press, 2002.

Mehlman, William. "A Case of Bad Faith: Jackson-Vanik-Mills and the Jewish Establishment." *Times of Israel* (August 1974): 26–31.

Moore, Deborah Dash. *At Home in America: Second Generation New York Jews.* New York: Columbia University Press, 1981.

Neuringer, Sheldon M. "American Jewry and United States Immigration Policy, 1881–1953." Ph.D. dissertation, University of Wisconsin, 1971.

Penkower, Monty N. "The 1943 Joint Anglo-American Statement on Palestine." *Herzl Year Book, Vol. VIII—Essays in American Zionism.* Edited by Melvin Urofsky. New York: Herzl Press, 1978, pp. 212–241.

Raab, Earl. "Are American Jews Still Liberal?" *Commentary* 107 (February 1996): 43–45.

Rosenbaum, David E. "Firm Congress Stand on Jews in Soviet Is Traced to Efforts by those in U.S." *New York Times,* April 6, 1973, 14.

Sachar, Howard M. *A History of the Jews in America.* New York: Alfred A. Knopf, 1992.

Shapiro, Edward S. Review of Thomas Kessner, *The Golden Door: Italian and Jewish Immigrant Mobility in New York City, 1880–1915.* In *American Jewish Historical Quarterly* 66 (March 1977): 461–462.

Solomon, Herbert L. "The Republican Party and the Jews." *Judaism* 37 (summer 1988): 276–287.

Sorin, Gerald. *The Prophetic Minority: American Jewish Immigrant Radicals 1880–1920.* Bloomington: Indiana University Press, 1985.

Szajkowski, Zosa. "The Jews and New York City's Mayoralty Election of 1917." *Jewish Social Studies* 32 (October 1970): 286–306.

Urofsky, Melvin I. *American Zionism from Herzl to the Holocaust.* Garden City, NJ: Anchor Press/Doublday, 1975.

———. *A Voice That Spoke for Justice: The Life and Times of Stephen S. Wise.* Albany: State Univeristy of New York Press, 1982.

Whitfield, Stephen J. "The Radical Persuasion in American Jewish History." *Judaism* 32 (spring 1983): 144.

———. *Voices of Jacob, Hands of Esau: Jews in American Life and Thought.* Hamden, CT: Archon, 1984.

Wyman, David S. *The Abandonment of the Jews: America and the Holocaust 1941–1945.* New York: Panthion, 1984.

5

Jews in Office

U ntil the twentieth century, relatively few American Jews were elected to public office, and most of those were in local elections. The influx of large numbers of Jewish immigrants from Eastern Europe in the early 1900s contributed to the election of many more Jewish candidates for office, especially to the House of Representatives from districts with large Jewish populations. The growing size of the Jewish electorate, the increased participation of Jews in American politics, and the gradual repudiation of anti-Semitism as a legitimate part of American culture, eventually paved the way for the election of a substantial number of Jews to the Senate and, in 2000, the first-ever nomination by a major party of a Jew for vice president.

Jews, like other non-Protestant minority groups, were generally prohibited from holding public office in Colonial America. A partial exception was New York, where the issue was a matter of dispute for some time; during the 1760s, Jewish candidates were on several occasions elected to the position of constable in New York City. On the eve of the American Revolution, Jews began to assume a higher political profile, and slowly they began to penetrate once-formidable barriers. In South Carolina, for example, a Jewish immigrant from England, Francis Salvador, was elected to the first two provincial congresses (in 1773–1776).

The earliest Jewish interest in competing for public office was typically dictated by business needs, Hasia Diner has found. During the nineteenth century, "Local politics in America rested heavily with the mercantile class, and Jews as merchants had a particular stake in the stability of their communities. Customers recognized their faces from behind clothing and dry-goods stores' counters, and the names on the ballots matched up with those emblazoned on store awnings. Reputation earned in business lent them the aura of upstanding men of substance." As a result, "through their entrepreneurship, Jewish businessmen served on county boards, city councils, school boards, in state legislatures, and as mayors in every region and community. In smaller communities and in the newly settled West, Jewish merchants were mainstays of town government." During this early phase in American Jewish history, "Jewish office holders rarely pursued politics as a career or won elections to further a particular ideology. Rather, they saw public service as befitting a merchant—custodian of public order." A second reason for the tendency of nineteenth-century American Jews to run for local, rather than regional or national, office was simply that "local governments dealt with issues that mattered most to Jews and non-Jews alike" (Diner 1992, 144).

There were additional reasons for the relative dearth of Jewish candidates for higher office during the nineteenth century. Irish-Americans often dominated urban political machines and were not eager to share power with Jews or other rival ethnic groups. Some potential Jewish candidates feared that if elected, they would at some point take politically unpopular positions that might trigger anti-Semitism. Others simply assumed that the prevalence of anti-Semitism among some voters made it unlikely that they would win election.

Indeed, anti-Semitic outbursts, while not common, did periodically greet Jews running for office. Jewish candidates for local office in Detroit in 1863 were denounced by a local newspaper, the *Commercial Advertiser,* as "hooked nose wretches" who "speculate on disasters. . . . [A] battle lost to our army is chuckled over by them, as it puts money in their purses." When the Democrats nominated a Jewish candidate for superior court in Chicago in 1879, the *Chicago Tribune,* which perceived the nomination as motivated strictly by a desire to attract Jewish voters, chastised the party leadership for assuming that "the rite of circumcision of itself qualifies a man to be a judge of the Superior Court of Cook County."

Deeply ingrained nativism made it especially difficult for Jewish candidates to succeed in certain parts of the country. In the Yankee culture of New England, for example, not more than a handful of Jews could win election to even relatively minor positions. In Boston, a Jew (Isaac Lopez) was elected city constable in 1720; another (Judah

Hays) was elected fire warden in Boston in 1805; and Godfrey Morse was elected to the Boston School Committee in 1875. It was not until 1876, a century after America's declaration of independence, that a New England state finally elected a Jew to Congress, Bavarian-born Leopold Morse, Democrat of Massachusetts.

In the South, too, few Jews were elected to higher office, and at long intervals. After a handful of Jews won election to Congress from the South during mid and late 1800s, not a single Jew was elected to higher office from the region between 1908 and 1973. Those who won election during the 1800s displayed little interest in Jewish matters. The first Jew elected to the Senate, David Levy Yulee, who served from 1845 to 1851 and 1855 to 1861, was a Southerner (a Floridian), but he refused to acknowledge his Jewish identity publicly, asserting instead that his forebears had come from Morocco, without explaining that they were Moroccan Jews. Despite his valiant attempts to hide his Jewishness, and despite his marriage to a Christian, Yulee frequently was the target of anti-Semitic barbs in Congress, and his critics in the press likewise often referred to his Jewishness. Similarly, the first Jew elected to the House of Representatives, Lewis Charles Levin, refused to acknowledge his Jewishness publicly. Elected in 1844 to his first of three terms in Congress, Levin was, ironically, a leader of the fanatically anti-immigrant and anti-Catholic Native American Party (the "Know Nothings").

The most prominent Jewish politician of that era likewise hailed from the South: Judah Benjamin, elected to the U.S. Senate from Louisiana in 1852. Although the 1850s controversy over Swiss discrimination against American Jews erupted during his service in the Senate, Benjamin was noticeably silent on the issue. Periodically the target of anti-Semitic remarks during congressional debates, Benjamin had a reputation for shooting back swiftly and fiercely. To one anti-Semitic barb he retorted, "It is true that I am a Jew, and when my ancestors were receiving their Ten Commandments from the immediate hand of the Deity, the ancestors of my opponent were herding swine in the forests of Great Britain." Benjamin went on to served as secretary of war, and later secretary of state, of the Confederacy. Eighteen years passed between the time that Benjamin left the Senate and the election of another Jew from the South to Congress—Benjamin Franklin Jonas, elected senator from Louisiana in 1878. Twelve years after that, former Confederate general Adolph Meyer was elected to Louisiana's delegation to the House of Representatives.

Jews enjoyed meager representation among the era's presidential appointees, as well. Throughout the 1800s, there had been a smattering of appointments of Jews as ambassadors: to Tunis (1813), The Hague (1853), Bucharest (1870), and Constantinople (1887). It was not until 1906 that the first Jew was appointed to a presidential cabinet, when President Theodore Roosevelt named Oscar Straus, his adviser and former minister to Turkey, to be secretary of commerce and labor. By choosing Straus, Roosevelt managed, in one fell swoop, to demonstrate his disapproval of Russia's anti-Jewish policies, to balance his recent first-ever appointment of a Catholic to the cabinet, and to have by his side a veteran public servant who on his own merits was more than qualified for the position, regardless of his ethnicity.

The handful of Jews elected to Congress in the 1800s were not elected from districts with significant Jewish populations. They represented only a minuscule number of Jewish voters, and hence did not consider themselves obliged to take a particular interest in matters of specifically Jewish concern. Some of them sought to deny their Jewish roots altogether. Although anti-Semitic prejudice did not succeed in blocking their path to Capitol Hill, that was usually because relatively few voters were even aware that the candidate in question was a Jew.

Jewish efforts to win election to political office in nineteenth-century America paralleled the broader experience of American Jews seeking to be accepted as an integral part of American society. Anti-Semitism was still a legitimate part of public discourse; it impeded both the ability of Jewish candidates to win elections and the ability of Jews in general to be seen as equal Americans. The few Jews who managed to penetrate the barrier of prejudice were, typically, those who were the most assimilated. As the Jewish community would grow in numbers and influence in the decades to follow, so too would its presence and impact on the political scene.

The Impact of East European Immigration on Jewish Political Office-Holding

The mass influx of East European Jewish immigrants during the late 1800s and early 1900s began to alter the electoral map in New York City first and foremost. Although the burgeoning Jewish populace of lower Manhattan at the turn of the century did not yet boast a sufficient number of registered Jewish voters to elect the city's first Jewish mayor, in 1901 they did choose Jacob Aaron Cantor as borough president, the first of seven Jews to be elected to that post.

There were several reasons why the waves of Jewish immigration did not immediately facilitate the success of many Jewish candidates for higher office. The seven-year delay between an immigrant's arrival and his eligibility to vote slowed the emergence of Jewish political power; so too did the fact that not all immigrants bothered to complete the voter registration process. There were not yet enough registered voters of the East European immigrant generation to send "one of their own" to Capitol Hill. Hence, those Jews elected to Congress prior to World War I typically were acculturated Jews of German descent who were selected by the local political machine on account of their wealth, connections, or appeal to a broad range of voters. Their involvement in Jewish communal affairs was limited, and they felt little obligation to take an interest in matters of specifically Jewish concern. Indeed, once in office, some of them consciously avoided involvement in areas of Jewish interest in order to avoid accusations of ethnocentricity. The most controversial Jew elected to Congress in the early 1900s, Socialist Party candidate Victor Berger of Milwaukee, owed his victory in 1910 to the fact that he was an Austrian-born socialist running for office in mostly German and heavily socialist Milwaukee. Berger's tumultuous career included being re-elected but denied his seat after being sentenced to prison for sedition, then having his conviction overturned by the Supreme Court and serving three more terms in Congress; but it was Berger's radicalism that shaped his political fortunes, not his Jewishness, to which he seldom drew attention. By contrast, the second socialist elected to Congress, Meyer London, was a Yiddish-speaking immigrant rights activist from the Lower East Side. His electoral triumph in 1914 marked a coming of age for the immigrant generation and the dawn of a new kind of Jewish public official.

The Russian-born London earned the admiration of the immigrant community as an attorney who worked long and hard, and often pro bono, for the heavily Jewish garment industry unions. London's socialist rhetoric was of less interest to immigrant voters than their perception of him as someone who spoke their language, understood their problems, and fought for their rights long before he sought their votes. Once in office, however, London found it difficult to please both his party colleagues and his constituents. Although he adhered to the Socialist Party's unbending pacifism during the first years of World War I, London infuriated the party leadership by refusing to vote against war appropriations measures in 1917. At the same time, London alienated some of his Jewish supporters by following the Socialist Party line against open immigration, which many labor leaders feared was creating unfair competition for jobs. London also refused to budge from the party's long-standing opposition to Zionism, even though the Balfour Declaration and the British liberation of Palestine from the Turks had aroused strong sympathy for Zionism among many Jews, including London's constituents. The socialist who had been sympathetically perceived by immigrant voters as a Jew first and a socialist second, now appeared to put doctrinaire socialism ahead of Jewish concerns. To make matters even more complicated, socialism was increasingly regarded by the American public as a dangerous and disloyal ideology, especially during wartime; this aroused fear among immigrants that London was giving the Jewish community a bad name. Press reports of London attending a session of Congress on Yom Kippur were by no means the most serious problem he faced, but they certainly did him little good in a community in which many people observed the strictures of Yom Kippur, even if they were less than scrupulous in their observance of other religious laws. Just as many Jews expect their rabbi to set the best possible example by being personally more religiously observant than his congregants, London was, in the minds of many Jews, a de facto Jewish leader, and therefore he was obligated to adhere to a higher standard of behavior.

London was defeated in 1918, but he then ran again in 1920 and won. Despite the government crackdown on suspected radicalism and the prevailing atmosphere of nativism and extreme anticommunism, London devoted much of his new term on Capitol Hill to seeking amnesty for violators of the espionage law and U.S. recognition of Russia's new communist government. Neither of these was an especially popular issue among voters nervous about being seen as un-American. London lost his final bid for re-election in 1922.

In smaller Jewish communities, too, the influx of East European immigrants facilitated the election of Jewish candidates. The political career of Hungarian-born Adolf Edlis illustrates how an aspiring politician could, with savvy and hard work, mobilize an unorganized immigrant community and turn it into a political force to be reckoned with. Although the number of Jews in turn-of-the-century Allegheny County, Pennsylvania—Pittsburgh and its environs—had swelled to an estimated 5,000 by the 1890s, their participation in local political life was minimal. Some potential Jewish voters were unaware of the registration process; others had neglected to complete all of their citizenship requirements. Edlis, an Orthodox Jew who ran a barber supply business, launched a political awareness campaign in the Jewish community in 1896, sponsoring advertisements in the local Yiddish newspaper urging Jews to register to vote, and personally coaching candidates for citizenship on their naturalization tests. A major ally in his campaign was the newspaper's publisher, Joseph Glick, who filled his paper with political news and advice, as well as frequent and enthusiastic coverage of Edlis's own candidacy for a seat on the local Common Council. "Every Jew should bring along his friends and acquaintances on election day and should go with joy to the ballot box to vote for a Jew and to make a shehechiynu [a special blessing on the occasion of a new accomplishment]," Glick editorialized shortly before election day, "because God has given us the zichus [privilege] to have officials from among our own brothers for which we would spend millions in Russia and other dark countries if only we were allowed." By contrast, Edlis received no support from the English-language Pittsburgh Jewish weekly, the *Jewish Criterion*, which reflected the perspective of the acculturated, German-born segment of the community. Edlis won his council seat by a large margin.

One of his first actions in office was to establish a Hebrew Political Club, to encourage Jews to become more politically active. That earned Edlis the wrath of the *Jewish Criterion*, which warned that such partisan Jewish political organizing would cause non-Jews to wonder if "the Jew is a foreigner and to which nation he belongs." The *Criterion* pleaded with its readers to emphasize that "in State affairs we are Americans; in religion we are Jews." Despite these divisions within the community, Edlis's own political career continued to advance. He ran for the Pennsylvania State Legislature, losing by less than one hundred votes the first time, and winning by 5,600 the second, in 1904. In the legislature he fought, albeit without success, on behalf of Jewish Sabbath observers who were frequently penalized for violating the state's Blue Laws by conducting business on Sundays. Edlis fared better with his campaign against houses of prostitution operating in Pittsburgh, including in mostly Jewish neighborhoods. The Edlis Act, which became law in 1905, was credited by the police with "obliterating" much of the local prostitution trade. Edlis later served as Pittsburgh's city treasurer, but after losing a race for state treasurer, he opted to leave politics and return to his business and Jewish community affairs. Edlis's years of political organizing left an indelible impact on Pittsburgh's Jews, showing them how to make their presence felt in local politics and laying the foundations for the community's political influence for years to follow.

Case Study: A Minor Politician Takes on a Major Issue

Chapter 2 of this volume mentioned a controversy in New York City in 1937 that illustrated the accelerating division of mood between the cautious Jewish leadership and the increasingly militant grassroots Jewish community. When a city-owned radio station, WNYC, broadcast anti-Zionist speeches by three proponents of the Palestinian Arab cause, both the radio station and the mayor's office faced a barrage of protests from Orthodox and militant Zionist groups, a flood of angry phone calls from Jewish listeners, and scathing editorials in the Yiddish-language press.

The episode also illustrated how in a city with a significant Jewish population, a Jewish political office-holder who held even a relatively minor post could, if he possessed sharp political instincts and sufficient public relations savvy, thrust himself into an issue with international implications. One of the leaders of the protest campaign against WNYC was Samson Inselbuch, a Republican alderman—the equivalent of a city council member—from a district with a sizable number of Jewish residents, the Williamsburg–Fort Greene area of Brooklyn. Inselbuch was a young man with considerable political ambition and a keen awareness of the value of every vote. At age twenty-seven, he had been elected to the New York State Assembly by a margin of just ninety-three votes, and two years later lost his seat by fifteen votes. He then ran for the city board of aldermen, and won with 51 percent of the ballots. Inselbuch used his position to introduce bills on a wide variety of issues, from legislation to protect city employees who observed Saturday as their Sabbath to a resolution calling for the resignation of Justice Hugo Black from the Supreme Court after the revelation of his membership in the Ku Klux Klan.

When the WNYC controversy erupted in June 1937, the board was just six months away from its scheduled dissolution, and Inselbuch had already declared his candidacy for one of the nine Brooklyn seats on the board of aldermen's successor, the New York City Council. As a Republican seeking votes from Jews who, for the most part, usually cast their ballots for Democrats, Inselbuch could scarcely afford to squander the political advantage that the WNYC controversy offered. As the son of an Orthodox rabbi, a graduate of the (Orthodox) Rabbi Jacob Joseph High School, and a former student at the Rabbinical College of America, Inselbuch was very much a part of the sizable traditionalist segment of Brooklyn Jewry and well positioned to take its pulse on political affairs. He immediately understood that a battle against Arab anti-Zionists could only enhance his city council candidacy.

The peculiarities of New York City politics also worked to Inselbuch's advantage. By a fortunate coincidence, the Democrats on the Board of Aldermen—who held a majority of the seats—had just recently accused the Republican LaGuardia administration of exploiting WNYC to broadcast programs that reflected favorably upon the mayor. When Inselbuch introduced a resolution condemning WNYC's Arab broadcast and demanding that it give equal time to the Zionist viewpoint, his Democratic colleagues unanimously supported him, delighted at the opportunity to simultaneously champion an issue of concern to Jewish voters and take a poke at the LaGuardia administration.

Mainstream Jewish organizations, however, took WNYC's side. B'nai B'rith, the National Council of Jewish Women, the American Jewish Committee, and the American Jewish Congress argued that the broadcast fell within the bounds of free speech. Frederick Kracke, the city commissioner responsible for supervising WNYC, made potent use of the Jewish groups' stance in his testimony before the board of aldermen, and the board had little choice but to file his report of the incident without further action. But Inselbuch and his colleagues refused Kracke's request to retract the original aldermanic resolution condemning WNYC. Unbeknownst to Inselbuch, the controversy even impacted on Middle East diplomacy. At that moment, Arab representatives—including one of those whose speeches were broadcast on WNYC—were conducting secret negotiations with several prominent American Jews about the future of Palestine; the Arabs asked their Jewish interlocutors to help ensure that the WNYC official who supervised the broadcast not be fired as a result of the affair.

Jewish political office-holders at the level of their local city council do not normally have many opportunities to play a role in matters of specifically Jewish interest, particularly those related to international controversies such as the Middle East conflict. Their attention is naturally occupied with pedestrian matters of purely local concern. But New York City is unique for its large and ethnically conscious Jewish community, and as a consequence, the lines between local, national, and international issues can sometimes be blurred. In such an environment, even a city councilman can sometimes assert a public role in areas normally reserved for members of Congress.

Jews on the Supreme Court

If Meyer London was widely perceived as the Jewish community's elected representative in Washington, Louis Brandeis emerged simultaneously as Jewry's senior unelected representative. The son of nine-teenth-century German Jewish immigrants, Brandeis was a successful Boston lawyer known as "the people's attorney" for his involvement in progressive politics and his legal battles against big business. Brandeis was a profoundly assimilated Jew who strove mightily to be part of Boston's Brahmin culture. The fact that he was denied full acceptance in New England society because of his Jewishness was one factor in propelling Brandeis toward discovering and embracing his ethnicity. Another factor was the anti-Semitic element of the opposition that erupted in 1912–1913 when he was under consideration for either secretary of commerce or attorney general in the Woodrow Wilson administration. Wilson confidant Colonel Edward House wrote to the president of the "curious Hebrew traits of mind" that raised questions as to whether or not Brandeis belonged in the cabinet. His path to Washington temporarily blocked, Brandeis turned his attention, with renewed vigor, to the American Zionist movement, becoming chair of the Provisional Executive Committee for General Zionist Affairs in 1914.

Two years later, Wilson named Brandeis the first Jewish justice of the Supreme Court, a decision made at least partly from political motives, although having nothing to do with Jewish voters. "It was a recognition of the jurist's extraordinary qualifications and an expression of personal regard as well as token compensation for the rebuff of 1913," Ben Halpern has noted. "But it was also intended to win over progressives for whom Brandeis was a hero. . . . [W]ith new elections approaching . . . the president realized the need to win over the progressive Republicans" (Halpern 1987, 103–104). Although the more assimilated elements in the Jewish community were nervous that the prominence of Brandeis could provoke anti-Semitism, for most American Jews his ascent to a seat on the highest court in the land was a badge of pride and yet another indication that Jews were at home in America. For American Zionists, the choice of their leader for the Supreme Court infused their movement with unprecedented legitimacy. In the eyes of many American Jews who had heretofore worried that affiliation with Zionism would raise questions about their loyalty to America, the fact that the most prominent Zionist in the country had received America's stamp of approval meant that, in effect, so had Zionism itself. The membership ranks of the American Zionist movement swelled accordingly.

Fifteen years later, a second Jew was named to the Supreme Court, this time by President Herbert Hoover: Benjamin Cardozo, a descendant of seventeenth-century Sephardic Jewish immigrants to Dutch-ruled New York. Like Brandeis, Cardozo had little in common with the East European Jewish immigrants who now constituted the bulk of American Jewry. Still, most Jews felt a sense of pride and accomplishment at his success. Moreover, the nomination of a second Jew to the Supreme Court demonstrated that the choice of Brandeis was not merely some historical fluke, and it helped solidify the idea that Jews belonged on the highest court. On the eve of Brandeis's retirement, Franklin Roosevelt named a third Jew to the Supreme Court: Felix Frankfurter. Although Brandeis and Cardozo came from privileged families whose Jewishness was tenuous at best, Frankfurter was an Austrian Jewish immigrant who had lived on the Lower East Side and studied, like so many of his compatriots, at the City College of New York before going on to Harvard Law School. The idea that there was an informal "Jewish seat" on the Supreme Court began to take hold, and when Frankfurter stepped down from the bench in 1962, President John F. Kennedy deliberately chose another Jew, Arthur Goldberg, to replace him. Nor was it coincidental that Goldberg's successor, appointed by President Lyndon Johnson, was Abe Fortas. But when Fortas resigned in 1969, President Richard Nixon did not appoint a Jew to replace him, and the concept of a "Jewish seat" gradually faded from public discourse, especially after President Bill Clinton named two Jews to the Supreme Court, Ruth Bader Ginsburg (in 1993) and Stephen Breyer (in 1994).

Anti-Semitism in Congress

The number of Jews in Congress increased significantly after World War I, as large numbers of Jewish immigrants from the prewar period became eligible to vote for the first time. By 1922 there were eleven Jews in the House of Representatives. Henry Feingold points to another factor that facilitated the entry of Jews into politics: the demise of urban political machines, often dominated by Irish-Americans, that often excluded Jews. "The growing social welfare role assumed by the federal government during the Depression delivered yet another blow to the influence of the political machine, so that by 1945 it had become a mere shadow of itself" (Feingold 1992, 201). The Jewish political profile was changing, too. In 1922 all but two of the Jewish members of Congress were Republicans; but of the Jews elected to Congress during the Roosevelt victory of 1932, all but two were Democrats.

As the Jewish community became firmly ensconced as part of American society, and as part of Washington political life as well, those who regarded Jews as a threat to their way of life felt more menaced than ever before. In the halls of Congress, a small but vocal minority openly expressed anti-Semitic sentiments. Edward Shapiro maintains that anti-Semitism in Congress was closely linked to isolationism; as the possibility of war in Europe grew, so did fears among a broad range of members of Congress that certain elements were seeking to drag the United States into Europe's conflict. "Congressional anti-Semitism [in the late 1930s and early 1940s] encompassed the far right and the far left, the deep South and the northern Plains states, and rural and urban Congressmen. . . . [It] included such prominent western and southern progressives as Senators Burton K. Wheeler of Idaho, Gerald P. Nye of North Dakota, and Ernest Lundeen of Minnesota and Congressman John E. Rankin of Mississippi. . . . They were part of that vast majority of Americans who, during the 1920s and most of the 1930s, firmly believed America had been tricked into entering World War I" (Shapiro 1984, 49).

Rankin openly accused Jews of conspiring to facilitate a communist conquest of the world. In one especially horrific incident, an anti-Semitic Rankin speech on the House floor in June 1941 so riled his colleague E. Michael Edelstein, a Polish Jewish immigrant who represented the Lower East Side, that Edelstein suffered a fatal heart attack in the middle of a shouting match with Rankin. Unlike Rankin, the aforementioned Senator Wheeler did not attack Jews per se; neither did Nye or Lundeen. Instead, they focused their anger on the "international bankers," "Hollywood moguls," and unwashed immigrants who, they said, were trying to push America into Europe's affairs. Yet the individual culprits whom they publicly denounced frequently bore identifiably Jewish surnames. Such rhetoric easily led listeners to the conclusion that Jews were to blame. Anti-Semitism emanating from the halls of Congress reached much wider audiences than the anti-Semitism of streetcorner hate-mongers, and carried a certain aura of credibility, since it came from a government source. It was particularly incendiary in the heated atmosphere of 1939–1940, as Americans struggled to recover from the Great Depression, worried about the rise of communism, and grew increasingly fearful of involvement in a world war.

Jewish members of Congress naturally abhorred those of their colleagues who expressed such sentiments, and mainstream Jewish organizational leaders kept their distance from the extreme isolationists on Capitol Hill. Maximalist Zionists, by contrast, found that they and some of the isolationists—although not those who had openly expressed anti-Semitism—could find common ground, especially around the realization that every Jew who settled in Palestine was one less refugee clamoring for admission to the United States. "I set [Wheeler] thinking along the road that if he doesn't want us here, he must find for us a State somewhere," Benjamin Akzin, the Washington representative of the militant New Zionist Organization of America, reported to his colleagues in early 1940. Nye even wrote an essay for the monthly *American Jewish Chronicle,* which Akzin edited; after his standard call to maintain tight U.S. immigration restrictions and keep the United States out of the European conflict, Nye proceeded to criticize Britain for breaking the pro-Zionist promises it had made in the Balfour Declaration. Zionist politics made strange bedfellows—for those in the Jewish community who were willing to make common cause on the Palestine issue with those with whom they strongly disagreed on other issues.

Once again, the experience of American Jews seeking political office paralleled the efforts of American Jews in general to secure a place in American society and culture. As their numbers increased on account of the mass immigration of Eastern Europe, Jews began to acquire the political muscle needed to elect larger numbers of Jews to higher office, especially the U.S. House of Representatives. It was not merely the sheer number of Jews that was shaping this new reality but also the quality and prominence of their contributions to American life—in the areas of law, medicine, science, journalism, and entertainment—that helped begin to cement their status, in the minds of most Americans, as equal partners in the country's political life and culture. Despite the continuing prevalence of anti-Semitic prejudice as well as cultural barriers that partly blocked the advance of Jews and other minorities, it could reasonably be said that on the eve of World War II, Jews at last had a foot in the door, both in Washington and in American society as a whole. Widening that opening would be the challenge of the years ahead.

Jewish Members of Congress and the Immigration Question

The Johnson Immigration Act of 1921, passed by an overwhelming majority of Congress, restricted entry to 3 percent of the number of members of each nationality present in the United States as of 1910. Jewish members of Congress fought unsuccessfully to limit the bill's impact. Representative Isaac Siegel, a Republican representing a heavily Jewish section of northern Manhattan, introduced an amendment to exempt from the quota restrictions those who could demonstrate that they sought admission to the United States "to avoid religious persecution." Faced with mounting opposition to the Siegel amendment, another member of Congress from New York, James Husted, offered a less sweeping version, which would require applicants to show that they were not merely seeking to avoid persecution but had also actually endured "suffering and hardship" because of such persecution. In the intensely anti-immigration atmosphere of the 1920s, even Husted's bill went down to defeat.

In late 1923, Representative Johnson introduced legislation to further tighten the restrictions on immigration, by reducing the maximum number of immigrants from 3 percent of the 1910 census to 2 percent of the census of 1890, when the size of the various nationality groups in the United States was considerably smaller. The House Immigration Committee endorsed the new measure in early 1924, notwithstanding a dissenting minority report from two Jewish members of Congress, Samuel Dickstein (D-NY) and Adolph Sabath (D-IL), denouncing the "pseudo-scientific" racial theories that served as the rationale for the quota system. Realizing that they were fighting a losing battle, congressional opponents of restrictionism endorsed the 1921 Johnson Act in the hope of holding off the new, tougher version of the law: "Keep the 1910 basis and I am sure that the immigration calm will not be disturbed," Emanuel Celler offered during the debate on the House floor. "The majority of Jewish spokesmen by 1924 would have regarded the retention of the main feature of the Immigration Act of 1921 [the provision stipulating 3 percent of the 1910 population] as a victory, even though they had bitterly denounced that measure just three short years before," Sheldon Neuringer (1969) notes (158–159). Representative Sabath even introduced a bill to extend the 1921 law until the end of 1925 and establish a government commission to review immigration policy. It was to no avail.

In the aftermath of the passage of the 1924 Johnson Act, Jewish members of Congress and other antirestrictionists concentrated on trying to amend some of the law's most objectionable features. In early 1926, Representative Nathan Perlman (R-NY) introduced legislation granting nonquota admission to the spouses and minor children of aliens already residing in the United States. At a hearing on the Perlman bill, restrictionists charged that the amendment would bring in at least half a million additional immigrants; Congressmember Celler countered that State Department officials had told him they put the figure at 200,000. Perlman eventually offered a watered-down version limiting the number admitted to a maximum of 35,000 annually, but restrictionists managed to bury it in committee. In early 1931, restrictionists put forward a drastic new measure to reduce the quota totals by 90 percent. Samuel Dickstein, the ranking Democrat on the House Immigration Committee, led a desperate, last-ditch effort to block the bill by offering to accept it if it were amended to "let the little babies and the old people come in"—that is, to permit the reunion of families that had been divided when the husband emigrated but other family members remained behind. Despite Dickstein's protests, the 90 percent reduction bill passed, 299 to 82, and likely would have become law if not for the fact that it had been introduced late in the session and could not be acted upon by the Senate before adjourning.

After Dickstein advanced to the position of chairman of the House Immigration Committee in late 1931, he again explored ways to ease the immigration of relatives of aliens. His first initiative was a bill granting a right of appeal to American relatives of would-be immigrants whose visa applications were rejected. But the State Department's opposition kept Dickstein's bill bottled up in committee. At the same time, legislation introduced by Emanuel Celler sought to grant nonquota admission to elderly parents and recently married husbands of U.S. citizens. The provision to aid parents failed, but the one for husbands passed, primarily because it was expected to bring about the immigration of just a few hundred people at most.

Some small consolation could perhaps be derived from the fact that Palestine remained open to Jewish immigration during the 1920s and 1930s. Palestine as a haven for Jewish refugees from Nazi Germany offered a soothing reassurance to Jewish leaders and Jewish members of Congress, who fretted over their own inability to alter America's immigration policies. The Lodge-Fish Resolution of 1922, which Congress passed by an overwhelming majority, put the United States squarely in favor of the Balfour Declaration, with its promise to foster Jewish immigration to the Holy Land. When, in the late 1920s, England began to backtrack from its earlier pro-Zionist stance, Jewish members of Congress were concerned but had little practical recourse, since Washington played no role in governing the Palestine Mandate. In the wake of the Palestinian Arab pogroms of 1929, representatives Celler and Dickstein urged the Hoover administration to intervene, and Dickstein in January 1930 introduced a resolution calling for an international inquiry into the Palestine conflict. Those initiatives went nowhere, however, because few of their colleagues were interested in seeing the United States entangled in Middle Eastern hostilities.

Jewish members of Congress occasionally found themselves in the confusing position of speaking out against foreign governments that mistreated their Jewish citizens, only to have American Jewish leaders urge them to desist from protesting. In response to the escalating persecution of Romanian Jews during the 1920s, AJ Committee president Louis Marshall raised the issue with both U.S. government officials and the Romanian ambassador in Washington. At the same time, Marshall pleaded with other Jewish groups to refrain from vocal protests, which he feared might provoke the Romanians to treat their Jewish citizens even more harshly, or cause them to accuse American Jewry of trying to undermine U.S.-Romanian relations. His only public appearance relating to the issue was a speech at a mass meeting of Jewish college students, at which he urged them to tone down their protests. Marshall urged Congressmember Emanuel Celler to refrain from any expressions of opposition to American loans to Romania, and he pressured Congressmember William Sirovich (D-NY) to withdraw his 1927 resolution criticizing Romania's mistreatment of its Jews. Naomi Cohen notes that Marshall believed his behind-the-scenes diplomacy was crowned with success when "he arranged for Sirovich to meet [Romanian ambassador George Cretziano], and the promises elicited from the minister were widely publicized." In Marshall's mind, the diplomat's private acknowledgement of anti-Semitic excesses was significant and showed that congressional action would have been unduly hasty. "What he refused to admit," Cohen explains, "was that simultaneously Cretziano brazenly undercut his promises by circulating contradictory statements that minimized the persecution and foisted the blame for anti-Semitism upon the Jews" (N. Cohen 1995, 23).

A Jewish member of Congress who, on his own initiative, takes the lead in publicly protesting the mistreatment of Jews abroad assumes that his action is in concert with the sentiments of the Jewish community; indeed, part of his motive may be to demonstrate to his constituents that he is articulating their concerns. Pressure from an established Jewish leader—especially one as prominent, widely respected, and politically well connected as Louis Marshall—places the member of Congress in a quandary. Defying the pressure means risking a rift with a leader of the very community whom the member of Congress is seeking to impress. Succumbing to the pressure means risking appearing to his constituents as if he were not seriously interested in the issue. Backing down on an issue that he loudly championed can also harm the congressmember's reputation in general, by making him appear impulsive, indecisive, or even ignorant.

Whichever way he goes, it is an experience that will likely make that member of Congress more wary the next time about getting involved in a public Jewish matter without first canvassing his Jewish associates to gain a more detailed understanding of where the Jewish community stands on that particular issue.

Case Study: Only in New York

The heavy concentration of Jewish voters in New York City has created an unusual political environment in which candidates for higher office routinely compete to demonstrate that they are the most sympathetic to Jewish concerns, and rival Jewish candidates sometimes seem to be seeking to prove that they are more devoted to the Jewish people than their opponents. The 1922 race in Manhattan's twentieth congressional district provided an unintentionally comic illustration of this peculiar political phenomenon. The Republican nominee was Fiorello LaGuardia, a prominent New York City political figure who had previously served in Congress, representing a district on the Lower East Side; LaGuardia was the first Italian-American to serve in Congress. Technically, he was also a Jew, since his mother was Jewish, and he even spoke Yiddish. But La-Guardia considered himself Italian and was widely regarded by the public as such. One of the rare instances in which LaGuardia made public reference to his Jewish heritage came in the 1922 congressional contest, after the Democratic candidate, Henry Frank, distributed an election-eve pamphlet describing LaGuardia as "a pronounced anti-Semite and a Jew-hater" and Frank as "a Jew with a Jewish heart." LaGuardia responded by publicly challenging Frank to "openly debate the issues of the campaign, the debate to be conducted by you and me entirely in the Yiddish language." Frank's self-serving declarations about his Jewishness rang hollow in the face of his inability to accept LaGuardia's challenge, since he spoke no Yiddish. LaGuardia's gumption, wit, and facility in the Yiddish language earned him the endorsement of the *Forverts,* one of the city's most important Yiddish newspapers, which undoubtedly aided him in securing his 168-vote margin of victory over Frank. During his subsequent tenure as mayor of New York (1934–1946), LaGuardia earned the strong support of Jewish voters with his early, frequent, and pointed denunciations of Hitler, which more than once prompted vicious attacks on him in the Nazi press as well as formal diplomatic protests by Berlin.

The rise of Hitler to power in Germany in January 1933 and his swift implementation of anti-Jewish policies stimulated several Jewish members of Congress to reopen the immigration issue. In March, Representative Dickstein introduced a bill to revoke Herbert Hoover's 1930 executive order to consuls abroad to strictly apply the legal requirement that would-be immigrants prove that they were not "likely to become a public charge" once they reached America. By frequently invoking the public charge provision, the consuls had reduced immigration to levels far below that which even the restrictive quota system permitted. As chairman of the Immigration Committee, Dickstein scheduled hearings on his bill, only to find himself the target of pressure from the AJ Committee to scrap the legislation, on the grounds that "it will be charged that America's Jews want to sacrifice America's obvious and essential interests on behalf of their co-religionists." The AJ Congress and other leading Jewish organizations soon joined the AJ Committee in opposing the measure; Dickstein, deprived of what he had assumed would be his primary base of support, abandoned the bill. Searching for a way to alleviate the suffering of German Jewry but wary of extending himself much further than the mainstream Jewish groups, Dickstein in May 1933 reintroduced his earlier, unsuccessful legislation to permit relatives to appeal visa rejections. The State Department's vehement opposition doomed the bill again.

The Jewish organizations' role in stopping the Dickstein "public charge" initiative illustrates the complicated and sometimes uneasy relationship that obtained between some Jewish leaders and the Jewish congressional delegation. Breitman and Kraut (1987) maintain that those American Jews who hoped that Jewish members of Congress would lead a campaign for German Jewry "placed their faith in a weak reed," citing Stephen Wise's assessment of the Jewish delegation in a private letter in 1933:

> Sabath, who is a thick and thin supporter of the President and who I believe did much to nominate him by securing Cermak's support for him; Celler, who is blatant but insignificant; Mrs. Kahn who has probably the best head of the whole crowd—though that does not mean very much; Dickstein, who can best be characterized as Dickstein; Sirovich, a super-articulate charlatan; Bloom, former vaudeville manager and real estate speculator, who as a result of his success in having put George Washington on the map is now become one of the statesmen of Washington; Ellenbogen of Pittsburgh, a Viennese lad who must wait another two months before he can be

sworn in, because seven years have not elapsed since he became a citizen . . . [M]uch of what they imagine to be anti-Semitism in general is nothing more than contempt and loathing for them personally, which of course they rationalize away in the self-protective terms of anti-Semitism. . . . Bloom and Sabath and those poor little colleagues of theirs, require indoctrination almost as much as C.H. [Secretary of State Cordell Hull] did on other grounds. (91)

Wise's irritation at the failure of Jewish members of Congress like Dickstein to consult him before taking action on Jewish-related matters was typical of the imperial style of Jewish communal leadership for which Wise was well known. But his critical view also reflected Wise's own failure to recognize the bind in which Jewish members of Congress found themselves, which was to some extent of the Jewish leadership's own making. On the one hand, men like Dickstein and Celler represented heavily Jewish districts in which there was intense sympathy for German Jewry, and in which the desire for some kind of U.S. action to alleviate the refugees' plight was substantial. Naturally these members of Congress were interested in responding to their constituents' wishes, while Jewish members of Congress from districts with small numbers of Jews typically exhibited much less interest in specifically Jewish concerns. At the same time, Dickstein and Celler regularly conferred with Jewish organizational leaders who urged them to, in effect, ignore their constituents' sentiment and refrain from introducing bills that, they feared, might provoke anti-Semitism by tampering with the extremely popular restrictions on immigration. Torn between grassroots Jewry's preference for action and the Jewish leadership's preference for caution, Dickstein and Celler sometimes leaned one way, sometimes the other. During the mid-1930s, they refrained from introducing new bills to facilitate refugee immigration and looked elsewhere for ways to respond to the Nazis. Dr. Joseph Tenenbaum, who was in charge of the boycott of Nazi goods organized by the AJ Congress, helped Celler draft an amendment to the Customs Tariff Law to hamper the marketing in America of goods whose production was subsidized by foreign governments, something the Hitler regime did routinely. The bill, introduced in early 1936, did not actually mention Germany, but its aim was clear. But like so many of the well-intentioned bills submitted by Dickstein or Celler, the trade measure never made it out of committee; congressional isolationists were loath to take any steps that might draw the United States closer to a conflict with Germany.

Case Study: Congress Investigates
American Nazis

In early 1934, Congress agreed to a proposal by Samuel Dickstein to investigate Nazi propaganda activities in America. The year-long inquiry, chaired by House Speaker John McCormack (D-MA) with Dickstein as vice chair, included a series of public hearings as well as closed executive sessions, and accomplished more or less what Dickstein intended: to expose Nazi front groups and draw the public's attention to the menace of Hitlerism. When Dickstein sought authorization for a follow-up investigation, however, he ran into opposition from, among other sources, the AJ Committee, which feared that if the new inquiry failed to recommend legislation, that could "be used unfavorably by the Nazis and anti-Semitic groups, and result in a boomerang."

It did boomerang, but not in the way the AJ Committee imagined. When Dickstein's measure floundered, Congressmember Martin Dies, an extreme conservative from Texas, introduced his own version of the bill, which Dickstein supported. Although Dies argued that a new investigating committee was needed to expose communists, Dickstein lobbied for the bill on the assumption that it would focus unflattering attention on domestic Nazis. Congress agreed to the Dies proposal and created the House Un-American Affairs Committee, which Dies chaired and from which Dickstein was excluded. Its focus was primarily on subversion by communists, and anti-Semitic groups used it to continue harping on the idea of a link between Jews and communism.

After the March 1938 German occupation of Austria (the *Anschluss*) and the accompanying persecution of Austrian Jewry, these Jewish members of Congress felt compelled to act again on the immigration issue. Celler presented a bill to permit the unrestricted immigration of all victims of religious or political persecution; Dickstein introduced legislation to give German and Austrian Jewish refugees all of the unused quota slots, of which there were many because of the strict application of the "public charge" clause. The major Jewish organizations once again succeeded in pressuring Celler and Dickstein to withdraw their bills.

The mass anti-Jewish violence of the November 1938 Kristallnacht pogroms convinced some Jewish leaders to quietly modify their position on immigration. Joining hands with several private humanitarian groups, they established a nonsectarian committee to press for legislation that would aid refugee children. Convinced that such a measure could pass only if its Jewish aspects were downplayed, they arranged for it to be sponsored by non-Jewish members of Congress, Senator Robert Wagner and Representative Edith Rogers; Dickstein and other Jewish members of Congress took a back seat, in the hope of attracting a broad range of support on general humanitarian grounds. Proponents of the measure deliberately omitted the word "Jewish" from both the bill and their arguments on its behalf. These tactics notwithstanding, the child refugee bill was staunchly opposed by nativist and restrictionist groups, and it was buried in committee in the summer of 1939.

Responding to reports of the brutal persecution of Jews in German-occupied Poland in early 1941, Dickstein tried a new approach to the immigration issue: he introduced legislation to allocate unused quota spaces to European refugees for the specific purpose of colonizing Alaska. He hoped to counter the usual restrictionist arguments by emphasizing America's national defense and economic needs: settling the vulnerable Alaska territory would fortify it against foreign enemies, and developing its vast natural resources would aid the economy. But Dickstein found it impossible to overcome the obstacles created by restrictionists trying to kill the bill and worried Jewish organizations refusing to support it. "As with the Wagner-Rogers Bill, the Alaska Development Bill foundered on the rocks of nativism, anti-Semitism, and economic insecurity that in the late thirties and early forties loomed in the way of all refugee legislation," David Wyman concludes (1984, 111). "Nativists saw the proposal as a means of slipping thousands of aliens in through the Alaskan frontier. And anti-Semites concluded that it was a bill to expose Alaska to an influx of Jewish immigrants. The claim that another move was afoot to dump penniless refugees in the country fed on economic fears which had matured through ten years of depression."

The only Jewish member of Congress whose immigration-related legislation succeeded was a supporter of restrictionism, Sol Bloom. A vaudeville comedian turned realtor, Bloom, a Democrat, was in 1922 elected by Manhattan's upper West Side district to the first of thirteen consecutive terms in Congress. As chairman of the powerful House Foreign Affairs Committee, he was theoretically in a position to influence America's refugee policy—and influence it he did, to the detriment of the refugees. Anxious to demonstrate his loyalty to both America and the Roosevelt administration, Bloom in 1941 sponsored legislation to give consular officials abroad more power to further reduce the already underutilized quotas, by authorizing them to reject the visa request of any applicant whom they had "reason to believe" might "endanger the public safety." The bill gained quick congressional approval and was signed into law by Roosevelt in June of that year.

Jewish Members of Congress Face the Holocaust

The diametrically opposed positions of Dickstein and Celler, on the one hand, and Bloom, on the other, demonstrated the growing division of opinion among Jewish members of Congress with regard to the wisdom and propriety of challenging Roosevelt's policies on Jewish-related matters. Although Dickstein and Celler repeatedly took issue with the administration's immigration restrictions, Bloom distinguished himself as one of the State Department's staunchest defenders on Capitol Hill and certainly its most loyal supporter among the Jewish members of Congress; even as strong a supporter of the administration as Stephen Wise contemptuously dubbed Bloom "the State Department's Jew." When reports of the Nazi genocide were confirmed by the Allied leadership in late 1942, Bloom was as shocked and horrified as were Celler, Dickstein, and the other Jewish members of Congress. But they responded to the crisis in sharply different ways.

Like most American Jews, the Jewish members of Congress were slow to grasp the enormity of the Holocaust and the need for extraordinary measures by the Allies to halt the murders. Anguished by the mounting reports of atrocities, the seven Jewish members of Congress secured a meeting with President Roosevelt on April 1, 1943, but did not present him with any dramatic or imaginative proposals. Instead they focused on the need for the State Department to simplify the manner in which immigration restrictions were applied so that a larger portion of the quotas would be filled; at that point, the number of immigrants actually entering the country was less than 10 percent of the maximum allowed by the law. "Although simplification would certainly have been a help, the failure of the congressmembers to focus on the major policy issues enabled Roosevelt to avoid the pressure they might otherwise have been able to put on him," David Wyman points out; FDR directed them to the State Department's immigration chief, Breckinridge Long, and he "could be depended upon to respond courteously to the congressmembers, to offer to consider whatever suggestions they would submit, and perhaps eventually to make a few superficial modifications. In that way,

Long could largely neutralize their potential for forcing the administration to make any real policy changes regarding the rescue of Jews" (Wyman 1984, 100–101). The hesitancy of the Jewish members of Congress resembled that of the mainstream Jewish leaders, who throughout much of 1943 refrained from advocating much more than liberalization of the existing quotas, verbal warnings to the Nazis of postwar punishment for war crimes, and other modest proposals. For Jewish members of Congress and Jewish organizational officials alike, this timidity was the result of loyalty to Roosevelt, fear of rocking the boat during wartime, and an inability to break free of traditional patterns of political strategy and action.

In the spring of 1943, the administration tried to defuse criticism of its refugee policy by announcing that it would sponsor an Anglo-American conference in Bermuda on the refugee problem. Bloom was chosen as a member of the U.S. delegation to the conference. Dickstein, who asked the administration for permission to be part of the delegation, or at least to attend as an observer, was turned down. From the State Department's perspective, Bloom was the perfect choice. As a prominent member of Congress, his presence would undermine attempts to lobby Congress on the refugee issue. As a Jew, his support of the administration's position at the conference could help counteract the growing criticism in the Jewish community of U.S. policy toward European Jewry. Although the conference ended without any indication that concrete steps would be taken to aid the refugees, Bloom announced, "I as a Jew am perfectly satisfied with the result," and he warned Jewish organizations to remember that "[t]he security of winning the war is our first step. We as Jews must keep this in mind." By contrast, Dickstein blasted the Bermuda conference's "sterility," and Celler accused the conferees of perpetrating "a diplomatic mockery."

Increasingly, Celler was becoming known for his brief, tart critiques of the administration's policy—what in later years would become known as sound-bites. He accused the State Department of having "a heartbeat muffled in protocol"; its refugee policy was so "cold and cruel" that it was "glacier-like." Even his explanation of why he employed sharp rhetoric was artful: "I do not measure my words because the hangmen of Europe do not tarry." It was indicative of the fact that Celler's position was shared widely in the Jewish community and its leadership that even Stephen Wise complained of "the ineptitude and worse of Bermuda." Yet when Celler asked Wise to help him bring together a group of senators and representatives to put "extreme pressure" on FDR for "active and genuine rescue," Wise demurred. For all his private jabs at the Jewish members of Congress, it was Wise whose unwavering loyalty to Roosevelt made it difficult for him to muster the political courage that the refugee crisis demanded.

Wise framed his position as a strategic necessity to preserve channels of political influence: public criticism of FDR by Jews "will shut every door and leave us utterly without hope of relief as far as FDR is concerned," Wise wrote to a colleague after Bermuda. Celler and Dickstein adopted a more skeptical approach.

Although concurring that access to the White House was crucial if American Jews were to have influence on the administration, they grew increasingly concerned that for Wise it had become a matter of access for the sake of access, not access that led to influence. Thus while Wise instinctively held back, waiting for a green light from the White House before undertaking any significant political initiative, Celler and Dickstein were more willing to get out in front of public opinion in the hope of stirring up public interest in order to create pressure on the administration. They were quicker than Wise to sense that the tide was turning during the spring and summer of 1943, that public awareness of the extent of the atrocities was generating support for a rescue initiative and creating political leverage to use on the administration. In early September, the presidents of the Democratic and Republican national clubs jointly called for temporary, unrestricted immigration for all victims of persecution. Dickstein moved swiftly to capitalize on their announcement; within days he had introduced a resolution urging that all political or religious refugees be permitted to enter the United States and remain until six months after the end of the war. The resolution never made it to a vote. Neither the administration nor Congress was yet prepared for such a drastic change in immigration policy, and the response of major Jewish organizations ranged from the brief and lukewarm support of Wise's AJ Congress to the staunch opposition of the AJ Committee, which continued to fear that large-scale immigration would provoke anti-Semitism in America. Still, Dickstein's politically bold proposal helped keep alive public interest in the refugee issue; it reinforced the idea that there were steps America could take to aid the persecuted, thus helping to pave the way for future rescue action; and it demonstrated that when Jewish communal leaders hesitated to act, they created a vacuum that an energetic and imaginative member of Congress could fill.

Celler was a politician, but the extent of his involvement in Holocaust rescue issues and his unusual willingness to propose bills that were politically unpopular suggest that general humanitarianism and a specific sense of moral obligation to his fellow Jews soon outweighed more narrow considerations, such as which stance would aid his personal political fortunes. In his autobiography, Celler wrote: "It is difficult to describe the sense of helplessness and frustration that seized one when streams of letters poured in from constituents asking help for a sister, brother, mother, child caught up in the Nazi terror." One episode in particular seems to have left a deep and permanent impression upon the young congressmember. An old rabbi came to his office one day, with "his hat which he didn't remove, his long black coat and patriarchal beard, the veined hands clutching a cane. . . . Trembling and enfeebled," the elderly scholar pleaded for congressional intervention to help rescue Jews from the Nazis. Celler referred to some of the logistical problems involved in mass rescue, and described how he had raised the issue at the White House, without success. "But the rabbi kept interrupting, striking his cane on the floor of the office. 'If six million cattle had been slaughtered,' he cried, 'there would have been greater interest. A way would have been found'" (Celler 1973, 89–91).

The dramatic contrast between Celler and Dickstein, as advocates for Allied rescue of refugees, and Bloom, as an advocate for the administration's hands-off approach, repeatedly manifested itself. While Celler and Dickstein were among the speakers at the July 1943 Emergency Conference to Rescue the Jewish People of Europe, sponsored by the activist Bergson group (see Chapter 2), Bloom tried to dissuade a group of rabbis from taking part in a Bergson-organized protest march in Washington on the grounds that it would be "undignified" for such "un-American-looking" individuals to be marching through the nation's capital. (Bloom's insulting remark appears to have only strengthened the rabbis' determination to join the protest.) While Celler was charging that, under the policies of the State Department's Breckinridge Long, "[it] takes months and months to grant the visa and then it usually applies to a corpse," Bloom was bringing in Long as one of the star witnesses at the congressional hearings on the rescue issue in November and December of 1943. (Once again, Bloom's actions backfired. Long's testimony was so egregiously misleading that it ignited a firestorm of controversy in the press and Jewish community, severely embarrassing the administration. See Chapter 2.)

The rescue hearing was one of the few occasions on which Bloom specifically used his position as committee chair to influence U.S. policy concerning the Holocaust. In order to undermine the resolution, which was introduced by the Bergson group's congressional allies and which called for creating a government rescue agency, Bloom insisted on a quick hearing before the sponsors were fully prepared, and he then diverted much of the hearing to his own unfriendly questioning of Peter Bergson. "Bloom's actions probably were also motivated by loyalty to the Roosevelt administration," David Wyman concludes. "If the resolution had reached the floor of the House, it could have touched off an embarrassing debate on the administration's record concerning the European Jews. In addition, Bloom's own prestige was at stake. For him to acknowledge the need for a new rescue commission would amount to repudiation of his role at Bermuda and his long-standing claim that the Bermuda Conference had exhausted all practical avenues of relief" (1984, 202).

Bloom's attitude was depicted in stark language by Leon Feuer, one of the American Zionist movement's senior lobbyists, who later recalled a meeting that he, his fellow lobbyist and former newspaperman Leo Sack, and Zionist leader Abba Hillel Silver held with Bloom in 1944:

Bloom remained deaf to all of our arguments, even expressing skepticism about the extent of the Holocaust, and was therefore oblivious to the opportunity of saving thousands of Jewish lives by keeping open the doors of immigration to Palestine. His information, which had been officially provided and which he did not question, did not jibe with our gloomy prognosis of the number of Jews already dead or on their way to the gas chambers. Suddenly, to the astonishment of Silver and myself, Leo threw himself on his knees and begged Bloom for even a small token, some indication that there was a pittance of Jewish feeling in a remote corner of his heart. Real tears were streaming from the eyes of this supposedly tough and often profane newspaperman. But they had no perceptible effect on Bloom. (Feuer 1976, 112)

Sometimes the State Department used Bloom as an instrument of pressure against potential Jewish critics. In the autumn of 1943, on the eve of a visit to the United States by the son of Saudi Arabian leader Ibn Saud, State Department officials persuaded Bloom to ask Nahum Goldmann, leader of the World Jewish Congress and confidant of Stephen Wise, to use his influence to ensure that no Jewish organization or newspaper would publicly criticize the Arab visitor. Goldmann agreed to do so, since, he said, "it would certainly be bad taste and bad politics to attack a man who comes here as a guest of the President." Convincing Jewish leaders to remain silent proved easier than trying to silence Emanuel Celler. At a meeting of the Jewish congressional delegation, Bloom pleaded with his colleagues to leave the Saudis alone, but Celler said that he intended to deliver a radio speech criticizing both Ibn Saud and his son. Goldmann promised to "ask Dr. Wise to discuss the matter with Mr. Celler and warn him not to make any public attack on Ibn Saud or his son."

Jewish Members of Congress in the Postwar Era

During the immediate postwar period, Jewish members of Congress were united in their strong support for the creation of a Jewish state. This was a striking change from the Holocaust years, when the rescue issue deeply divided the Jewish congressional delegation. The new unity resulted from several factors. First, the inability of Jewish members of Congress to bring about any significant intervention by the United States on behalf of refugees from Hitler increased their feeling—and the feeling of many American Jews in general—of bearing a special moral responsibility to facilitate the establishment of a homeland in Palestine for the survivors of the Holocaust. Second, the campaign for Jewish statehood attained widespread sympathy among the American public after newsreel footage of the Allied-liberated death camps helped illustrate the magnitude of what the Jews had suffered; this increased level of public support for Zionism meant that Jewish members of Congress could champion statehood without fearing accusations that they were pursuing special-interest causes. In addition, the extremely high levels of Zionist sentiment that prevailed in the postwar American Jewish community meant that a Jewish member of Congress from a district with a significant number of Jewish voters could not distance himself from Zionism without risking his political future.

Sol Bloom became one of the lead sponsors of the 1944–1945 Taft-Wagner resolution supporting Jewish statehood, although at one point, when Stephen Wise was urging postponement of the resolution (at the administration's request), a bewildered Bloom complained to the Zionist Organization of America's Israel Goldstein that he did not know which way to go, since "one moment Rabbi Silver tells [me] to go ahead with the hearings, and the next Rabbi Wise tells [me] to delay." Bloom also initially joined Emanuel Celler in his 1946 attempt to use America's postwar reconstruction loan to England as leverage to change British policy in Palestine, although, in an echo of some of the conflicts and divisions that riddled the Jewish community during the war, Bloom dropped his opposition after fervent lobbying by Stephen Wise.

With Bloom partly discredited—in the eyes of many in the Jewish community—by virtue of his close association with the State Department during the war, Celler emerged as the de facto leader of the postwar Jewish congressional delegation, which ranged in size from eleven to fourteen members from 1945 to 1948. Samuel Dickstein had left Congress at the end of 1945 to take a seat on the New York State Supreme Court, and although Illinois Democrat Adolph Sabath technically had more seniority than Celler, Celler's high public profile, especially when it came to Palestine affairs, cemented his position as the most prominent Jew in Congress during those years. His steady drumbeat of pro-Zionist speeches, press conferences, and protests to the British government helped galvanize Jewish and American public opinion against British policy in the Holy Land. Celler's warning that "[y]ou can't carry New York without Brooklyn, and you might not carry Brooklyn without a [pro-Zionist] plank" had succeeded in convincing the 1944 Democratic convention leaders to endorse Jewish statehood. Similarly, Celler helped keep the Truman administration from accepting the State Department's anti-Zionist line, by constantly reminding Truman's advisers that Democratic candidates in New York and elsewhere would be defeated in the 1946 midterm congressional elections if the Democratic administration was perceived to be opposed to Jewish statehood.

A significant addition to the Jewish congressional roster during the period prior to Israel's creation was Leo Isaacson. A child of Romanian Jewish immigrants who had been raised in a secular, politically leftwing but Yiddish-speaking home in the Bronx, Isaacson was an attorney active in the American Labor Party. Elected to the New York State Assembly in 1944, Isaacson lost his bid for re-election two years later. But the sudden resignation of a Bronx congressmember resulted in the scheduling of a special election for February 17, 1948, and Isaacson became the American Labor Party's candidate in a field of four. Isaacson's campaign slogan, "Peace, Prosperity and Palestine," cast the race as something of a referendum both on Truman's Palestine policy and on the potential presidential candidacy of former vice president Henry Wallace, of whom Isaacson was a passionate supporter. The pundits were stunned when Isaacson won with 56 percent of the vote. Isaacson did not disappoint his constituents. Living up to his troublemaker image from day one, Isaacson's first speech in Congress was a blistering denunciation of the Truman administration's arms embargo on the Middle East. On day two, he introduced legislation to require U.S. recognition of a Jewish state in Palestine. Visiting newborn Israel in June, Isaacson was the first member of Congress to meet David Ben-Gurion, and he undertook a widely publicized meeting with European Jewish refugees who were still being detained by the British on Cyprus. On the Fourth of July, in what Isaacson later called "one of the great moments of my life," he delivered an address about U.S. and Israeli independence on the Voice of Israel radio station. The feisty congressmember also got a firsthand taste of the perils of Middle East warfare when Jerusalem's King David Hotel, where he was staying, was shelled; he had to take shelter under a bed, next to a bearded gentlemen who turned out to be Israel's chief rabbi. Isaacson's political career was colorful but short-lived. Resentful at his victory in February, the Republican, Democratic, and Liberal parties jointly endorsed a rival candidate and defeated Isaacson at the polls in November 1948.

Jewish members of Congress were also active in the postwar struggle to permit Displaced Persons to immigrate to the United States (see Chapter 2). The first major postwar immigration bill to be enacted, the Displaced Persons Act of 1948, disappointed Jewish organizations because it permitted the entry of only 200,000 persons, with 30 percent of the places reserved for agricultural laborers and 40 percent for individuals whose countries had been conquered by the Soviets—two provisions that were likely to reduce drastically the number of immigrants who would be Jews; in addition, the list of those eligible for admission included pro-Nazi ethnic Germans who had settled in Nazi-occupied areas of other countries and had been expelled after the war. As noted in Chapter 3, Jewish organizations decided not to challenge the latter provision, for fear of alienating Catholic groups that supported admission of DPs, and out of concern that Jewish groups would be accused of casting aspersions on all ethnic Germans. Not all Jewish members of Congress were willing to swallow this compromise. During the debates over the various amendments to the DP bill, Representative Isidore Dollinger, the Bronx Democrat who had unseated Leo Isaacson, denounced the stipulation regarding ethnic Germans, charging that it gave "preference to the very people who helped Hitler in his tyrannical rise to power. . . . Are our memories so poor that we have forgotten Buchenwald and Dachau?"

It was Congressmember Celler who, in early 1949, introduced a liberalized version of the immigration act, intended to increase the number of those permitted to enter and eliminate the reserved places for agricultural workers and residents of Soviet-occupied areas. It passed the House in June. But Senator Pat McCarran of

Nevada, chairman of the Senate Judiciary Committee, opposed the bill as too liberal. He stalled it until early 1950, at which point he introduced his own, more restrictive version that reinstated the provisions that Jewish groups, and Celler, had sought to jettison. Liberal members of Congress succeeded in attaching a variety of amendments to the Senate version, but when the Celler and McCarran bills came before the House-Senate conference committee to be reconciled, the amendments that Jewish organizations favored were eliminated. The new senator from New York, Herbert Lehman—the first Jew elected to the U.S. Senate in more than forty years—defended inclusion of special privileges for ethnic Germans on the grounds that it was the only way to appease those senators who wanted to go even further and grant the ethnic Germans the official status of Displaced Persons.

Case Study: Debating How to Treat Postwar Germany

The complex issue of how to treat postwar Germany bedeviled and divided Jews in high office just as it did the broader American Jewish community. Samuel Dickstein, in his capacity as chairman of the House Immigration Committee, headed a 1945 study intended as a basis for overhauling the U.S. immigration system. Among Dickstein's unheeded recommendations was prohibiting immigration by all Germans except victims of Nazi oppression; the proposal found little support either on Capitol Hill or in the Jewish community.

Toward the end of the war, Treasury Secretary Henry Morgenthau Jr. argued that to prevent the Germans from again menacing the world, postwar Germany should be divided, demilitarized, deindustrialized, and turned into an agricultural country. His proposal was blocked by the State Department and Secretary of War Henry Stimson, who derided the Morgenthau Plan as "Jewish vengeance." Like Congressmember Dickstein's proposal, Morgenthau's plan was not supported by major American Jewish organizations. They feared American Jews would be accused of being vindictive against Germans. They were also concerned that Jews would be criticized for failing to fall in line with the administration's view that postwar Germany should be treated not as an enemy deserving severe punishment but as an ally of the United States against the Soviet Union.

During the early 1950s, West German diplomats in Washington actively cultivated Jewish members of Congress, hoping to soften their critical view of Germany and thereby improve German-U.S. relations. Senator Lehman of New York was probably the least receptive. He had irritated the Germans with his support for the 1950 proposal for a congressional examination of the U.S. relationship with Germany, and he had been unenthusiastic about permitting Germany to rearm. Lehman also opposed efforts to unfreeze German property seized by the Allies and was outspoken in his criticism of the paroling of some Nazi war criminals. But other leading Jewish members of Congress gradually softened. Emanuel Celler, for example, had, in 1952, opposed early admission of West Germany to NATO, but over the next few years he reversed his position and came to favor a complete rapprochement between Washington and Bonn. Jacob Javits, a rising young liberal Republican member of Congress from New York City, initially opposed West German rearmament, urged the long-term stationing of U.S. troops in West Germany, and was the only U.S. representative to refuse to vote for ending America's state of war with Germany. But faced with pressure from the administration to strengthen ties to West Germany as part of the Western alliance against Soviet expansionism, Javits supported U.S. aid to Germany. After West Germany agreed, in 1951, to negotiate with Israel on Holocaust reparations, Javits became a consistent and increasingly enthusiastic proponent of normalizing relations between West Germany, the United States, and world Jewry.

The shifting positions of Jewish members of Congress like Celler and Javits paralleled shifting attitudes toward West Germany in the American Jewish community at large. In the prevailing anticommunist atmosphere of the 1950s, major Jewish organizations were reluctant to strongly oppose normalization with West Germany, for fear of appearing to hamper America's efforts to build an anti-Soviet alliance. Many rank-and-file American Jews might have taken issue with the Jewish leadership's attitude if not for Israel's decision, stemming from its desperate economic situation, to accept Holocaust reparations from the West German government. Israel's willingness to negotiate with Bonn and gradually normalize relations with it made it legitimate, in the eyes of most American Jews, for American Jewish leaders to do likewise. Soon there was widespread acceptance in the Jewish community of the idea that Israel's economic needs and America's strategic needs justified a rapprochement with the Germans sooner than many would have preferred.

Postwar Patterns in Jewish Political Office-Holding

The postwar period witnessed significant developments in patterns of Jewish political office-holding, coinciding with sociological and demographic trends in the American Jewish community. There was, to begin with, a gradual but significant increase in the number of Jews in office, especially in the House of Representatives. This was a reflection of several factors. Perhaps most significantly, anti-Semitism was—at least for the time being—thoroughly discredited by virtue of its association with America's just-defeated enemies. Anti-Semitism was further hampered by the nation's postwar prosperity, scientific advancement, and social environment of optimism. Hence voters were more willing than ever before to support Jewish candidates.

At the same time, a greater number of Jews were interested in running for office. This was partly because they felt less intimidated, now that anti-Semitism was in obvious decline. But in addition to the retreat of the bigots, there was a growing sense in the Jewish community that most Americans now accepted Jews as full partners in American society, that it was permissible for Jews to take a more forthright role in areas such as political life. The sociologist Will Herberg, in his landmark book of the era, *Protestant-Catholic-Jew,* argued that Protestantism, Catholicism, and Judaism had become America's three established, and equally respected, religions—an especially remarkable achievement for Jews, since their numbers were so much smaller than those of the adherents of the other major faiths.

What also made it more possible for Jews to seek office was the coming of age of the children of immigrants. During the interwar period, immigrant parents typically labored in blue-collar occupations, struggling to make it in the New World despite the obstacles of the Depression years. Their children, reaching young adulthood in the 1930s and 1940s, worked their way through college in pursuit of white-collar careers. Many went into medicine, business, education, or the arts; but many others became attorneys, a common jumping-off point for political careers. Those who served in World War II returned from overseas and attended college on the GI Bill, giving them a boost that often proved crucial to their professional success and, in some cases, helped pave the way for future political involvement.

Another factor was the impact of the intense anticommunism that dominated American political culture throughout the 1950s and into the 1960s. The relegation of communists and fellow-travelers to the fringes of political life meant that many talented young Jewish political activists and intellectuals who otherwise might have been attracted to the radical left instead opted for the mainstream—typically the liberal wing of the Democratic Party—rather than risk being labeled subversives and treated as pariahs.

Demography also helped dictate Jewish political trends. During the 1950s and early 1960s, the Jewish populace of the New York City area reached its peak (approximately 2.3 million) and began to level off, while Jewish communities in the South and West experienced huge population surges. Los Angeles, which had an estimated 130,000 Jews in 1940, had more than 400,000 by 1960. The Jewish communities of southeastern Florida, which numbered in the vicinity of 50,000 in 1950, had quadrupled in population twenty years later. The Jewish community of Phoenix more than tripled between 1950 and 1970, and the Jews of San Diego more than doubled in number during the same period. The Jewish population of the greater Washington, D.C., area increased from 45,000 in 1950 to about 110,000 in 1970, which reflected less a pursuit of warmer climate—a common reason for Jews to relocate to places like Florida and California—than an increase in the number of Jews working in government and government-related businesses, another indication of the social and professional success of postwar American Jewry. What these demographic trends meant for Jewish office-holding was that there was an increasing number of areas of the country in which Jewish candidates now had a natural base of support and, therefore, a better chance of being elected than previously. It was not a coincidence that the postwar Jewish members of Congress hailed from a much larger variety of states than did their predecessors. Prior to 1965, the Jews in Congress never represented districts in more than six states. Between 1979 and 2001, by contrast, the representation ranged from sixteen to twenty-two different states.

The size of the Jewish congressional delegation has steadily grown throughout the years. Prior to 1897, there had never been more than five Jews in Congress at any one time. Between 1897 and 1921, with the advent of mass immigration from Eastern Europe, the figure ranged from five to nine, and from 1921 to 1939, with the political maturation of the immigrant generation, it reached eight to twelve. After a slight decrease during the war years, Jewish representation in Congress climbed to between twelve and sixteen members at any one time between 1949 and 1965, and from fourteen to twenty during the next ten years. It has continued to grow since then, ranging from twenty-five to thirty-three from 1975 to 1983, and from thirty-three to forty-one between 1983 and 2001.

Although 150 Jews have been elected to the House of Representatives, only 30 have been elected to the Senate. The competition for Senate seats is far more severe than for the House, not only because of the smaller number of seats in the Senate (currently 100, as opposed to 435 in the House) but also because its influence, prestige, and lengthier terms of office (six years rather than two in the House) naturally make the Senate more desirable. In the case of a Jewish candidate with specific ethnic appeal, election to the House from a single, heavily Jewish district is likely to be far more achievable than attracting sufficient support throughout an entire state.

Even among the relatively few Jews elected to the Senate, some trends are discernible. Of the three Jews elected to the Senate from 1949 to 1957, two were from New York—Herbert Lehman and Jacob Javits—and they received substantial Jewish electoral support specifically because of their records on matters of Jewish concern. New York has always been one of the few states in which the Jewish population is sufficiently numerous to play a consistently significant role in statewide races, although Lehman and Javits were the only two Jewish senators from New York until the election of Charles Schumer in 2000.

Of the nine Jews elected to the Senate from 1949 through 1979, seven were Democrats and another was a liberal Republican, one of the many indications of the strongly liberal leanings of many American Jews. Not one of the five Jewish senators elected during the 1970s came from the Northeast. They hailed from Minnesota, Ohio, Florida, Nebraska, and Michigan—perhaps a reflection of the aforementioned Jewish geographic diversity of the post–World War II era. On the other hand, there is nothing to be deduced from the fact that a Jew, Ernest Gruening, represented Alaska in the Senate from 1959 to 1969; since he had no connection to Jewish religious or communal life and did not even mention his Jewish identity in his autobiography, it is likely that few of Gruening's constituents were even aware he was a Jew.

The six Jews elected to the Senate during the 1980s were divided evenly between Democrats and Republicans. This may be attributed, at least in part, to the new prominence of Jewish conservatives as well as the increased willingness of some Jewish voters to stray from the Democratic Party, especially in nonpresidential elections. Of the six Jewish senators elected in the 1990s, two were women, a reflection of the growing prominence of women both in the Jewish community and in American political life.

Overall, the Jewish presence in both houses of Congress has been overwhelmingly Democratic and liberal. Of the 150 Jews who have been elected to the House of Representatives (through 2000), 74 percent were Democrats; 67 percent of the 30 Jews who have served in the Senate were Democrats. In modern times, those percentages were even more heavily weighted to the Democrats, since the aforementioned figures include the many Republican Jewish members of Congress who served during the 1800s or early 1900s, before American Jewry's close and enduring relationship with the Democratic Party had taken shape. Most Jewish members of Congress have accumulated liberal voting records, typically receiving high ratings from liberal political action groups such as the Americans for Democratic Action and low scores from its conservative counterparts. In the 104th Congress (1998–1999), for example, 15 of the 25 Jews in Congress received a rating of zero on the Christian Coalition Congressional Scorecard. However, if the recent Jewish demographic and voting trends discussed in Chapter 3 continue, it seems likely that the percentage of moderate and even conservative Jews in Congress will gradually increase in the years ahead.

Outside the Northeast, Jews have had little success in gubernatorial or mayoral races. It is true that, on occasion, a Jew has been elected governor of a state that lacked a substantial Jewish population. Georgia, for example, chose a Jewish governor in 1801; Louisiana did so in 1864, as did Idaho in 1915 and Utah two years later. During the 1930s there were Jewish governors in New Mexico, Oregon, and Alaska, and also in two states in which it was not quite as surprising a phenomenon, Illinois and New York. In 1954, Connecticut's voters chose Abraham Ribicoff as their governor, and not because they did not know he was Jewish; in addition to his distinctive name, Ribicoff's best-known speech from the campaign described his roots as the son of poor immigrants struggling to succeed in America. Despite his obvious Jewishness, Ribicoff triumphed and, indeed, was the only Democratic candidate to be elected to statewide office in Connecticut that year. New York has had only one Jewish governor in its history, Herbert Lehman (he served from 1933 to 1942). Another Jewish gubernatorial candidate in New York, Democrat Arthur Goldberg, was defeated by Nelson Rockefeller in the 1970 race. In recent decades, Jews have served as governor in Illinois, Rhode Island, Maryland, Pennsylvania, Vermont, and Oregon. Madeleine Kunin, who was elected governor of Vermont in 1985, was the first Jewish woman ever to win a gubernatorial contest.

Likewise, not many Jews have been elected mayors of major cities. San Francisco, Portland, Denver, and Jersey City had Jewish mayors in the late 1800s. During the 1970s, Jews served as mayors in Atlanta and Portland. More recently, there were Jewish mayors in San Francisco, Tucson, Indianapolis, and Dallas. Yet Miami, despite its large Jewish population, has had a Jewish mayor only once, from 1953 to 1955. The city that has had the most Jewish mayors is Cincinnati, which had three prior to 1930, one in the 1960s, and three more in the 1970s. Given the fact that Cincinnati's small Jewish population has never exceeded 25,000, the larger number of Jewish mayors in that city would seem to have been a fluke. Interestingly, two cities with especially large Jewish populations did not have their first Jewish mayors until quite recently. Ed Rendell, the first Jewish mayor of Philadelphia, served from 1992 to 2000. New York City did not have an identifying Jew as mayor (inasmuch as Fiorello LaGuardia, although technically Jewish, did not consider himself as such and was commonly regarded as Italian-American) until the election of Abraham Beame in 1973. He was succeeded by another Jewish mayor, Edward Koch, who served from 1978 to 1989.

Koch demonstrated how New York City, because of its unique demography and political significance, can catapult a local Jewish political office-holder into controversies pertaining to national or even international affairs. This is because of the unique combination of several factors: New York's huge Jewish populace; the fact that it is home to the headquarters of the world's most important news media; and the city's pivotal role, every four years, in the New York presidential primaries, which award the second-largest bloc of electoral votes in the nation and are held early enough in the primary season that they typically have significant impact on the outcome of the presidential race. We have seen how Samson Inselbuch, a minor Jewish politician in Brooklyn, turned a 1937 dispute over anti-Zionist speeches on a local radio station into a headline-grabbing controversy that involved national Jewish leaders and Arab spokesmen, one that was even raised in the context of Arab-Jewish diplomatic contacts regarding Palestine. Although the idea of Koch, as a local politician, being able to play a role in a national or international issue somewhat parallels the Inselbuch experience, in Koch's case his influence was much more significant because of his status as both the most important political figure in New York City and the most prominent Jew.

Koch, the son of Polish Jewish immigrants, was one of the most brash and colorful mayors in New York's history. After a term on the

New York City Council (1966–1968), Koch had been elected to the House of Representatives, where he served until his election as a mayor in 1977. It was during Koch's first term, just as the 1980 presidential primary season was getting underway, that his most memorable Israel-related moment occurred. As noted in Chapter 3, in late 1979 and early 1980, tensions between the Carter administration and the American Jewish community increased as a result of statements made by the president and his aides criticizing Israel's positions in its ongoing negotiations with Egypt. Less than four weeks before the New York primary election, the U.S. ambassador to the United Nations voted in favor of a UN Security Council resolution that harshly criticized Israel and characterized Jerusalem as "occupied Arab territory." The vote set off an avalanche of protests from Jewish organizations angry both at Carter's embrace of the Arab position on Jerusalem and the specter of the United States siding with the Arabs at the same time that the country was serving as a mediator in Israeli-Arab peace negotiations. Two days later, the White House issued a statement claiming that the vote had been cast "by mistake," because of a "miscommunication" between the president, the secretary of state, and the ambassador. This explanation did little to mollify the Jewish community, where it was increasingly suspected that the "mistake" did, in fact, represent Carter's true feelings. Crowds of pro-Israel demonstrators suddenly began showing up at speeches by Carter representatives in New York, brandishing signs that declared: "Carter—You're the Mistake!" and "Carter Stabbed Israel in the Back!"

It was Mayor Koch who set much of the tone of the Jewish community's response, when he publicly ridiculed the U.S. ambassador to the UN and Carter's other advisers on Middle East issues as "an anti-Israel Gang of Four." Koch, a master of sound bytes and pithy phrases, deliberately chose an instantly recognizable phrase, based on the Chinese government's description, at that time, of a "gang of four" senior government officials who supposedly had been leading their country astray. For the mayor of New York City to adopt such a strongly worded position in effect legitimized similar responses throughout the New York Jewish community. It also packed an especially emotional punch because Koch coincidentally made his statement just hours before a raucous pro-Israel demonstration was held outside a Manhattan club where Carter aides were meeting with Jewish community leaders. At one point during the rally, a brief clash took place between the police and some of the demonstrators, and one youth suffered head injuries. New York's newspapers the next day printed Koch's denunciation of Carter alongside dramatic photos of one young pro-Israel demonstrator bleeding profusely and a second protester lying on the ground with a policeman's shoe on his face. The combination of these graphic photos and the mayor's strong words left an indelible imprint on the mood of the Jewish community in New York and beyond. That autumn, on the eve of the presidential election, Koch caused a second sensation with his comments about Carter's unreliability when it came to Israel: "I don't know if he will keep his commitments [to Israel] after he is elected," the mayor declared. "If he doesn't he should rot in hell."

With his willingness to speak his mind and the bully pulpit afforded him as mayor of the city with the largest Jewish population in the world, Koch was able to inject himself into an international political controversy and help shape the Jewish community's response. He also demonstrated how in specific situations, a Jew in political office, although elected to serve a constituency that has a majority of non-Jews, can also serve, at least temporarily, as a de facto Jewish leader. Although there is no evidence to suggest that this was Mayor Koch's intention, his position of prominence, sense of timing, ability to attract the media spotlight, and emotional articulation of the concerns that many grassroots Jews were feeling made him, in effect, the leading spokesman for a large segment of American Jewry.

The Persistence of Anti-Semitism

Although, as noted earlier, America's war with Germany did much to delegitimize anti-Semitism in postwar America, some anti-Jewish prejudice inevitably persisted and has occasionally surfaced in the political arena. Anti-Semitic violence, such as the burning of a cross on the front lawn of Jewish mayoral candidate Sam Massell in Atlanta in 1969, has been rare. A somewhat more common experience was that of Frank Licht, who was serving on the Rhode Island Superior Court in 1964 when the local Democratic Party bosses considered offering him the nomination for governor but then decided not to because he was Jewish. Licht said that he received the gubernatorial nomination in 1968 only because nobody else wanted to run against the popular Republican incumbent, whom Licht then defeated. Jacob Javits appears to have had a similar experience when he privately expressed interest in the Republican nomination for mayor of New York City in 1953; the party bosses turned him down, according to some reports, because they regarded his Jewishness as a liability among likely Republican voters.

The 1966 Democratic gubernatorial candidate in Pennsylvania, Milton Shapp, accused his opponents of orchestrating "a vicious anti-Semitic campaign in certain parts of the state," by using the slogan "Don't put Shapp-iro in Harrisburg." Shapp's advisers tried to counter that tactic by playing up their candidate's experience as a U.S. soldier who participated in the liberation of Nazi concentration camps. Shapp lost that race by 240,000 votes; his campaign aides estimated that he lost 50,000 of those votes because of his Jewishness. The more significant factor was probably the general anti–Johnson administration trend that resulted in the defeat of every Democratic senatorial candidate, and all but one of the Democratic gubernatorial candidates, in 1966.

Howard Metzenbaum, the Democratic nominee for senator from Ohio in 1970, attributed his loss in part to his opponent's constant thrusting of Metzenbaum's Jewishness into the media spotlight through the tactic of loudly and frequently denying that it was an issue. Metzenbaum, the first Jew to run for high public office in Ohio, did beat a national hero, astronaut John Glenn, in the Democratic primary and came within 1 percentage point of defeating his Republican opponent, Robert Taft, Jr., despite the fact that Taft was the biggest name in Ohio Republican politics. Metzenbaum eventually did make it to the senate, where, during one 1981 debate on the Senate floor, he had to endure the indignity of having Senator Ernest Hollings of South Carolina refer to him as "the Senator from B'nai B'rith." In a similar vein, Representative Abner Mikva, Democrat of Illinois, who served in the House from 1968 to 1972 and 1974 to 1979, later recalled that every time he asked for recognition to speak from House Speaker John McCormack, McCormack would declare, in a mock Jewish–New York tone, "The gentleman from New YAWK!"

Jewish Members of Congress on Soviet Jewry, Israel, and Vietnam

As the plight of Soviet Jewry became an issue of significant public concern in the late 1960s and early 1970s, Jewish members of Congress took an increasingly high profile role. Many spoke out in the halls of Congress against Soviet persecution and took part in public rallies. Some went further. James Scheuer (D-NY) traveled to the Soviet Union to meet personally with Soviet Jews who had applied to emigrate, and the furious Soviet authorities expelled him for doing so. Bertram Podell (D-NY) not only met with refuseniks but also, at the request of Israeli officials, smuggled documents (hidden in his wife's clothing) out of the USSR. Joshua Eilberg (D-PA, from 1966 to 1978) used his position as chairman of the House Judiciary Subcommittee on Immigration to facilitate extra Soviet Jewish refugee immigration to the United States.

The first congressional resolution about Soviet Jewry was initiated by Senator Ribicoff in 1963. It urged that Jews in the USSR be permitted freedom of religion and culture but did not mention the issue of emigration; at that point, there had been little public indication that many Soviet Jews desired to leave. The resolution gained 70 cosponsors in the Senate and 140 in the House before stalling under pressure from the State Department and Senator J. William Fulbright, chairman of the Senate Foreign Relations Committee, a longtime critic of Israel and the Jewish lobby. They succeeded in watering down the wording so that it would refer to Eastern Europe in general, rather than the USSR specifically, and to the mistreatment of all people living there, not just Jews. The final version was so disappointing to the chief sponsors that they withdrew the resolution rather than see it passed in such neutered form. The following year, Ribicoff tried a different route: he and sixty-nine senatorial colleagues signed a public statement—not a congressional resolution—urging freedom of religion for Soviet Jewry. A similar statement by more than 300 members of the House was issued in 1967. Finally, in April 1972, the House passed, in a near-unanimous vote, a resolution calling for freedom of emigration for Soviet Jewry. By that time, however, the terms of the debate had changed: Soviet Jews were actively clamoring to emigrate—a group of them had tried to steal a plane to fly out of the USSR in 1970, and they had been sentenced to long prison terms for treason—and Congress addressed the issue accordingly.

The first congressional effort to provide concrete assistance to the Soviet Jewish emigration movement was a proposal for a special allocation of $85 million to Israel to help in absorbing new immigrants from the USSR. Sponsored in the Senate by Edmund Muskie (D-ME), Ribicoff, Javits, Richard Schweiker (R-PA), and 46 fellow senators, and in the House by Seymour Halpern (R-NY), Jonathan Bingham (D-NY), and 67 colleagues, it was reduced to $50 million during budget negotiations and enacted in March 1972.

When it came to the major legislative initiative to aid Soviet Jewry, however, Jewish members of Congress deliberately took a back seat for tactical reasons. After Podell drafted the original version of what was to become the Jackson-Vanik amendment, officials of the National Conference on Soviet Jewry and the Greater New York Conference on Soviet Jewry persuaded him to remove his name as the chief sponsor for fear that it would be seen as "serving Jewish self interest as opposed to serving American interests."

Not surprisingly, pro-Israel lobbyists have traditionally turned to the Jewish congressional delegation with regard to matters concerning Israel. They have provided support, and often leadership, on Israel-related legislation since the very first attempt to secure a small amount of U.S. financial assistance to the Jewish state in 1951. Javits and Ribicoff, who were then members of the House, successfully defeated an amendment by then-Representative John F. Kennedy to reduce drastically all U.S. aid to the Middle East that year, for budgetary reasons. As U.S. policy toward Israel grew progressively colder during the early and mid-1950s, it was Javits who repeatedly approached Secretary of State John Foster Dulles, sometimes accompanied by American Jewish leaders, to protest the shift.

In 1956, Jewish members of Congress Sidney Yates (D-IL) in the House, and Lehman and Javits in the Senate, initiated resolutions denouncing Saudi Arabia's refusal to permit Jewish American GIs to be stationed at the U.S. military base at Dhahran. The nature of the controversy made it possible for these members of Congress to present their position as a means of protecting all Americans against possible discrimination, not just Jews, and in 1959 they and like-minded colleagues proposed an amendment denying U.S. aid to countries that discriminated against American citizens on the basis of religion or race. Facing opposition from the ubiquitous Senator Fulbright, the sponsors eventually accepted a compromise version by Senator Kennedy that urged the president to apply the principle of nondiscrimination in dealing with foreign countries but did not require him to suspend aid if discrimination was practiced.

Despite the support and involvement of Jewish members of Congress, attempts to alter U.S. policy in the Mideast often made little headway. Javits, in the Senate, and Emanuel Celler, in the House, issued statements protesting the Eisenhower administration's pressure on Israel to unilaterally withdraw from the Sinai peninsula in early 1957; such congressional protests notwithstanding, the pressure continued and the Israelis felt compelled to pull out. Javits was active on behalf of a 1960 Sense of Congress resolution protesting Egypt's blockade of ships carrying Israeli produce, and another Jewish congressmember, Leonard Farbstein (D-NY) spearheaded the resolution on the House side. Its passage, however, was "a splendid paper victory," as AIPAC director I. L. Kenen put it. "Despite the action taken by Congress, aid to Egypt continued. So did the blockade of the Suez

Canal and so did the U.S. courtship of Egypt's Nasser." The most Kenen could say was that "this clash marked the beginning of a more
articulate role for Congress in the conduct of U.S. foreign policy in
the Middle East" (Kenen 1981, 153).

Another Farbstein amendment, introduced in 1963 (and simultaneously introduced in the Senate by the only two Jewish senators,
Javits and Gruening), responded to Egypt's involvement in the
Yemeni civil war and its continuing hostile actions against Israel by
requiring the suspension of U.S. aid to any country that the president
determined to be undertaking or preparing aggression against another recipient of U.S. aid. The amendment passed, but, because the
final wording conditioned the aid suspension on a presidential determination, it was never implemented.

On the eve of the 1967 war, it was Celler to whom AIPAC turned
to serve as the point man for appeals to the Johnson administration
to prevent the Arabs from again invading Israel. Celler, then seventy-
nine years old and serving his forty-fourth year in the House of Representatives, still displayed the vigor and passion for which he was
well known. "Celler never needed prompting from us," AIPAC's Kenen recalled. "On the contrary, we often had to restrain him. Celler's
long record on Israel's Washington struggle is virtually a day-to-day
chronicle of the concerns of the Jewish people of his generation."
Celler met with Johnson to press his case, and he initiated a congressional letter urging the administration to intervene against "aggression in the Middle East." Two of the newest Jewish members of
congress, Herbert Tenzer (R-NY) and Benjamin Rosenthal (D-NY), collected 110 signatures on the statement. But AIPAC was unable to persuade Javits to organize a similar letter on the Senate side and to approach the president on the issue.

In response to the post-Six Day War rearmament of Syria and
Egypt by the Soviet Union, Israel expressed interest in purchasing
American Phantom F-4 fighter aircraft. When the Johnson administration stalled on the Israeli request, two Jewish members of
Congress, Seymour Halpern (R-NY) and freshman Lester Wolff (D-
NY), introduced legislation urging provision of the F-4s. It succeeded
in prodding the administration to move ahead with the sale. The
campaign for the F-4s helped pave the way for the provision of much
larger quantities of U.S. military aid to Israel in the years following
the 1973 Yom Kippur War.

Once again reflecting opinion trends in the American Jewish community at large, a segment of the Jewish congressional delegation
grew uneasy over some aspects of Israeli policy during the 1980s. In

early 1988, Jewish critics of Israeli policy persuaded two Jewish senators, Rudy Boschwitz and Carl Levin, to initiate a letter mildly critical
of statements by Israel's prime minister indicating reluctance to make
additional territorial concessions to the Arabs. Three other Jewish
senators signed it, as did twenty-five of their colleagues. But two
other Jewish senators, Arlen Specter and Chic Hecht, publicly criticized the letter. "The people of Israel elected their own leadership,"
Hecht said. "Israel is our most important ally in the Middle East and
we should not interfere."

Major Jewish organizations also denounced the letter, and when a
delegation of Jewish critics of Israel met with ten Jewish members of
the House of Representatives several days later to sign a similar letter,
they declined. "After the Senate letter, many of us could see it was a
mistake," noted Henry Waxman (D-CA). "However well-intentioned
the letter may have been, it signaled to the Arab world that the
United States may pressure Israel into making concessions without
any reciprocal concessions on the part of the Arabs." In an indication
of the extent to which non-Jewish members of the House rely on the
judgment of their Jewish colleagues on Israel-related matters, no
other members of the House were willing to undertake such a letter
without the involvement of Jewish members of Congress. "Without
their leadership, none of us is going to do it," as Don Edwards (D-CA)
put it. Many non-Jewish members of Congress assume both that their
Jewish colleagues are more informed concerning Israel and that they
are best positioned to assess American Jewish public opinion. Months
later, Jewish senators who were among the signatories to the controversial letter reported encountering considerable difficulty in their efforts to raise funds in the Jewish community, where grassroots sentiment has always been largely unsympathetic to the idea of Jewish
members of Congress publicly criticizing or pressuring the Jewish
state.

Although Jewish members of Congress have consistently worked
to secure U.S. military aid to Israel, they simultaneously assumed a
leading role in the movement to end America's military assistance to
South Vietnam. Conservative supporters of American involvement in
Vietnam derided the Jewish congressional delegation's position as inconsistent. Jewish members of Congress argued that the two situations differed because Israel is a democracy, while South Vietnam was
not; and because the United States was being asked to send only
weapons, not soldiers, to the Middle East.

Sidney Yates (D-IL) was a leader of the congressional effort to halt
appropriations for U.S. military action against communist forces in

Cambodia, while Congresswoman Elizabeth Holtzman (D-NY) used the courts in pursuit of the same goal, filing suit in U.S. District Court to have U.S. military action in Cambodia declared unconstitutional. A federal judge initially ruled in her favor, although it was overturned on appeal. James Scheuer (D-NY) was one of the few members of Congress to vote in favor of an unorthodox measure that would have prohibited the government from using defense budget funds for military action against North Vietnam. Lester Wolff (D-NY), for his part, cited the Vietnam issue as "the one basic reason" why he decided to remain in Congress after seriously considering retiring in 1968.

Abner Mikva (D-IL) was so vocal in his opposition to U.S. policy in Vietnam that conservative congressmember Wayne Hays dubbed him "an emissary from Hanoi" and "a dupe of the Viet Cong," and U.S. Army intelligence briefly put Mikva under surveillance. Allard Lowenstein (D-NY), a frequent participant in antiwar protests who was elected to Congress in 1968, was denounced by the Republican who defeated him two years later as "an encourager of draft-card burners." Another Jewish member of Congress who was particularly close to the antiwar protest movement was Benjamin Rosenthal (D-NY), one of the first and most outspoken congressional opponents of U.S. involvement in Vietnam. That was, as he recalled, "a very lonely road" to take when he first spoke out in 1965. When masses of college students rallied outside the Capitol to protest the war in 1969, Rosenthal led the move to keep the House of Representatives open all night long as an expression of solidarity with the protesters. The following year, when protesters again massed at the Capitol, he made his office available to them as a message center.

Although Jewish members of Congress were almost unanimous in their opposition to U.S. military action in Southeast Asia, attitudes in the American Jewish community in general and among the Jewish congressional delegation toward U.S. military action abroad had shifted considerably by the time the United States next prepared for a major, sustained military conflict. On the eve of the Persian Gulf War, the House of Representatives voted narrowly to authorize the use of military force to liberate Kuwait from its Iraqi occupiers. Most American Jews agreed that it was justified and appropriate for the United States to take military action in a case involving undisputed aggression by a reckless (and, incidentally, anti-Israel) dictator whose actions posed a threat to America's supply of overseas oil; only a small minority believed that the conflict could still be resolved through diplomacy. The Jewish congressional delegation was split. Holocaust survivor Tom Lantos (D-CA) called Saddam Hussein "a new Hitler," evoking powerful memories of an era when the international community had been slow to confront an aggressive dictator. Howard Berman (D-CA) warned, "If we do not deal with Saddam Hussein now, the United States and the world will be facing a more heavily armed, a more powerful, more dangerous Saddam Hussein five or ten years from now." The most liberal of the Jewish members of Congress, however, remained instinctively reluctant to authorize military action. Anthony Beilenson (D-CA), for example, voted against the Gulf War resolution on grounds that it would mean "systematically inflicting great violence and punishment on another people" and "killing thousands of human beings."

Jewish Women in Congress

Although the election of the splashy Bella Abzug to the House of Representatives in 1970 caused a minor sensation, actually the first Jewish woman was elected to Congress in 1924, when Florence Prag Kahn, the daughter of Polish Jewish immigrants and wife of Congressmember Julius Kahn of San Francisco, ran for his vacant seat after he died. Elected then and to five consecutive terms until 1936, Kahn was a conservative Republican although, bucking trends in her party, she favored military preparedness and opposed prohibition. "There is no sex in citizenship and there should be none in politics," Mrs. Kahn was fond of saying, but it would be many years before her dream would become reality. Women had only recently won the right to vote—something that, ironically, the conservative Mrs. Kahn had opposed—and she remained the only woman in Congress during the fifteen years she spent there. Although Florence Kahn's electoral victories were important for their symbolism, they did not indicate a trend or a major, lasting breakthrough for Jewish women; no other Jewish woman would be elected to Congress until Bella Abzug's triumph more than forty years later.

Abzug, an attorney and liberal political activist in the 1950s, became a prominent antiwar activist and fighter for women's rights in the 1960s, helping to found, among other things, "Women Strike for Peace," one of the earliest organizations devoted to an American withdrawal from Vietnam. She was elected to the House from a heavily Jewish district of Manhattan, despite pre-election media reports that she had said she did not favor selling more planes to Israel. Abzug ran on a slogan that typified her feisty approach to life and politics: "This woman's place is in the house—the House of Representatives." Once in office, Abzug lived up to her reputation, and then some. She spoke out loudly and frequently against U.S. involvement in the Vietnam War, was the first member of Congress to call for the impeachment of President Richard Nixon, and introduced legislation to broaden abortion rights, combat gender discrimination, and require the release of FBI records to the public. After narrowly losing a race for the 1976 Democratic nomination for the Senate, Abzug ran for mayor of New York, and twice more for the House of Representatives, but was unsuccessful each time. Two other Jewish women were elected to the House in the meantime, Elizabeth Holtzman in New York (1972) and Gladys Spellman in Maryland (1974), and others have continued to win elections to the House on occasion. As a rule, the Jewish women in Congress have been liberal Democrats, the exception being Roberta "Bobbi" Fiedler, a California Republican who during her terms in the House (1980–1986) earned a 100 percent rating from the American Conservative Union.

The first two Jewish women in the Senate, San Francisco mayor Dianne Feinstein and Congresswoman Barbara Boxer, were both elected from California in 1992. Analysts attributed their victory in part to backlash from the hearings for Supreme Court nominee Clarence Thomas. The manner in which an all-male Senate committee treated Anita Hill, the professor who accused Thomas of sexual harassment, was considered to have galvanized many female voters to become politically active and to promote female candidates for higher office.

"Most politics is local, not national, and Jewish women's activism at the neighborhood level set the stage for the relatively small number who would achieve national renown," Deborah Dash Moore has noted. Linking contemporary Jewish activism to precedents in turn-of-the century urban neighborhoods, Moore contends that:

> Jewish women entered politics to solve problems they faced as wives and mothers, as workers and daughters. Radical ideologies colored their understanding of why they suffered: why kosher meat cost so much, or why they endured constant pregnancies; why they worked endlessly and earned so little, or why large companies discriminated against them. Both socialism and anarchism recruited working-class, immigrant Jewish women and schooled them in politics, teaching the values of solidarity, organizing, direct action, and militancy. Jewish women's organizations taught middle-class, second generation women similar lessons. To change the world, even to make modest improvements, you needed to learn to exercise power. Men were not going to step aside for women; women would have to push their own agenda to the forefront.

Some of that agenda can be seen in the host of political causes espoused by Jewish women, from consumer protections to birth control, from civil rights to peace movements. (Moore 2000, 15)

Recent Trends and Developments

Recent years have witnessed a number of notable trends concerning Jews in political office. In addition to the aforementioned growth in the size of the Jewish delegation in both houses of Congress, numerous Jews were appointed to cabinet posts during the Clinton years— Robert Rubin as secretary of the treasury, succeeded by another Jew, Laurence Summers; Dan Glickman, as secretary of agriculture; Mickey Kantor, secretary of commerce; and Robert Reich, secretary of labor. (Although Secretary of State Madeleine Albright was discovered to be technically Jewish, she chose not to identify herself as such.)

The heightened interest in Holocaust education in the Jewish community in recent years coincided with the election to the House of Representatives, in 1980, of Holocaust survivor Tom Lantos, Democrat of California, and Sam Gejdenson, Democrat of Connecticut, a child of Holocaust survivors who was himself born in a Displaced Persons camp in Germany. (Gejdenson served for twenty years before losing in 2000; Lantos remains in office.) Lantos was successful in his highly publicized campaign to have Holocaust rescue hero Raoul Wallenberg given the rare distinction of being awarded honorary U.S. citizenship. An achievement of more practical value was U.S. Representative Elizabeth Holtzman's 1979 initiative to establish the Office of Special Investigations, a Justice Department unit charged with the task of pursuing Nazi war criminals who took refuge in the United States after World War II.

Perhaps it is an indication of the extent to which Jews now feel comfortable in American political culture that a race for the U.S. Senate in 1990 would involve a Jewish candidate challenging the Jewish bona fides of his Jewish opponent. Interestingly enough, the episode took place in Minnesota, a state that at the time had only about 35,000 Jews. The incumbent since 1977, conservative Republican Rudy Boschwitz, facing a tough race against liberal Democrat challenger Paul Wellstone, ignited a controversy by sending a pre-election mailing to Jewish voters that said that "in this first senate race between two Jewish candidates," Boschwitz was preferable because "Wellstone took no part in Jewish affairs and had not raised his children as Jews." Unflattering news media coverage of the episode, accusing Boschwitz of engaging in "negative campaigning" by inappropriately raising questions about Wellstone's Jewish credentials, helped to swing the narrow election in Wellstone's favor.

At the same time, religious and ethnic assertiveness by Jews in Congress is far more common than ever before. Gary Ackerman, a liberal Democrat who has represented a Queens, New York, district since 1983, and Charles Schumer, a longtime representative from New York who was elected senator in 2000, initiated regular prayer and study group sessions known as the "Congressional Minyan [a traditional Jewish prayer quorum]." The door to Ackerman's office bears a mezuzah, a small case containing parchment with passages from the Hebrew Bible. Peter Deutsch, an observant Jewish member of Congress from Florida (since 1993), has made arrangements to cast nonelectronic votes in Sabbath or holiday sessions of the House.

Joseph Lieberman (D-CT), first elected to the U.S. Senate in 1988, was the first (and remains the only) observant Jew in the Senate. Lieberman's road to Capitol Hill was typical of young, aspiring politicians, as he went from law school to congressional intern to the Connecticut State Senate, then was elected state attorney general in 1981. In 1988 he was made the Democratic nominee for the U.S. Senate, at a convention he declined to attend because it took place on the Sabbath. After his election to the Senate, Lieberman generally refrained from Senate business on the Sabbath, except for occasional urgent matters, which he dealt with by walking from his home to Capitol Hill, using the stairs rather than the elevator, and casting votes by nonelectronic means so as not to transgress the prohibitions against using automobiles, elevators, or other electric devices on the Sabbath.

Indeed, the Senate session on Lieberman's first Friday in Washington ran so late that he made plans to sleep in his office rather than violate the religious prohibition against traveling on the Sabbath—only to have Tennessee senator Al Gore insist that he stay at Gore's parents' apartment, which was within walking distance. Aware that Lieberman was not permitted, by Jewish religious law, to switch lights on or off on the Sabbath, Gore did it for him—leading Lieberman to quip that he had "the most distinguished Shabbos goy in history"—referring to a non-Jew who performs minor tasks forbidden to Jews on the Sabbath. The Gore-Lieberman friendship would reach its pinnacle twelve years later, when Gore would select Lieberman as his vice presidential running mate.

No Jew has ever been nominated by a major party for president, and, until Lieberman, none had been nominated for vice president, although Senator Abraham Ribicoff reportedly declined George Mc-Govern's offer to be his running mate in 1972. Only two Jews have ever declared their candidacy for their party's presidential nomination, but in both cases they withdrew from the race within a short time: Pennsylvania governor Milton Shapp, a Democrat, in 1976, and Senator Arlen Specter, Republican of Pennsylvania, in 1996. Their candidacies were, in a sense, a declaration of defiance of the conventional wisdom among political professionals that latent anti-Semitism would make it impossible for a Jew ever to be elected to either of the two highest posts in the government. Although neither Shapp nor Specter made it very far as candidates, they helped put an end to the long-standing taboo against Jewish candidates for the presidency. By helping to accustom the American public to the legitimacy of a Jewish president or vice president, they played an important role in paving the way for the Lieberman nomination in 2000.

Al Gore may have been personally comfortable with Lieberman in part because of their long-standing friendship, but Gore's choice of Lieberman as his running mate had everything to do with political calculation—and Lieberman's religiosity was very much a part of that calculation. Lieberman was the first Democrat to chastise President Clinton publicly during the Monica Lewinsky episode; his rhetoric broke ranks, even if he later voted against impeachment. Lieberman's stance concerning Clinton and Lewinsky was widely hailed as an admirable demonstration of moral conviction. The choice of Lieberman as his vice presidential running mate thus enabled Gore to put some distance between himself and a president whom he was reluctant to criticize directly. The fact that Lieberman is religiously observant reinforced his public image as a man of moral stature, which implicitly contrasted with Clinton's moral lapses in the Lewinsky affair. The Gore-Lieberman campaign went out of its way to invoke terms such as faith, tradition, and morality, in an effort to branch out beyond the Democratic Party's usual pool of liberal support and seek the backing of moderately conservative Americans to whom religion is a matter of significance. Although Gore maintained standard liberal Democratic positions on church-state issues such as voluntary prayer in schools, Lieberman's more centrist approach on school prayer and affirmative action, together with his denunciations of excessive violence and sexuality on television, gave Gore the ability to make inroads among some traditionally Republican voters.

Some liberal Jewish circles regarded the Democrats' deliberate emphasis on their vice presidential candidate's religious faith as an unacceptable breach of church-state separation. The Anti-Defamation League, which had on many occasions criticized Christian conservatives for attempting to inject religious issues into the political arena, felt compelled to do the same in response to the unexpected appearance of such rhetoric at the other end of the political spectrum. From the standpoint of the Gore-Lieberman campaign, however, the temporary discomfort experienced by some of their liberal allies was a small price to pay for the centrist votes they might be able to win away from the Republicans.

In previous years, a potential vice presidential candidate's Jewishness would have been regarded as a major disadvantage because of latent anti-Semitic prejudice among some voters, and it would have proven to be a major obstacle to his being selected as the nominee. In Lieberman's case, however, the opposite was true. His well-publicized religious behavior turned out to be a major asset to the ticket. In earlier times, even being thoroughly assimilated would not have helped a Jewish candidate reach the vice presidential slot on the ticket, since the fact that he was Jewish would have been widely reported in the press regardless of his level of religious observance. In the year 2000, however, because of the Clinton-Lewinsky scandal, and thanks to the generally increased level of religious tolerance in America, the more visibly Jewish the vice presidential candidate was, the better.

During the election campaign, Lieberman went to considerable lengths to scotch any perception that any of his views as a Jew might ever conflict with his priorities as an American political leader. His efforts in that regard sometimes involved making controversial statements that set off ripples of dismay in a Jewish community that for months was fairly bursting with pride at the fact that one of its own had finally risen to become nominee for the second highest position in the land. At one point, for example, Lieberman declared his readiness in principle to meet with Louis Farrakhan, the anti-Semitic Black Muslim leader; on another occasion, he told an interviewer that Judaism does not prohibit marriages between Jews and non-Jews. Neither the mass media nor most voters paid much attention to these statements, and even most Jewish voters seem to have excused them as the sort of compromises a Jewish candidate for office might find necessary in the heat of an election campaign. Certainly Lieberman's remarks about Farrakhan and intermarriage appeared to have made no dent in the level of Jewish support he and Gore received, which was in the 80 percent range, comparable to most Democratic presidential tickets.

The Lieberman nomination also said something significant about American political culture at the dawn of the twenty-first century. "The Lieberman nomination did not create a climate of decency in America; it confirmed such a climate," the *New Republic* remarked (August 21, 2000):

> This is not another exercise in "diversity." It is an exercise of the philosophical disposition of America, which is a country that does not demand an erasure of self or an erasure of tradition as a condition for citizenship; that does not recoil before the particular as the enemy of the universal; that assumes the rights of individuals and groups, and does not condescend to grant them; that defeats tribalism with pluralism; that prefers equality to tolerance . . . Gore-Lieberman! Our open society just became a little more open.

At the dawn of the twenty-first century, American Jews could confidently assess the history of Jews in political office as one of steady and definable progress. This success can be measured in the number of Jewish candidates elected, the near disappearance of anti-Semitism as a factor in elections, and the broad range of offices to which Jews have been elected. The nomination of a Jew for vice president by one of the two major political parties was a dramatic statement of the extent to which a candidate's Jewishness is no longer regarded as a detriment to a ticket's chance of success; indeed, it may even be considered an asset in certain circumstances. How long it will be until the final psychological hurdle, the nomination of a Jew for president by a major party, remains to be seen.

References

Breitman, Richard, and Alan M. Kraut. *American Refugee Policy and European Jewry 1933–1945*. Bloomington: Indiana University Press, 1987.

Celler, Emanuel. *You Never Leave Brooklyn*. New York: Day, 1973.

Cohen, Naomi W. "Faces of American Jewish Defense in the 1920s." In *An Inventory of Promises: Essays on American Jewish History in Honor of Moses Rischin*, edited by Jeffrey S. Gurock and Marc L. Raphael, pp. 15–30. Brooklyn, NY: Carlson, 1995.

Diner, Hasia R. *A Time for Gathering: The Second Migration 1820–1880*. Baltimore, MD: Johns Hopkins University Press, 1992.

Feingold, Henry. *A Time for Searching: Entering the Mainstream 1920–1945*. Baltimore, MD: Johns Hopkins University Press, 1992.

Feuer, Leon. "The Birth of the Jewish Lobby." *American Jewish Archives* 28, no. 2 (November 1976): 107–118.

Halpern, Ben. *A Clash of Heroes: Brandeis, Weizmann, and American Zionism.* New York: Oxford University Press, 1987.

Kenen, I. L. *Israel's Defense Line: Her Friends and Foes in Washington.* Buffalo, NY: Prometheus, 1981.

Moore, Deborah Dash. "A Century of Jewish Women in American Politics." *Women's League Outlook* 71 (summer 2000): 15–17.

Neuringer, Sheldon. "American Jewry and United States Immigration Policy, 1881–1953." Ph.D. dissertation, University of Wisconsin, 1969.

Selavan, Ida Cohen. "Adolph Edlis—A Hungarian Jew in Pittsburgh Politics." *American Jewish Archives* 36, no. 1 (April 1984): 1–10.

Shapiro, Edward S. "The Approach of War: Congressional Isolationism and Anti-Semitism, 1939–1941." *American Jewish History* 74 (September 1984): 45–65.

Wyman, David S. *The Abandonment of the Jews: America and the Holocaust, 1941–1945.* New York: Pantheon, 1984.

Documents

George Washington: "To Bigotry No Sanction"

In a letter dated August 17, 1790, President George Washington publicly affirmed that the new United States of America "gives to bigotry no sanction, to persecution no assistance." Elsewhere around the world, equality for Jews had come—when it came at all—after lengthy and difficult struggles. From its very inception, America embraced the principles of tolerance.

Washington's statement came in the form of a reply to a letter he had received from the Hebrew Congregation of Newport, Rhode Island.

Gentlemen:

While I receive with much satisfaction your address replete with expressions of affection and esteem, I rejoice in the opportunity of assuring you that I shall always retain a grateful remembrance of the cordial welcome I experienced in my visit to New Port from all classes of citizens.

The reflection on the days of difficulty and danger which are past is rendered the more sweet from a consciousness that they are succeeded by days of uncommon prosperity and security. If we have wisdom to make the best use of the advantages with which we are now favored, we cannot fail, under the just administration of a good government, to become a great and a happy people.

The citizens of the United States of America have a right to applaud themselves for having given to mankind examples of an enlarged and liberal policy, a policy worthy of imitation.

All possess alike liberty of conscience and immunities of citizenship. It is now no more that toleration is spoken of, as if it was by the indulgence of one class of people that another enjoyed the exercise of their inherent natural rights. For happily the government of the United States, which gives to bigotry no sanction, to persecution no assistance, requires only that they who live under its protection should demean themselves as good citizens, in giving it on all occasions their effectual support.

It would be inconsistent with the frankness of my character not to avow that I am pleased with your favorable opinion of my administration and fervent wishes for my felicity.

May the children of the stock of Abraham who dwell in this land continue to merit and enjoy the good will of the other inhabitants, while every one shall sit in safety under his own vine and fig-tree, and there shall be none to make him afraid.

May the Father of all mercies scatter light and not darkness in our paths, and make us all in our several vocations useful here, and, in his own due time and way, everlastingly happy.

G. *Washington*

Grant's Expulsion Order

The 1862 directive by Union General Ulysses S. Grant to expel all Jews from the Kentucky-Tennessee-Mississippi region stands as a unique document in the history of anti-Semitism in the United States. With its references to "the Jews as a class" and its use of the extreme measure of mass expulsion, Grant's order is reminiscent of anti-Semitic steps taken by governments in the medieval era. At the same time, the final outcome of the affair illustrates just how far the status of Jews in the United States had advanced: Jewish protests to President Abraham Lincoln persuaded him to countermand Grant's order.

General Orders,

No. 11

The Jews as a class violating every regulation of trade established by the Treasury Department, and also department orders, are hereby expelled from the department within twenty-four hours from the receipt of this order.

Post commanders will see that all of this class of people be furnished passes and required to leave, and anyone returning after such notification will be arrested and held in confinement until an opportunity occurs of sending them out as prisoners, unless furnished with permit from headquarters.

No passes will be given these people to visit headquarters for the purpose of making personal applications for trade permits.
By order of Maj.-Gen. U.S. Grant
Jno A. Rawlins,
Assistant Adjutant-General

The Maryland "Jew Bill" of 1826

The only instance in which state legislators engaged in a formal and detailed debate on the merits of extending full civil equality to Jews took place in Maryland in 1818–1825. The final version of the bill that was adopted by the Maryland General Assembly on January 5, 1826, focused specifically on "people professing the Jewish Religion," in contrast with an earlier version of the bill, which had proposed to grant all "civil rights and religious privileges" to all of the state's citizens. Legislators wary of granting equality to Muslims, atheists, and other "infidels" blocked the universal version and ultimately adopted the bill that referred to Jews alone. The bill also replaced the previous, explicitly Christian oath of office with one affirming "belief in a future state of rewards and punishments," a formula with which Jews would be comfortable.

To extend to the sect of people professing the Jewish Religion the same rights and privileges that are enjoyed by Christians.

Section 1: Be it enacted by the General Assembly of Maryland, that every citizen of this state professing the Jewish Religion, and who shall hereafter be appointed to any office or public trust under the State of Maryland, shall in addition to the oaths required to be taken by the constitution and laws of the United States, make and subscribe to a declaration of his belief in a future state of rewards and punishments, instead of the declaration now required by the constitution and form of government of this state.

Section 2: Be it enacted, that the several clauses and section of the declaration of rights, constitution and form of government, and every part of any law of this state contrary to the provisions of this act, so far as respects the sect of people aforesaid, shall be, and the same is hereby declared to be repealed and annulled on the confirmation hereof.

Section 3: [summarizes the procedure by which one must undertake to amend the state constitution]

Pittsburgh Platform (1885)

Although not an official platform of Reform Judaism, the Pittsburgh Platform accurately reflected the consensus among Reform rabbis and lay leaders in late-nineteenth-century America. The document illustrates the dominant ideological trends among this key segment of the American Jewish elite, emphasizing the perceived commonality of beliefs between Jews and non-Jews, the need to abandon traditional religious rituals, opposition to the creation of a Jewish state, and the Reform movement's interest in social action.

First. We recognize in every religion an attempt to grasp the Infinite, and in every mode, source or book of revelation, held sacred in any religious system, the consciousness of the indwelling of God in man. We hold that Judaism presents the highest conception of the God-idea as taught in our Holy Scriptures and developed and spiritualized by the Jewish teachers, in accordance with the moral and philosophical progress of their respective ages. We maintain that Judaism preserved and defended, midst continual struggles and trials and under enforced isolation, this God-idea as the central religious truth for the human race.

Second. We recognize in the Bible the record of the consecration of the Jewish people to its mission as priest of the one God, and value it as the most potent instrument of religious and moral instruction. We hold that the modern discoveries of scientific researches in the domains of nature and history are not antagonistic to the doctrines of Judaism, the Bible reflecting the primitive ideas of its own age, and at times clothing its conception of Divine Providence and justice dealing with man in miraculous narratives.

Third. We recognize in the Mosaic legislation a system of training the Jewish people for its mission during its national life in Palestine, and to-day we accept as biding only the moral laws, and maintain only such ceremonies as elevate and sanctify our lives, but reject all such as are not adapted to the views and habits of modern civilization.

Fourth. We hold that all such Mosaic and rabbinical laws as regulate diet, priestly purity and dress originated in ages and under the influence of ideas altogether foreign to our present mental and spiritual state. They fail to impress the modern Jew with a spirit of priestly holiness; their observance in our days is apt rather to obstruct than to further modern spiritual elevation.

Fifth. We recognize in the modern era of universal culture of heart and intellect the approaching realization of Israel's great Messianic hope for the establishment of the kingdom of truth, justice and peace among all men. We consider ourselves no longer a nation, but a religious community, and, therefore, expect neither a return to Palestine, nor a sacrificial worship under the sons of Aaron, nor the restoration of any of the laws concerning the Jewish state.

Sixth. We recognize in Judaism a progressive religion, ever striving to be in accord with the postulates of reason. We are convinced of the utmost necessity of preserving the historical identity with our great past. Christianity and Islam being daughter religions of Judaism, we appreciate their providential mission to aid in the spreading of monotheistic and moral truth. We acknowledge that the spirit of broad humanity of our age is our ally in the fulfillment of our mission, and, therefore, we extend the hand of fellowship to all who cooperate with us in the establishment of the reign of truth and righteousness among men

Seventh. We reassert the doctrine of Judaism that the soul of man is immortal, grounding this belief on the divine nature of the human spirit, which forever finds bliss in righteousness and misery in wickedness. We reject, as ideas not rooted in Judaism, the beliefs both in bodily resurrection and in Gehenna and Eden (Hell and Paradise) as abodes for everlasting punishment and reward.

Eighth. In full accordance with the spirit of Mosaic legislation, which strives to regulate the relation between the rich and poor, we deem it our duty to participate in the great task of modern times, to solve, on the basis of justice and righteousness, the problems presented by the contrasts and evils of the present organization of society.

The Johnson Immigration Act

In 1921, Congress adopted the Johnson Immigration Act, which established stringent quotas for the admission of immigrants to the United States. Three years later, those quotas were tightened even further. As a result, during the years of Hitler's persecution (1933–1945), very few Jews were able to escape to America. The statement to the House Immigration Committee by Congressman Johnson excerpted below, which accompanied the introduction of his bill, makes clear that excluding Jews was a primary intention of the legislation.

The flow of immigration to the United States is now in full flood. The need for restrictive legislation is apparent. The accommodations at Ellis Island are not sufficient for the avalanche of new arrivals;

larger cities have not houses for them; work cannot be found for them; and, further, the bulk of the newer arrivals are of the dependent rather than the working class. . . .

Members of your committee, as a result of personal investigation at Ellis Island . . . found the new immigration at Ellis Island to consist practically of all nationalities except Orientals. It found by far the largest percentage of immigrants to be people of Jewish extraction. On the steamship *New Amsterdam,* sailing from Rotterdam, the committee found that 80 percent of the steerage passengers were from Galicia, practically all of Jewish extraction. On the *New Rochelle,* arriving from Danzig, the committee estimated that more than 90 percent were of the Semitic race. The committee is confirmed in the belief that the major portions of recent arrivals come without funds. It was apparent to the committee that a large percentage of those arriving were incapable of earning a livelihood. These are temporarily detained, causing great congestion, much delay, and pitiful distress, until relatives or others arrive to give bonds that the newcomers will not become public charges. . . . [T]he largest number of Jews coming to the United States before the war in a single year was 153,748 (1906); while during the one month of October 1920, it is estimated that of the 74,665 immigrants arriving at Ellis Island, more than 75 percent were of the Semitic race.

Treasury Secretary Henry Morgenthau's "Report to the President" (1944)

In 1943 senior aides to Treasury Secretary Henry Morgenthau Jr. discovered that the State Department had been deliberately sabotaging attempts to rescue Jews from Hitler. They compiled a detailed report on the State Department's actions—which they originally entitled —"Report to the President on the Acquiescence of This Government in the Murder of the Jews"—and Morgenthau presented it to President Franklin Roosevelt on January 16, 1944. In the preamble to the report, excerpted below, Morgenthau cites a congressional resolution on rescue that Jewish activists had initiated, and warns the president that "a nasty scandal" could ensue if the administration should fail to take some action. As a result, Roosevelt decided to create a special government rescue agency—as the congressional resolution sought—which rescued many tens of thousands of Jews during the final eighteen months of the war. This document illustrates how the combination of Jewish activism, insider lobbying by a cabinet minister, and the political interests of a president soon to face re-election brought about the only meaningful American response to the Holocaust.

One of the greatest crimes in history, the slaughter of the Jewish people in Europe, is continuing unabated.

This Government has for a long time maintained that its policy is to work out programs to save those Jews and other persecuted minorities of Europe who could be saved.

You are probably not as familiar as I with the utter failure of certain officials in our State Department, who are charged with actually carrying out this policy, to take any effective action to prevent the extermination of the Jews in German-controlled Europe.

The public record, let alone the facts which have not yet been made public, reveals the gross procrastination of these officials. It is well known that since the time when it became clear that Hitler was determined to carry out a policy of exterminating the Jews in Europe, the State Department officials have failed to take any positive steps reasonably calculated to save any of these people. Although they have used devices such as setting up intergovernmental organizations to survey the whole refugee problem, and calling conferences such as the Bermuda Conference to explore the whole refugee problem, making it appear that positive action could be expected, in fact nothing has been accomplished.

The best summary of the whole situation is contained in one sentence of a report submitted on December 20, 1943, by the Committee on Foreign Relations of the Senate, recommending the passage of a Resolution (S.R. 203), favoring the appointment of a commission to formulate plans to save the Jews of Europe from extinction by Nazi Germany. The Resolution had been introduced by Senator Guy M. Gillette in behalf of himself and eleven colleagues, Senators Taft, Thomas, Radcliffe, Murray, Johnson, Guffey, Ferguson, Clark, Van Nuys, Downey and Ellender. The Committee stated:

"We have talked; we have sympathized; we have expressed our horror; the time to act is long past due."

Whether one views this failure as being deliberate on the part of those officials handling the matter, or merely due to their incompetence, is not too important from my point of view. However, there is a growing number of responsible people and organizations today who have ceased to view our failure as the product of simple incompetence on the part of those officials in the State Department charged with handling the problem. They see plain Anti-Semitism motivating the actions of these State Department officials and, rightly or wrongly, it will require little more in the way of proof for this suspicion to explode into a nasty scandal.

The 1944 Democratic and Republican Party Platforms Embrace Zionism

As a result of energetic lobbying by American Zionists, the party platforms adopted by both the Republican and Democratic parties in 1944 for the first time embraced the cause of Jewish statehood in Palestine. This represented a significant departure from the 1930s, when American Zionist leaders had focused their lobbying attention almost exclusively on the Democrats, to whom they felt ideologically close. It also signaled a new awareness in both parties of the growing significance of American Jews in presidential elections, because of their concentration in states with large numbers of electoral votes.

The timing of the two conventions is also significant. The Democratic platform plank on Palestine was adopted in part as a response to the Republicans' strong statement on the subject the previous month. The fact that the Democrats felt obliged to take such a step, even though it was a departure from President Roosevelt's traditional hands-off stance regarding Palestine, is indicative of the party's recognition of the increasing importance of Jewish voters.

Republican Plank, June 27, 1944:

In order to give refuge to millions of distressed Jewish men, women and children driven from their homes by tyranny, we call for the opening of Palestine to their unrestricted immigration and land ownership, so that in accordance with the full intent and purpose of the Balfour Declaration of 1917 and the resolution of a Republican Congress in 1922 Palestine may be constituted as a free and democratic commonwealth. We condemn the failure of the President to insist that the mandatory of Palestine carry out the provision of the Balfour Declaration and of the mandate while he pretends to support it.

Democratic Plank, July 21, 1944:

We favor the opening of Palestine to unrestricted Jewish immigration and colonization and such a policy as to result in the establishment there of a free and democratic Jewish commonwealth.

The Jackson Amendment

On March 15, 1973, following the most comprehensive lobbying campaign ever undertaken by the American Jewish community, Senator Henry

M. Jackson (D-WA) and seventy-three of his colleagues introduced an amendment to deny "most favored nation" status, a category from which a foreign country might accrue particular benefits from trade with the United States, from countries prohibiting freedom of emigration. The amendment was aimed at pressuring the Soviet Union to permit the emigration of its Jewish citizens. It was enacted by Congress in late 1974, and although the Soviet Union publicly denounced the Jackson amendment, it is widely credited with forcing the Kremlin to permit increased emigration in the years to follow.

Amendment on East-West Trade and Freedom of Emigration

(a) To assure the continued dedication of the United States to fundamental human rights, and notwithstanding any other provision of this Act or any other law, after October 15, 1972, no nonmarket economy country shall be eligible to receive most-favored-nation treatment or to participate in any program of the Government of the United States which extends credits or credit guarantees or investment guarantees, directly or indirectly, during the period beginning with the date on which the President of the United States determines that such country—

(1) denies its citizens the right or opportunity to emigrate; or

(2) imposes more than a nominal tax on emigration or on the visas or other documents required for emigration, for any purpose or cause whatsoever; or

(3) imposes more than a nominal tax, levy, fine, fee, or other charge on any citizen as a consequence of the desire of such citizen to emigrate to the country of his choice, and ending on the date on which the President determines that such country is no longer in violation of paragraph (1), (2), or (3).

(b) After October 15, 1972, a nonmarket economy country may participate in a program of the Government of the United States which extends credits or credit guarantees or investment guarantees, and shall be eligible to receive most-favored-nation treatment, only after the President of the United States has submitted to the Congress a report indicating that such country is not in violation of paragraph (1), (2), or (3) of subsection (a). Such report with respect to such country, shall include information as to the nature and implementation of emigration laws and policies and restrictions or discrimination applied to or against persons wishing to emigrate. The report required by this subsection shall be submitted initially as provided herein and semi-annually thereafter so long as any agreement entered into pursuant to the exercise of such authority is in effect.

Key People,
Laws, and Terms

Abzug, Bella (1920–1998): An outspoken feminist and antiwar activist, Abzug was elected to the House of Representatives from Manhattan in 1970, becoming the first Jewish woman elected to Congress since the 1930s. She was elected to two additional terms but then lost her 1976 bid for the U.S. Senate and was defeated in several subsequent races for mayor of New York and the House of Representatives.

America Endorses Zionism: In the summer of 1944, both major political parties for the first time adopted planks supporting the establishment of a Jewish state in Palestine, a major turning point in Zionist lobbying efforts. Two years later, President Truman for the first time expressed support for the creation of a Jewish state, and in 1947 the Truman administration led the effort to have the United Nations support partitioning Palestine into Jewish and Arab states.

American Jewish Conference: In an effort to achieve American Jewish unity in dealing with matters of pressing concern, more than 500 delegates from Jewish communities around the United States representing major Jewish organizations—some elected, some appointed—gathered in New York City on August 29, 1943. The highlight of the conference was the adoption of a resolution calling for the establishment of a Jewish state. The non-Zionist American Jewish Committee withdrew from the conference as a result. During subsequent Zionist lobbying efforts in Washington, the American Jewish Conference's Palestine resolution was frequently cited as evidence of broad American Jewish support for Zionism. The AJ Conference itself, however, never evolved into a significant force in the Jewish community.

American Jewish Congress: Jewish activists convened the first American Jewish Congress, in 1918, as a democratically elected grassroots alternative to the established Jewish organizations. The 400 delegates, most of them chosen by more than 300,000 voters in Jewish communities around the United States, endorsed the creation of a Jewish national home in Palestine and resolved to send representatives to take part in the Paris Peace Conference and to press for Jewish rights in postwar Eastern Europe. Organized as a permanent body in 1922, the AJ Congress addressed a broad range of Jewish concerns, domestic and international, and spearheaded the boycott of German goods during the 1930s. It also played a prominent role in the American Zionist movement.

American Zionist Emergency Council: On the eve of World War II, the World Zionist Organization established the Emergency Committee for Zionist Affairs (ECZA) in the United States, to become the main Zionist center for the duration of the war. An umbrella group for the major U.S. Zionist organizations, the council changed its name to the American Zionist Emergency Council in 1943 and elevated the activist Rabbi Abba Hillel Silver to its leadership. Silver undertook a national campaign of rallies, lobbying, and political pressure that helped win public sympathy for the Zionist cause and used congressional pressure to counteract the State Department's attempts to turn President Truman against Zionism.

Anti-Nazi Boycott: After Adolf Hitler became chancellor of Germany in 1933, the Jewish War Veterans of America and the American League for the Defense of Jewish Rights organized a public boycott of German goods; they were later joined by the American Jewish Congress.

Anti-Semitism: Prejudice against Jews. The term was actually coined by nineteenth-century Europeans who were hostile to Jews as a people (whom they considered "Semites") but wanted to distinguish themselves from those whose hatred of Jews was rooted in a hatred for Judaism as a religion. Today the term "anti-Semitism" is commonly used to refer to bigotry against Jews and Judaism alike.

Benjamin, Judah (1811–1884): Elected to the U.S. Senate from Louisiana in 1852, Benjamin later served the Confederacy as its secretary of war, and then secretary of state.

Berger, Victor (1860–1929): Austrian-born Jewish immigrant Victor Berger, of Milwaukee, in 1910 became the first Socialist Party candidate elected to the House of Representatives. Berger's writings against American participation in World War I resulted in his conviction, in 1919, of violating the Espionage Act, and he was prevented from taking his seat in Congress. After the Supreme Court overturned his conviction, Berger was re-elected to the House three more times.

Bermuda Conference: In response to mounting public criticism of the Allies' failure to aid the Jews in Nazi-occupied Europe, the U.S. and British governments held a conference to discuss the refugee problem, in Bermuda in April 1943. The conference ended without any concrete plans to aid the Jewish refugees, prompting strong criticism from the American Jewish community.

Black-Jewish Rift: Anti-Semitic outbursts by black militants at the 1967 National New Politics Convention, a major gathering of New Left activists, caused a permanent split between black activists and many of their Jewish allies, and contributed to a broader rift between the black and Jewish communities that continued for years afterward.

Bloom, Sol (1870–1949): A former vaudeville comedian turned realtor, Bloom was elected to the House of Representatives in 1922 from Manhattan. In 1939 he became chairman of the House Foreign Relations Committee. Bloom served as a U.S. delegate to the Anglo-American refugee conference in Bermuda in 1943, and he angered many in the Jewish community with his defense of the conference despite its failure to produce any rescue plans. Later that year he attempted to block a congressional resolution urging the administration to create a refugee rescue agency.

Brandeis, Louis D. (1856–1941): Social reform advocate Louis D. Brandeis, known in Boston as "the People's Attorney," was named chairman of the Provisional Executive Committee for General Zionist Affairs, the top position in the American Zionist leadership, in 1914. His personal prestige significantly increased the popularity of Zionism in the American Jewish community, especially after he became the first Jew appointed to the U.S. Supreme Court, in 1916.

Celler, Emanuel (1888–1981): A Brooklyn attorney who was first elected to the House of Representatives in 1922, Celler served continuously for fifty years. During the 1930s and 1940s, Celler repeatedly sought, without success, to have America's immigration quotas liberalized to permit the entry of more refugees, and he was blunt in his criticism of the Roosevelt administration's failure to rescue Jews from Hitler. He was perhaps the most outspoken advocate of Zionism on Capitol Hill, and, after 1948, the most vocal defender of the state of Israel.

Conservative Judaism: A movement originating in the United States in the early 1900s, positioning itself as more traditional in its beliefs and ritual practices than Reform Judaism but less strict than Orthodox Judaism. Approximately one-third of American Jews are affiliated with Conservative synagogues.

Dickstein, Samuel (1885–1954): Russian-born attorney, Samuel Dickstein served in the New York State Assembly from 1918 until his election to Congress in 1922. He served twelve consecutive terms, during part of which time he chaired the House Committee on Immigration and Naturalization. During the Hitler era he fought unsuccessfully to have more Jewish refugees admitted to the United States. In 1945 he left Congress to assume a seat on the New York state Supreme Court.

Frank Lynching: In a trial laced with anti-Semitism, Atlanta pencil factory owner Leo Frank was falsely convicted of murdering a Christian girl in 1913 and was then lynched by a mob. The episode prompted the Jewish fraternal order B'nai B'rith to establish the Anti-Defamation League for the purpose of actively combating anti-Semitism.

Grant's Expulsion Decree: In 1862, Union general Ulysses Grant responded to popular resentment over Jewish merchants, allegedly taking advantage of the cotton shortage to sell cotton in war zones, by issuing General Order 11, which expelled all Jews from the region known as the Tennessee Department. The entire Jewish community of Paducah, Kentucky, was ordered to depart on twenty-four hours' notice. Local Jewish leaders, together with local dignitaries, among them Paducah Union League president Cesar Kaskel, protested directly to President Lincoln, who eventually revoked Grant's directive.

Holocaust: The systematic mass murder of approximately six million European Jews by the Nazi regime between 1941 and 1945. Most were killed in specially constructed gas chambers in death camps to which Jews were deported en masse in sealed cattle cars.

Intermarriage: Marriage between a Jew and a non-Jew. Intermarriage is prohibited by biblical law and has always been regarded by most Jews as a grave threat to Jewish communal survival. As religious observance among Jews has plummeted since the 1800s, the rate of intermarriage has gradually risen, reaching 50 percent in the United States in recent years.

Isaacson, Leo (1910–1996): In a closely watched special election in the Bronx, New York, American Labor Party candidate Leo Isaacson was elected to Congress on a platform emphasizing the issue of Jewish statehood in Palestine. His victory was widely interpreted as a warning signal to the Truman administration that its failure to support Jewish statehood could have serious electoral consequences.

Jackson-Vanik Amendment: Introduced in 1972 and adopted by Congress two years later, the Jackson-Vanik legislation, named after lead sponsors Senator Henry Jackson (D-WA) and Charles Vanik (R-OH), linked U.S.-Soviet trade to freedom of emigration for Soviet Jews. It is widely credited with pressuring the Soviet authorities to permit increased Jewish emigration.

Javits, Jacob (1904–1986): New York attorney Jacob Javits, a liberal Republican, was first elected to the House of Representatives in 1946, where he served until becoming attorney general of New York state in 1954. Elected to the U.S. Senate in 1956, Javits remained there until 1980, making him the longest serving Jewish senator.

Kook, Hillel (1915–2001): A disciple of the militant Zionist leader Vladimir Ze'ev Jabotinsky, Kook left Palestine in 1940 for the United States, where, under the pseudonym Peter Bergson, he organized a number of Jewish activist groups: the Committee for a Jewish Army of Stateless and Palestinian Jews (est. 1941) sought to convince the Allies to establish a Jewish military force to fight in World War II; the Emergency Committee to Save the Jewish People of Europe (est. 1943) pressed the Roosevelt administration to aid Jewish refugees; the American League for a Free Palestine (est. 1943) and the Hebrew Committee of National Liberation (est. 1944) sought to rally American support for the creation of a Jewish state. Kook's efforts were instrumental in bringing about the creation of the U.S. government's War Refugee Board, although he was criticized by mainstream American Jewish leaders for operating beyond the regular bounds of Jewish communal activity.

Lehman, Herbert (1878–1963): Elected lieutenant governor of New York as Franklin Roosevelt's running mate in 1928, Herbert Lehman became the first Jewish governor of New York state in 1932. During World War II he chaired the UN Relief and Rehabilitation Administration, after which (in 1949) he became the first Jew to serve in the U.S. Senate since World War I, a position he held until 1956.

Lieberman, Joseph (b. 1942): A five-term Connecticut state senator, Joseph Lieberman, an observant Jew, also served as the state's attorney general before being elected to the U.S. Senate in 1988. In 2000 he was selected as the running mate of Democratic presidential nominee Al Gore, making Lieberman the first Jew nominated for vice president by a major political party.

London, Meyer (1871–1926): The Yiddish-speaking East European immigrants of Manhattan's Lower East Side finally elected "one of their own" when, in 1914, they chose Socialist Party candidate Meyer London for the House of Representatives. He was re-elected in 1916 but defeated in 1918, then elected again in 1920, only to be defeated, for the final time, in 1922.

March of the Rabbis: More than 400 rabbis marched to the White House, in early October 1943, to protest the Roosevelt administration's failure to help Jewish refugees from Hitler. Shortly afterward, Congress held hearings concerning the issue of rescuing Jews from Hitler, and President Roosevelt responded, in January 1944, by creating a government agency to aid the Jews: the War Refugee Board.

Marshall, Louis (1856–1929): A founder and leader of the American Jewish Committee and prominent Republican Party activist, Louis Marshall led the campaign for abrogation of the Russo-American treaty, as well as other Jewish defense efforts and communal enterprises. As the most prominent non-Zionist in the American Jewish community, Marshall negotiated the 1929 inclusion of non-Zionists into the expanded Jewish Agency for Palestine, thus legitimizing the Palestine development project among an important segment of the Jewish community.

Maryland's "Jew Bill": After the only major public debate in early America on whether Jews should be given the right to vote, Maryland's "Jew Bill" was finally enacted in 1826.

Nathan, Maud (1862–1946): Social worker and women's rights activist Maud Nathan was well known for her oratorical ability, organizational know-how, and imaginative protest tactics. A prominent member of the National Council of Jewish Women and the National Consumer League, Nathan successfully mobilized Jewish immigrant women to join the woman's suffrage movement.

New York State Civil Rights Act: Introduced in response to anti-Semitic discrimination in resort hotels, the New York State Civil Rights Act, enacted in 1913, was the first legislation to prohibit resort hotels from advertising restrictions on admission based on race or religion.

Orthodox Judaism: The theology and way of life of Jews who believe in the divine origin of the Hebrew Bible and adhere to traditional religious strictures as detailed in the Talmud and related religious literature. Between 5 and 10 percent of American Jews today regard themselves as Orthodox. This figure includes Hasidic Jews, those Orthodox Jews who belong to small religious factions centered around a charismatic spiritual leader known as a "rebbe."

Reconstructionist Judaism: A small movement established by American Jewish intellectuals in the 1930s that argues that Judaism should be defined not by religious beliefs but in accordance with the culture and way of life practiced by most American Jews—what Reconstructionists call "Jewish civilization."

Reform Judaism: A movement originating in central Europe in the early 1800s that rejects those biblical and Talmudic laws that its adherents regard as distasteful or inconsistent with modernity. Approximately one-third of American Jews are affiliated with Reform synagogues.

Russo-American Treaty Abrogated: Years of American Jewish protests over Russia's treatment of its Jewish citizens resulted in the U.S. abrogation of a Russo-American treaty in 1913, significantly reducing American trade with Russia.

Silver, Abba Hillel (1893–1963): A dynamic orator, Abba Hillel Silver became spiritual leader of Cleveland's Temple, one of the country's most prominent Reform congregations, in 1917. Silver gained increasing prominence as a Zionist activist in the 1930s, and in 1943 he was elevated to the leadership of the American Zionist Emergency Council, from which post he led a nationwide activist campaign to rouse public support for the creation of a Jewish state. Among the council's notable successes was the adoption by the two major political parties of planks in their 1944 platforms endorsing Jewish statehood. It also played a major role in the decision of the Truman administration to support the establishment of a Jewish state and to recognize the new state of Israel just minutes after its creation.

Straus, Oscar (1850–1926): After serving as U.S. minister to Turkey during the 1880s, Oscar Straus became the first Jew appointed to a presidential cabinet, when President Theodore Roosevelt named him secretary of commerce and labor in 1906. In 1909 he again became ambassador to Turkey, but he left the post in 1910 and went on to help Roosevelt create the Progressive Party.

Struggle for Soviet Jewry: As the Soviet Jewry issue became an increasing focus of American Jewish activists, more than 1,000 Jewish protesters were arrested in Washington in 1971, in the first mass civil disobedience on behalf of Soviet Jewry. In 1987 an estimated 250,000 Soviet Jewry protesters gathered across from the White House, in one of the largest demonstrations in American history.

Wise, Stephen S. (1874–1949): Reform rabbi and social activist, Stephen S. Wise was one of the earliest leaders of American Zionism, as well as a cofounder of the National Association for the Advancement of Colored People (1909) and the American Civil Liberties Union (1920). Wise's ties to Franklin D. Roosevelt gave him a level of access to the White House that no other Jewish leader enjoyed, but his inability to influence Roosevelt's policies on Palestine and Jewish refugees disillusioned many in the Jewish community and led to the elevation of Abba Hillel Silver, in 1943, as the most prominent American Zionist leader in Wise's stead.

Resources

American Jewish Historical Society
15 West 16 St.
New York, NY 10011
Tel. (212) 294-6100 / fax (212) 294-6161 / e-mail: ajhs@ajhs.org
web site: http://www.ajhs.org

The AJHS is the premier national Jewish organization devoted to the preservation and dissemination of American Jewish history, as well as the leading archival repository of documents pertaining to the history of American Jewry. It publishes a quarterly scholarly journal, *American Jewish History*, and a quarterly members-only newsletter, *Heritage*.

American Jewish Archives
3101 Clifton Ave.
Cincinnati, OH 45220
Tel. (513) 221-1875 / fax (513) 221-7812 / e-mail: aja@cn.huc.edu
web site: http://www.huc.edu/aja

The AJA is an important archival institution and publisher of the semiannual scholarly journal *American Jewish Archives Journal*. It is not a membership organization.

Feinstein Center for American Jewish History
Temple University
117 S. 17th St., Suite 1010
Philadelphia, PA 19103
Tel. (215) 665-2300 / fax (215) 665-8737 /
e-mail: isserman@astro.ocis.temple.edu

Established in 1990, the Feinstein Center is "a resource center and clearing house for information concerning American Jewish history." It sponsors research, conferences, and publications, mostly of a scholarly nature, as well as a semiannual members-only newsletter, *News from the Feinstein Center for American Jewish History.*

Jewish-American History on the Web-http://www. jewish-history.com

This is a web site specializing in nineteenth-century American Jewish history; it includes a helpful page of links to related web sites.

Jewish Women's Archive
68 Harvard St.
Brookline, MA 02445
Tel. (617) 232-2258 / fax (617) 975-0109 /
e-mail: webmaster@jwa.org
web site: http://www.jwa.org

The JWA aims "to uncover, chronicle, and transmit the rich legacy of Jewish women and their contributions to our families and communities, to our people and our world."

National Jewish Democratic Council
777 N. Capital St. N.E., Suite 305
Washington, DC 20002
Tel. (202) 216-9060 / fax (202) 216-9061 /
e-mail: njdcon-line@aol.com
web site: http://www.njdc.org

The NJDC defines its purpose as "strengthening Jewish participation in the Democratic party" and "promoting Jewish values and interests in the Democratic party." It publishes two occasional bulletins, *Capital Communique* and *Extremist Watch.*

National Museum of American Jewish History
56 N. 5th St., Independence Mall East
Philadelphia, PA 19106-2197
Tel. (215) 923-3811 / fax (215) 923-0763 /
e-mail: nmajh@nmajh.org
web site: http://www.nmajh.org

The largest museum on Jewish history in the United States.

Philadelphia Jewish Archives Center
18 S. 17 St.
Philadelphia, PA 19106
Tel. (215) 925-8090 / fax (215) 925-4413 /
e-mail: pjac@balchinstitute.org
web site: http://www.libertynet.org/pjac

The PJAC is part of Philadelphia's Balch Institute for Ethnic Studies.

Religious Action Center of Reform Judaism
2027 Massachusetts Ave. N.W.
Washington, DC 20036
Tel. (202) 387-2800 / fax (202) 667-9070
web site: http://www.rj.org/rac.html

The Washington arm of the Commission on Social Action of Reform Judaism, the RAC advocates liberal political and social positions from a Jewish perspective. It defines its goal as "the pursuit of social justice and religious liberty by mobilizing the American Jewish community and serving as its advocate in the capitol of the United States." The RAC publishes an electronic newsletter, *RAC News.*

Republican Jewish Coalition
415 Second St. N.E., Suite 100
Washington, DC 20002
Tel. (202) 547-7701 / fax (202) 544-2434 / e-mail: rjc@rjchq.org
web site: http://www.rjchq.org

The RJC was founded in 1985, as the National Jewish Coalition, to "foster and enhance ties between the Republican Party and the American Jewish community." It publishes a bimonthly members-only newsletter, *RJC Bulletin.*

Southern Jewish Historical Society
P.O. Box 5024
Atlanta, GA 30302
web site: http://www.jewishsouth.org

Devoted to the history of the Jewish experience in the Southern United States, the SJHS publishes an annual scholarly journal, *Southern Jewish History,* and a quarterly members-only newsletter, *The Rambler.*

Toward Tradition
P.O. Box 58
Mercer Island, WA 98040
Tel. (206) 236-3046 / e-mail: towardtradition@towardtradition.org
web site: http://www.towardtradition.org

Toward Tradition advocates conservative political and social positions from a Jewish perspective. Defines itself as "a national coalition of Jews and Christians devoted to fighting the secular institutions that foster antireligious bigotry, harm families, and jeopardize the future of America." It publishes the quarterly magazine *Toward Tradition*.

Chronology

1654   Twenty-three Jews of Dutch origin flee Brazil and establish the first permanent Jewish settlement in North America, at New Amsterdam (New York).

1790   President George Washington, in a letter to the Jews of Newport, Rhode Island, promises that the United States will give "to bigotry no sanction, to persecution no assistance."

1826   Maryland, the only state to hold a comprehensive public debate on the right of Jews to vote, finally passes its so-called Jew Bill.

1844   David Levy Yulee of Florida becomes the first Jew elected to the U.S. Senate.

1844   Lewis Charles Levin of Pennsylvania becomes the first Jew elected to the U.S. House of Representatives.

1852   Judah Benjamin is elected to the U.S. Senate from Louisiana; later serves as secretary of war, and then secretary of state, of the Confederacy.

1859   The international controversy over the kidnapping and forced baptism of an Italian Jewish infant galvanizes twenty-four synagogues to establish the first national American Jewish defense organization, the Board of Delegates of American Israelites.

1862   General Ulysses Grant orders the expulsion of all Jews from the region known as the Tennessee Department, but after Jewish protests, President Lincoln revokes the decree.

1869   Jewish protests over Russia's plans to expel 2,000 Jews from their homes prompt the Russian authorities to suspended the expulsions.

1876   Bavarian-born Leopold Morse, Democrat of Massachusetts, becomes the first Jew elected to the U.S. Congress from a New England state.

1877   New Hampshire becomes the last state to grant non-Christians the right to hold public office.

1901   New York City elects its first Jewish mayor, Jacob Aaron Cantor.

1906   Oscar Straus becomes the first Jew appointed to a presidential cabinet, when President Theodore Roosevelt names him secretary of commerce and labor.

1906   The American Jewish Committee is established to defend the rights of Jews around the world through diplomatic intercession and education.

1910   Austrian-born Jewish immigrant Victor Berger, of Milwaukee, becomes the first Socialist Party candidate elected to the House of Representatives.

1913   New York state passes the first legislation to prohibit resort hotels from advertising restrictions on admission based on race or religion.

1913   In a trial laced with anti-Semitism, Leo Frank of Atlanta is falsely convicted of murdering a Christian girl, and is then lynched by a mob. The episode prompts the Jewish fraternal order B'nai B'rith to establish the Anti-Defamation League for the purpose of actively combating anti-Semitism.

1913   Hadassah, the American women's Zionist organization, is established.

1913   Years of American Jewish protests over Russia's treatment of its Jewish citizens result in the U.S. abrogation of a Russo-American treaty, reducing U.S. trade with Russia.

1914   The Yiddish-speaking East European immigrants of Manhattan's Lower East Side elect "one of their own," Socialist Party candidate Meyer London, to the House of Representatives.

1916   Louis D. Brandeis becomes the first Jewish justice of the Supreme Court.

1918   The first American Jewish Congress is held, in Philadelphia, attended by 400 delegates, most of them chosen by more than 300,000 voters in Jewish communities around the United States.

1922   The American Jewish Congress transforms itself into a permanent body devoted to addressing a broad range of Jewish concerns, domestic and international.

1924   Florence Prag Kahn of San Francisco becomes the first Jewish woman elected to the House of Representatives, succeeding her husband, the late Congressman Julius Kahn.

1932   Herbert Lehman becomes the first Jewish governor of New York state.

1933   After Adolf Hitler becomes chancellor of Germany, the Jewish War Veterans of America and the American League for the Defense of Jewish Rights organize a public boycott of German goods; they are later joined by the American Jewish Congress.

1941   U.S. representative E. Michael Edelstein, a Polish Jewish immigrant who represented the Lower East Side in Congress, suffers a fatal heart attack in the middle of a shouting match with anti-Semitic congressmember John E. Rankin of Mississippi.

1943   The dismal results of an Anglo-American conference on the refugee problem, held in Bermuda in May, galvanize some American Jews to take a more activist approach to the plight of European Jewry.

1943   Mainstream Jewish organizations hold the American Jewish Conference in New York City, in August, at which the activist Rabbi Abba Hillel Silver is elevated to the helm of the American Zionist movement.

1943   More than 400 rabbis march to the White House, in early October, to protest the administration's failure to help Jewish refugees from Hitler. Shortly afterward, Congress holds hearings concerning the issue of rescuing Jews from Hitler. Roosevelt responds, in January 1944, by creating a government agency to aid the Jews: the War Refugee Board.

1944   Both major political parties for the first time adopt planks supporting the establishment of a Jewish state.

1947   The Truman administration leads the effort to have the United Nations support partitioning Palestine into Jewish and Arab states.

1948   In a closely watched special election in New York City, American Labor Party candidate Leo Isaacson is elected to Congress on a platform emphasizing the issue of Jewish statehood in Palestine.

1948   The United States becomes the first country to grant recognition to the newborn state of Israel.

1948   Herbert Lehman of New York becomes the first Jew elected to the U.S. Senate since World War I.

1955   Establishment of the Conference of Presidents of Major American Jewish Organizations, to serve as American Jewry's primary spokesman on foreign affairs; and the American Israel Public Affairs Committee (AIPAC), the first registered pro-Israel lobby in the nation's capital.

1967   Repeated expressions of anti-Semitism by black militants at the National New Politics Convention cause a permanent split between black activists and many of their Jewish allies.

1970   Bella Abzug of New York, an outspoken feminist and anti-war activist, becomes the first Jewish woman elected to Congress since the 1930s.

1971   More than 1,000 Jewish protesters are arrested, in Washington, D.C., in the first mass civil disobedience on behalf of Soviet Jewry.

1972   Introduction of the Jackson-Vanik Amendment, linking U.S.-Soviet trade to freedom of emigration for Soviet Jews.

1973   New York City elects its first Jewish mayor, Abraham Beame.

1976   Pennsylvania governor Milton Shapp becomes the first Jewish candidate for the Democratic presidential nomination.

1980   Tom Lantos of California becomes the first Holocaust survivor elected to Congress.

1987   An estimated 250,000 Soviet Jewry protesters gather across from the White House, in one of the largest demonstrations in American history.

1992   Philadelphia elects its first Jewish mayor, Ed Rendell.

1992   Election of the first Jewish women to the U.S. Senate, both from California: San Francisco mayor Dianne Feinstein and Congresswoman Barbara Boxer.

1996   Senator Arlen Specter of Pennsylvania becomes the first Jewish candidate for the Republican presidential nomination.

2000   Senator Joseph Lieberman, Democrat of Connecticut, becomes the first Jew nominated for vice president by a major political party.

Annotated Bibliography

Chapter 1

Feingold, Henry. *Zion in America*. New York: Hippocrene, 1974.
    A general survey of the history of U.S. Jews.
Hertzberg, Arthur. *The Jews in America*. New York: Simon and Schuster, 1989.
    A general survey of the history of U.S. Jews.
Marcus, Jacob R. *United States Jewry 1776–1985*. 4 vols. Detroit: Wayne State University Press, 1989.
    An encyclopedia-length history of U.S. Jews.
Sachar, Howard M. *A History of Jews in America*. New York: Knopf, 1992.
    A general survey of the history of U.S. Jews.

Chapter 2

Alexander, Edward. "Twenty-Four Hours with the KGB." *Alternative: An American Spectator* 10 (May 1977): 22–23.
    Memoir of an American Jewish activist's attempt to make contact with Jewish dissidents in the USSR.
Ben-Ami, Yitshaq. *Years of Wrath, Days of Glory: Memoirs from the Irgun*. New York: Shengold, 1983.
    A Bergson Group activist's autobiography.
Best, Gary Dean. "The Jewish 'Center of Gravity' and Secretary Hay's Romanian Notes." *American Jewish Archives* 32 (April 1980): 23–34.
    American Jewish protests on behalf of Romanian Jewry in the late 1800s.

Bloom, Leonard. "A Successful Jewish Boycott of the New York City Public Schools, Christmas 1906." *American Jewish History* 67 (December 1980): 180–188.

> A turn-of-the century Jewish protest campaign against Christian programming in public schools.

Cohen, Naomi W. "Faces of American Jewish Defense in the 1920s." In *An Inventory of Promises: Essays on American Jewish History in Honor of Moses Rischin.* Edited by Jeffrey S. Gurock and Marc L. Raphael, pp. 15–30. Brooklyn, NY: Carlson, 1995.

> Surveys the variety of protest tactics employed by interwar Jewish defense organizations.

Dinnerstein, Leonard. *The Leo Frank Case.* New York: Columbia University Press, 1968.

> Recounts the anti-Semitism that motivated the prosecution and lynching of a Jewish businessman in Georgia.

Dodek, Joan, and Ruth Newman. "Washington Jewry's Activities on Behalf of Soviet Jews, 1968–1991." *Record* 18 (1991): 7–16.

> An anecdotal survey of one community's involvement in Soviet Jewry protests.

Feingold, Henry L. "The Jewish Radical in His American Habitat." *Judaism* 22 (winter 1973): 92–105.

> Explores the reasons for the disproportionate level of American Jewish involvement in radical political protest activity.

Finger, Seymour Maxwell, ed. *American Jewry during the Holocaust.* New York: Holmes and Meier, 1984.

> The report of a commission that examined the responses of American Jewry to news of the Holocaust.

Friedman, Murray, and Albert D. Chernin, eds. *A Second Exodus: The American Movement to Free Soviet Jews.* Hanover, NH: Brandeis University Press and University Press of New England, 1999.

> A collection of essays on different aspects of American Jewry's protest campaigns to aid Soviet Jewry.

Gartner, Lloyd P. "Romania, America, and World Jewry: Consul Peixotto in Bucharest, 1870–1876." *American Jewish Historical Quarterly* 58 (September 1968): 25–116.

> American Jewish protests in behalf of Romanian Jewry in the late 1800s.

Greenberg, Evelyn Levow. "An 1869 Petition on Behalf of Russian Jews." *American Jewish Historical Quarterly* 55 (March 1965): 278–295.

> An early American Jewish protest campaign to aid Russian Jewry.

Gurock, Jeffrey S. "The Americanization Continuum and Jewish Responses to Christian Influences on the Lower East Side, 1900–1910." In *Christian Missionaries and Jewish Apostates,* edited by Todd Endelman, pp. 255–271. New York: Holmes and Meier, 1987.

> Jewish protests against Christian missionizing in turn-of-the-century New York.

———. "Jacob A. Riis: Christian Friend or Missionary Foe?: Two Jewish Views." *American Jewish History* 71 (September 1981): 29–47.
Divisions within the New York Jewish community over protesting against Christian missionizing during the early 1900s.

———. "Why Albert Lucas Did Not Serve in the New York Kehilla." *Proceedings of the American Academy for Jewish Research* 51 (1984): 55–72.
Lucas was a leader of the Jewish protests against Christian missionizing in New York during the early 1900s.

Hecht, Ben. *Child of the Century.* New York: Simon and Schuster, 1954.
A lively autobiographical account of Hecht's life as an author, playwright, and controversial Jewish political activist.

Helzner, Robyn. "Still Vigilant after All These Years." *Record* 18 (1991): 17–21.
Memoir of an American Jewish musician's involvement in protests in behalf of Soviet Jewry.

Kahn, Douglas. "Advocacy on the Community Level: A Personal Perspective." In *A Second Exodus: The American Movement to Free Soviet Jews.* Edited by Murray Friedman and Albert D. Chernin. Hanover, NH: Brandeis University Press and University Press of New England, 1999, pp. 181–199.
Recollections of a Sovieet Jewish activist.

Klein, Naomi, and Henry Klein. "Present at the Creation." *Jewish Exponent of Philadelphia,* January 2, 1997, 8.
Memoir of a Philadelphia couple's involvement in protests in behalf of Soviet Jewry.

Korff, Baruch. *Flight from Fear.* New York: Elmar, 1953.
A militant Zionist rabbi recalls his 1940s activism.

Kritz, Francesca Lunzer. "A Child of Sharansky Searches for Ways to Rally Her Own." *Forward,* January 3, 1997, 14.
Memoir of a young activist's involvement in protests in behalf of Soviet Jewry.

Kuzmack, Linda Gordon. *Woman's Cause: The Jewish Woman's Movement in England and the United States, 1881–1933.* Columbus: Ohio State University Press, 1990.
Jewish involvement in protest campaigns for women's rights.

Lookstein, Haskel. *Were We Our Brothers' Keepers?* New York: Hartmore House, 1985.
Examines American Jewish responses to the Holocaust, through the eyes of the Jewish press.

Medoff, Rafael. *The Deafening Silence: American Jewish Leaders and the Holocaust.* New York: Steimatzky, 1987.
The first comprehensive study of how American Jewish organizations responded to the Holocaust.

———. "'A Foolish Encroachment upon the Allied High Command'? American Jewish Perspectives on Requesting U.S. Military Intervention against the Holocaust." *Modern Judaism* 20, no. 3 (October 2000): 299–314.
Explores the sociological factors shaping the debate over Jewish protests against Allied policy during the Holocaust.

348 ■ Annotated Bibliography

———. *Militant Zionism in America: The Rise and Impact of the Jabotinsky Movement in the United States, 1926–1948.* Tuscaloosa: University of Alabama Press, 2002.
 The first history of the Jabotinsky movement in America.
———. "New Perspectives on How America, and American Jewry, Reacted to the Holocaust." *American Jewish History* 84, no. 3 (September 1996): 253–266.
 Historiographical survey of American Jewry's response to the Holocaust.
———. "'Retribution Is Not Enough': The 1943 Campaign by Jewish Students to Raise American Public Awareness of the Holocaust." *Holocaust and Genocide Studies* 11, no. 2 (fall 1997).
 Chronicles a protest campaign mounted by Jewish student activists in behalf of European Jewry in the 1940s.
Mervis, Leonard J. "The Social Justice Movement and the American Reform Rabbi." *American Jewish Archives* (June 1955): 171–185.
 A survey of the involvement of the Reform rabbinate in social action protests.
Orbach, William W. *The American Movement to Aid Soviet Jews.* Amherst: University of Massachusetts Press, 1979.
 Survey of American Jewish protests in behalf of Soviet Jewry, through the mid-1970s.
Peck, Sarah E. "The Campaign for an American Response to the Nazi Holocaust, 1943–1945." *Journal of Contemporary History* 15 (1980): 367–400.
 An early and valuable account of the events leading to the creation of the War Refugee Board.
Penkower, Monty N. "In Dramatic Dissent: The Bergson Boys." *American Jewish History* 70, no. 3 (March 1981): 281–309.
 Seminal essay on the 1940s activists.
Porter, Jack Nusan, and Peter Dreier, eds. *Jewish Radicalism.* New York: Grove Press, 1973.
 A collection of essays and interviews focusing on U.S. Jewish radicals in the early 1970s.
Rabinovich, Abraham. "Borrowing Tactics from Campus Blacks." *Jerusalem Post* (August 8, 1969): 8.
 How Jewish student protesters engineered change on their campuses in the late 1960s and early 1970s.
Rafaeli, Alex. *Dream and Action.* Jerusalem: Achva, 1993.
 Memoirs of a Bergson group activist.
Rapoport, Louis. *Shake Heaven and Earth: Peter Bergson and the Struggle to Rescue the Jews of Europe.* Jerusalem: Gefen, 1999.
 A journalistic account of the Bergson group's activism.
Ruby, Walter. "The Role of Nonestablishment Groups." In *A Second Exodus: The American Movement to Free Soviet Jews.* Edited by Murray Friedman and Albert D. Chernin. Hanover, NH: Brandeis University Press and University Press of New England, 1999, pp. 200–223.
 A journalist's account of the role of activist groups in the struggle of Soviet Jewry.

Ruchames, Louis. "Jewish Radicalism in the United States." In *The Ghetto and Beyond: Essays in Jewish Life*. Edited by Peter I. Rose. New York: Random House, 1969, pp. 228–252.
  Explores the reasons for the disproportionate level of American Jewish involvement in radical political protest activity.
Sorin, Gerald. *The Prophetic Minority: American Jewish Immigrant Radicals 1880–1920*. Bloomington: Indiana University Press, 1985.
  Interprets Jewish immigrant radicalism as an expression of traditional Jewish values.
Urofsky, Melvin I. *We Are One! American Jewry and Israel*. Garden City, NY: Anchor Press/Doubleday, 1978.
  A history of relations between the U.S. Jewish community and Israel from 1948 to the 1970s.
Zaar, Isaac. *Rescue and Liberation: America's Part in the Birth of Israel*. New York: Bloch, 1954.
  The role of American Jewish protests in shaping 1940s American policy on the Jewish statehood question.

Chapter 3

Abbott, David W., Louis H. Gold, and Edward T. Rogowsky. *Police, Politics, and Race: The New York City Referendum on Civilian Review*. New York: American Jewish Committee, 1969.
  Sheds light on changing Jewish voting patterns in response to racial crises in New York.
American Jewish Committee. *The "Jewish Vote."* New York: American Jewish Committee, 1972.
  A summary of the reasons for Jewish electoral trends.
American Jewish Committee Information and Research Services. *Jewish Voting in Recent Elections*. New York: American Jewish Committee, 1969.
  An analysis of Jewish voting patterns in the 1969 municipal elections in Los Angeles, Minneapolis, and New York City.
———. *Jewish Voting in the 1984 Democratic Primaries*. New York: American Jewish Committee, 1984.
  An analysis of trends in the 1984 primaries.
———. *Jewish Voting in the 1968 Presidential Election: A Preliminary Report*. New York: American Jewish Committee, 1968.
  A study of Jewish voting patterns in the 1968 presidential primaries and the general election.
American Jewish Committee—Jewish Information Service. *Elections, 1963 (Civil Rights and White Reaction)*. New York: American Jewish Committee, 1963.
  An analysis of voting trends among various ethnic groups in the 1963 Boston School Committee election and the Philadelphia mayoral race.
Brenner, Saul. "Patterns of Jewish-Catholic Democratic Voting and the 1960 Presidential Vote." *Jewish Social Studies* 26 (1964): 169–178.

A comparison of how these two segments of the American electorate voted in 1960.

Dalin, David G. "Louis Marshall, the Jewish Vote, and the Republican Party." *Jewish Political Studies Review* 4, no. 1 (spring 1992): 55–84.

A history of Marshall's use of the Jewish vote as a lobbying tool.

Dawidowicz, Lucy. *Jewish Voting in the 1968 Presidential Election: Preliminary Report.* New York: American Jewish Committee, 1968.

An analysis of Jewish voting trends in the 1968 presidential race.

Diner, Hasia R. *A Time for Gathering: The Second Migration, 1820–1880.* Baltimore, MD: Johns Hopkins University Press, 1992.

A history of nineteenth-century Jewish immigrants to the United States from central and western Europe, and their role in the evolution of U.S. Jewry.

Featherman, Sandra. *Philadelphia Elects a Black Mayor: How Jews, Blacks, and Ethnics Vote in the 1980s.* Philadelphia: American Jewish Committee, 1984.

A comparative analysis of Jewish and black voting patterns in several Philadelphia elections.

Friedman, Murray. "Are American Jews Moving to the Right?" *Commentary* 111 (April 2000): 50–52.

Interprets late–1990s Jewish voting trends as indicative of gradually increasing conservatism.

Fuchs, Lawrence H. *The Political Behavior of American Jews.* Glencoe, IL: Free Press, 1956.

An interpretation of Jewish voting patterns as an expression of traditional Jewish values.

———, ed. *American Ethnic Politics.* New York: Harper & Row, 1968.

A collection of essays about voting patterns among various U.S. ethnic groups.

Guysener, Maurice G. "The Jewish Vote in Chicago." *Jewish Social Studies* 20 (October 1958): 195–214.

Surveys Jewish voting trends in 1950s Chicago.

Himmelfarb, Milton. "American Jews: Diehard Conservatives." *Commentary* 100 (April 1989): 44–49.

Contends that Jewish voting trends in the late 1980s indicate growing conservatism on some issues.

———. "The Jewish Vote (Again)." *Commentary* 84 (June 1973): 81–85.

An examination of Jewish voting in the 1972 presidential election.

Himmelfarb, Milton, and Howard W. Yagerman. *Preliminary Report on Presidential Voting by Jews in 1972.* New York: American Jewish Committee, 1972.

Analyzes U.S. Jewish voting patterns in the Nixon-McGovern presidential race.

Hochbaum, Martin. "The Jewish Vote in the 1984 Presidential Election." New York: American Jewish Congress, 1984.

Surveys Jewish voting trends in the 1984 presidential primaries and general election.

Howe, Irving. *World of Our Fathers*. New York: Harcourt, Brace, Jovanovich, 1976.
  A history of the eastern European Jewish immigrants who settled on the lower east side of Manhattan.
Isaacs, Joakim. "Candidate Grant and the Jews." *American Jewish Archives* 17 (April 1965).
  Explores how Grant's policies were affected by his interest in attracting Jewish electoral support.
Isaacs, Stephen D. "The Jewish Vote in '74." *Hadassah Magazine* 56 (December 1974): 11, 29.
  Summarizes how Jews voted in congressional and gubernatorial races in 1974.
———. *Jews and American Politics*. Garden City, NY: Doubleday, 1974.
  A collection of essays on various aspects of U.S. Jewish political behavior.
Lefkowitz, Jay P. "Does the Jewish Vote Count?" *Commentary* 112 (March 2001): 50–53.
  Analyzes the impact of Jewish voters on recent U.S. politics.
———. "Jewish Voters and the Democrats." *Commentary* 104 (April 1993): 38–41.
  Surveys developments in relations between U.S. Jewry and the Democratic Party.
Levine, Charley J. "The Jewish Electorate." *Practical Politics* 1, no. 4 (May–June 1978): 5–7.
  A broad survey of the U.S. Jewish electorate in the mid-1970s.
Levy, Mark R., and Michael S. Kramer. *The Ethnic Factor: How America's Minorities Decide Elections*. New York: Simon and Schuster, 1972.
  Includes one chapter on Jewish voting trends.
Lipstadt, Deborah, Charles Pruitt, and Jonathan Woocher. "Election '84: Where Are the Jews?" *Moment* 9 (October 1984): 35–38.
  Analyzes U.S. Jewish voting patterns in the 1984 presidential race.
Maller, Allen S. "Class Factors in the Jewish Vote." *Jewish Social Studies* 39, nos. 1–2 (winter–spring, 1977): 159–162.
  An analysis of Jewish voting patterns in mayoral elections in New York and Los Angeles, emphasizing variances in voting preferences among different socioeconomic levels in the Jewish electorate.
Raab, Earl. "Are American Jews Still Liberal?" *Commentary* 107 (February 1996): 43–45.
  Discusses signs of a shift among U.S. Jews away from liberalism.
Schechtman, Joseph B. "There *Is* a Jewish Vote." *Congress Bi-Weekly* 27 (October 24, 1960): 4–6.
  An early appeal for more forceful use of the Jewish vote as a political tool.
Szajkowski, Zosa. "The Jews and New York City's Mayoralty Election of 1917." *Jewish Social Studies* 32 (October 1970): 286–306.
  A detailed study of Jewish voting trends in the 1917 New York City mayoral race.

Solomon, Herbert L. "The Republican Party and the Jews." *Judaism* 147 (summer 1988): 276–287.

A survey of the history of Jewish attitudes toward the Republican Party.

Chapter 4

Berman, Aaron. *Nazism, the Jews, and American Zionism 1933–1948.* Detroit: Wayne State University Press, 1990.

An analysis of American Zionist responses to the persecution of European Jewry, including 1940s lobbying efforts.

Bierbrier, Doreen. "The American Zionist Emergency Council: An Analysis of a Pressure Group." *American Jewish Historical Quarterly* 60 (September 1970): 82–105.

A detailed examination of 1940s American Zionist lobbying efforts.

Cohen, Michael J. *Truman and Israel.* Berkeley: University of California Press, 1990.

A history of the interrelationship between American Zionists and U.S. foreign policy in the late 1940s.

Cohen, Naomi W. *The Year after the Riots: American Responses to the Palestine Crisis of 1929–1930.* Detroit, MI: Wayne State University Press, 1988.

Describes the responses of the U.S. government and American Jewry to the Palestinian Arab pogroms of 1929, including lobbying efforts.

Dollinger, Marc. *Quest for Inclusion: Jews and Liberalism in Modern America.* Princeton, NJ: Princeton University Press, 2000.

American Jewry's lobbying campaigns for civil rights and related causes.

Feingold, Henry. "'Courage First and Intelligence Second': The American Jewish Secular Elite, Roosevelt, and the Failure to Rescue." *American Jewish History* 72 (June 1983): 424–460.

How the Jews closest to Roosevelt grappled with the dilemma of lobbying for Jewish concerns during the Holocaust.

Feuer, Leon. "The Birth of the Jewish Lobby." *American Jewish Archives* 28, no. 2 (November 1976): 107–118.

The early days of the 1940s American Zionist lobbying campaign.

Ganin, Zvi. "Activism versus Moderation: The Conflict between Abba Hillel Silver and Stephen Wise during the 1940s." *Studies in Zionism* 5 (spring 1984): 71–95.

Differences among American Zionist leaders on the goals and methods of lobbying in Washington.

———. *Truman, American Jewry, and Israel, 1945–1948.* New York: Holmes and Meier, 1979.

Includes material on American Zionist lobbying in the 1940s.

Goldstein, Judith. "Ethnic Politics: The American Jewish Committee as Lobbyist, 1915–1917." *American Jewish History* 65 (September 1975): 36–58.

A survey of the American Jewish Committee's early lobbying campaign.

Gurock, Jeffrey S. "The 1913 New York State Civil Rights Act." *AJS Review* 1 (1976): 95–113.
  Background to the passage of a landmark antidiscrimination bill, including efforts by Jewish lobbyists.
Hunnicut, Benjamin Kline. "The Jewish Sabbath Movement in the Early Twentieth Century." *American Jewish History* 69 (December 1979): 196–215.
  Early 1900s Jewish lobbying on legislation affecting Sabbath observance.
Kenen, I. L. *Israel's Defense Line: Her Friends and Foes in Washington.* Buffalo, NY: Prometheus, 1981.
  Anecdotes from the front lines of pro-Israel lobbying in Washington, from the 1940s through the 1970s.
Leonard, Henry B. "Louis Marshall and Immigration Restriction, 1906–1924." *American Jewish Archives* 24 (April 1972): 6–26.
  Early 1900s Jewish lobbying efforts on the immigration issue.
Neumann, Emanuel. *In the Arena.* New York: Herzl, 1978.
  Autobiography of a long-time American Zionist leader.
Neuringer, Sheldon. "American Jewry and United States Immigration Policy, 1881–1953." Ph.D. dissertation, University of Wisconsin, 1969.
  History of American Jewish lobbying on the immigration issue.
Penkower, Monty N. "The 1943 Joint Anglo-American Statement on Palestine." *Herzl Year Book* 8 (1978): 212–241.
  The role of American Jewish lobbyists in averting a drastic change in U.S. policy regarding Palestine during World War II.
Polier, Justine Wise, and James Waterman Wise. *The Personal Letters of Stephen S. Wise.* Boston: Beacon, 1956.
  Includes some material on Wise's lobbying efforts in Washington during the 1930s and 1940s.
Proskauer, Joseph M. *A Segment of My Times.* New York: Farrar, Straus and Giroux, 1950.
  Autobiography of the one-time president of the American Jewish Committee, including material on Jewish lobbying.
Raphael, Marc Lee. *Abba Hillel Silver.* New York: Holmes and Meier, 1989.
  A compelling biography of an American Zionist leader and leader of the 1940s lobbying effort in Washington.
Reznikoff, Charles, ed. *Louis Marshall: Champion of Liberty.* 2 vols. Philadelphia: Jewish Publication Society of America, 1957.
  Includes material on Marshall's extensive lobbying efforts in Washington during the early 1900s.
Shapiro, Edward S. "The Approach of War: Congressional Isolationism and Anti-Semitism, 1939–1941." *American Jewish History* 74 (September 1984): 45–65.
  Explores the connection between isolationism and anti-Semitism among members of Congress from 1939 to 1941.
Urofsky, Melvin I. *American Zionism from Herzl to the Holocaust.* Garden City, NY: Anchor Press/Doubleday, 1975.

A survey of the rise and impact of the U.S. Zionist movement from the 1890s to the 1930s.

Wise, Stephen S. *As I See It*. New York: Jewish Opinion, 1947.
Includes some material on Wise's lobbying efforts in Washington during the 1930s and 1940s.

Zuroff, Efraim. *The Response of Orthodox Jewry in the United States to the Holocaust*. Hoboken, NJ: Ktav, 2000.
Includes material on efforts by American Orthodox Jews to lobby in Washington for rescue of Jews from the Holocaust.

Chapter 5

Bloom, Sol. *The Autobiography of Sol Bloom*. New York: G. P. Putnam's Sons, 1948.
The autobiography of the long-time chairman of the House Foreign Affairs Committee.

Celler, Emanuel. *You Never Leave Brooklyn*. New York: Day, 1973.
The autobiography of one of the longest-serving Jewish members of Congress.

Chyet, Stanley. "The Political Rights of the Jews in the United States." *American Jewish Archives* 10 (April 1958): 14–75.
A broad survey of the history and evolution of the political rights of U.S. Jews.

Koch, Edward I. *Mayor*. New York: Putnam, 1995.
The autobiography of one of the most prominent Jewish office-holders in modern times.

Maisel, L. Sandy, and Ira N. Forman. *Jews in American Politics*. Lanham, MD: Roman and Littlefield, 2001.
A collection of essays on aspects of Jewish involvement in American politics.

Moore, Deborah Dash. "A Century of Jewish Women in American Politics." *Women's League Outlook* 71 (summer 2000): 15–17.
Surveys the history of American Jewish women in politics.

Selavan, Ida Cohen. "Adolph Edlis—A Hungarian Jew in Pittsburgh Politics." *American Jewish Archives* 36, no. 1 (April 1984): 1–10.
A useful case study of local ethnic politics.

Seretan, Glen. "Daniel De Leon: Wandering Jew." *American Jewish Historical Quarterly* 63 (March 1976): 245–256.
Includes material on attempts by Jewish socialists to win elections for public office.

Stone, Kurt. *The Congressional Minyan: The Jews of Capitol Hill*. Hoboken, NJ: Ktav, 2000.
Brief anecdotal histories of every Jewish member of Congress.

Index

About the Author

Rafael Medoff is Visiting Scholar in Jewish Studies at Purchase College, The State University of New York. He has also taught Jewish history at Ohio State University, Touro College, and elsewhere, and has served as consulting historian to the Jewish Historical Society of Greater Washington, the Jewish Historical Society of Maryland, and the Interfaith Holocaust Council.

His previous books are *Militant Zionism in America: The Rise and Impact of the Jabotinsky Movement in the United States, 1926–1948; Baksheesh Diplomacy: Secret Negotiations between American Jewish Leaders and Arab Officials on the Eve of World War II; The Secret Beneath the Hill: Memoirs of a Haganah Veteran* (with Zvi Yarom); *Historical Dictionary of Zionism* (with Chaim I. Waxman); *Zionism and the Arabs: An American Jewish Dilemma, 1898–1948;* and *The Deafening Silence: American Jewish Leaders and the Holocaust, 1933–1945.*

Dr. Medoff is associate editor of the scholarly journal *American Jewish History,* and a member of the editorial boards of *Southern Jewish History, Shofar,* and *Menorah Review.* His essays and reviews have appeared in numerous encyclopedias and other reference volumes, as well as journals such as *American Jewish Archives, Modern Judaism, Jewish Culture and History, Judaism, Studies in Zionism, the Journal of Israeli History, Holocaust and Genocide Studies,* and *Holocaust Studies Annual.* He has also been the recipient of prestigious fellowships, including a Lady Davis Graduate Fellowship, a Herbert Hoover Presidential Association Research Fellowship, a Marguerite R. Jacobs Postdoctoral Fellowship from the American Jewish Archives, and a Board of Trustees Fellowship from the American Jewish Historical Society.